The
Political
Experience

MICHAEL A. WEINSTEIN, EDITOR

The Political Experience

Readings in Political Science

ST. MARTIN'S PRESS   NEW YORK

right, 1964, by Editions Gallimard, reprinted by permission of the American publisher, The Bobbs-Merrill Company, Inc.

III STUDYING POLITICS: APPROACHES

"What Is Political Philosophy," by Leo Strauss. Reprinted with permission of The Macmillan Company from *What Is Political Philosophy? and Other Studies* by Leo Strauss. © by The Free Press of Glencoe, 1959.

"The Historical Approach," by Edward Hallett Carr. Chapter 1 of Edward Hallett Carr's *The New Society* (New York: St. Martin's Press, 1956). Copyright © 1956 by St. Martin's Press, Inc.

"The Origins of the Behavioral Movement," by Don R. Bowen. Chapter 1 of Don R. Bowen's *Political Behavior of the American Public* (Columbus, Ohio: Charles E. Merrill Publishing Company, 1968). Reprinted by permission.

"Sense and Non-Sense in Politics," by Marvin Surkin. Chapter 1 from *An End to Political Science: The Caucus Papers*, edited by Marvin Surkin and Alan Wolfe. © 1970 by Basic Books, Inc., Publishers, New York. Reprinted by permission.

"Creating Political Reality," by Henry S. Kariel, in *American Political Science Review*, 64, No. 4 (December 1970), 1088-1093. Reprinted by permission of the American Political Science Association and the author.

IV ALTERNATIVE FUTURES: POLICY

"The End of Ideology?" by Seymour Martin Lipset. From *Political Man* by Seymour Martin Lipset. Copyright © 1959, 1960 by Seymour Martin Lipset. Reprinted by permission of Doubleday & Company, Inc.

"The New American Dilemma," by David E. Apter. Reprinted with permission of The Macmillan Company from *Ideology and Discontent* by David E. Apter. Copyright © 1964 by The Free Press of Glencoe, a Division of The Macmillan Company.

"Mass Responses to Political Symbols," by Murray Edelman. Chapter 9 of Murray Edelman's *The Symbolic Uses of Politics* (Urbana, Ill.: University of Illinois Press, 1964). Reprinted by permission.

"The Artificial Majority," by Theodore J. Lowi, in *The Nation,* December 7, 1970. Reprinted by permission of *The Nation.*

"Corporate Responsibility: Politics by Other Means," by Hazel Henderson, in *The Nation,* December 14, 1970. Reprinted by permission of *The Nation.*

V COMMITMENT TO A FUTURE: DECISION

from *Who Governs?* by Robert A. Dahl (New Haven: Yale University Press, 1961). Copyright © 1961 by Yale University. Reprinted by permission.

"An Alternative Approach," by Peter Bachrach. From *The Theory of Democratic Elitism,* by Peter Bachrach, pp. 93-106. Copyright © 1967 by Little, Brown and Company, Inc. Reprinted by permission.

"The Higher Circles," by C. Wright Mills. From *The Power Elite* by C. Wright Mills, Copyright © 1956 by Oxford University Press, Inc. Reprinted by permission.

"The New Class," by Milovan Djilas. From Milovan Djilas' *The New Class* (New York: Frederick A. Praeger, 1957). Reprinted by permission.

from *Technocracy,* by Jean Meynaud. Reprinted by permission of Faber and Faber Ltd.

VI SHAPING THE FUTURE: ADMINISTRATION

from *Formal Organizations,* by Peter M. Blau and W. Richard Scott (San Francisco: Chandler Publishing Company, 1962), pp. 242-253. Reprinted by permission of Intext Educational Publishers.

"Dramaturgy," by Victor A. Thompson. From *Modern Organization,* by Victor A. Thompson. Copyright © 1961 by Victor A. Thompson. Reprinted by permission of Alfred A. Knopf, Inc.

VII Judging the Past: Evaluation

VIII Prospects of Political Action

To Greenlee, Seibold, Deena et al.

Preface

The objective of this volume is to convey the quality of political experience as it is lived in the complex structures of the post-modern world. The attainment of this objective requires that three conditions be met. First, it is necessary to show that the contemporary political experience contains abundant diversity, conflict and, particularly, ambiguity. There are multiple perspectives through which human beings attempt to understand and to cope with their current situations. Examples of these perspectives are presented in the following pages, spanning the traditional left-right spectrum and going beyond it to newer organizational and existential modes of analysis. The second condition for conveying the lived quality of political experience is to avoid getting bogged down in particular debates and discussions about specific institutions. The political process must be interpreted in a wide enough way to allow each person to relate it to his own situation, and to situations that he has never directly experienced. There is an attempt to meet this requirement in the following pages by dividing the political process into four broad phases of policy, decision, administration, and evaluation, each of which includes more than activities within governmental institutions and provides the student with a way of analyzing political activities wherever they occur. Finally, it is necessary to discover some provisional unities in the present public situation. Tying together many of the selections that follow is the idea that there is a contemporary conflict between creative freedom and the domination of free activity by complex organizations, or conglomerates. Thus, the unity is interpreted as a debate or a conflict, rather than as a single tendency or direction in history. During the last half of the nineteenth century many thinkers believed that mankind was continually advancing to ever higher levels of liberty and happiness. During the first half of the twentieth century this optimism frequently turned to pessimism, and there were dismal predictions of the decay of civilization. While optimism and pessimism are still with us, a new attitude seems to have taken precedence in the second half of the twentieth century. This is the attitude that humanity is at a crossroads between conflicting futures: freedom and oppression, cooperation and conflict, civilization and barbarism. It is a time of ambiguity and choice, and the selections that follow are meant to reflect this complexity.

Political science best clarifies the public situation when it enables a person to grasp the fundamental characteristics of the political experience. Details float in a meaningless void unless there is a basic context to which to relate them. This is why this introduction to political science concentrates on presenting and analyzing general interpretations of the current political process. With a firm understanding of these interpretations at the outset of his education in political science, the student will have a framework in which more advanced work will make sense. In addition, grasping these general interpretations will aid the student in organizing the political events that go on around him and in taking action with respect to them.

Many people have helped me work out the ideas that have guided the design of this volume. Dr. Deena Weinstein of DePaul University has helped conceive and perfect the project at every stage of its development. Ms. Judy Green has been a skilled and sympathetic editor and friend, and Ms. Tuyet Hofman has been a valued assistant. Dr. Philip Haring has provided many fresh ideas about theory and an extraordinary intellectual friendship. Most important, however, was the informal theory discussion circle which grew up at Purdue University during the academic year, 1970-71. The members of that circle, Jim Caldwell, Art Kroker, Randy Triplett, and Tim Witsman, provided a year of intellectual stimulation that I will never forget. It was through their keen, thoughtful, and lively discussion that the idea of a political experience took shape.

Tippecanoe County, 1972

Contents

Introduction   1

I The Human Condition

Big Brother Is Dead Too, *Kenneth Melvin*   41
Brave New World, *Frank S. Meyer*   46
The Welfare Non-Issue, *James Burnham*   48
Moral Bewilderment, *from* On the Diversity of Morals,
    Morris Ginsberg   50
Learning To Be Radical, *from* The New Democratic Theory,
    Kenneth A. Megill   56
The Pillage of the Earth, *from* The Failure of Technology,
    Friedrich Georg Junger   64
Protean Man, *from* History and Human Survival,
    Robert Jay Lifton   68

II The Nature of Politics

Politics As the Master Science, *from* Politics As the Master Science:
    From Plato to Mao, *Herbert J. Spiro*   84
Political Power, *from* Politics Among Nations,
    Hans J. Morgenthau   89
The General Problem of Human Existence, *from* Political Morality:
    A General Theory of Politics, *Philip S. Haring*   98
Process and Polity, *from* Political Violence, *H. L. Nieburg*   104
The Two Faces of Janus, *from* The Idea of Politics,
    Maurice Duverger   111

III Studying Politics: Approaches

What Is Political Philosophy? *from* What Is Political Philosophy?
    and Other Studies, *Leo Strauss*   119
The Historical Approach, *from* The New Society,
    Edward Hallett Carr   126
The Origins of the Behavioral Movement, *from* Political Behavior
    of the American Public, *Don R. Bowen*   133
Sense and Non-Sense in Politics, *Marvin Surkin*   145
Creating Political Reality, *Henry S. Kariel*   160

IV Alternative Futures: Policy

The End of Ideology? *from* Political Man, *Seymour Martin Lipset*   173
The New American Dilemma, *from* Ideology and Discontent,
    David E. Apter   178
Mass Responses to Political Symbols, *from* The Symbolic Uses
    of Politics, *Murray Edelman*   185
The Artificial Majority, *Theodore J. Lowi*   191
Corporate Responsibility: Politics by Other Means,
    Hazel Henderson   197

V   Commitment to a Future: Decision

from Who Governs? *Robert A. Dahl*   209
An Alternative Approach, *from* The Theory of Democratic Elitism,
    Peter Bachrach   218
The Higher Circles, *from* The Power Elite, *C. Wright Mills*   226
The New Class, *Milovan Djilas*   232
from Technocracy, *Jean Meynaud*   238

VI   Shaping the Future: Administration

from Formal Organizations, *Peter M. Blau and W. Richard Scott*   251
Dramaturgy, *from* Modern Organization, *Victor A. Thompson*   261
The Technostructure, *from* The New Industrial State,
    John Kenneth Galbraith   265
The Sickness of Government, *from* The Age of Discontinuity,
    Peter F. Drucker   272
Normative Theory and Public Administration, *Michael M. Harmon* 279
Comment: On a Redefinition of Administrative Responsibility,
    John Paynter   289

VII   Judging the Past: Evaluation

Political Stability: Civic and Praetorian Polities,
    from Political Order in Changing Societies,
    Samuel P. Huntington   297
The Performance of Political Systems, *from* Politics and
    Government, *Karl W. Deutsch*   303
from The Supreme Court and American Capitalism,
    Arthur Selwyn Miller   314
The Ethical Society, *from* The Structure of Evil, *Ernest Becker*   321
A Fourth Branch of Government: For Whom?
    Michael A. Weinstein   325

VIII   Prospects of Political Action

The Self-Fulfilling Prophecy, *from* The Future of Conservatism,
    M. Stanton Evans   341
A Strategy for Radical Liberals, *Arnold S. Kaufman*   346
The Transition to Socialism, *Paul M. Sweezy*   360
A Nightmare, *Morton A. Kaplan*   372
The Institutional Spectrum, *from* Deschooling Society, *Ivan Illich*   378

The
Political
Experience

Introduction

There are many different reasons why people become interested in studying political activity. Some follow day to day political conflicts in the same way that their friends keep up with sports. For them, politics is an entertainment to which the admission fee is the price of a newspaper. Others are more serious about politics and study it so that they can learn to be effective participants in public life, as defenders of the existing order, as reformers, or as revolutionaries. Still others study politics to find out why certain events like wars and revolutions have occurred in the past and whether they are likely to occur in the future. Some people, however, are less interested in explaining what actually happens than in determining what ought to be. They study politics in an effort to find the purpose of life.

Is it possible to make sense out of this wide variety of motivations? Is there a common link among them—treating politics as an entertainment, seeking to become a political actor, trying to understand why political events occur, and attempting to determine the purpose of life? It seems that in order to reach any of these particular goals a person must already have a certain kind of knowledge. He must have a general image of the *public situation*—the larger environment in which he lives and acts.

Human existence is always bounded by particular frames of space and time and filled up by particular objects, meanings, and relations. There are no human beings in general, only particular people in specific situations. There is a Vietnamese villager slowly dying from a wound inflicted by a bombing attack and an American suburbanite watching him die on a television screen. Both are human because both can imagine themselves moving from the present into the future. However, the two futures that they project are very different. The Vietnamese villager worries about what will become of his family when he is gone and anticipates with dread the stroke of death. The suburbanite is mentally preparing himself for his weekly night out playing cards. Thus, each one is a particular human being in a specific situation. They are brought together through a vast network of worldwide electronic media, but their lives scarcely touch and they have no concern for one another. However, both the Vietnamese villager and the American suburbanite have some ideas about where they stand in history and what their personal lives mean in the light of larger trends. The Vietnamese villager may believe that he is a victim of American aggressors seeking to control the destinies of his people. He may view history as a struggle between white imperialists and oppressed colored peoples. The American suburbanite may believe that he is part of a great nation attempting to extend freedom in the world. He may view current history as a struggle between world communism and Western democracy. Each one makes sense of what happens in the world in terms of his image of the public situation.

Before a person can study political activity—for whatever reason—he must have an image of the public situation. He must be aware that he is living at a particular place and in a particular time, and he must have some idea of what activities are most important at the historical juncture at which he stands. A person who enjoys the "great game of politics" may view political affairs as a contest between liberals and conservatives, workers and managers, blacks and whites, or any other pair of adversaries. However, he needs some framework in which to place his information about the day to day conflicts. The need for an image of the public situation is equally obvious for the person who wants to participate effectively in politics. The side that he chooses and the type of action that he takes will generally make sense in terms of his view of what human activities are crucial at a given time and place. The same holds true for the person who wants to explain political events. For example, many political scientists study racial conflict while few, if any, study the frequency with which politicians stutter. This is because they themselves, or the people who give them research grants, believe that racial conflict is a more important part of the current public situation than stuttering politicians. Finally, the person who wants to know what human life ought to be also needs this larger image. He does not search for meaning in a vacuum but is motivated by his sense of current conditions and their deficiencies.

Most people are not fully aware of their own images of the public situation, and even less are aware of the content or even the existence of alternatives. Frequently, a person's image of the public situation remains implicit, in the sense that it is better revealed in the way he acts and feels than in what he thinks. For example, the person who votes in an election is usually implying that the vote is an important part of the public situation, whether or not he has a conscious opinion about its importance. Of course, some people who believe that the vote is insignificant continue to go to the polling booth out of habit or out of vague feelings of guilt. It is also important to note that many people hold images of the public situation which have been fabricated for them by propagandists, teachers, parents, or friends. They simply accept these images without thinking about them and assume that they are correct. In short, it is probably fair to say that most people shape their political opinions and actions in terms of categories that they have never consciously evaluated. They think and act politically in terms that other people have figured out.

Political conflicts usually involve competing images of the current public situation and clashing visions of future ones. For example, many white Americans believe that black Americans are savages and parasites living off tax dollars supplied by hard-working whites. These people look forward to a future in which blacks will find it difficult, if not impossible, to receive welfare checks. On the other hand, many black Americans believe that powerful whites are drawing up plans for the mass murder of blacks. These people dream of a future in which they will "get whitey off our backs" and "gain control of our own communities." Without images of the present and dreams of the future, politics would be merely physical collision. It is such images and visions that make politics human activity rather than animal behavior.

POLITICAL SCIENCE AND THE PUBLIC SITUATION

Political science is, before anything else, an attempt to clarify the public situation. This effort involves two main steps. First, the political scientist must criticize the various images actually held by people in their everyday lives. Second, he must attempt to create an image more adequate than the ones he has criticized. This means that the political scientist must have standards to guide his criticism and creation. While there are many sets of standards, five of them seem particularly important—accuracy, consistency, comprehensiveness, felt adequacy, and fruitfulness.

Images of the public situation can be judged by their factual accuracy. For example, it is possible to find out how many black Americans actually are drawing welfare checks and make some determination about whether or not welfare clients are motivated by the desire to be parasites. Similarly, it might be possible to find out whether or not powerful whites are plotting the mass murder of blacks and even to make some determination of the conditions in which mass murders are likely to occur. It is important to note, however, that even if a person is shown that his image of the public situation is inaccurate he may not give it up. Instead, he may ignore the evidence, insist it is not true, or claim it is unimportant.

A second standard is consistency. Two statements are inconsistent when one statement affirms what the other denies. For example, some whites claim that blacks are stupid. However, these same whites frequently also claim that blacks are exceptionally crafty when it comes to getting on welfare rolls. Since one cannot be stupid and crafty at the same time, the two claims are inconsistent. As in the case of accuracy, however, it would be a mistake to believe that people will give up an image of the public situation just because they are shown that it contains inconsistencies.

A third standard is comprehensiveness—the scope of what is being described. For example, some people view the public situation solely in terms of the population explosion. They are concerned that overpopulation will lead to the impoverishment of the human race, the depletion of natural resources, and eventually to the destruction of humanity. Convinced of their view, they seize upon information that can be related to the population explosion and ignore information that has little to do with this problem. Thus, their image lacks breadth, even though it may have depth in one or several areas. At the other extreme are images containing vague, general, and untestable statements about the human condition. For example, some people express an image of the public situation composed of the single statement, "Everybody has got their own racket." This kind of statement does little to help one think about specific political events or act with respect to them. When political scientists strive for comprehensiveness, they do not attempt to include every event in their descriptions, but only the important trends and problems. But, how does one define what is important? There is no easy answer to this question, and the best that can be said now is that people generally define what is important according to their interests.

A fourth standard is felt adequacy. Here the question is whether or not a particular image helps the person orient himself better to political events, see the relations of his activity to other activities, and better grasp his possibilities for future action. Felt adequacy is a more personal standard than the others and it is difficult to describe precisely, but some attempt can be made to show what it means. It may appear to some people that there is something wrong with an image of the public situation based entirely upon the population explosion, besides its narrowness of scope. Such an image may strike one as distorted, petty, and even silly or grotesque. From one point of view, it seems to lack nobility and to see human beings merely as breeding animals. From another point of view, it seems to lack seriousness because it minimizes the importance of racial, class, and national conflicts. Such terms as distorted, petty, silly, and grotesque are taken from the vocabulary of taste. And while such terms lack precision, they point to the important standard of felt adequacy. Many political scientists, who are very much concerned with accuracy, consistency, and comprehensiveness, disregard felt adequacy. This is, perhaps, one reason why their critics claim that their work is irrelevant.

A final standard is fruitfulness. Here the question is whether or not an image gives rise to new possibilities for acting to transform the public situation. For example, there are images of the public situation which include the ideas that human beings are becoming more and more the servants of machines and that this tendency is fated to continue until all are reduced to robots. Such images may have a certain felt adequacy for some people, but they certainly do not provide human actors with fresh possibilities. In order to use the standard of fruitfulness a person must believe that human beings are capable of actively transforming their situations. Those who do not hold this belief will generally confine themselves to using the standards of accuracy, consistency, comprehensiveness, and felt adequacy, and will reject the standard of fruitfulness.

In its fullest development political science aims at clarifying the public situation through accurate, consistent, comprehensive, adequate, and fruitful images of that situation. In so doing, it also undertakes the critical task of judging the images held by people as they act in daily life. Both the critical and constructive tasks are fundamental to political science.

WHAT GOOD IS POLITICAL SCIENCE?

Many people enter political study with the expectation that they will be entertained by the great game of politics, that they will learn how to change the world, or that they will learn to distinguish right from wrong. Relatively few begin studying political science with the expectation that they will seek to explain political events or to clarify the public situation. This is the case because most people take their own views for granted. They do not look beyond their particular opinions and preferences to the context in which those opinions and preferences have meaning. And, if they do become aware that their judgments are embedded in a particular image, many people do not want to find out whether the image that they hold is accurate, consistent, comprehensive, and fruitful. They are satisfied with the fact that it has some felt adequacy for them, and they are more interested in learning how to satisfy their preferences than in questioning them. If this is the case, then it is necessary to ask whether political science can do any good for most people.

One position on this question is that political science can only cause trouble and discomfort for the majority of people and that teaching it to large numbers of people may even lead to social disorder and tragedy. Odd as this position may seem, it must be taken seriously. As we have already noted, bringing people to an awareness of their images of the public situation, criticizing those images, and showing alternatives is not very important to most people. (It also may be uncomfortable to learn about such things.) However, much more important is the fact that once a person learns that his image is one among many and is open to criticism, he may become disoriented and embittered or fanatically embrace a new image of the public situation. This can lead to unhappiness, turmoil, and even violence.

There is no direct argument against this position. There is some truth in every one of its claims. However, instruction in political science does not inevitably lead to the destruction of human good. Learning about images of the public situation and the ways that they can be criticized can lead to freedom just as well as it can produce disorientation. Realizing that the views one holds are relative to other views and thus imperfect may cause a person to take greater responsibility for his actions. Further, it may convince a person to undertake the open-ended and never ending task of creating an accurate, consistent, comprehensive, adequate, and fruitful image of the public situation.

THE CURRENT PUBLIC SITUATION

It would, perhaps, be useful at this point to present a specific image of the current public situation—the image, in fact, which has guided the selection of the readings in this book. This image does not represent the only way of looking at the current public situation, and many people find it neither adequate nor fruitful. However, thought about the public situation must start somewhere, and it is always best to start with the events and trends that one finds most compelling. It is particularly important to begin with the concrete experiences that one considers most important in his daily life and in the larger events of which he becomes aware. This concern with concrete experiences will be the standard guiding the following discussion.

THE EXPERIENCES OF PARADOX AND AMBIVALENCE

It seems to be a hallmark of the present that many people are unsure of what the future holds for them and how their own courses of action relate to that future. In a relatively superficial sense, this uncertainty is frequently expressed in the idea that since World War II people have been living with the knowledge that nuclear and other modern weapons have the capacity to destroy humanity. Applied to nuclear weapons there is little comfort in the statement that weapons do not kill people, people kill people. More recently, the uncertainty has been expressed in the notion that it is quite possible that humanity will be destroyed through overpopulation, famine, air pollution, water pollution, the accumulation of solid wastes, micro-organisms from other planets, the accumulation of pesticides, or any combination of two or more of these factors and a multitude of others. Many commentators on the current scene have constructed an image of the public situation by putting together all of these factors and tying them up in a package labeled "technology out of control." There is, of course, no way of proving that humanity will not be poisoned to death by the waste products of industry. However, the image summed up in the phrase "technology out of control" does not provide an answer to the question of why there has been a general lack of concern with industrial by-products in the past. It is certainly true that a portion of the current lack of confidence in the future is a result of fear about the possible consequences of technology. But, it also appears true that this uncertainty has a deeper dimension.

One of the dictionary definitions of paradox is "something inconsistent with common experience or having contradictory qualities." The dictionary definition of ambivalence is "the simultaneous existence of conflicting emotions, as love and hate, in one person toward another person or thing." The basis of the image of the public situation to be presented here is that contemporary human experience is marked by paradoxes and that the contemporary response to that experience is ambivalent. In brief, people are unsure of what the future holds for them and how their own courses of action relate to that future, because their present experience is paradoxical and their current choices are governed by mixed motives.

One does not have to look very far to find paradoxes in contemporary public life; a very partial listing will show how the very structure of current experience contains paradox. A convenient starting point is the "technology out of control" argument. There is, of course, nothing paradoxical about humanity choking to death in its polluted air or drowning in its own poisoned effluent. However, while a great many spokesmen are warning their constituents that catastrophe is beyond the next turn in the road, other commentators are hailing the dawn of an economy of abundance in which machines will do the drudge work and human beings will lead an existence of creative leisure. When the "technology out of control" and "economy of abundance" images are put side by side and experienced at the same time, there is a paradox in experience. This paradox cannot be resolved simply by saying that technology contains a promise and a peril, and it is not simply a point of accentuating the promise and eliminating the peril. There is, in fact, a haunting notion that the promise and the peril may be inseparable. It is conceivable that both images will be proven correct. At the very moment that people begin to lead a life of creative leisure they may begin to choke on their polluted air.

Faced with such paradox, attitudes toward technology are ambivalent. On the one hand, people do not want to give up the comforts and opportunities for expanding horizons provided by many of the new technologies. On the other, they do not want life to be imperiled on the planet. These ambivalent desires and the mixed emotions associated with them lead to behaviors that might appear paradoxical to an outside observer. Anti-pollution editorials are carried in mass circulation newspapers, the raw materials for which are produced in paper mills which dump mercury into rivers and lakes. People insist upon eating only "organic" foods, to which no synthetics have been added, but refuse to spend the money to have their automobiles equipped with anti-pollution devices. People join communes to get "close to nature" but bring electric guitars and stereo sets along with them. Businessmen join anti-litter campaigns, while their factories produce tons of solid waste. These examples are not meant to show that people are either stupid, selfish, or evil. Instead, they are meant to show that when people experience paradox they often become ambivalent, and that when they become ambivalent their behavior frequently appears to be paradoxical. The current love-hate relation with technology is a result of the paradoxes contained in experiencing technology.

Getting away from technology, which is only one part of human experience, one finds paradoxes in contemporary race relations. Government agencies are continually publicizing statistics to show that the economic conditions of racial minorities are improving. Yet at the very time that these statistics are released, there is an outcry that more and more members of racial minorities are on welfare rolls, evidence that social services are deteriorating in the ghetto, and fear of a race war. Those who look at the economic improvement sometimes counsel "benign neglect" of minority groups and contend that time will be a great healer of divisions. Others, who are more impressed by rising welfare costs and fears that their children will be "bussed across town," prepare to defend themselves against a rising tide of color. Still others urge that the public sector redouble its efforts to bring economic development to America's "internal colonies." These notions by no means exhaust the ideas that people have about race relations. However, when even these are put together, experience becomes paradoxical, and the paradoxes lead to ambivalence. Many blacks state that they are through being treated like animals and demand that they be treated as human beings. Yet, at the same time, some of them claim that they are special kinds of human beings possessed of "soul," which gives them far greater sensitivity than the white "pigs." Many whites are staunch defenders of equal rights for blacks, but they resist attempts of blacks to move into their neighborhoods. They say that their "hands are tied" because they cannot let the property value of their homes fall. Has there been progress in race relations? How would one define that progress? The difficulty in answering these questions reveals the paradox in contemporary experience.

Still other paradoxes appear in military affairs. At the very moment that the military has risen to the height of its importance and influence in the United States, it is subjected to increasing criticism and abuse. At the very time the military services are making a concerted effort to show that they are "professional," the public is told of atrocities committed by ill-trained American soldiers in Vietnam. These paradoxes give rise to ambivalence. A familiar experience of ambivalence is that felt by the young man confronted by the draft. He may not want to be a law breaker, but he also does not believe that he should serve in a war that he considers immoral. He wonders whether he is motivated by cowardice or principle. At one and the same time he may feel an obligation to "serve when called" and an obligation to refuse military service. By no means do all people confronted by the draft feel this way, but many do.

The discussion above merely contains a small sample of the paradoxes characteristic of contemporary human experience. These paradoxes and many others, however, are not unrelated to one another. Basic to the image of the public situation presented here is the idea that one central paradox in current affairs can be used to make sense out of many of the more obvious paradoxes. It is not comprehensive enough to cover all of the aspects of human experience that people consider significant at the present time. However, it goes a long way toward showing why so many people today are unsure of what the future holds for them and how their own courses of action relate to that future.

FREEDOM AND REGIMENTATION

The central paradox in the contemporary public situation is that at the very time more and more human beings are becoming aware of themselves as free actors capable of making their own decisions, they are being called upon to live much of their lives in vast organizations possessed of impressive means of regimentation. The head-on clash between freedom and regimentation is the central paradox of the present time.

An appreciation of the interplay between freedom and regimentation, and how it is expressed in the current public situation, requires that these two central ideas be given precise meanings. It is best to start with freedom, because it is in terms of freedom that one defines regimentation. In the current public situation, freedom can be defined as a series of stages between the limits of silent rebellion and creativity. Throughout their social lives, human beings are presented with a wide variety of rules that they are supposed to follow, images that they are supposed to believe in, and models that they are supposed to imitate. The first glimmer of freedom in human existence comes when a person holds himself apart from the rules, images, and models, and recognizes that they may not be right, true, or good. The person may continue to follow the rules, espouse the accepted beliefs in conversation, and outwardly imitate the models, but he will keep a private self independent of these activities. For example, a student may do all of his assignments just as his instructor wants them done and believe that what he is writing is false. The instructor has received what he has "asked for," but he has had no lasting effect on the student's belief structure.

Beyond silent rebellion is more overt rebellion, in which the person refuses to obey a rule or a command, to espouse an accepted belief, or to imitate a pre-existing model. This ability to say "No" has been stressed by many twentieth-century thinkers who hold that people in organizations have the responsibility to judge whether or not the orders that they receive are moral and the obligation to disobey those orders that they judge to be immoral. According to this viewpoint, one is in bad faith if he claims that the individual's responsibility to make decisions can be transferred to an organization. During the twentieth century people have been ordered to commit mass murders as part of their organizational roles. Is it convincing for such people to plead that as long as they are getting paid they have to follow orders, that the organization is wiser than they are, that they face punishment if they do not carry out the order, or that someone else would have carried out the order if they did not? Of course, mass murder is merely the extreme case. What does one say about the salesman who is encouraged to engage in false advertising, the executive who is encouraged to engage in price fixing, or the politician who makes secret deals with those who he publicly proclaims are his enemies? Every day many people are confronted with the choice of going along or saying "No." Once people sense that they should make this choice consciously, it is no longer possible for organizations to appear to work automatically. This is the point of Michael Harmon's article and of John Paynter's reply.

Beyond the stage of overt rebellion is choice among alternatives. While it is true that in overt rebellion there is a choice between going along and refusing to obey, the refusal often leads to embracing an alternative project. Once people realize that they can say "No" it is usually not long before they become aware of alternative courses of action that have been suggested by others. During the 1960's a number of young people learned that they could refuse to go along with such organizations as the military, business firms, and universities. Some of them became aware of alternatives, like living in communes, and embraced one or another of the alternatives.

The stage of choice among alternatives can become the stage of the fullest expression of freedom, creation of alternatives. The selections of Ivan Illich, Ernest Becker, Peter Bachrach, Henry Kariel, Kenneth A. Megill, and Robert Jay Lifton emphasize various aspects of the drive for creative freedom. They believe that human existence is not a game in which one plays by the rules or simply breaks the rules. The presence of alternatives shows this to be the case. However, human existence also is not a supermarket or a television listing from which one chooses among pre-existing alternatives. The alternatives have to come from somewhere, and experience seems to teach that they come from human beings imaginatively working upon the world and themselves. In the twentieth century many thinkers have come to interpret creative freedom as the fullest development of human freedom. They see the human condition as one of self-transcendence, in which the human being is capable of surpassing pre-existing definitions of his nature. This is a far more ambitious definition of freedom than definitions that have appeared in past centuries, when freedom was thought of as following an objective moral law or being able to satisfy one's desires. Creative freedom demands far more of human beings than the other types. E. H. Carr, whose work appears in this volume, explains this:

And if I were asked to define freedom, I do not think I could do better than the definition of Berdyaev . . .: "The opportunity for creative activity." This definition includes within itself the old and unsatisfyingly negative definition of freedom as "the recognition of necessity"; for creative activity implies an understanding of the conditions in which such activity can be pursued.[1]

The fact that creative freedom has become an important ideal in the twentieth century shows that human beings have come to expect more from themselves and others than they did before. Those who deem creative freedom important are satisfied neither to accept existing conditions nor to follow slavishly someone else's lead in changing them. Instead they demand a role in changing those conditions, as full participants. It is such a demand that is sparking the current liberation movements—the women's movement, the black movement, the student movement, and others. There is nothing paradoxical about this demand for creative freedom and this new confidence in human possibility and social experimentation. The paradox arises from the fact that at the very moment in history when the vision of human possibility is fuller and more demanding than ever before, nightmares of mass regimentation abound.

Regimentation begins where freedom ends. Like freedom, it has its degrees. The weakest form of regimentation appears when the possibility for creativity is not recognized, or if it is recognized, is not encouraged. Repressing creativity cuts off an entire mode of human experience, but it may still leave people with alternatives from which to choose. Regimentation intensifies as alternatives are progressively eliminated through force, censorship, constraint on production, or propaganda. At the point where there is only one alternative, the person has the choice of going along or saying "No" (and taking the consequences). However, this is not the limit of regimentation. In the twentieth century, many thinkers have begun to fear that it is now becoming possible to wipe out the most elementary form of freedom, the ability to keep part of oneself at a distance from his social relations and the roles that he is called upon to play. Complete regimentation would come when human beings, in robot fashion, were brought to perform tasks blueprinted for them in advance by a power elite controlling advanced technologies. This obedient herd would not know of any reality but the one programmed for it by the elite. Individuals would not rebel because they would not have any selves apart from the program that had been imposed upon them. C. Wright Mills summed up the problem expressed in this nightmare:

The ultimate problem of freedom is the problem of the cheerful robot, and it arises in this form today because today it has become evident to us that *all* men do *not* naturally *want* to be free; that all men are not willing or

1. E. H. Carr, *The New Society* (New York: St. Martin's Press, Inc., 1960), p. 118.

not able, as the case may be, to exert themselves to acquire the reason that freedom requires.[2]

Never before in history has the problem of freedom and regimentation been put so starkly and severely, and in such extremes. The choice appears to be between an expansion of human freedom into entirely new domains or a contraction of freedom to its very disappearance. It is this clash between freedom and regimentation, between complete manipulation and the burgeoning of creativity, which is the central paradox of contemporary political experience. It is this paradox which explains the widespread uncertainty about the future and the bewilderment about how one's own course of action relates to that future.

THE CONTEXT OF THE PARADOX

The paradox posed by the twin possibilities of an expansion of creative freedom and a world of complete manipulation does not appear in a vacuum. Most of the selections chosen for this book can be interpreted as attempts to fill in the social and cultural context of the paradox. Many of the authors, of course, do not interpret the current public situation in terms of paradox and ambivalence. They seize upon the theme of creative freedom *or* regimentation, and ignore the other theme. However, even when the paradox itself is not grasped, an attempt to appreciate the background of one side of it can be quite useful.

Several themes seem to recur continually in discussions of the contemporary public situation. Perhaps the first and most important of these is planning. In Europe and the United States during the nineteenth century, it was generally felt that economic enterprise unhindered by government control and freely competitive assured continually greater levels of prosperity. Public morality could be summed up in the term "enlightened self-interest." As long as he respected the lives and property of others, a person was considered moral if he strove to make the best bargain for himself in the marketplace. In the twentieth century the beliefs in free enterprise and enlightened self-interest have come under severe attack and have been abandoned in practice, even if some people still pay lip service to them or even believe that they act upon them. In place of competition has come planning, whether by governments or large corporations.

There are many reasons why planning has progressively replaced competition in the twentieth century, and some of these are given in the selections that appear in this book. Kenneth Melvin, for one, argues that planning is needed because people have demanded guarantees of security in their enjoyment of the necessities of life. According to Melvin, large numbers of people rejected the notions of free competition and enlightened self-interest when they seemed to lead to depressions and extreme inequalities of wealth. They demanded, instead, a welfare state that would regulate the economy and prevent periodic impoverishment of

2. C. Wright Mills, *The Sociological Imagination* (New York: Grove Press, Inc., 1961), p. 175.

broad sections of the population. Another argument is provided by Friedrich Georg Junger, who claims that the modern fascination with technology and mechanism leads to treating human beings and their relations with one another as objects that can be engineered. John Kenneth Galbraith maintains that an objective of huge economic enterprises is to reduce risk and guarantee a stable rate of return on investment. Since new technologies are very costly and specialized, corporations try to guarantee a market in advance and plan how to exploit that market efficiently. In pursuing these goals they call on government for help. E. H. Carr traces planning back to wartime economic mobilization. There is no need to choose among these explanations for the "correct" one. Each of the factors mentioned above has been important in the progressive growth of planning. It is, however, important to note that planning by large organizations is a significant part of the contemporary experience of paradox.

In planning, future actions are not left to chance or spontaneity, but an attempt is made to control them. Thus, planning is a realm in which the paradox of freedom and regimentation appears with particular intensity. On the one hand, planning is the social activity that seems to come closest to the exercise of creative freedom. It is in planning that human beings become conscious of themselves as actors capable of taking charge of their destinies. The future does not just happen to them, but they attempt to exert control over it. On the other hand, planning is the social activity that seems to come closest to complete manipulation. Planning has been made possible in the twentieth century partly because of new management techniques, the development of the social sciences, and impressive media of communication. All of these developments allow for increased control over human activity and open up the possibility that people will be more and more manipulated by propaganda, bribery, and coercion into performing tasks that have been programmed by the planner. Thus, planning appears to be paradoxical. It seems to offer a new expansion of creative freedom at the very time it promises to take all freedom away.

Another theme that recurs in contemporary discussions of the public situation is the confrontation between elitism and democracy. Political thinkers have always been interested in ruling classes, but only recently have they become acutely aware of the linkages between these ruling classes and complex organizations. According to many commentators, like C. Wright Mills, Milovan Djilas, and Jean Meynaud, the elites of today are made up of those who hold the highest positions in the wealthiest and most powerful organizations. They claim that such elites make major decisions that affect the lives of masses of people and that they do not consult these masses. Other observers, like Robert Dahl, acknowledge the existence of elites but stress that there are multiple elites associated with a wide variety of different special interest groups. Thus, a group will attempt to exert pressure and influence policy when an issue comes up that concerns it but will usually refrain from action on problems that have little to do with its stability or expansion. For example, labor unions are likely to try to influence minimum-wage laws, but they are much less likely to take stands and commit resources on the issue of whether or not prayers should be said in public schools.

Some current thinkers oppose elitism in the name of democracy and participation. They agree that the present public situation is characterized by the existence of elites at the top of organizations and interest groups, but they claim that the current arrangement is neither necessary nor desirable. They maintain that many people, particularly the poor, are not represented by any powerful interest groups and, therefore, get lost in the shuffle. Further, they hold that people who do not have a say in making decisions that affect them are deprived of dignity. Political thinkers like Peter Bachrach urge that a democracy of participation be extended to the complex organizations in which people spend much of their lives.

Demands for greater participation in making decisions are an important part of many current social movements. Some welfare clients have demanded a greater voice in the content and administration of benefits, some students have demanded a greater role in the formulation of curriculum and dormitory rules, some consumers have claimed a right to exercise control over the quality of products they buy. These are only a few examples of the movement for greater participation, which extends from the action of parent groups in local school districts to the demands of United States Senators for a greater role in shaping foreign policy. Thus, the call for "participatory democracy" is not merely an idea of some political thinkers but a working hypothesis for an entire complex of current social movements.

The confrontation between elitism and participation in both thought and action is another source of paradox in the current public situation. Year by year governments, corporations, and other complex organizations get larger and larger and take up more and more of people's space and time. They also take on more and more functions and interpenetrate with one another through complicated links. For example, the large American university (sometimes called a "multiversity") may conduct military research, produce dairy products on its farm, provide space for business and labor conventions, run psychiatric clinics, offer mass entertainments in the form of sports and variety shows, run a publishing house, offer courses to students, and do a wide variety of other things. What is the purpose of such a university? Often it seems to be a "conglomerate" with no purpose but to grow as large as it can in any direction which presents itself. Most of the enormous organizations of today are conglomerates with many and varying functions, tied together by a concern with growth and prestige. The large organizations of today are elitist in the sense that the power of making policy decisions is concentrated in the hands of relatively few people at the top. They are a factor of increasing importance in the current public situation.

However, the conglomerate is not alone on the present scene. Simultaneous with the growth of complex organizations has been an increasing interest in frameworks of social life aimed at encouraging participation, like communities and various other communal experiments. Some people have "dropped out" of complex organizations just at the time that these organizations have been reaching new heights of power, wealth, and prestige. Some people have formed experimental communes, in both urban and rural areas, to see whether they could create more satisfying alternatives than those offered by the conglomerates. These communes often attempt to carry participation in common decisions to its maximum and to see that the burdens of keeping the commune going are shared equally. Other people have chosen to experiment with the possibilities of the local community rather than with communes. Community clinics and law offices have been opened up by young doctors and lawyers who are dissatisfied with organized medicine and law, and there has also been a spurt of community organization in minority neighborhoods.

Generally, these various communal experiments are poorly funded and weak, which puts them at a serious disadvantage in relation to the large organizations. However, for some people, particularly a number of the young, the commune already has more prestige than the conglomerate. This interest in the possibilities of community at a time when complex organizations seem to be gaining in importance presents a paradox. The complex organizations may have most of the wealth and power, but they can no longer be confident of loyalty. Their impressive array of material rewards and punishments was not able to prevent the emergence of an active "quest for community" in the 1960's.

At least part of the paradoxical quality of contemporary experience is due to a tendency to separate the issues of planning and democracy. Many people believe that planning necessarily goes along with elitism, and this leads them to conclude that the public situation is moving in a direction of regimentation. One of the most striking events of the twentieth century has been the emergence of totalitarianism, a form of rule combining comprehensive planning implemented by advanced technology with elitist decision-making. Those who believe that planning and elitism are inseparable point to the examples of totalitarian social orders and warn that humanity is only at the beginning of a new dark age. However, there is no universal agreement that planning and elitism are necessarily combined. According to observers like Dahl, the public situation is made up of a series of competing interest groups, and there is little likelihood of comprehensive planning. Still others do believe that planning and elitism are associated with one another but maintain that both should be abolished in favor of a system of small communities. Finally, there are those who would advocate a future public situation based on linking planning with participation. It does not at all seem necessary to hold that planning and elitism are always found together, or will be found together in the future. There is nothing in the idea of planning (self-conscious effort to control the future) that necessitates elitism (exclusion of certain human beings from participation in decisions that affect them). Perhaps a challenge of the current public situation is to break any links between planning and elitism.

AMBIVALENCE AND THE PUBLIC SITUATION

The image of the public situation discussed above takes as its central feature the paradox that at the very time many people are coming to an awareness of the possibilities for creative freedom, fear is spreading that humanity will be reduced to an army of robots. This paradox appears in a political context characterized by the growth of large-scale planning by complex organizations and control of these organizations by elites. Further, the elitism is being seriously challenged by social movements calling for a democracy of participation, and the effectiveness of the planning is being questioned by observers who see the most carefully laid plans fail because of mismanagement or the conflict of interest groups. It is important to note that the paradox outlined here is not built into the human condition. As has been noted, a future public situation may be characterized by democratic planning opening up large areas for creative freedom. In the present public situation, however, paradox seems to color much of political experience.

The paradox of freedom and regimentation leads to a deep-seated ambivalence in many people. Some individuals are able to throw themselves wholeheartedly into careers in one or another of the complex organizations. Others reject these organizations outright and make a firm commitment to creating alternative ways of life. However, many feel themselves caught between the conglomerate and the community—in transition between an old self accepting social models and a new self yet unknown. They are unwilling to surrender the seeming security provided by the organization and, for those at the higher levels, its opportunities for interesting work. Yet they are not satisfied with the values produced by these organizations and are uncomfortable that they may be involved, at long range, in actions that they would never perform personally. Such people may alternate between cynicism and enthusiasm, between hope and fear, between shows of independence and expressions of total dependency. In other cases, they may make a conscious effort to keep "cool" and remain uninvolved. In all cases they are ambivalent. They can neither accept nor reject the present and, thus, they are pulled in both directions at once. A striking example of this ambivalence is the situation of many young women at the present time. A woman who has graduated from college has the opportunity for a career of her own. She has learned too much to be satisfied with simply being a housewife and a mother, but she has vague feelings that she will not be "fulfilled" if she gives up the traditional role. She has her own aspirations, but she is not sure that she will have security outside of a traditional marriage. At the same time, she even feels some physical distress in looking forward to a life of cleaning house and catering to the needs of others. Description of just this one example of ambivalence could go on for pages. Readers can surely think of many others.

It will probably not be soon that the intense paradox and ambivalence of the current public situation will be alleviated. However, these characteristics of experience can best be surpassed if they are fully understood. Such understanding can be gained through an appreciation of the political process and its bearing on the central dilemmas of human existence. All of the significant problems in the current human condition are linked to political processes.

THE POLITICAL PROCESS

Political activity appears within every public situation and provides an important key to clarifying that situation. There are many different ideas about the nature of politics, some of the most important of which are discussed in articles that appear later in this book. One great debate over the definition of politics involves those who view the study of politics as the "master science" and those who view it as the "science of power." Some, like Herbert J. Spiro, who claim that political science is the master science, define politics as the activity in which human beings decide upon the purposes of their communities and how to implement those purposes. Spiro believes that politics at its best is a process of rational discussion about the nature and possibilities of the good life. Others, like Hans Morgenthau, who claim that political science is the science of power, define politics as the activity through which some human beings come to dominate their fellow human beings. Thus, politics becomes the process through which the interests of some are satisfied at the expense of the desires of others.

A second great debate over the definition of politics involves those who view political activity as "care of the community" and those who see it as a process of continuous conflict. Philip Haring, who defines politics as care of the community, holds that the general problem of human existence is the maintenance of cooperation. Since human beings are not self-sufficient, they depend upon one another for the continuation of existence. At its best, politics sustains and enhances this interdependence. H. L. Nieburg takes the view that politics is a process of incessant conflict, in which diverse groups and individuals strive to attain their particular objectives. Methods of conflict vary from peaceful discussion to sustained violence, but the process of conflict itself is always present.

The two debates are closely related to one another. Those who define politics as the master science also tend to view political activity as care of the community. Similarly, those who define politics as the science of power also tend to view political activity as a process of conflict. However, there is no logical necessity behind this tendency. A person can define politics as the master science and claim that the purposes of communities are arrived at through a process of bargaining and competition among groups. A person can define politics as the science of power and claim that the exercise of power is the only way human beings can assure that their web of interdependence will be maintained. Ruling groups frequently take this last view, while movements favoring change often adopt the view that politics is the science of power and political activity is a process of conflict.

Many political thinkers hold that it is false to say that political science is either the master science or the science of power, or that political activity is either cooperation or conflict. These thinkers, like Maurice Duverger, hold that politics is Janus-faced, in that it includes both elements of each pair. From this viewpoint, politics is a tension set up between opposite poles. Since this tension can never be fully resolved, wisdom resides in avoiding commitment to any polar position.

The idea that politics actually embraces both sides of each debate is attractive because it seems to accord with everyday political experience. However, simply stating that in each case both sides are partly right does not go very far. It would be far better if a common basis for each of the competing definitions could be found. Such a common basis is provided by the idea of politics as active reflection on the pattern of human activity.

POLITICS AS ACTIVE REFLECTION

Each of the four major definitions of politics described above includes the idea of politics as active reflection on the pattern of human activity. When politics is defined as the master science, or as the activity in which human beings decide upon the purposes of their communities and how to implement these purposes, politics is being viewed as a debate about which human activities should be encouraged and which human activities should be discouraged. Thus, politics is being seen as a process of active reflection. When politics is defined as the science of power, or as the activity through which some human beings come to dominate their fellows, politics is being viewed as a set of relations in which some activities are encouraged at the expense of others. This also is active reflection, but from another viewpoint. Similarly, when politics is defined as a process of caring for the community, it is clear that seeing to the maintenance of interdependence involves actively reflecting upon what people are doing. Finally, when politics is defined as a process of conflict, it is clear that conflict arises when human beings attempt to encourage some activities at the expense of others. Such conflict involves active reflection on the pattern of human activity, because the demands of some are being compared to the demands of others.

Each of the four major definitions of politics stresses a different phase of a continuous political process. These phases are policy, decision, administration, and evaluation. In the phase of policy alternative futures are offered to a community, in decision one of these futures is chosen as a basis for action, in administration there is an attempt to put the chosen future into effect, and in evaluation the success of that attempt is judged. Together, the four phases describe a process of active reflection.

The first phase—*policy*—emphasizes politics as a process of conflict. Here the primary question is, "What competing policies are being promoted and who is promoting them?" As active reflection on the pattern of human activity, politics is partly a process of individuals and groups advocating, through methods ranging from violence to discussion, alternative definitions of the future. These alternative definitions are policies, and clusters of policies are frequently associated with opposed social groupings. When politics is defined as conflict the phase of policy is emphasized.

The second phase of the political process—*decision*—stresses politics as a set of power relations. In this case the primary question is, "Which of the competing policies will be put into effect, how is this decision made, and who makes it?" Thus, in the second phase of the political process choices are made among futures. These choices can be made in various ways and by various groups and individuals. It is here that the issue between elitism and participation is most clearly present.

In the third phase of the political process the emphasis is on politics as care of the community. Here the primary question is, "How are policies applied in particular cases?" Thus, while the second phase of the political process was a phase of decision, the third phase is one of *administration*. There are many difficulties involved in making a policy concrete, and seldom do particular applications fully meet the expectations of decision-makers. There are many reasons for this lack of fit, including the possibility that administrators are more concerned with preventing than they are in encouraging its success.

Finally, the fourth phase of the political process emphasizes politics as the master science, or reflection on the purposes of the community. This is the phase of *evaluation*, in which the major question is, "Is the present political process a good one?" In order to answer this question there must be one or more standards available against which to measure political practice. It is also clear that the phase of evaluation leads directly back into the phase of policy. When the public situation is evaluated negatively there will be calls for new policies, while when it is evaluated positively there will be efforts made to continue existing policies. Thus, the political process is a continuous process of active reflection on human activity, which links the four phases of policy, decision, administration, and evaluation.

POLITICS AND GOVERNMENT

The view of politics sketched above applies to activities that take place both inside and outside of governmental institutions. At one time, however, it was normal for political thinkers to hold that political activity was concentrated solely in the institutions of government. Government was seen as a set of institutions which specialized in the political process, and its specialization was based on the fact that it held a monopoly on the "legitimate" use of force. This view, which is still held by many people in everyday life, has some serious problems associated with it.

The first problem concerns the idea of "legitimate" use of force. Particularly in the large states of the contemporary world, there is no unanimous agreement that any government has the right to use force. In every state there are revolutionaries of various stripes who deny that the existing government is legitimate. These revolutionaries and their followers believe that they have the right to use force, not the state. Further, in every state there are people who deny that any person, group, or organization has the right to use force. Finally, in every state there are large numbers of people who do not give any thought to whether or not the use of force by the state is legitimate. This is not to mention the great numbers of people who believe that while in general the state may have the right to use force, its particular uses of force are wrong. All of these observations do not mean that there are no governments in the present world. Instead, they mean that government cannot sensibly be defined as a set of institutions *holding* a monopoly on the legitimate use of force. It is closer to the facts to define a government as a set of institutions *claiming* a monopoly on the legitimate use of force. This means that in a given territory there may be more than one government. Such is the case in South Vietnam, where an American-backed government vies with a communist-backed government.

Once one agrees that government does not hold a monopoly on the legitimate use of force, a second problem arises: It becomes difficult to argue reasonably that political processes are concentrated in governmental institutions. In the present world, governments perform many activities besides active reflection on human activity. For example, they run postal services, munitions plants, railroads, research laboratories, educational organizations, and museums. What sense does it make to state that these are secondary activities of government but that its activities with respect to policy, decision, administration, and evaluation are primary? Like all conglomerates of the contemporary world, government has no specific primary function. However, if governments perform many activities besides political activities, then political processes are found outside of governments. In any organization there are conflicts over policy, power relations and ways of making decisions, administrative activities, and evaluation. Even in families these processes occur. For example, a major policy issue in the family is frequently where to live. One side may favor an apartment and the other side may favor a private home. A decision on this issue may be reached through negotiation, the dictate of one side (sometimes backed up by force), discussion aimed at consensus, or some other method. The policy decided upon will likely be put into effect through a search for an appropriate dwelling unit followed by occupancy. Finally, as the family lives through the consequences of the decision, the members will evaluate those consequences in terms of some implicit or explicit standard of a decent life. This does not mean that politics embraces everything human. There are several human processes besides politics, such as creating objects, appreciating the world, and inquiring into events. However, where alternative goals appear, or where there are different ways of attaining a goal, the stage is set for politics.

Beyond the fact that governments perform other than political activities and that all organizations perform political activities, there is still another reason why the study of politics should not be confined to the activities that take place in and around governmental institutions. When the study of politics is identified with the study of government there is a tendency to ignore the possibility that important decisions may be made about the general pattern of human activities in economic and other nongovernmental organizations. This is the point made by Hazel Henderson in her article on corporations and the political process in the United States. Through decisions on where to locate operations, what to produce, and who is to be hired, large corporations make decisions about the general pattern of human activities which may never be reviewed by any government. In many communities in the United States the local government is relatively unimportant. It may, in fact, be responsible only for administering some public services which most people in the area agree should be performed. However, in such communities there may be a factory upon which most of the residents depend directly or indirectly for their livelihood. The hiring policies and production decisions of that factory are far more important to the residents than the activities of the local, state, or even the federal governments. The people in the community may sometimes take strong action to influence corporate decisions. For example, when some shipyards were closed down in Scotland, the workers occupied the yards and continued to perform their normal tasks. Few, if any, decisions made by their local government would have resulted in such action.

POLICY

With the understanding that politics is not to be confused with government, it is possible to discuss the political process in greater detail. As already noted, the first phase of the process is policy, or the advocacy of alternative, and often clashing, definitions of the future. Policy is the most creative part of politics, because it centers about visions of the form that social relations might take. Policy is closely linked to human self-transcendence, because it expresses the possibility that people can reject their present conditions and self-consciously move on to a new future. It is in the formulation of alternative policies that human beings become aware of a relatively open future over which they have some control. Thus, policy is a phase of the political process essential to the recognition and expansion of human freedom.

Since policy is made up of visions of the future, the value most closely associated with it is freedom of expression. Without freedom of expression it is impossible for people to become aware of the full range of possibilities available for future action and of the strengths and weaknesses of these possibilities. However, it is clear that nowhere in the world does complete freedom of expression exist, in the sense that nowhere in the world do all visions of the future get an equal hearing. The self-designated Emperor of the World residing in a mental hospital does not get equal television time with the President of the United States. The political opinions of a movie star gain far more publicity than those of a scholar. The program of the Democratic Party gets headlines, while the program of the Socialist Workers Party does not even gain mention on the back pages. At least in the United States, it is the wealthiest and best organized groups that have the best chance of making their visions of the future, or policies, well known. However, it would be misleading to simply describe a positive relationship between the ability to gain a hearing, and wealth and organization. The problem of free expression and the range of policy alternatives available at any given place and time can only be understood by analyzing the relation of thought and imagination to other human activities.

The policies proposed by individuals and groups vary from specific demands for particular rights to general proposals for changing the basic ways in which people act. Most policy in the United States is on the level of specific demands for particular rights. For example, a manufacturer troubled by foreign competition may decide that he should appeal to the Federal government for an import quota on the goods of his competitors. He is proposing a future in which he will prosper more, his competitors will lose money, and consumers will have less goods to choose from and will have to pay a higher price for what they buy. When policy is advocated on this low level it is quite boring to most people and of great concern to those specially interested. The manufacturer will follow avidly the response to his demand and attempt to influence that response. His competitors will also try to exert whatever pressure they can muster. However, the vast majority of people will not even be aware that there is a struggle going on, the result of which could spell financial success for some and ruin for others.

Frequently, a number of specific demands for particular rights will be compatible with one another, and this compatibility will form the basis of a coalition of special interests. For example, the manufacturer seeking an import quota may not care very much whether or not prayers should be said in public schools. A candidate for office may put together a program composed of policies favoring import quotas, prayer in public schools, opposition to school busing to achieve racial integration, tax credits for businesses undertaking pollution control, more expenditures on defense, and other proposals. This program is meant to appeal to people with the wealth to support his election campaign and ultimately to a majority of those who vote in the election. The key to a successful program of this sort is that it contains policies that are compatible with one another, in the sense that appeals to special interests are not cancelled out by policies that offend those interests. For some political thinkers, like Robert Dahl, the core of policy is the construction of such winning programs by political actors.

In the United States it is common to think of policies in the kinds of terms we have just described—as specific demands for particular rights or as loosely related sets of such demands strung together by candidates for office or office holders. This approach to policy, however, is not always fully satisfactory. The coalitions and programs that actually appear in the political process seem to be knit together by more than mere compatibility and expediency. They seem to have in common certain general ideas about the desirable direction of social life shared by broad social groupings. It is in terms of such general ideas and the activities represented by them that many of the more specific demands for particular rights make sense. Thus, broad and important social groupings frequently share images of the public situation in terms of which they propose plans for the future. When images of the public situation function as reference points for the policies proposed by social groupings, it is convenient to call them ideologies. Ideologies normally function to justify claims for the maintenance and expansion of rights made by broad and important social groupings.

Pluralism, an example of an ideology, is based on the idea that a good political process is one in which a large number of special interest groups make specific demands for particular rights and in which political actors attempt to put together winning coalitions of such groups. The desirability of such a political process is frequently defended on the grounds that it promotes stability and a certain type of freedom. Supposedly, this pluralist political process promotes stability because it insures that the most intense and powerful interests are satisfied and, therefore, will not resort to civil or revolutionary war. It is also supposed to promote the freedom of most individuals to live private lives unconcerned with politics, because the professional politicians are taking care of balancing the various interests in a "dynamic equilibrium." For this process to work well it is necessary to have general agreement on the principle that groups should not promote policies aimed at driving rivals out of existence and that losers should not resort to force to change a decision. This agreement, in turn, rests upon a situation in which no intense and powerful group is continually defeated and in which a large number of people belong to several groups, some of which are frequently opposed to one another and none of which absorbs the complete loyalties of a given individual. The fact that no intense and powerful group is continually defeated is a safeguard against any group resorting to revolution or civil war to change a decision. The fact that a large number of people belong to several cross-cutting groups is a safeguard against any single group or coalition attempting to promote policies aimed at driving rivals out of existence. According to the pluralist, politics is a balancing act performed by skilled professional politicians.

Pluralism is both a description of the public situation and a justification of that situation. It is this combination of description and justification that makes it an ideology. However, if pluralism is an ideology, it is necessary to determine which social groupings use it as a reference point for policies. The first step in this determination is to recognize that the core of pluralism is the idea of a continuous competition between interest groups, balanced by professional politicians. The second step is to recognize that such "free" competition favors the wealthiest and best-organized groups over the less well-endowed and more dispersed groups. Thus, pluralism is an ideal way of disguising and justifying the position of the most powerful interest groups. It makes such groups appear to be equal competitors in the political arena, when in fact they enter the arena with distinct advantages.

Not surprisingly, the directors and officials of the major complex organizations are the people most likely to hold and defend a pluralist ideology. They believe that the growth of these organizations in wealth, power, influence, and ability to mold opinion is in the "public" interest, because this growth has resulted from a "healthy competition" between groups which insures that only reasonable policies are put into effect. Since the directors and high officials of complex organizations and conglomerates are members of an important contemporary social grouping, the ideology of pluralism plays a significant role in current debates over policy. Specifically, it is called upon to justify the assumption of new functions by existing organizations, to defend the existing rights of these organizations against attack, and to convince people that their freedom lies in cooperating with one or another of these organizations. For example, pluralism is used to justify government contracts to large corporations for research and development of weapons, to defend corporations against proposals to regulate them advocated by consumer groups, and to convince people that the best hope for social change lies in a career in a civic-minded corporation which "gives a damn."

The discussion of pluralism brings out several important features of ideology. First, many of those who publicly espouse the ideology believe in its claims. They believe that their organizations are serving the public interest and that the best political process is one that balances the claims of intense and powerful interest groups. Second, whether or not people actually believe that their proposals are in the "public" interest, it is important for the student of policy to determine which groups will gain most if the proposals are put into effect. Only a minority of those who hold an ideology may be consciously using it as a weapon to gain advantage. But, the ideology may operate to gain an expansion of rights for the whole group. In the case of pluralism, it is clear that competition among interest groups works out to the benefit of the strongest interest groups and to the distinct disadvantage of the weakest ones. Thus, it is not surprising that members of the more disadvantaged social groups frequently are not pluralists.

A second important set of social groupings in the contemporary United States is made up of those who are dispossessed and in the process of asserting their rights. This group, composed of many members of racial and ethnic minorities, a number of women, some segments of youth, some consumers, and some of the aged, views politics in terms of a "power structure" dominated by an elite. According to this view, the elite makes most of the important social decisions, such as those on broad economic and military policy, and these decisions keep the disadvantaged in a permanent position of inferiority. The goal of this group is frequently expressed in the demand for "participation" in making decisions that affect the course of one's existence. This runs head on into the pluralist idea that participation is best limited to professional politicians skilled in balancing interests. Clearly, the idea that there is an oppressive power elite and the demand for guaranteed participation are useful to the weaker groups in their drive for expanding their rights. The officials of complex organizations already have effective participation, so they do not have to demand guaranteed participation. They are already on top, so they have every interest in spreading the idea that there is free competition among organizations rather than a power elite. Members of weaker groups, without effective participation, must demand guaranteed participation if they are to expand their rights. They are on the bottom, so they have every interest in spreading the idea that there is a single "repressive" power structure. As far as this idea is accepted, they gain keener focus to their struggle and greater support. When officials of organizations state that members of protest groups should "lower their voices" and "engage in reasoned dialogue" they are inviting these groups to engage in an unequal competition in which the organizations have most of the resources. Historically, protest groups have always used the tactic of "polarization" to give focus to their struggles and to unify their movements against a common enemy. It is not likely that they will give up this tactic simply on account of pleas made by those they do not trust.

The directors and the dispossessed are not the only two important social groupings on the current scene. A third group is composed of the specialists who fill positions in the middle levels of complex organizations. The major ideology of this group differs from the two views discussed above. For the specialist, current social existence is governed by the "technological imperative." Human beings are surrounded by more and more complicated machines that only experts can understand. In a world of such complexity, the people in charge of organizations have lost the ability to make rational decisions. Yet those who would solve major social problems (defined by this group as environmental pollution, overpopulation, and other conditions arising from the unintended effects of technology) through confronting a nonexistent power structure are misguided. It is necessary to harness technology and direct it toward the solution of the major social problems. This can only be done by recognizing the importance of experts in the contemporary world and allowing them the opportunity to turn their talents to meeting "reordered priorities." The politics of the present revolves around whether or not an effective majority can be molded in favor of the use of national wealth and expertise to clean up the environment, end poverty, maintain a sound national defense, and guarantee full employment. The experts are the effective decision-makers in contemporary society. But, their hands are tied by the lack of clarity in national purpose and by the selfish demands of certain powerful interest groups. According to the spokesmen for the specialists, "if we could send men to the moon, we ought to be able to solve our social problems here on earth." In short, the specialist sees human existence as a technical problem.

It is clear that the specialist's ideology is as useful to him as the other ideologies are to their proponents. If the major issues of contemporary life are seen to revolve around the proper use of technology, then the specialists are likely to gain greater power and privilege. If directors come to believe that they are helpless without the specialist's judgment, then they are likely to give specialists more rights. A good example of the specialist's ideology is David Apter's article in this volume. Apter argues that the great ideological struggle of the present is between those who aim at applying scientific knowledge to the solution of social problems and those who are not experts and distrust the specialist. Apter believes that in the future social scientists will become more and more important in political decision-making. He argues that if they do not gain this social significance human existence is likely to enter a new dark age. Whatever merits this position might have, it is clearly in the interest of social scientists seeking greater influence to believe in it.

A fourth and final important social grouping on the current scene is composed of the "middle Americans," those people who are neither experts nor directors but who do not consider themselves dispossessed. These people, who range from blue-collar workers with relatively secure jobs to white-collar workers in nontechnical positions, view politics primarily in terms of their private lives. They are concerned with economic issues, such as unemployment and inflation, and generally endorse those parts of the welfare state which benefit them, such as social security and medical insurance. They are also concerned with so-called social issues such as race relations, in the sense that they distrust racial minorities and fear for the property values of their homes and the safety of their neighborhoods in case of integration. Many of them strongly identify with the American nation and support an anti-communist foreign policy. Generally they are also very opposed to the movements of the dispossessed, perhaps because these movements threaten their hard-won respectability and promise to disrupt their private lives. They also have a tendency alternately to worship and to distrust and fear specialists. It is this tendency which lies behind Apter's warning of an impending struggle between the experts and those who have not had the benefits of specialized training.

The ideology of the "middle American," which is not as well worked out as the other three ideologies, fits well with the aspirations of this group. They are most concerned with the maintenance of a secure private life and throw their support to those political tendencies which promise to give them this security. However, their emphasis on private life makes them less concerned than any of the other three groups with analyzing the dynamics of the conglomerates which provide the context for much of their working and recreational activity. It is reasonable to predict that if their security becomes gravely threatened they will revise their image of the public situation and perhaps become a far more active political force than they have been previously.

The analysis of the content of ideologies and of the relations of that content to the aspirations of important social groupings provides an effective way of studying the broad outlines of the policy phase of the political process. With a framework describing the major ideologies it becomes possible to fit specific demands for particular rights into a more general pattern. For example, demands for prayer in public schools can be associated with the quest of the "middle American" to maintain a traditional respectability and to defend his way of life against the scientific rationality of the specialist. The demand for import quotas can be considered an attempt by certain directors to expand profits and defend markets in the face of competition. Demands for a council of social science advisers to the President can be interpreted as a push for greater specialist influence in decision-making. Demands for local control of schools in black neighborhoods can be seen as an assertion of group identity by people who feel that they have been dispossessed. Thus, interpreting policies through broader ideologies allows one to make sense out of the kaleidoscopic progression of specific issues that forms the substance of the everyday political process in the United States.

Returning to the beginning of the discussion of policy, it should be easier now to understand the main limits on the free expression of policy alternatives in the contemporary United States. Those policy alternatives compatible with or derived from the aspirations of major social groupings gain the greatest attention, while those proposals unrelated or contrary to the leading ideologies are relatively ignored. Further, those groupings with the most access to means of communication, such as the mass media, will attempt consciously or merely as a matter of course to advocate policies compatible with or derived from the ideologies that they hold. This means that one of the most important steps in gaining political freedom is to understand the relativity of one's own ideologies and the relativity of the ideologies that one is exposed to in the mass media and in everyday life.

The ideologies, groupings, and policies discussed above are based on the image of the public situation presented earlier. They assume the importance of complex organizations in contemporary life and reflect the paradoxical experience and ambivalent response to that experience associated with existence in these organizations. However, whether or not one accepts this description of the major groupings and the ideologies associated with them as relatively accurate, the discussion of the policy phase of the political process should lead one to ask "What are the major social groupings, on what futures are they acting, and how do these futures bear on the attainment of rights for the different sectors of social life?" It is seriously asking this question that can take one beyond the narrow confines of his everyday life and allow him to appreciate the more long-range consequences of his daily action.

DECISION

The policy phase of the political process flows directly into the phase of decision. In various ways and in various institutions, human beings decide which of the available futures they will attempt to put into effect. Decision cannot be kept clearly separate from policy, because some of the most important policies involve proposals on how decisions should be made. This is particularly the case in the twentieth century, when political activities have attracted more interest than they did in the preceding century. In the nineteenth century, the most vital issues in policy revolved around economics. The major social groupings were based on ownership and economic function, and the broadest policy alternatives and ideologies were concerned with whether industrial property was to be kept in private hands or whether it was to be socialized. There was general agreement that some kind of representative government was the proper form of decision-making. In the twentieth century, however, the broadest policy alternatives and ideologies concern the ways in which decisions are to be made.

The importance of the phase of decision in the contemporary political process was stressed earlier in the discussion of the paradox of elitism and participation. It was brought out even more in the discussion of policy. Pluralism, one of the chief ideologies of the directors of complex organizations and powerful interest groups, is essentially a doctrine of how decisions are and should be made. It states that within organizations decisions should be made by those at the top of the heap, so long as the decisions concern the solvency, power, influence, and prestige of the organization. Decisions on the technical aspects of the organization's performance are supposed to be made by appropriate specialists. When decisions involve conflicts between organizations, they should be made through negotiation or through the intervention of professional politicians skilled in balancing off interests against one another. Many of the pluralists claim that not only should decisions be made in these ways, but that decisions actually do conform to these patterns in the contemporary United States. They point to such events as complex labor-management struggles in which attempts are made at negotiation, with intervention later by government if the negotiations fail. Many current conflicts do seem to conform to the pluralist pattern, but others do not fit as well into the mold. Violent racial conflicts, for example, are not always resolved by negotiation and bargaining.

Like pluralism, participatory democracy, the ideology of the dispossessed groups, centers on a desired form of decision-making. The pluralist believes that those who have succeeded in getting to the top of complex organizations have both the right and obligation to make decisions about the future of the organizations and the people involved with them. He holds that the daily job of the directors of these organizations is to lead the competitive struggle for wealth, power, influence, and prestige. This involves negotiating with allies and rivals, approving new projects and evaluating old ones, influencing public and private agencies to grant special rights and privileges, and projecting an image of service in the "public interest." For the pluralist, the place of elections in a democratic system is not so much to influence specific policies as it is to support or reject a particular leadership and a very general line of policy. The advocate of participatory democracy rejects almost every one of the pluralist's claims. He holds that far from having a right and an obligation to make decisions affecting the lives of people involved with a complex organization, the director has usurped the right of the people affected by decisions to have a say in making those decisions. Thus, while the pluralist has diminished the role of elections to the point where they are evaluations on the performance of leaders, the participatory democrat holds that elections are not democratic enough. He wants enough decentralization of decision-making to insure that each person affected by a decision has some say in making that decision.

Advocates of participatory democracy claim that the present system of making decisions is not as dispersed as the pluralist thinks it is. They frequently agree with the ideas of such thinkers as C. Wright Mills, Milovan Djilas, and Jean Meynaud, each of whom has pointed to the importance of elitism in contemporary politics. Mills claimed that despite the forms of representative democracy, major decisions on the direction of the economy and military and foreign policy are made in the United States by an elite composed of high officials in large corporations, top military officers, and high government officials. He called this group the "power elite" and claimed that they were wielding their power irresponsibly and only to increase the prestige of their organizations. Although he did not name it by this term, Mills was one of the first thinkers to call attention to the military-industrial complex, which has received so much attention during recent years. Milovan Djilas, a Yugoslavian thinker imprisoned several times for speaking out, coined the term "new class" to characterize the elite of Communist Party officials that he saw appearing throughout Eastern Europe after World War II. Djilas argued that despite the Communist doctrine insisting upon social equality, Party leaders everywhere were granting themselves special privileges and excluding all others from participation in decisions. Finally, Jean Meynaud has argued that in the future an elite of technocrats, or specialists, may emerge which will govern in the name of a mindless efficiency. He notes that there are signs of this elite already in western Europe and elsewhere in the industrialized world. Thus, following such thinkers as Mills, Djilas, and Meynaud, participatory democrats repudiate the regimes of both the industrialized East and West on the grounds that they are elitist. Part of their alternative is spelled out in the article by Peter Bachrach.

The ideologies of the other two groups, specialists and "middle Americans," are less well focused than those of the directors and the dispossessed. Specialists tend to favor decision by experts, and they frequently note a tendency in this direction in contemporary life. However, at least in the United States, specialists appear to be willing to function within the framework of a mixed pluralist and representative democracy. Perhaps the lack of any distinctive proposal for a method of decision-making by specialists is due to the fact that expertise is confined to narrow slices of human activity and contains no principle within it for integrating its contribution into a larger whole. Thus, the specialist normally functions as an expediter of work within any system of decision-making. It is, of course, possible that a regime of technocrats will arise which will allocate resources according to the ease with which problems can be resolved by technical means.

"Middle Americans" tend to be the most committed of the four groupings to the traditional notion of representative democracy, in which two parties articulating alternative programs vie for the majority of votes. Concerned with the maintenance of security, they either vote out of party identification (often "inherited" from parents) or out of a judgment about which party is most likely to maintain their security and the nation's.

Today the phase of decision in the political process is dominated by the interplay between the principles of organizational elitism and participation. Elitists argue that participatory democracy and decentralization would cause such a lack of coordination and resulting chaos that the present complex social life would be impossible to maintain. Participatory democrats answer that elites are becoming so "unresponsive" to the pleas of those affected by their decisions that "business as usual" will not continue for very much longer. Is the choice of the present generation between a decisional system of unresponsive coordination and one of chaotic participation? How much coordination is actually provided in the contest between powerful interest groups? Would a system of communities stressing participation along with other values do any worse? All of these are central questions about the phase of decision in the contemporary political process.

ADMINISTRATION

Just as the phase of policy flows into decision, so the phase of decision flows into administration. Once a decision has been made—once one attempts to make a certain image of the future concrete—the problem arises of how to coordinate the efforts of human actors to attain the goal. It is this problem of coordination which is at the center of the theory and practice of administration.

Administration must be distinguished from the actual production, distribution, and use of goods and services. For example, a decision may be made to try to produce a supersonic transport plane. The specifications of that plane, and the construction and testing of it, are not administration, but production or creation. However, the system of rewards and punishments used to keep people on the job and the network of rights and duties of the people involved in the project *are* matters of administration. Thus, administration includes two aspects: a system of incentives and a blueprint for coordination.

Since the twentieth century has thus far been an era of politics, rather than an age of economics, religion, or some other area of human activity, it is not surprising that along with concern about policy and decision has come great interest in administration. It is only in the twentieth century that political thinkers have become used to speaking in terms of organization in general, rather than in terms of specific types of organizations. While even in the nineteenth century few would have thought it fruitful to compare hospitals with business enterprises, today government agencies, business firms, universities, hospitals, and other units are often considered together as organizations. One writer has compared mental hospitals, prisons, ships, monasteries, tuberculosis sanatoria, military units, and other organizations, because they are all total institutions—they attempt to impose an entire life style on those within them.[3] The earlier discussion of conglomerates goes along with this tendency in contemporary thought. At present, it is useful to consider many large and complex organizations as conglomerates which have no single purpose, but which combine enterprises ranging from nursing homes to oil refineries under a single umbrella, and which strive for such abstract ends as growth and profitability. Thus, in the conglomerate each specific enterprise or agency is highly specialized and adapted to performing a particular task. However, the central directorate, which ties together the various agencies, is very unspecialized and performs the two tasks of monitoring the agencies through budgetary controls and expanding the conglomerate in competition with other organizations.

Human beings always carry on their production of goods and services

3. Erving Goffman, *Asylums* (New York: Anchor Books, 1961).

within some form of organization, and the patterns of organization present at a given time are the focal point of the administrative phase of the political process in that era. At the present time the major social groupings—directors, the dispossessed, specialists, and "middle Americans"—seem to be based on relation to complex organizations. In general, pluralism is the image of the public situation held by those who are high officials in large organizations, participatory democracy is the ideology held by those who consider themselves abused by and excluded from these organizations, technocracy is the view held by those who perform specialized tasks within the organizations, and the middle American perspective is held by those who are primarily clients of the organizations. Thus, it is very difficult to make a clear distinction between the policy, decision, and administrative phases of the political process, at least in the twentieth century. Major policy alternatives are expressed by groups rooted in organizational forms, and the content of these policies concerns desirable ways of making decisions. This kind of interlinking and overlapping is bound to appear when political activity becomes the central human activity.

As on questions of policy and decision, the major social groupings differ in their views of administration according to their relationship to organizations. The dominant view, which represents the mentality of directors, sees the organization on the model of a computer programmed by those at the top. According to this way of thinking, the job of the director is to set the general goals of the organization, make sure that there are adequate incentives to keep people working efficiently to attain the goals, maintain a set of rights and duties adapted to efficient performance, and increase the competitive advantage of the organization. Under this description of administration, the directors, who are formally accountable for the performance of the organization, must be the ones who exercise ultimate oversight on operations and determine the general direction of the unit. However, they exercise this oversight and set these goals within the framework of an organizational aim which is not determined by them. For example, in corporations the aim is turning a maximum profit, in government agencies it is fulfilling goals set in law, and in hospitals it is providing certain health services for a given range of clients. The existence of these aims is often used by directors to let themselves off the hook when they are criticized for such things as failing to curb environmental pollution or refusing to hire members of minority groups. However, the aims are usually so general that a multitude of actions probably would be compatible with them.

The idea that directors exercise a stewardship over complex organizations leads to the view that neither specialists, clients, nor dispossessed groups should participate in supervision. Specialists are considered essentially as hired hands who are kept within the organization by the rewards (salary and interesting work) and sometimes the punishments (legal action for failure to perform duties) dispensed by it. They are not supposed to question whether the work that they are asked to do is more or less important than alternative work that they might be doing. At most they are encouraged to make suggestions on how to improve operations. They are, however, expected in most cases to bargain, either collectively or individually, for wages and fringe benefits. If they believe that they can get a better deal elsewhere, it is expected that they will leave. Similarly, clients, such as consumers, patients, and students, are not supposed to participate in supervision. If they are not satisfied with goods or services, it is expected that they will "vote with their feet" by going to a competitor. Where there are no competitors (for example, where there is only one hospital in town) there are laws to protect clients from the most flagrant abuses. As for the dispossessed, it is unfair, according to the pluralist view, to ask any particular organization to shoulder the burden of social reconstruction. Aid to the dispossessed should be a "public" concern in which "everyone" should participate.

In recent years, the dominant pluralist view of organization and administration has been challenged by members of the other three groupings. In many cases it is not as easy as it sounds to "vote with your feet," and the law is often a quite inefficient and tedious way to redress grievances. Once the two major props of the pluralist argument were shaken, demands for greater participation in supervision began to be expressed by some specialists, clients, and dispossessed minorities. These demands have been met by the argument that if participation is to be so widely diffused all accountability for performance will be lost. This argument, in turn, has been answered by the claim that in contemporary complex organizations the directors have essentially become accountable to themselves, and that this has encouraged them to abuse their power. Some specialists have suggested that this dispute misses the essential point, and that only through the deliberate creation of counter-organizations, which will compete with and challenge existing conglomerates, can accountability be retrieved and goals such as pollution control be realized.[4] For example, if there is a strong "military-industrial complex" composed of powerful conglomerates, it should be challenged by the creation of a "social-industrial complex" dedicated to social problem-solving. Such counter-organizations would probably result in greater rights for specialists, but they would be unlikely to encourage very much participation by clients and the dispossessed. At the very least, these current debates should show that the future of the administrative phase of the political process is by no means settled.

The differing views of administration present in current political life show that it is impossible to distinguish sharply between "politics" and "administration." Many people believe that politics is the activity in which decisions are made on what goals to pursue and that administration is the activity of attaining those goals. While a similar conception guides the present discussion, it is important to keep in mind that the phases of the political process are continuous with one another and overlap with each other. Interest groups find it just as important, if not more vital, to influence the actions of administrative agencies as to exert pres-

4. I am indebted to Don Kash of the University of Oklahoma for the idea of counter-institutions and for his able defense of this notion in several discussions. I am also indebted to Philip Haring of Knox College and Deena Weinstein of DePaul University for correspondence and conversations about many of these ideas.

sure on legislatures. Decisions on general directions of policy are not at all like computer programs. Often they give only the broadest guidelines for implementation. It is in the administrative phase, rather than in policy or decision, that the political process touches most people. This is why it seems contrived to argue that the function of administration is to put into effect policies that have been decided by the vote of a "democratically" elected legislature, whatever the effects on those touched by the action. Similarly, it is contrived to argue that the function of "management" is to put into effect general policies that have been decided by a board of directors acting as "trustees" for the stockholders. Such formulations may appeal to the tidy mind, which would like to think of politics as a series of boxes on an organizational chart. However, in recent years more and more people have come to understand that formal chains of command and publicly expressed explanations of accountability are often very far removed from the experiences actually encountered in complex organizations. A great many of the policies voted on by legislatures or approved by boards of directors or trustees originate in the minds of administrators. Thus, it may even be true in some cases that the fastest way to influence legislation is to work through administration. Further, in the simple model of administration, the specialist is obliged to carry out an order whether or not he believes that it is moral. Many people find such an obligation unacceptable in the face of crimes against humanity which have been ordered by some administrators in the twentieth century. It is such considerations as these which have opened up the current debate about administration in the West, and which promise to result in continued organizational transformation.

EVALUATION

A political process composed only of policy, decision, and administration would be incomplete. Policy defines alternative futures. Decision selects a future to act upon. Administration attempts to make that future come about. However, after the administrative phase of the political process it comes time to judge the success of the experiment. This act of judgment is the evaluative phase of the political process, and it is the consummation of the other three phases. It is in evaluation that the other three phases find their justification, because if the future-put-into-effect turns out to be evil, then the policies espoused by the dominant groups, the ways in which decisions are made, and the ways in which activities are coordinated are all thrown into question. Thus, without evaluation the political process would be a random walk leading nowhere.

In human existence, the simplest evaluations are made in terms of feelings such as pleasure and pain, and experience of tension and release of tension. However, through social and cultural learning, human beings come to hold standards of evaluation that are far more complex and sophisticated than the judgments of immediate feeling. Such standards are often thought of as "values," or idealizations of the good life in terms of which people judge their present conditions. While there is some merit in looking at values as yardsticks against which experience is measured, this view leaves out an important consideration. Why do people find a particular idealization of the good life worthy to be a standard of evaluation? It is likely that they hold certain standards because they can make a connection between the ideal image and some concrete experience that they have had before or that they can imagine themselves having. For example, many people evaluate the present situation in terms of an ideal society based on universal love. They hold this ideal because some time in their lives they have either experienced love or have imagined what love would be like. Thus, it is important to remember that values are rarely bloodless abstractions and sets of ritual words. Instead, as they function in political life they are images pointing toward concrete experiences, emotions, and feelings. When the black revolutionary demands "freedom now" the word *freedom* does not refer to an abstraction but to a situation in which blacks will no longer be confined to ghettos, in which they will be treated with respect, and in which they will have access to the materials necessary to create a distinctive way of life. The black revolutionary will evaluate the political process according to this standard of freedom.

Historically, too, demands for freedom have been demands for the liberty to engage in certain specific activities. For an early capitalist, freedom meant the liberty to originate and manage a business enterprise without being bothered too much by state controls and the vested interests of landowners. For an American teen-ager, freedom may mean the liberty to take certain drugs, go to certain entertainments, dress in a certain way, and have one's own car. The teen-ager would be as little interested in the freedom to originate a business enterprise as the early capitalist would be in the freedom to attend a rock concert.

There are two cases in which values become detached from relatively concrete experiences and situations. First, such detachment sometimes occurs when values are discussed in conversations and classes. When an attempt is made to define a value such as freedom abstractly, as "the ability to do what one wants so long as one does not infringe on the equal freedom of others," values seem far removed from concrete experiences. However, abstract definitions of values do have an important use. They show the general framework in which debate over standards of evaluation is taking place. Thus, in the present world it is important to know whether somebody means by freedom the ability to develop creative talents, the ability to keep some mental distance from social requirements, a degree of freedom between these, or something else entirely. However, it is always important to keep in mind that these abstractions have their origin in particular problems encountered by human beings in their daily existence. For example, the current debate over freedom arises from the experiences of people in complex organizations. Earlier definitions of freedom, such as the ability to follow God's law, had implications for another set of specific conditions. The discussion of abstract principles of value becomes far more interesting when their connection with concrete experiences is not forgotten.

The second way in which values become detached from concrete experiences and situations is far more significant. Frequently, terms such as *freedom, equality, justice, democracy,* and *participation* are used by political actors to disguise policies aimed at gaining greater advantage for themselves or their group. An import quota may be sought in the name of "fair trade" or "economic justice," an agricultural subsidy may be sought in the name of "equality of treatment" or "economic democracy," representation on a regulatory commission may be sought in the name of "free expression," "participation," and "justice." In such cases it is quite difficult to determine any meaning for these terms which goes beyond the meaning implied in the particular demand being put forward by the interest group in question. Yet it is obvious that the spokesman for the interest group does not intend people to believe that he defines justice in terms of a specific demand. Instead, he would like people to be left with the feeling that satisfaction of the specific demand would be consistent with or derived from a much wider ideal of justice. However, that ideal is never spelled out in concrete terms, and the people who are persuaded by the propaganda are left with a feeling and a word but no definite meaning.

The importance of such propaganda in contemporary political life has led some people to state that no rational standards of evaluation can be worked out. According to them, all the words in the vocabulary of political value are smoke screens hiding the pursuit of narrow interest. This position has the merit of recognizing that value terms refer to concrete situations and aspirations. However, it has the defect of blurring the distinctions between widely different claims and standards. Some demands aim simply at greater power and profits for organizations, while others aim at increasing the creative freedom of certain groups. While both types of claims can be considered merely as demands, it is sometimes important to make distinctions between the content of demands. It may not be possible to "prove" that creative freedom is a "higher" value than organizational power, but it is possible to define both of these standards in terms of concrete situations and then leave it to people to experience these situations imaginatively and choose which one they prefer. The problem with propaganda is that it makes such choice between alternative futures and standards of evaluation impossible. Since propaganda is frequently consciously intended to split off values from concrete situations, it becomes an important factor in stifling the imagination and preventing conscious choice among alternatives. However, even when there is no conscious intent to deceive, political statements can divorce values from experiences and thereby function like propaganda. Thus, one condition of gaining political freedom in the contemporary world is learning to trace back values to the concrete situations and aspirations that they represent. Concerted effort to do this tracing will eventually immunize one to the appeals of propaganda without forcing one into the condition of permanent cynicism about the realization of any values.

The phase of evaluation is continuous with the phase of policy. The aspirations characteristic of a group are, from another point of view, the very situations that they would evaluate positively. Of course, there is some difference between the phases of policy and evaluation. When a group succeeds in realizing its aspirations, its members may find that they are dissatisfied with the situation. The world may not seem as rosy as they expected it to be. Thus, they may question their standard of evaluation and attempt to formulate a new one to express their new experience. Along with the new standard of evaluation will come new policies and ideologies. Such revision is continually going on in human affairs, and at its most open and experimental, the political process can be pictured as a spiral which rises to a new level each time evaluations give rise to new plans for the future. Of course, the political process is not always open and experimental, and it can sometimes be pictured as a circle in which activities repeat themselves over and over again or as a downward spiral tending toward regimentation.

The continuity of evaluation with policy can be illustrated by con-sidering briefly the standards of evaluation used by the four major contemporary groupings. The pluralists evaluate political activity according to two standards. Their ideal political process is one in which the competition between interest groups is disrupted neither by losers fomenting revolution or civil war nor by some groups forcefully attempting to eliminate other groups. They deplore the use of force because they are in the position to win in most "peaceful" competitions. Their ideal of success is one in which the organizations that they represent grow in wealth, power, influence, and authority over opinion. The dispossessed evaluate the political process in terms of how many opportunities it gives them to escape from poverty, do interesting work, expand the range of choices available in planning their lives, and gain self-respect and the respect of others. They judge success in terms of how much they and the other members of their group have gained control over the conditions of their lives. The specialists believe that a good political process is one in which maximum intelligence and skill are being used to "solve" certain social problems. The problems with which they are concerned vary according to perceived threats to their way of life and perceived opportunities for increasing the influence of their group. The current issue of ecology and the environment is a good example of a problem that meets both of these standards. Environmental pollution threatens the specialist's enjoyment of his privileges and provides many specialists with an argument that their talents should be utilized more fully. The specialist judges success in terms of the prestige of his profession, his standing in that profession, the intrinsic interest of his work, and the degree of contribution that he can make to solving problems he deems significant. Finally, the "middle Americans" believe that a good political process is one that allows them to devote most of their attention to their private lives. They are concerned with the maintenance of secure employment, the prevention of inflation, the ability to prevent intrusion by those they define as undesirable into their neighborhoods and daily lives, and the freedom to enjoy their leisure time with family and friends. They judge success in terms of the degree to which these goals are met. Thus, the standards of evaluation of the four major groupings are built directly into their ideologies.

SUMMARY

Political science is an attempt to clarify the public situation, or the public world in which human beings are enfolded whether they like it or not. It undertakes this clarification by attempting to create factually accurate, consistent, comprehensive, adequate and fruitful images of that situation.

The materials for these images are found in the observation of the political process, which includes the four phases of policy, decision, administration, and evaluation. In the phase of policy, different social groupings present alternative visions of the future and advocate those visions through methods ranging from debate to violence. At their broadest, those visions of the future are ideologies, and these ideologies are themselves images of the public situation. Although there is often no attempt to make ideologies factually accurate, consistent, or fruitful, they are frequently quite compelling and comprehensive. In the phase of decision choices are made among competing futures, while in the phase of administration activities are coordinated toward the realization of a future. Finally, in the phase of evaluation the results of the other three parts of the political process are judged in terms of some standard of value. This judgment in turn gives rise to new visions of the future.

In studying the political process it is important to remember that the various phases are not disconnected boxes on a chart, but overlapping and interpenetrating activities. The articles that appear in the following pages make this quite evident, as familiar themes are repeated and elaborated in new contexts.

I
The Human
Condition

The beginnings of political thought are found in images of the public situation, through which human beings attempt to grasp the broader dimensions of the problems they encounter and the hopes they have for the future. Each human being has at least an implicit image of the larger environment which he uses to interpret the events in which he takes part. Such images are not idle speculations with little meaning for everyday life. Instead, they are the very stuff of which human possibilities and projects are made, and in which these projects have meaning.

During the twentieth century several distinctive images have appeared, and these are represented in the articles composing this section. First, there are the images associated with the conservative tradition. For the conservatives represented here the most important recent development has been the welfare state, which claims to guarantee for its members at least a minimum level of economic and social security. Conservatives are concerned about the fate of individual enterprise and personal choice in such a state, which must resort to standardizing broad areas of human activity. Thus, Kenneth Melvin argues that the welfare state is here to stay and that the best hope for personal freedom lies in intelligent conformity to the requirements of economic security. Frank Meyer disagrees and calls for greater individual enterprise and courage in resisting state encroachment. James Burnham adds a third voice to the debate, agreeing with Melvin that the welfare state is here to stay but adding that care must be taken to resist total state power in the service of fanatics.

The second image grows out of the liberal tradition. Here the significant development is seen as bewilderment and the loss of traditional meanings. Morris Ginsberg holds that religious accounts of human destiny are no longer convincing to many people, that people are becoming aware of the great diversity of moral standards, and that many people perceive a gap between the proclaimed standards of conduct and what actually is done. Ginsberg believes that we should respond to bewilderment by applying intelligence to the reconstruction of human affairs. Through intelligence people may find a common ground uniting diverse moral systems and, thus, prepare the way for a new consensus.

A third image grows out of the radical tradition and is represented here by Kenneth A. Megill. He describes how people who begin acting for social reform often find that such reform cannot easily be realized, if at all, within existing political institutions. Frequently these people become convinced that only by transforming institutions can their ideals be put into effect. Thus, for contemporary radicals the most important aspect of the current public situation is the presence of massive hierarchical organizations which suppress human potential. They believe that these organizations should be eliminated in their present form or, at the very least, be run democratically.

Yet a fourth image of the current public situation stresses the importance of technology in the world today. Friedrich Georg Junger argues that the increasing significance of machines in human existence tends to diminish the role of human spontaneity and vitality. According to Junger, the machine threatens to turn the human condition into a deadly monotony of processes repeating themselves over and over again in a predetermined progression. Directly opposed to this image is a fifth one, represented here by Robert Lifton's article. Lifton believes that the most important recent development has been the appearance of masses of people who are willing to experiment continually with their personalities and transform them from one day to the next. These people have emerged from Ginsberg's age of bewilderment and have abandoned themselves to flux. What the appearance of such people means for the future is an open question.

Several important similarities link these five images together. All note the effects of large-scale organizations on personal existence, all pose the problem of the meaning of freedom and regimentation in contemporary life, and all are concerned with the future of democracy. Thus, while specific diagnoses may differ, all seem to be speaking about the same public situation.

Big Brother Is Dead Too

KENNETH MELVIN

Lord Jebb wrote a book a year or so ago to remind us that we are now past the half-way mark to Orwell's *Nineteen Eighty-Four*. Aldous Huxley's *The Island* gave us his private idea of hell ahead in a society reduced to mindless conformity by subliminal coercions. Nobody need doubt that the ambient air throbs constantly with suggestion and chilling menace; but where it might have seemed prophetic in the Fifties and perhaps even in the early Sixties we have become bored with the Cassandras. In a state of constant if undeclared warfare we have supped too full of horrors: tales of terror are over-told. We are now resistant. The whole idea was wrong-headed from the start and for unsuspected reasons. We see now that the myth of Circe's swine can be enacted without Big Brother, without any vast and villainous conspiracy against the person. It was a mistake to think that men have to be terrorized into obedience in an affluent society.

Hindsight enables us to see what misled the prophets of an early doom. After the Second World War, which was to reassert individualism and personal freedom after the long night of totalitarianism, the millennium was delayed somewhat. The real reason was that the age of individualism had gone beyond recall, and its going had to do with technology, not ideology. Let men believe what they will; technological dynamism will bring them to heel. Industrialization and urbanization will complete the rout of twentieth-century militarism. It is the collective solution of social and economic disorder which yields the dividends collective security, collective prosperity, collective conformity; the sequence is inevitable because of the comfort it brings. Wicked men do not have to arrange matters; it is the logic of our age. The planned economy, the welfare society, the benevolent bureaucracy—this is the structure, and it is all so far from needing some infernal Big Brother to manipulate it, demonstrably so very far from being an evil machination that it *is* positively benevolent toward the masses depicted as its victims. It makes a purple passage to decry conformism and denounce *anomie;* but from the campus up (or down) to the Senate the battle cry of freedom is so much fustian. It does not fit the facts of the provident society and the kind of supportive commitment which is indispensable for its maintenance.

ENTER CONFORMISM

We have lived through the end of ideology. The welfare society is not a doctrinaire creation of either the political Left or Right; it just had to happen under the economics of surplus. It took its rise in the post-Depression years, and by the end of the Thirties, New Zealand had enacted the prototype social service state of the western world. The United

States embarked upon it under Franklin D. Roosevelt's New Deal, but being the United States it never regarded that Administration as more than a temporary receiver. With returning prosperity welfarism was shelved, and only in the Sixties is the logic of events compelling America to resume the pattern of collective responsibility for human need. The pattern of welfarism has had varied applications in Sweden, Great Britain, and Holland; but the common denominator is its bipartisan acceptance everywhere. Any differences between the political parties tend to be the little more or the little less. Repudiation of the provident society spells political hara-kiri. The ideologue is strictly for the museum. In demanding individual liberty in any other terms than those of collective responsibility, the "with-it" generation is just not with it at all.

If welfarism is to operate it requires pervasive bureaucracy and conformity for the effective discharge of its ever-widening tasks. This is where Orwell et al. missed the point. They believed that human nature is intrinsically individualistic, and that men would therefore resent and rebel against conformism in even its benign forms. The stubborn fact is that mankind has an inveterate mass-disposition to prefer the comfort of security to the loneliness of self-sufficiency. The bureaucratic state suits most men for most of the time. The protest of today's youth reflects ignorance of their actual and inescapable dependence as substantial beneficiaries of the society they affect to despise. University students in particular and in the main have yet to give their hostages to fortune—children to be cared for and a job to be kept. Those two great stabilizers will teach them the facts of life from which the campus largely protects them. At that stage they will need no Big Brother to subdue them: they will become voluntarily part of that great panjandrum. Nor is social man any less significant than the solitary man youth seems so to admire. Both have a legitimate role; the myth of the "either/or" was played out some time ago.

This compliance of social man has long been observed, though the first consequential books about it seem to date only from the mid-nineteenth century. Tocqueville's classic study of democracy in America explained this phenomenon with clarity. In briefest summation his exposition is that with the overthrow of aristocracy in the late eighteenth and early nineteenth centuries came the end of federations of lordships and franchises. Society tended now to become a mass of individuals, theoretically equal before the law and in the ballot box, enjoying a new freedom for which they had neither training nor taste. Into the power vacuum thus artificially created in the democracies, grew the modern state, affecting to act in the interests of all and exacting, in return, reasonable obedience by all. Conformism entered, therefore, as a concomitant of leveling society. The timeless problem of freedom and order was to be resolved in the balancing scales of social justice. Economic security, political liberty, process of law, protection of person and property, systems of communication and transport, health and social services—even statutory leisure, guaranteed wages, and the sponsorship of the arts—all these provisions have flourished far beyond Tocqueville's notions of democracy. How could public education—chief of the social services—manage without the capacious public purse? How could any of this collective provision operate without bureaucracy?

THE WRIT OF BUREAUCRACY

Nor is this machinery a sinister invention of some Big Brother. The absolutist states of the fifteenth and sixteenth centuries formed major bureaucracies; clerks and inspectors, tax-gatherers and law-enforcement agents so multiplied that Hobbes was scared out of his wits by Leviathan. Since then, parliaments have moderated monarchies in the public interest without being able to dispense with the growing machinery of government. Rousseau declared cynically in his time that the English people had a voice only during elections; in between, bureaucracy took over, to be disciplined only when its growth was too rank or the central power became too predatory. Nor have communized societies been spectacularly successful in enlarging individual freedom against collective responsibility. So it is clear that nobody had to invent bureaucracy as a criminal conspiracy. It grew because it was inescapable in the kind of society most men want—the provident kind no less than the exploitative. From absolutism, through representative government to the social service state runs the writ of bureaucracy as the instrument of social order. The manifest danger, of course, lies in too much of a good thing. Where social controls cease to be imposed by autocrats and are devised and directed by the popular will, collective solutions of personal need can assume a sanctity they do not necessarily possess. *Vox populi* never has been *vox dei*. But this is not the point, which is rather that social man must come to terms with social power and social efficiency—and pay due price in social conformity. What modern man cannot do is to have the fruits of collective provision without the entail of collective solidarity.

This would all be but a tedious exposition of the obvious were it not for the fact that the half of the American people under the age of 28 is only partially persuaded of it, and the quarter of the nation under the age of 25 and still being educated is not persuaded of it at all. This may prove to have been the central issue of the Sixties. The cooperative commonwealth—the redistributive society—the social service state—has been a signal triumph of social engineering, applied technology, political acumen, and responsible citizenship. But to hear it told on the university campus—even by renegade "visiting scholars" who should know better—the only life worth living is that of completely dissident individualism. On this sick thinking, the examined life can only be one of total social repudiation and the escape into bizarre minorities of atomized eccentricity. Here alone may be found personal authenticity and existential integrity. Yet it is this sector of the nation—university youth—which is the chief beneficiary of the sustaining society. Whatever fees it may pay for tuition and/or board and lodging are fractions of the actual cost being borne by either the taxpayer or philanthropy or both together. The direct annual cost per student of American higher education stands currently at about $1,300, quite apart from the costs of research and auxiliary items. Over $1 billion per year are spent on educational technology, and publishers in the U.S. issue some 400 technical and educational books and 3,500 articles per week. A higher proportion of young Americans proceed to a college or university education than in any other country, backed by the unique resources of the great philanthropic foundations. As a result of all this, the graduate may expect to earn, on the average, $180,000 more during a working life than the average individual with only a high school diploma.

SCANDALOUS SWINDLE

In the antic indignation of campus protest, however, higher education is described as a scandalous swindle, the luckless student as an exploitee, and the faculty as shameless players of an academic numbers racket. The older generation, willing provider of educational opportunities that never came its own way, is neither edified nor amused. Having grown bored with its advocacy of external causes such as civil rights and antiwar sit-ins, the authentic student-style is now to be had in psychedelic adventures, *The Harrad Experiment,* riots about parietal rules, something gracefully called "the bitch-in," and any new version of the tired alienation theme. Everywhere there is an aching longing for a successor to those profound insights called "Grooks" wherein students found a spokesman for their ennui in such lines as "I'd like to know/what this whole show/is all about/before it's out." The academic death-wish reached its apogee at Berkeley, but campus defiance as a way of university life occurs clear across the nation, is endemic, and predictably as bizarre as perverse ingenuity can make it. Nobody bothers about the peccadilloes of students until they become victims of their own propaganda. At that point student leaders become a social nuisance in their own constituency and place higher education at risk of having the tune called by the piper who pays. If the beleaguered American people, forced to cut back antipoverty programs in order to sustain an unwanted war, should curtail educational appropriations at university levels on the ground of irresponsible student leadership there would be a rough justice and a tough logic about it.

INTELLIGENT ACCOMMODATION

Over against the Orwellian theme of man as naturally individualistic and intolerably coerced by society ought to be set Thomas Mann's precautionary tale *Dr. Faustus.* Therein, the hero demands and gets absolute freedom, enjoys a staggering series of intellectual and aesthetic adventures, and ends by plunging into insanity. Most of us would find absolute liberty insupportable, including the student gauleiters whose slogan is "Trust no one over thirty." It is the ugliness of this senseless repudiation of that senior half which is the provident half of the nation which denies rebel youth more sympathetic hearing of its legitimate grievances. It is the inalienable right of students to make fools of themselves, but not by inept leadership to make fools of the whole university membership—student body and faculty alike. Universities are places where men think differently, and it did not remain for this raw generation of students to invent protest in order to save the soul of academe. Equality of opportunity, which turns out to be equality of educational opportunity, may be impossible in any absolute sense. But the United States has achieved its close approximation by a triumph of collective responsibility.

Orwell and Aldous Huxley and the whole heavenly host of existentialist thinkers hold that the price of security—political, social and economic security—is too high. It is an equally cogent case that the price of the old order of anarchy was higher still. Whether one regards welfarism altruistically as social justice or cynically as insurance against revolution, it yields by far the better deal for all. Rebellion against social controls, bureaucracy, and collective planning is no more than a vote for anarchy. It is at least arguable that integrity lies less with the denunciator, the agitator, the rebel, the misanthrope, the pilgrim or the anchorite than with the involved intelligence bent upon the improvement rather than the repudiation of collective compromises. The American society, close to anarchy at home and abroad, stands divided because it will not face the facts of social power and efficiency in the technological age for which it is so largely responsible. America presents itself to the European observer as pursuing freedom and order in unrelation as though there is little recognition of necessity.

On this view, there is no need to terrorize or hypnotize society into conformity by the control mechanisms of some great conspiracy. *Conformity is necessity.* The degree of conformity will always be the test of intelligence; and mindless movements, whether of conformity or disaffiliation, of Left or Right, of youth or maturity, of Watts or Berkeley, fail of that test. These splinter drives cohere because individual man no longer means anything or can find meaning in anything; it is social man that counts. The crucial point is that social man can be mindful or mindless, and it is identification with the human situation—not rejection of it—that makes man mindful and society meaningful. Where there are no penalties upon opinion there can be no premium upon protest. The most rabid denouncers of community, whether students or black powerites, Birchers or Communists, draw followers not because they are moved by compassion *for* their fellows, not because they are alienated, but *because they have alienated themselves from* their fellows.

It is not accidental that in some parts of the world psychiatrists are called alienists; or that the socially estranged reveal so many features of the disordered mind. It is to Karen Horney that we owe this perception;

that the ideal of self-fulfillment becomes a cult when it is withdrawn from social context. This is not to say life should be merely passive accommodation; it is to say the opposite, namely, that life should be intelligent accommodation.

Brave New World

FRANK S. MEYER

It would hardly seem necessary, after twenty years of intense discussion in the American conservative movement, to reiterate in these pages one of the central political axioms of that movement—that the modern state, in its massive growth, is the primary instrumentality of liberal utopianism and the greatest contemporary enemy of man's freedom and spiritual growth. Yet the appearance . . . of Mr. Kenneth Melvin's dithyramb of the welfare state, "Big Brother is Dead Too," proves that even in conservative circles old errors never die, that intellectually as well as politically "eternal vigilance is the price of liberty."

In an apparent hope that our disgust with the nihilistic students and black revolutionaries around us will have deadened our critical faculties and blotted every lesson of history from our minds, Mr. Melvin presents to us, not only as the sole alternative to threatening anarchy, but as the ultimate haven of human hopes—the totalizing bureaucratic state:

If welfarism is to operate, it requires pervasive bureaucracy and conformity for the effective discharge of its *ever-widening tasks*. This is where Orwell et al. missed the point. They believed that human nature is intrinsically individualistic, and that men would therefore resent and rebel against conformism in even its benign forms. The stubborn fact is that mankind has an inveterate mass-disposition to prefer the comfort of security to the loneliness of self-sufficiency. The bureaucratic state suits most men for most of the time. [My emphasis.]

Shades of Wittfogel! Shades of Voegelin! So ran the writ of every oriental despotism, every cosmological civilization. It is the very glory of the West, and of its Hellenic and Hebraic civilizational ancestry, that we have always raised the standard of the person against this age-old nostalgia of mass-men for slavish security. So the murmuring Jews in the wilderness railed against Moses:

Would to God we had died by the hand of the Lord in the land of Egypt, when we sat by the flesh pots, and when we did eat bread to the full.

It is clear, both from history and from theory: the greater the security, the closer to slavery; the firmer the self-reliance, the deeper the freedom; the deeper the freedom, the wider the human achievement.

The massive bureaucratic state is and always has been the polar opposite of freedom and self-reliance. For obvious reasons. Power breeds power, and state control over the economy and over the lives of human beings limits liberty more and more drastically.

Acton has been quoted and requoted till perhaps the edge has been rubbed off his apothegm, but so long as ideologists of collectivism like Mr. Melvin exist, he cannot be quoted too often: "Power tends to corrupt and absolute power corrupts absolutely." Acton meant that it corrupts not only its holders but the entire society where it is exercised in centralized form. He knew what the founders of this republic had taught him, that only the division of power (not that laughable concept "democratic" control over holders of massive power) can tame power and leave men free.

Mr. Melvin presents us with the statist prescription for tyranny characteristic of the ideology of the twentieth century in all its manifestations, from the brutality of Communism and Nazism to the insidious seductivity of European social democracy and American welfarism. He does it, what is more, under the guise of an attack on ideology. No ideologist he, just pragmatic, down-to-earth, as offended as you or I by the posturings of revolutionary students.

It would be a neat trick, except that in his eagerness to prove that he is not motivated by ideology—only by the way things are—he introduces a second ideological myth dear to the twentieth century: the myth of economic and social determinism. "The welfare society," so it appears, "just had to happen under the economics of surplus." It is predetermined by social and economic developments, and you'd better put up with it, or else. . . .

"Conformity is necessity," says Mr. Melvin—or, as Hegel and Marx put it more elegantly, "Freedom is the recognition of necessity." This is the helpless surrender to material conditions that Marxism and quasi-Marxism have preached to us incessantly these hundred years or more.

But the spirit of the West is a different spirit. It recognizes that, within broad limits, men can guide and shape society upon the foundations of principle and civilizational tradition. Of course the mode of such a society will differ in differing economic situations. They will be different today than they were in feudal federated Europe or in federated agrarian America—but they will be modes that free men from subservience to the state. And they will be modes that will restore motivation to those who produce and show initiative and provide for themselves and their families, lifting from them an ever increasing burden of taxation and regulation.

I do not argue against the spirit of charity by which men take care of the unfortunate among them, but Mr. Melvin's welfarism destroys charity as surely as it destroys freedom, seizing the surplus of the productive to build the rigid social structures of a bureaucracy, leaving men neither the material substance nor the motivation for charity. It is a pattern for a society as spiritually arid as it is politically tyrannical.

The Welfare Non-Issue

JAMES BURNHAM

Frank Meyer's excommunication of Kenneth Melvin . . . was stirringly pronounced, but he managed to avoid the main point. I do not pretend to speak for Mr. Melvin (who does well enough on his own), but I want to set down a few of the things that his article . . . prompted me to think about, and rethink.

First and most important: *Welfarism is not a real issue.* It is a pseudo-issue, with obsolescent meaning for rhetoric and ideology but none or very little in relation to the real world.

I use the word, "welfarism," in a wide sense: "acceptance of public responsibility for many important needs and wants of the citizens."

The list of needs and wants varies from country to country, and tends, as we know, to expand. Among the more prominent: education, sewage, water, roads (these four dating back, in many places, to long before the days of "the welfare state"), food, housing, medical care, security against the hazards of unemployment, disability and old age.

"Public responsibility," in this rough definition, has also a wide reference. The responsibility can be exercised—and in fact is currently being exercised—in any of a great number of ways, ranging from performance of the function (e.g. medical care) directly by the central state apparatus to the mere noting by the public authorities that the function is being sufficiently carried out by private means.

WELFARISM IS ALWAYS WITH US

Welfarism need not mean and in many countries has not meant "government medicine," "state farming," "government housing," etc. But it does mean that the organs of government, and in the last analysis the sovereign, that is the central government, recognizes (or takes) a responsibility, over and above any private responsibility, for dealing with these needs and wants.

Welfarism does not mean a sharp break with either the theory or practice of government in the past. *Some* welfarist responsibility has always been recognized by every government. What is distinctive (though not unprecedented) about government in our age is the enlargement of the range of that responsibility. But there is nothing surprising in this. The enlargement is obviously correlated with a) the population explosion, b) the disappearance of agricultural society, and c) the technological revolution which, on the one hand, underlies those first two changes and, on the other, provides the material possibility for public welfarism.

Frank Meyer inadvertently expresses the purely ideological nature of his rhetoric. "Mr. Melvin," he writes, "presents us with the statist prescription for tyranny characteristic of the ideology of the twentieth century in all its manifestations, from the brutality of Communism and Nazism to the insidious seductivity [*sic*] of European social democracy and American welfarism." In more prosaic moments I feel sure Frank Meyer would never have slipped into that careless equating of Nazism, Communism, social democracy and the American system. Nevertheless, the facts from which that sentence takes off are indeed significant for an understanding of modern welfarism. All modern nations are welfarist, no matter what their forms of government and economy: Communist, socialist, capitalist or mixed; dictatorial, republican, fascist and clerical; Christian, Jewish, Buddhist or atheist; conservative, labor, liberal or radical; one-party, two-party or multi-party. Surely this suggests that modern welfarism is brought not by a plot or by any special doctrine or political movement, but as one consequence of the twentieth-century human condition. Or do we conclude, in the words of a World War I song, that they're all out of step but Frank?

Several generations ago, classical economists and libertarians believed socialism to be like pregnancy. Once impregnated even the least tiny bit, the body politic would inevitably breed the monstrous offspring, totalitarian Communism. They were wrong. Communism never comes as a "development" within a non-Communist society, but only as a deliberately engineered revolution. We know that some-socialism does not inevitably mean all-socialism, that welfarism does not inevitably mean socialism in the classic sense of government monopoly, and that freedoms can coexist with social democracy and welfarism—in some cases, more freedoms than before, indeed, for the masses. Intellectuals may not be able to draw a clear metaphysical line between Communism, social democracy and welfarism, but the masses have no difficulty seeing it: nowhere have the masses, however conditioned by welfarism and socialism, opted voluntarily for Communism.

FREEDOM AND FATE

In scornfully rejecting "economic and social determinism," Frank Meyer perhaps slips into a conception of human freedom closer to that of our anarchism of the New Left than to Aristotle. Correctly understood, Engels was near to a profound truth when he wrote that "Freedom is the knowledge of necessity." Man's freedom is narrowly limited by man's fate—by the human condition, by his own organism, the physical universe and the historical circumstances in which he finds himself. A man's significant choices must indeed be made within the framework of these necessities; if not, the proclaimed choices become just talk, fustian.

It in no way follows from what I have written that conservatives must simply resign themselves to any and every welfarist project and proposal. It does not follow that the only solution to each major welfare program is to turn it over to the central government—though that is where it will end if nothing is done at other levels, public or private, to solve it. By undiscriminating resistance to *welfarism*, conservatives may have indirectly nurtured the welfare *state*.

What does follow is that no serious politics in our time can be based on a simplistic anti-welfarist doctrine. Granted that axiom, there remains an enormous field of dispute and choice. Do you doubt whether choice thus circumscribed has much significance? Ask the Czechs.

Moral Bewilderment

MORRIS GINSBERG

The period between the wars is frequently described as one of disillusion. The peoples of western Europe were suffering, it is said, from decay, moral and intellectual. In the sphere of politics this was visible in widespread loss of faith in the efficiency of democratic forms of government. The arts, it is alleged, reflected the growing sense of the aimlessness of existence and the futility of ideals. Even science no longer held out the hope that by its methods an interpretation would be reached of the ultimate structure of the world. The traditional doctrines both of religion and morality were shaken by the growing influence of the theory that all knowledge was relative and that no judgments could claim absolute validity. There was, in short, a general loss of the sense of direction and this appeared not only in the sceptical utterances of the intellectuals but in the conduct of the masses of the people which revealed, so it is said, a lack of zest and alertness and of confidence in their own future and the future of civilization itself.

Diagnoses of this kind which pretend to sum up the entire mentality of an age are easily made. By giving prominence to certain tendencies and ignoring others, by assuming causal links between movements which in fact may not be causally connected, in particular by taking the utterances of literary men as reflecting the mental state of the masses of the people, it is not difficult to make out a plausible case for any particular theory. But if such diagnoses are easily made they are as easily refuted. Consider the alleged moral decay. There is no proof that doctrines of the relativity of moral judgments are especially characteristic of the present age or are dominant among present-day philosophers. There is no evidence that doctrines of this kind necessarily affect the working code of the people who teach them. For philosophical analysis is one thing, actual morality another. There is still less evidence that such doctrines are at all widely accepted by non-philosophers or that they make articulate a widely-diffused belief that the distinctions between right and wrong are ephemeral and arbitrary. To attribute political or economic "crises" to moral factors mainly is particularly dangerous. The collapse of France for example has often been taken to indicate a wide prevalence of moral and political cynicism or at the least of a state of moral weariness. But careful

observers have noted that despite the "moral Hamletism" of some intellectuals the sources of devotion, enthusiasm and readiness for self-sacrifice
had by no means run dry in France. It would be as misleading to attribute
the revival of France to a moral renaissance as to explain its collapse as
due to a decay of morals. There is no evidence of widespread changes of
moral temper and outlook in either direction.

There is no reason for believing that the men of this age are lacking
in moral fibre. The experience of the two world wars shows that men are
no less responsive to ideals or less tenacious of purpose than were men of
former ages. The difficulty of dealing with this problem is made evident
by the fact that régimes of very different character appear to be equally
capable of evoking qualities of the very highest order. Russians and
Japanese, Germans and their opponents, have all alike revealed astonishing powers of devotion, readiness for self-sacrifice, indomitable courage
and endurance. Are we to conclude that the social systems of these peoples
are of equal intrinsic value or are these peoples fighting not for any particular social system but for something much more elemental—the survival
of their group?

It is clear that if we attempt to estimate the moral quality of an entire
people we set ourselves an impossible task. We must begin by a study of
the groups within the people and even then our information is woefully
scanty. In Germany, for instance, we can distinguish between the Nazis,
their supporters and their opponents. Among the former we can, according to the most plausible accounts, recognize three different groups.
There were the Nazi leaders and their immediate followers. These appear
to have been moral nihilists. They made power their end and ruthless
violence their instrument. They could talk of justice and reasonableness
when it suited them, but this was a mere ruse to be discarded as soon as
other methods became available. There were, secondly, the indoctrinated.
Among these there were undoubtedly many who by their training became
as amoral as their leaders, brutal and without any moral scruple. But
there were others who perhaps are more correctly described as moral
fanatics. They accepted a set of beliefs which to them was the one true
guide to life and which they regarded as so precious that by comparison
nothing else was of any importance. All ordinary moral standards lost
their significance and, in practice, such moral fanaticism led to acts which
cannot be distinguished from the acts committed by those whom I have
called the moral nihilists.

There were, thirdly, the loyal citizens. These were people who had
not abandoned their wonted moral standards but who were accustomed
to follow and obey the recognized and accepted authority. Among these
there was perhaps a large group who are more correctly described as
bewildered and apathetic. They found themselves in the grip of forces
they could not control and they followed their leaders for fear lest even
worse might befall. In the opposition too no doubt various sub-groups
can be distinguished, which need not here be examined. In non-totalitar-
ian countries there are no exact parallels to the amoralists, nor is there any
evidence of fundamental moral scepticism among the masses of the people. But there is a good deal of political apathy on the one hand and of

moral bewilderment on the other. This bewilderment is not, as it seems to me, evidence of moral decay but rather of moral ferment and it reflects genuine moral difficulties and not merely ignorance or mental confusion.

The moral malaise of our times is not yet articulate but certain elements in it may, I think, be discerned. To begin with, there is a widespread feeling that the religious authorities have not succeeded in showing how the moral tenets which they teach can be applied to the complex situations of modern life. Consider, for example, the attitude of the churches to war. There are at least three views, for each of which Christian warrant is claimed. There is, first, the view that war is always sinful and must be absolutely renounced. There is, secondly, the view which distinguishes between wars which are just and those which are unjust, and here there are wide differences of opinion as to the criteria of just wars. There is, thirdly, the view of those who think that normally it is a duty of a Christian to obey the orders of his government and therefore he must fight if so commanded, though here some authorities would admit that individuals may feel justified in refusing if they are convinced that the fighting is in a wrong cause. At a conference of Christian Churches held before the war it was clear that those who took part felt overwhelmed by the difficulty of the problem. It was even suggested that the perplexity was "a sign of the sins in which the members of the Church were implicated." What they meant is that they were no wiser than other people. Similar illustrations could easily be given from the attitude of Christianity to the problems connected with the institutions of property and economic organization. The fundamental moral principles are perhaps not seriously questioned but their application to complex issues is felt to be vague and uncertain and this shakes belief in their workability. The difficulty cannot be resolved by a separation of zones, one concerned with the individual and the family and the other with public life. For the zones interpenetrate, and apathy towards or abstraction from public life must sooner or later, under modern conditions, lead to an enfeeblement of the entire structure of morals.

Another source of moral difficulty is to be traced to the close interweaving of ethical questions with questions of fact. I believe that a larger proportion of the population than in any other previous epoch is now eager for justice in social and economic relations. But the lack of accurate knowledge of the facts involved tends to obscure the ethical aspects of the problem and, in particular, to suggest greater differences of opinion regarding ethical standards than would exist if the factual issues were more clearly grasped. The believer in "capitalism" and the believer in a socialized economy are apt to think that they are divided by a difference of view regarding ends and values. But it is perfectly possible that both sides, for example, attach equal value to the full and harmonious development of individual personality, but that each is convinced that the policy advocated by the other would lead to slavery. In such a controversy there are certainly involved ethical questions in the proper sense of the word; for example, the grading and balancing of different kinds of freedom, such as the relative importance of basic security in the conditions of life, the exercise of initiative, the freedom of expression and the like.

Such grading involves a conception of a hierarchy of values and is thus a proper matter for ethical analysis. But even here questions of fact are involved, since we need to be able to estimate the likely effects of the policy to be followed on each kind of freedom and on each other. Futhermore the difference between the socialists and their opponents turns also on differences of view regarding the motives or incentives of action, the possibility of changing the direction of motives by changes in institutions and the probable effect of different systems of distributing the products of industry on the total produced. These are questions mainly of economics and sociology and not so much of ethics. But people are apt to think they differ about ethics, when in reality the root of the difference may well be due to the obscurity and complexity of the facts and the difficulty of estimating in advance the consequences likely to follow from the line of policy pursued.

A third cause of moral malaise is to be found in the use made of the moral appeal in modern propaganda. The confusions thus arising are very widespread and the source of much bewilderment. Marxist literature, for example, is infused with moral passion and idealism, while at the same time suggesting that morals like religion are only opium for the people. The contradiction is more blatant in fascist literature. Here appeal is constantly made to justice and reasonableness, while in the same breath the fundamental principles of humanity and justice are dismissed with contempt. Above all, war propaganda, in which both sides claim to be fighting for the highest ideals, cannot but engender a suspicion of insincerity and a tendency to dismiss all ideals as illusions or shadowy epiphenomena of a struggle between forces in their essence non-moral. No doubt, while in the midst of war, most people come to feel that right is on their side. The political disillusion that follows wars is, however, only too apt to revive moral doubts that during a war are latent or suppressed.

A fourth tendency which appears in many forms is a manifestation not so much of moral bewilderment as of moral fanaticism. One of the most alarming things in our time is the demand so frequently made on the Left and the Right for unquestioning faith. In the Nazi writings the word fanaticism has become a term of praise, but the longing for an intensification of certitude, for an assured conviction which will withstand all challenges and be beyond all discussion, is by no means confined to the Nazis. We can recognize in this connexion types well-known in the study of religious fanaticism. There is the brooding ascetic type, obsessed by his conviction, incapable of tolerating any conflicting ideas, often paranoid, a persecuted persecutor, ready for anything, however cruel. There is, secondly, the weak and unstable type, hunting his own doubt in others, the man who cannot believe in himself so long as others doubt him. This type too tends to seek reassurance in exaggerated self-assertion and to overcome his own weakness in cruelty and destructiveness. There are, thirdly, the excessively loyal, those who, as William James puts it, suffer from "a loyalty carried to a convulsive extreme." Such people tend to idealize the devotion itself and they too may go to any length, of cruelty especially, to avenge a slight, imaginary or real, to their hero or cause.

There are others, themselves uncertain and incapable of resolute action, who admire what they take to be the strength and confidence of the fanatics and are ready to condone in them acts of which they themselves are quite incapable. In times of social confusion all these types come to the surface. The demand for an assured faith which will kill all doubt and inspire speedy action gives the fanatics their chance. The resort to violence is the natural outcome.

We are here concerned not so much with the psychology as with the ethics of violence. We need not consider those who glorify violence as an end in itself. But the problem of the limits of the use of force as a means for attaining ends deemed of supreme value is one that deeply troubles many of the younger generation who have no sympathy at all with the romantic view of violence familiar in fascist literature. Do revolutionary ideals justify the use of violent methods deemed to be necessary for their attainment? Has a minority convinced that it is acting for the well-being of the community as a whole the right to impose its will on an indifferent or apathetic or hostile majority? Is there a fundamental difference between the use of force in war and its use in a revolution? These are questions which in different forms are very frequently raised, and they are the more pressing because in the background is a feeling of impatience with the liberal spirit and a longing for decisive action, which may easily pass into the admiration of action as such, characteristic of many fascists. The arguments adduced often imply an unreal separation of ends and means. There are no doubt many forms of conduct in which the two can be clearly distinguished, but in complex social activities the means employed frequently affect the nature of the end sought and means and ends must therefore be considered together for the purposes of ethical evaluation. If force is used to bestow freedom the probability is that the mentality of those who apply the force and of those who suffer from it will be pauperized and that both will be made unfit to act freely. This is not to say that force can never be rightly used, but merely to suggest that in dealing with the use of force as a means for the attainment of valuable ends attention must be given to the question how far force can attain these ends without distorting their nature or producing consequences incompatible with them. The history of revolutions shows how difficult such questions are to answer. Who can say even in retrospect whether any of them were worth the price and whether the price was necessary? In prospect the problems involved in grading values and in estimating the probable consequences are even more difficult. It is not surprising that they lead to bewilderment, or that refuge from bewilderment is sought in fanaticism.

There is another group of problems which occasion much perplexity. These are connected with the growing realization of the discrepancy between public and private morals. Some philosophers indeed have thought that ethically there is a gulf between the two worlds and that states in their relations to one another cannot be judged by the same standards as those which are held to bind individuals. The ordinary man finds the situation bewildering. He realizes that on behalf of their state men are expected to do acts which in the sphere of private relations they would regard as monstrous. Yet he would certainly not admit that in the behavior of states the distinction between what is fair and unfair, just and unjust, right and wrong, does not hold good. A philosophical analysis of common-sense morality would probably show that underlying it is an assumption that there can be no two moralities and the same ethical principles must bind groups as individuals. The differences, common-sense morality would say, lie rather in the conditions under which the principles have to be applied, in the greater complexity of the relations between states, the greater difficulty of foreseeing the consequences of action, in particular, the absence of an impartial and effective legal order guaranteeing the minimum conditions of a common life, and so forth. Up to a point, analysis along these lines would clarify the issues involved and it would show, I think, that ordinary men have become increasingly conscious of their personal responsibility for the action taken by states in their behalf. Such an analysis would, however, also reveal the appalling vagueness of what may be called the secondary principles of international morality such as are expressed in words like "national self-determination," the "equality of states" and the principle of "trusteeship" in its application to the treatment of backward areas. There is an equal vagueness in our knowledge of the relevant facts. The consequence is that in ordinary times it is easy to satisfy idealistic cravings in repeating these phrases without making any effort to work out their implications. In times of crisis their inadequacy becomes painfully evident and there is frequently a tendency to reject them wholly. The scepticism that results not only shakes our confidence in these secondary principles, but it raises the doubt whether there are any moral principles at all which can effectively guide the relations between states. Yet on the whole it is probable that among large numbers of individuals there is now a greater interest in the moral aspects of international relations than in any previous epoch.

It is sometimes said that in the present age two opposed ideals are striving for mastery: that which assigns supreme value to the individual and that which claims supremacy for the community. Can it be this which really divides people? Formally, even the Nazi writers, who are commonly cited as representing the view which claims supremacy for the community in the shape of the *Volk*, would not admit that they deny the value of individual personality. In practice, of course, their policy leads to the ruin of personality, but then it also fails to achieve the good of the community. The trouble about the Nazis is that their so-called ethical theory lacks all sincerity, whether they talk in terms of individual or social welfare. Their aim is power as such. They talk occasionally of the ends which power is to serve, but that is only because they believe this to be psychologically necessary in order to inculcate obedience or inspire enthusiasm. The emphasis on the community is no doubt useful as serving to appeal to the individual's capacities for devotion and self-sacrifice, but it is doing the Nazi writers too much honor to attribute to them an ethical theory in which communal goods are consistently defined as different from individual goods. Power for them requires no justification save as a ruse for the multitude.

When we review the examples of moral malaise that have been

briefly sketched above, we can see, I think, that they are not all due to ignorance or lack of moral courage in applying known moral principles, or to the vagaries of passion and the distortion due to selfish interests. There are perplexities which would remain, granted goodwill, due in the main to the complexity of the problems which have to be faced and the difficulty of applying highly general moral principles to concrete situations of great intricacy. Those who stand for a cult of violence and inculcate it through violence are clearly beyond ethical argument. The moral fanatics are on a different level. They are carried away by an overwhelming motive, a conviction so profound that ordinary moral standards cease to operate. They too are perhaps not open to argument, but no one can pretend that the problems which the revolutionary idealist, for example, is confronted with are simple or unreal. They involve a grading of values and an analysis of social facts for which there exists at present no exact method. They can only be conjured to "remember the possibility that they might be mistaken." For the rest, the problems of the morally bewildered will not be resolved by their acceptance of an unquestioning faith, religious or other, for which there is now so much clamor. What is needed is greater moral courage and above all greater knowledge of social facts and a development of ethical theory equal to the task of evaluating and interpreting them.

Learning To Be Radical

KENNETH A. MEGILL

The chief end [of civil society] is the preservation of property.—J. Locke

Democracy in the United States and Western Europe is understood as a system in which a representative government is elected and controlled by the majority in such a way that the rights of minorities are protected. Social disputes, according to this liberal democratic theory, are resolved by integrating minorities within the system. With integration it becomes possible for minorities to participate in the electoral process, through which decisions are made. The liberal democratic theory is a democratic theory because the people are able to control their fate through elections, but in order to do so they must enter into the bargaining process which goes on among the various minorities.

The development of a radical political theory in the United States has come not from the educational and academic institutions, but began as a practical reaction to discrepancies within the liberal society. Only recently has there begun to be a theoretical discussion to accompany the revolt against the liberal democratic theory. For several years, even though students and faculty members have been involved during their free time with the problems of civil rights and the war in Viet Nam, involvement in political affairs has seldom been carried into the classroom and research room, where a theoretical understanding of the failure of the liberal society could be investigated. Radicalism in the United States has had to be learned, not at the university, but in the process of trying to solve particular problems within the existing order which claims to be democratic.

Two practical issues united the democratic forces in the United States and served as a learning process for the new democrats. The civil rights struggle and the organized opposition to the war in Viet Nam have created a large number of young people who are disillusioned with the society in which they live and who have made practical efforts to bring about by persuasion changes in this society. It is precisely because persuasion has failed that the movement has developed from a pressure group demanding certain specific and minimal changes within the liberal democratic framework to a movement demanding fundamental changes in the social and economic system of the United States. The new democrats learned to adopt a position opposed to the prevailing social order only after the order had been tested and found to be wanting.

The summer of 1964, known as the Mississippi Summer, stands as the high point of enthusiasm for liberal democracy and is also the decisive moment when those who had become involved in the struggle for civil rights for the Negro began to realize that the liberal democratic society could not provide genuine freedom for him. The strategy guiding the activity during the early days of the civil rights movement was obvious to all Americans imbued with the ideals of liberal democracy. In Mississippi, and elsewhere in the South and North, the problem was thought to be simple: The blacks had not been allowed to vote; therefore if the fundamental rights of voting and access to public schools on an equal basis could be guaranteed, then all other necessary social changes would follow. Indeed, if democracy *means* the right to vote, then the securing of the vote was all that would be required for the institution of democracy. The task of the Mississippi Summer was to bring the blacks in the South within the political and social life of the United States. The project was welcomed by the liberals throughout the nation, and the enthusiasm among the singing, chanting workers was contagious for the whole country. There seemed to be hope that democracy really could be meaningful for the blacks, if only the right to vote could be won.

Several years and many elections later the failure of the strategy adopted in Mississippi has become obvious. Even though the number of black voters has increased considerably, there has been no significant improvement in the lot of the blacks. The election of a black to even a local office is still a major news story. The Southern racist senators, who have consistently killed or modified attempts at federal action to aid the blacks, are still chairmen of powerful committees. They still claim to represent states with large Negro populations.

If anything, the blacks have become even more alienated from society and are even more impoverished economically than before the liberal strategy was adopted. The civil rights struggle is dead, and instead the battle for black power in the cities of the North has begun; no one seriously holds that the strategy of the Mississippi Summer can provide the slightest hope of solving the problems of the blacks in the ghetto. Democracy conceived as a system of electoral politics has shown itself to be a farce for a substantial portion of the population. It has become obvious that only fundamental economic and social change can begin to meet the problem of the lack of freedom for the blacks in the United States.

Black power has become the theoretical expression of the realization that liberal democracy is bankrupt. Disorder in the cities has been the spontaneous, unorganized, and undirected expression of the realization on the part of the blacks that the liberal democrats cannot help them to gain control over their lives. Black power expresses clearly that revolution and power are necessary for a genuine freeing of the blacks. The panic-stricken reaction of the liberal democrats shows that the message of black power has been understood. Not integration, but the development of genuine integrity for the local community and power for all human beings to organize and plan their own lives is at the heart of black power. Community control can be developed only if the property relations which support the liberal democratic institutions are fundamentally altered. In short, black power is one of the first genuinely revolutionary theories to develop in the United States.

At first, black power was little more than a slogan, but it was a slogan which captured the failure of liberal democracy and began to provide the direction for a movement away from liberalism. Concretely, black power means local organization, new political institutions, and economic independence for the black community and also the development of the specialness of the black. The whites are told to work for their own freedom in their own community but to realize that they are responsible for the centuries of oppression of the blacks. Freedom requires the creation of a whole new set of political and social institutions, which are separate from the white power structure. An independent police and judicial system is already developing in black communities as it has been realized that the police and judicial system organized by the elected representatives can neither provide protection nor give justice to the people who live in the ghetto. The day-to-day life in the ghetto has come more and more under the rule of habit and informal pressure, rather than the rule of the white establishment. During the first rebellions in the ghettos it was understood which buildings should be burned down and which areas should be attacked, thus showing that even in moments apparently the most unorganized of all, there existed a set of genuine social institutions and customs that operated where the white man's police failed. The law and order of "whitey" failed, but a new kind of law and order was revealed.

Economic independence is the most important goal for the black man. The most significant part of the black power position is its focus on the oppressive economic system, which is supported by the liberal democratic theory. In the attempt to create new social and economic institutions, the black power advocates have insisted that these institutions be under community control. A kind of socialism absent from the American tradition is being established in the center of certain American cities. As the black power movement developed it was realized that in order to achieve genuine community control over the economic institutions, is was necessary to free the ghetto from outside interference and to bring about democratization in the economic affairs of the nation at large. For black power to be real, there had to be a change in the white community as well. The liberation of the blacks presupposes the liberation of the whites from racism and an unfree society.

There have been some attempts to organize the poor white community along the lines suggested by black power, but they have not been notably successful. The black revolution will continue to be led by the blacks. The success of the democratic movement in the United States will largely depend upon the ultimate victory of the black revolution and the successful creation of revolutionary movements in the ghetto, which can serve as examples for the rest of society. Because of the particularly open nature of the oppression of the blacks, they are beginning to develop radically new institutions more rapidly than the unorganized whites.

Had it not been for the war in Viet Nam, perhaps the black revolution could have been quickly suppressed, and a massive program of federal expenditures could have relieved the worst pressures on the black community. Perhaps many of the racial problems in the United States could have been solved within the framework of liberal democracy. Liberalism is a theory that has always argued for formal freedom from oppressive institutions. The original aim of the poverty program was to bring the black population within the liberal middle-class society and ideology. Had it not been for the war in Viet Nam, this strategy might well have succeeded, and black power would never have developed into an important revolutionary movement.

The failure of the Mississippi Summer project and similar liberal efforts to integrate blacks into white society and to bring about a genuine democratization produced the first wave of radicals in the United States who have expressed their rejection of the liberal theory by the black power argument. In 1968 a similar process of radicalization with regard to the Viet Nam war took place. In late 1967, Eugene McCarthy announced his candidacy for the presidency, with the expressed purpose of bringing the protest against the war and those engaged in these protests within the political system. The McCarthy campaign, particularly in its early stages, was an attempt to integrate a minority into the political system of the United States. Particular policies (such as the conduct of the war in Viet Nam) were questioned, but there was no discussion of the nature of the American society which had produced the war in Viet Nam. The McCarthy campaign mobilized thousands of people, particularly young people, and gave them hope that they could have a place within the political system.

Like the Mississippi Summer project of 1964, the McCarthy campaign of 1968 failed to integrate the protesters into the society and produced instead a new generation of radicals. The radicals of 1968 were made by the failure of the traditional political machinery, which the liberal theory and the liberal society claimed was adequate to make any necessary change. By the time the Democratic Convention was held in Chicago it had become clear to an increasing number of people that it was impossible for the war in Viet Nam to be brought to a close by working within the social and political institutions present in the United States. Even more important, a large number of people had begun to ask why the war could not be stopped and what caused the American society to participate in an imperialistic war in a far-off country. What began as an integration process turned out to be a radicalization process for a significant part of the population. By the end of the Chicago convention many McCarthy sympathizers understood that the system itself, and not merely a particular policy, needed to be attacked.

The final act of the McCarthy campaign, appropriately enough, took place in the streets, not in the convention hall, which had been established by the political authorities as the place where political decisions ought to be made. The police action against the demonstrators and the McCarthy campaign workers showed clearly that the United States governmental system rests ultimately on force and that if necessary this force will be used to suppress a movement which aims at changing the social and political system of the United States.

The failure of the final attempt to end the war in Viet Nam through the political process radicalized a large number of people and showed that the disillusionment with the existing order had become widespread. The new democrats have been created as they have tried to go through the existing channels, which are supposedly offered for changing the liberal society. The breakdown of the liberal ideology and the disillusionment with the liberal society have created the possibility for a genuinely new democratic theory to begin to develop.

The war in Viet Nam is a classic example of a war fought to "save" democracy and preserve the American sphere of influence. It began as a small police action supposedly designed to protect the rights of another country to remain free and to prevent the "international communist conspiracy" from a victory won by military means. Just as the events after the Mississippi Summer showed that racial problems cannot be solved with the framework of liberal democracy, so the past few years have shown that the war in Viet Nam is not against external aggression, but instead is being waged by the United States in order to protect its economic and political position in the world.

In the minds of the younger American generation, for the first time, the United States has clearly been on the wrong side in a war. This astounding fact has sent many young people back to the history books, and under a critical eye, the unemphasized imperialistic nature of the American political tradition has begun to emerge. The war in Viet Nam, to those who have looked again at the history of the United States, is no longer viewed as an isolated tactical mistake, but is seen as the most flagrant and obvious act of imperialistic aggression by a mighty nation with a long history of imperialism against smaller nations in Latin America and Asia. After repeated revelations concerning the role of the secret police (CIA) of the United States in the internal affairs of many nations and disclosures that the secret police have dominated many domestic organizations as well, little faith remains in the current order, which claims to be democratic. The loss of faith in the ability of the present government structure to provide a democratic order has perhaps been the most important result of the war in Viet Nam. The failure of liberal democracy in both the racial situation and in Viet Nam has revealed that a new way of understanding democracy is necessary if the problems of racial injustice at home and imperialism abroad are to be met. Just as the blacks have discovered that freedom will not come to them until the economic structure of the white community is altered, so the opponents of the war in Viet Nam have come to understand that there must be a fundamental change in the social and economic structure before wars such as that in Viet Nam can be eliminated.

While the development of the new democratic forces in the United States has been the result of the practical experience of seeing the collapse of the accepted institutions of society, the theoretical rejection of the liberal democratic theory, which was the basis for the social order in the United States, is only now being formulated. The significant fact is that merely the formulation of the premises of the liberal theory is almost sufficient to refute the theory itself. The problem is not to *refute* the liberal democratic theory, but to *portray* it and to show that it is meaningless—that it is simply irrelevant as a theory for a democratic society today.

It is generally held that liberal democracy is based upon two major principles: majority rule and minority rights. Undoubtedly the first principle is that the majority rules. In an assembly, whether it be the United States Congress, a ladies league for better schools, or any other small or large group, the assumption is that an organization is democratic if the majority rules. An important corollary to this principle is that in any sizable group, it is impossible for the majority to decide all matters directly; therefore, responsibility must be delegated. Parties, factions, and groups are built within the organization and play the most important role in decision making. In practice the principle of majority rule means that there must be at least two parties within a democratic organization or state and that these two parties must alternate in holding power; it must be possible for the party in power to be replaced. The principle of majority rule thus holds that a nation or organization is democratic if there is a possibility for the party in power to be replaced and if minorities can be integrated into the system.

The second crucial principle for the liberal democratic theory is that there are certain rights of the individual which cannot be violated. Even a majority cannot take them away from individuals and groups within the organization or state. Examples are freedom of speech, of the press, of assembly, of religion, and (traditionally) the right to property. Individual rights must be protected in order to leave the possibility open for new parties and other collectives to be formed which can replace the party in power.

It would, however, be misleading to conclude that liberal democracy means only that the majority rules and that the rights of individuals are protected. Equally important is the presence of a capitalist, or so-called free enterprise, economic system. Majority rule and minority rights are required as principles for political organizations if the capitalistic economic order is to function well. John Locke emphasized that the natural rights of man apply not only to individuals, but to private property as well, and he described the purpose of the liberal democratic government as being to protect private property. According to Locke, the individual, in order to protect his property, enters into a civil society, that is, a society which is ruled by laws. A state, a political power, is created to protect property, which includes man's life and liberty. In order to determine who rules, man must allow the majority to make political decisions, as long as the rights of property are not infringed upon. Since the purpose of government is to protect property, government has no right to infringe upon the property created by an individual.

The liberal theory of democracy, which received its classical formulation with Locke, links majority rule, natural rights, and private property. The ordinary understanding of democracy in the United States today is basically Lockean, and his conception of democracy is still repeated in most civics textbooks. It is important to notice that several assumptions are necessary if this view is correct in connecting majority rule, individual rights, and private property:

1. Man is, essentially, an individual who owns property.
2. Man can, by and large, determine what is in his best interests through an act of will, such as voting.
3. In order for man to act politically, political parties must be created which can express the will of the individuals in society.

All these assumptions necessary for the liberal democratic theory have been challenged since Locke wrote. Almost no one, whether he be a philosopher, a political scientist, or the man in the street, would seriously argue today that man is *essentially* a property-owning animal. Furthermore, the notion of man having a "will," through which he can directly and rationally express what is in his best interest, has also been widely rejected as being too simple-minded to be taken seriously as the foundation for a theoretical work. The will has proved to be notoriously difficult to locate, and almost all contemporary philosophers and scientists would reject a theory requiring man to have a will which he can express in a direct, rational manner.

The third fundamental assumption of liberal democracy, that political parties can express the will of individuals through the election process, has been the one most thoroughly investigated by empirical political scientists. Although this assumption is only one of the necessary elements of the democratic theory put forward by the liberals, it is the one assumption which can be more or less empirically tested. If it could be shown that it is possible, through the party machinery and voting, to control one's fate and protect one's property, then we would have to conclude that the liberal theory is at least an adequate, generalized description of an existing political system, even if we would not want to accept it on other grounds. However, from the studies made of voting behavior in liberal democratic societies, it can be concluded that the election mechanism does not provide a way by which the individual can control the political authorities. In political decision making, the results of the electoral process play a modest role. Public policy is primarily determined by the interests of the dominant economic class.

The importance of the discovery that the creation of a "fair" voting system does not ensure control of the government by the people has been largely ignored in the discussion of the nature of democracy. Almost all of the democratic movements in the United States at the beginning of this century were chiefly concerned with the introduction of direct democratic processes—such as initiative and referendum, where indirect procedures had been in effect—and with broadening the right to vote to include all segments of society. The political scientist Dahl has perhaps best expressed the conclusions of those working within the liberal democratic theory by stating that

We cannot correctly describe the actual operations of democratic societies in terms of the contrasts between majorities and minorities. We can only distinguish groups of various types and sizes, all seeking in various ways to advance their goals, usually at the expense, at least in part, of others. . . . A good deal of traditional democratic theory leads us to expect more from national elections than they can possibly provide.

While realizing that the principle of majority rule has never functioned as the liberal theory has contended, Dahl does not question the liberal theory. Instead, he speaks of an "American hybrid," which he insists "is not for export to others." At best, the democratic theory articulated by political scientists such as Dahl is a peculiarly American phenomenon, which cannot be exported to others and serves as a justification for the continuation of the capitalistic economic order in which those who control the property play the most important role in fixing public policy. Dahl and other liberal democrats begin with the assumption that the United States is democratic. The results he presents in his work reflect this assumption and constitute an ideology rationalizing and justifying the current political order. Unless parties can express directly the will of individuals, then the liberal democratic theory, at least in its traditional formulation, is no longer valid. Almost no one would today hold that the liberal theory is still adequate, either as an accurate description of the political process or as a proposal for reform; however, as an ideology—as a way to understand our political life—the liberal theory of democracy is still predominant.

The concepts of majority rule and minority rights fail to provide us with an adequate way of understanding the nature of democracy in an advanced industrial nation. They have become part of an ideology which supports the existing order and obscures the fact that man does not have control over his life and the society in which he lives. The practical and theoretical experience in the United States have shown that the liberal democratic theory can be taken seriously only as an ideology which supports the existing social and economic forces. It fails both as a way of understanding the current order of society and as a theory for a movement set on establishing a new democratic order.

The collapse of the liberal democratic theory as an adequate theory of democracy has also meant that the economic system based upon this theory cannot provide a democratic social order. The new democrats in the United States have a new theory of democracy because they understand that a change in the social system, and not merely a change in personnel, is necessary for there to be democracy. One of the most important tasks for the new democrats is to gain control of the economic system. Unless some kind of effective public control of the economic order can be established, a solution of the racial and military problems in the United States does not seem to be possible. Private ownership of the means of production exists best in a society dominated by a liberal theory of democracy. The new democrats in the United States have been radicalized and have begun to understand that only an economic system under public control can serve as the basis for a democratic political order.

The Pillage of the Earth

FRIEDRICH GEORG JUNGER

Industry is the daughter of poverty.—Rivarol

I love machines; they are like creatures of a higher order. Intelligence has freed them of all the woes and joys which are the lot of the human body in its activity and its exhaustion. Machines on their concrete bases act like serenely meditating Buddhas, squatting on their timeless lotus. They vanish when more beautiful, more perfect ones are born.—Henry van de Velde

Why does the contemplation of machines give us such pleasure? Because they manifest the fundamental form of man's intelligence, because before our very eyes this constructive and combining intelligence masters and amasses power, because they win a ceaseless triumph over the elements which they beat down, squeeze, and forge. Let us enter the workshop, then, to see what goes on.

The impression we gain as we observe technical processes of any sort is not at all one of abundance. The sight of abundance and plenty gives us joy: they are the signs of a fruitfulness which we revere as a life-giving force. Rooting, sprouting, budding, blooming, ripening, and fruition—the exuberance of the motions and forms of life—strengthen and refresh us. The human body and the human mind possess this power of bestowing strength. Both man and woman have it. But the machine organization gives nothing—it organizes need. The prospect of vineyard, orchard, or a blossoming landscape cheers us, not because these things yield profits, but because of the sensation of fertility, abundance, and gratuitous riches. The industrial scene, however, has lost its fruifulness; it has become the scene of mechanical production. It conveys, above all, a sense of hungriness, particularly in the industrial cities which, in the metaphorical language of technological progress, are the homes of a flourishing industry. The machine gives a hungry impression. And this sensation of a growing, gnawing hunger, a hunger that becomes unbearable, emanates from everything in our entire technical arsenal.

When we enter a factory, be it a cotton mill, a foundry, a saw mill, or a powerhouse, everywhere we get the same impression. The consuming, devouring, gluttonous motion racing through time restlessly and insatiably, reveals the never stilled and never to be stilled hunger of the machine. So obvious is this hunger that even the impression of concentrated power which we receive in the centers of heavy industry cannot overcome it. In fact, it is strongest in these centers, because precisely here we find the greatest greed for power. And the rational mind which stands behind the machine and keeps watch over its automatic, mechanical motion—it too is hungry, and hunger follows it everywhere. It cannot shake off hunger; it cannot free itself from it; it cannot be stilled, however hard it may try. And how, indeed, could that be possible! This mind itself is consuming, gluttonous, and it has no access to riches; it cannot conjure up abundance. No effort of ingenuity, not all the inventive power that is brought to bear here can do it. For rationalization only sharpens hunger, and actually increases consumption. This growing consumption is a sign not of abundance but of poverty; it is bound up with worry, want, and toil.

It is precisely the methodical, disciplined effort leading to the perfection of the technical processes which destroys the basis for the hopes that certain groups place in this perfection. Progress in its present rapid advance creates an optical illusion, deceiving the observer into seeing things which are not there. Technology can be expected to solve all problems which can be mastered by technical means, but we must expect nothing from it which lies beyond technical possibilities. Since even the smallest mechanical process consumes more energy than it produces, how could the sum of all these processes create abundance? There can be no talk of riches produced by technology. What really happens is rather a steady, forever growing consumption. It is a ruthless destruction, the like of which the earth has never before seen. A more and more ruthless destruction of resources is the characteristic of our technology. Only by this destruction can it exist and spread. All theories which overlook this fact are lopsided because they disregard the basic conditions which in the modern world govern production and economics.

In every healthy economy, the substance with which it works is preserved and used sparingly, so that consumption and destruction do not overstep the limit beyond which the substance itself would be endangered or destroyed. Since technology presupposes destruction, since its development depends upon destruction, it cannot be fitted into any healthy economic system; one cannot look at it from an economic point of view. The radical consumption of oil, coal, and ore cannot be called economy, however rational the methods of drilling and mining. Underlying strict rationality of technical working methods, we find a way of thinking which cares nothing for the preservation and saving of the substance.

What is euphemistically called production is really consumption. The gigantic technical apparatus, that masterpiece of human ingenuity, could not reach perfection if technological thought were to be contained within an economic scheme, if the destructive power of technical progress were to be arrested. But this progress becomes all the more impetuous, the larger the resources at its disposal, and the more energetically it devours them. This is shown by the concentration of men and machines in the great mining centers where the mechanization of work and the organization of man are most advanced. The rationality of technology, so impressively displayed here, becomes intelligible only when one has understood the conditions on which it depends. Its concomitant is waste and contempt for all rationality in the exploitation of the resources on whose existence technology depends, as the lungs depend on air.

Where wastage begins, there begins desolation, and scenes of such desolation can be found even in the early days of our technology, in the era of the steam engine. These scenes are startling by the extraordinary ugliness and the Cyclopean power which are characteristic of them. The machine invades the landscape with destruction and transformation; it grows factories and whole manufacturing cities overnight, cities grotesquely hideous, where human misery is glaringly revealed; cities which, like Manchester, represent an entire stage of technology and which have become synonymous with hopeless dreariness. Technology darkens the air with smoke, poisons the water, destroys the plants and animals. It brings about a state in which nature has to be "preserved" from rationalized thinking, in which large tracts of land have to be set apart, fenced off, and placed under a taboo, like museum pieces. What all museum-like institutions make evident is, that preservation is needed. The extension of protected areas, therefore, is an indication that destructive processes are at work.

Mining centers, in particular, are the focal points of organized pillage. The riches in the earth are being exploited and consumed. Human pauperization begins with the proletarization of the masses, who are indoctrinated to factory work and kept on a low level of existence. The exploitation of the factory worker (about which socialism is indignant only so long as it is in the opposition) is an inevitable symptom of the universal exploitation to which technology subjects the whole earth from end to end. Man no less than ore deposits belongs to the resources subject to consumption by technology. The ways in which the worker tries to evade this exploitation—associations, labor unions, political parties—are the very methods which tie him forever closer to the progress of technology, mechanical work, and technical organization.

The obverse side of technology is a pillage which becomes constantly better organized; this must not be overlooked when one speaks of technical progress. True, we have made a technical advance if by means of artificial fertilizers we succeed in squeezing uninterrupted crops out of our overburdened plough and pasture land. But this advance itself is at the same time the consequence of a calamitous deficiency, for if we did not have the fertilizer we should no longer be able to feed ourselves at all. Technical progress has deprived us of the free choice of nutriment which our ancestors possessed. A machine which trebles the output of a previous model constitutes a technical advance, for it is the result of a more rational design. But for this very reason it also possesses a more intense consuming and devouring power. Its hunger is sharper, and it consumes correspondingly more. In this way, the whole realm of the machine is full of a restless, devouring power that cannot be satisfied.

Closely linked to this is the rapid wear and tear the machine suffers. That most of our machines become junk so soon results from their design and purpose. Their durability, strength, and usability are lessened, restricted in the very degree to which technology approaches perfection. The consumption brought about by technology extends even to its own apparatus. The repairs and replacements these mechanisms constantly demand represent an immense amount of human labor. And the machine falls quickly into that state of disrepair in which we see it around us everywhere. Technical progress covers the earth, not alone with its machines and workshops, but also with junk and scrap. All this rusty tin, these twisted girders, these bent and broken machine parts and castaway tools—they remind the thoughtful observer of the fleeting impermanence of the process he witnesses. Perhaps they keep him from overestimating all this progress and help him to an understanding of what really goes on. Wear and tear is a form of consumption; it manifests itself preeminently where plundering goes on and so we find it in particular wherever technology is at work.

If two thousand years hence there should still be archaeologists— which is rather unlikely—who were to undertake excavations, say, in Manchester, Essen, or Pittsburgh, they would find but little. They would discover nothing as enduring as Egyptian burial chambers and classic temples. For the stuff with which the factory system works is not *aere perennius* ("more lasting than bronze"—Horace). These archaeologists might even be surprised at the paltriness of their discoveries. The earth-spanning power of technology is of an ephemeral kind—a fact easily overlooked by those engrossed in it. Everywhere it is threatened by decay, given over to decay, and decay follows upon its heels all the more insistently and closely, the faster it marches on towards new triumphs.

The machine does not create new riches. It consumes existing riches through pillage, that is, in a manner which lacks all rationality even though it employs rational methods of work. As technology progresses, it devours the resources on which it depends. It contributes to a constant drain, and thereby again and again comes to a point where it is forced to improve its inventory and to rationalize anew its methods of work. Those who deny this, claiming that it is the wealth of new inventions which made the existing apparatus obsolete, are confusing cause and effect. Inventions presuppose a need for improvement; their purpose is the rationalization of work. Nor can the technician legitimately blame the steadily growing deficits of the technical work process and the recurrent crises and disturbances it causes upon the political organization, charging that the competing political powers of this earth are burdening the industrial production with unjustifiable costs. Such is indeed the case; for the principle of competition is a political and economic rather than a technical one. However, even if the world were one single state—even then the machine would push the process of rationalization to the extreme. The process of rationalization would manifest itself in a free economy no less than in that kind of a planned economy which goes hand in hand with technology. When the engineer destroys free economy—that is, the economy in which the businessman rules autonomously—then he forces the economy to adopt a plan designed by the engineer. To any such planned economy there applies what we have said before about the end effects of organization.

When economic crises can no longer be overcome by economic means, human hopes turn towards stricter rationalization of technology: the idea of technocracy arises. But first we should examine whether it is not technology itself which brings about such crises. We should examine whether technology is capable of putting our economy in order and whether such an ordering falls within the scope of its tasks at all. What does "technocracy" mean? If the word has any meaning, it can only be that the technician rules, that he takes over government. But the technician is no statesman; he has no talent for politics. His knowledge is one of technical, functional effects. All technical knowledge is marked by an impersonalism that necessarily results from the purely material facts that it deals with. This impersonalism is reason enough to doubt whether the technician is capable of taking over and running the affairs of state.

Protean Man

ROBERT JAY LIFTON

I should like to examine a set of psychological patterns characteristic of contemporary life, which are creating a new kind of man—a "protean man." As my stress is upon change and flux, I shall not speak much of "character" and "personality," both of which suggest fixity and permanence. Erikson's concept of identity has been, among other things, an effort to get away from this principle of fixity; and I have been using the term self-process to convey still more specifically the idea of flow. For it is quite possible that even the image of personal identity, in so far as it suggests inner stability and sameness, is derived from a vision of a traditional culture in which man's relationship to his institutions and symbols are still relatively intact—which is hardly the case today. If we understand the self to be the person's symbol of his own organism, then self-process refers to the continuous psychic recreation of that symbol.

I came to this emphasis through work in cultures far removed from my own, studies of young (and not so young) Chinese and Japanese. Observations I was able to make in America also led me to the conviction that a very general process was taking place. I do not mean to suggest that everybody is becoming the same, or that a totally new "world-self" is taking shape. But I am convinced that a new style of self-process is emerging everywhere. It derives from the interplay of three factors responsible for human behavior: the psychobiological potential common to all mankind at any moment in time; those traits given special emphasis in a particular cultural tradition; and those related to modern (and particularly contemporary) historical forces. My thesis is that this third factor plays an increasingly important part in shaping self-process.

My work with Chinese was done in Hong Kong, in connection with a study of the process of "thought reform" (or "brainwashing") as conducted on the mainland. I found that Chinese intellectuals of varying ages, whatever their experience with thought reform itself, had gone through an extraordinary set of what I at that time called identity fragments—of combinations of belief and emotional involvement—each of which they could readily abandon in favor of another. I remember particularly the profound impression made upon me by the extraordinary history of one young man in particular: beginning as a "filial son" or "young master," that elite status of an only son in an upper-class Chinese family; then feeling himself an abandoned and betrayed victim, as traditional forms collapsed during civil war and general chaos, and his father, for whom he was to long all his life, was separated from him by political and military duties; then a "student activist" in rebellion against the traditional culture in which he had been so recently immersed (as well as against a Nationalist Regime whose abuses he had personally experienced); leading him to Marxism and to strong emotional involvement in the Communist movement; then, because of remaining "imperfections," becoming a participant in a thought reform program for a more complete ideological conversion; but which, in his case, had the opposite effect, alienating him, so he came into conflict with the reformers and fled the country; then, in Hong Kong, struggling to establish himself as an "anti-Communist writer"; after a variety of difficulties, finding solace and meaning in becoming a Protestant convert; and following that, still just thirty, apparently poised for some new internal (and perhaps external) move.

Even more dramatic were the shifts in self-process of a young Japanese whom I interviewed in Tokyo and Kyoto from 1960 to 1962. I shall mention one in particular as an extreme example of this protean pattern, though there were many others who in various ways resembled him. Before the age of twenty-five he had been all of the following: a proper middle-class Japanese boy, brought up in a professional family within a well-established framework of dependency and obligation; then, due to extensive contact with farmers' and fishermen's sons brought about by wartime evacuation, a "country boy" who was to retain what he described as a life-long attraction to the tastes of the common man; then, a fiery young patriot who "hated the Americans" and whose older brother, a kamikaze pilot, was saved from death only by the war's end; then a youngster confused in his beliefs after Japan's surrender, but curious about rather than hostile toward American soldiers; soon an eager young exponent of democracy, caught up in the "democracy boom" which swept Japan; at the same time a youthful devotee of traditional Japanese arts—old novels, Chinese poems, kabuki and flower arrangement; during junior high and high school, an all-round leader, outstanding in studies, student self-government and general social and athletic activities; almost simultaneously, an outspoken critic of society at large and of fellow students in particular for their narrow careerism, on the basis of Marxist ideas current in Japanese intellectual circles; yet also an English-speaking student, which meant, in effect, being in still another vanguard and having strong interest in things American; then, midway through high school, experiencing what he called a "kind of neurosis" in which he lost interest in everything he was doing and, in quest of a "change in mood," took advantage of an opportunity to become an exchange student for one year at an American high school; became a convert to many aspects of American life, including actually being baptized as a Christian under the influence of a minister he admired who was also his American "father," and returned to Japan only reluctantly; as a "returnee," found himself in many ways at odds with his friends and was accused by one of "smelling like butter" (a traditional Japanese phrase for Westerners); therefore reimmersed himself in "Japanese" experience—sitting on *tatami*, indulging in quiet, melancholy moods, drinking tea and so on; then became a *ronin*—in feudal days, a samurai without a master, now a student without a university—because of failing his examinations for Tokyo University (a sort of Harvard, Yale, Columbia and Berkeley rolled into one), and as is the custom, spending the following year preparing for the next round rather than attend a lesser institution; once admitted, found little to interest him until becoming an enthusiastic *Zengakuren* activist, with full embrace of its ideal of "pure Communism" and a profound sense of fulfillment in taking part in the planning and carrying out of student demonstrations; but when offered a high position in the organization during his junior year, abruptly became an *ex-Zengakuren* activist by resigning, because he felt he was not suited for "the life of a revolutionary"; then an aimless dissipator, as he drifted into a pattern of heavy drinking, marathon mah-jongg games and affairs with bargirls; but when the time came, had no difficulty gaining employment with one of Japan's mammoth industrial organizations (and one of the *bêtes noires* of his Marxist days) and embarking upon the life of a young executive or *sarariman* (salaried man)—in fact doing so with eagerness, careful preparation and relief, but at the same time having fantasies and dreams of kicking over the traces, sometimes violently, and embarking upon a world tour (largely Hollywood-inspired) of exotic and sophisticated pleasure-seeking.

There are, of course, important differences between the protean life styles of the two young men, and between them and their American counterparts—differences which have to do with cultural emphases and which contribute to what is generally called national character. But such is the intensity of the shared aspects of historical experience that contemporary Chinese, Japanese and American self-process turn out to have striking points of convergence.

I would stress two historical developments as having special importance for creating protean man. The first is the world-wide sense of what I have called *historical* (or *psychohistorical) dislocation,* the break in the sense of connection which men have long felt with the vital and nourishing symbols of their cultural tradition—symbols revolving around family, idea systems, religions, and the life cycle in general. In our contemporary world one perceives these traditional symbols (as I have suggested elsewhere, using the Japanese as a paradigm) as irrelevant, burdensome or inactivating, and yet one cannot avoid carrying them within or having one's self-process profoundly affected by them. The second large historical tendency is the *flooding of imagery* produced by the extraordinary flow of post-modern cultural influences over mass communication networks. These cross readily over local and national boundaries, and permit each individual to be touched by everything, but at the same time cause him to be overwhelmed by superficial messages and undigested cultural elements, by headlines and by endless partial alternatives in every sphere of life. These alternatives, moreover, are universally and simultaneously shared—if not as courses of action, at least in the form of significant inner imagery.

We know from Greek mythology that Proteus was able to change his shape with relative ease—from wild boar to lion to dragon to fire to flood. But what he did find difficult, and would not do unless seized and chained, was to commit himself to a single form, the form most his own, and carry out his function of prophecy. We can say the same of protean man, but we must keep in mind his possibilities as well as his difficulties.

The protean style of self-process, then, is characterized by an interminable series of experiments and explorations—some shallow, some profound—each of which may be readily abandoned in favor of still new psychological quests. The pattern in many ways resembles what Erik Erikson has called "identity diffusion" or "identity confusion," and the impaired psychological functioning which those terms suggest can be very much present. But I would stress that the protean style is by no means pathological as such, and, in fact, may well be one of the functional patterns of our day. It extends to all areas of human experience—to political as well as sexual behavior, to the holding and promulgating of ideas and to the general organization of lives.

I would like to suggest a few illustrations of the protean style, as expressed in America and Europe, drawn both from psychotherapeutic work with patients and from observations on various forms of literature and art.

One patient of mine, a gifted young teacher, spoke of himself in this way:

I have an extraordinary number of masks I can put on or take off. The question is: is there, or should there be, one face which should be authentic? I'm not sure that there is one for me. I can think of other parallels to this, especially in literature. There are representations of every kind of crime, every kind of sin. For me, there is not a single act I cannot imagine myself committing.

He went on to compare himself to an actor on the stage who "performs with a certain kind of polymorphous versatility"—and here he was referring, slightly mockingly, to Freud's term, "polymorphous perversity," for diffusely inclusive (also protean) infantile sexuality. And he asked:

Which is the real person, so far as an actor is concerned? It he more real when performing on the stage—or when he is at home? I tend to think that for people who have these many, many masks, there is no home. Is it a futile gesture for the actor to try to find his real face?

My patient was by no means a happy man, but neither was he incapacitated. And although we can see the strain with which he carries his "polymorphous versatility," it could also be said that, as a teacher and a thinker, and in some ways as a man, it served him well.

In contemporary American literature, Saul Bellow is notable for the protean men he has created. In *The Adventures of Augie March,* one of his earlier novels, we meet a picaresque hero with a notable talent for adapting himself to divergent social worlds. Augie himself says: "I touched all sides, and nobody knew where I belonged. I had no good idea of that myself." And a perceptive young English critic, Tony Tanner, tells us: "Augie indeed celebrates the self, but he can find nothing to do with it." Tanner goes on to describe Bellow's more recent protean hero, Herzog, as "a representative modern intelligence, swamped with ideas, metaphysics, and values, and surrounded by messy facts. It labours to cope with them all."

A distinguished French literary spokesman for the protean style—in his life and in his work—is, of course, Jean-Paul Sartre. Indeed, I believe that it is precisely because of these protean traits that Sartre strikes us as such an embodiment of twentieth-century man. An American critic, Theodore Solotaroff, speaks of Sartre's fundamental assumption that "there is no such thing as even a relatively fixed sense of self, ego, or identity—rather there is only the subjective mind in motion in relationship to that which it confronts." And Sartre himself refers to human consciousness as "a sheer activity transcending toward objects," and "a great emptiness, a wind blowing toward objects." These might be overstatements, but I doubt that they could have been written thirty years ago. Solotaroff further characterizes Sartre as

constantly on the go, hurrying from point to point, subject to subject; fiercely intentional, his thought occupies, fills, and distends its material as he endeavors to lose and find himself in his encounters with other lives, disciplines, books, and situations.

This image of repeated, autonomously willed death and rebirth of the self, so central to the protean style, becomes associated with the themes of fatherlessness—as Sartre goes on to tell us in his autobiography with his characteristic tone of serious self-mockery:

There is no good father, that's the rule. Don't lay the blame on men but on the bond of paternity, which is rotten. To beget children, nothing better; *to have* them, what iniquity! Had my father lived, he would have lain on me at full length and would have crushed me. . . . Amidst Aeneas and his fellows who carry their Anchises on their backs, I move from shore to shore, alone and hating those invisible begetters who bestraddle their sons all their life long. I left behind me a young man who did not have time to be my father and who could now be my son. Was it a good thing or bad? I don't know. But I readily subscribed to the verdict of an eminent psychoanalyst: I have no Superego.

We note Sartre's image of interchangeability of father and son, of "a young man who did not have time to be my father and who could now be my son"—which, in a literal sense refers to the age at which his father died, but symbolically suggests an extension of the protean style to intimate family relationships. And such reversals indeed become necessary in a rapidly changing world in which the sons must constantly "carry their fathers on their backs," teach them new things which they, as older people, cannot possibly know. The judgment of the absent superego, however, may be misleading, especially if we equate superego with susceptibility to guilt. What has actually disappeared—in Sartre and in protean man in general—is the *classic* superego, the internalization of clearly defined criteria of right and wrong transmitted within a particular culture by parents to their children. Protean man requires freedom from precisely that kind of superego—he requires a symbolic fatherlessness—in order to carry out his explorations. But rather than being free of guilt, we shall see that his guilt takes on a different form from that of his predecessors.

There are many other representations of protean man among contemporary novelists: in the constant internal and external motion of "beat generation" writings, such as Jack Kerouac's *On the Road;* in the novels of a gifted successor to that generation, J. P. Donleavy, particularly *The Ginger Man;* and of course in the work of European novelists such as Günter Grass, whose *The Tin Drum* is a breathtaking evocation of prewar Polish-German, wartime German and postwar German environments, in which the protagonist combines protean adaptability with a kind of perpetual physical-mental "strike" against any change at all.

In the visual arts, one of the most important postwar movements has been aptly named "action painting" to convey its stress upon process rather than fixed completion. And a more recent and related movement in sculpture, called Kinetic Art, goes further. According to Jean Tinguely, one of its leading practitioners, "artists are putting themselves in rhythm with their time, in contact with their epoch, especially with permanent and perpetual movement." As revolutionary as any style or approach is the stress upon innovation per se which now dominates painting. I have frequently heard artists, themselves considered radical innovators, complain bitterly of the current standards dictating that "innovation is all," and of a turnover in art movements so rapid as to discourage the idea of holding still long enough to develop a particular style.

We also learn much from film stars. Marcello Mastroianni, when asked whether he agreed with *Time* magazine's characterization of him as "the neo-capitalist hero," gave the following answer:

> In many ways, yes. But I don't think I'm any kind of hero, neo-capitalist or otherwise. If anything I am an *anti*-hero or at most a *non*-hero. *Time* said I had the frightened, characteristically 20th-century look, with a spine made of plastic napkin rings. I accepted this—because modern man is that way; and being a product of my time and an artist, I can represent him. If humanity were all one piece, I would be considered a weakling.

Mastroianni accepts his destiny as protean man; he seems to realize that there are certain advantages to having a spine made of plastic napkin rings, or at least that it is an appropriate kind of spine to have these days.

John Cage, the composer, is an extreme exponent of the protean style, both in his music and in his sense of all of us as listeners. He concluded a recent letter to the *Village Voice* with the sentence: "Nowadays, everything happens at once and our souls are conveniently electronic, omniattentive." The comment is McLuhan-like, but what I wish to stress particularly is the idea of omniattention—the sense of contemporary man as having the possibility of "receiving" and "taking in" everything. In attending, as in being, nothing is "off limits."

To be sure, one can observe in contemporary man a tendency which seems to be precisely the opposite of the protean style. I refer to the closing off of identity or constriction of self-process, to a straight-and-narrow specialization in psychological as well as in intellectual life, and to reluctance to let in any "extraneous" influences. But I would emphasize that where this kind of constricted or "one-dimensional" self-process exists, it has an essentially reactive and compensatory quality. In this it differs from earlier characterological styles it may seem to resemble (such as the "inner-directed" man described by Riesman, and still earlier patterns in traditional society). For these were direct outgrowths of societies which then existed, and in harmony with those societies, while at the present time a constricted self-process requires continuous "psychological work" to fend off protean influences which are always abroad.

Protean man has a particular relationship to the holding of ideas which has, I believe, great significance for the politics, religion, and general intellectual life of the future. For just as elements of the self can be experimented with and readily altered, so can idea systems and ideologies be embraced, modified, let go of and reembraced, all with a new ease that stands in sharp contrast to the inner struggle we have in the past associated with these shifts. Until relatively recently, no more than one major ideological shift was likely to occur in a lifetime, and that one would be long remembered as a significant individual turning-point accompanied by profound soul-searching and conflict. But today it is not unusual to encounter several such shifts, accomplished relatively painlessly, within a year or even a month; and among many groups, the rarity is a man who has gone through life holding firmly to a single ideological vision.

In one sense, this tendency is related to "the end of ideology" spoken of by Daniel Bell, since protean man is incapable of enduring an unquestioning allegiance to the large ideologies and utopian thought of the nineteenth and early twentieth centuries. One must be cautious about speaking of the end of anything, however, especially ideology, and one also encounters in protean man what I would call strong ideological hunger. He is starved for ideas and feelings that can give coherence to his world, but here too his taste is toward new combinations. While he is by no means without yearning for the absolute, what he finds most acceptable are images of a more fragmentary nature than those of the ideologies of the past; and these images, although limited and often fleeting, can have great influence upon his psychological life. Thus political and religious movements, as they confront protean man, are likely to experience less difficulty convincing him to alter previous convictions than they do providing him a set of beliefs which can command his allegiance for more than a brief experimental interlude.

Intimately bound up with his flux in emotions and beliefs is a profound inner sense of absurdity, which finds expression in a tone of mockery. The sense and the tone are related to a perception of surrounding activities and beliefs as profoundly strange and inappropriate. They stem from a breakdown in the relationship between inner and outer worlds—that is, in the sense of symbolic integrity—and are part of the pattern of psychohistorical dislocation I mentioned earlier. For if we view man as primarily a symbol-forming organism, we must recognize that he has constant need of a meaningful inner formulation of self and world in which his own actions, and even his impulses, have some kind of "fit" with the "outside" as he perceives it.

The sense of absurdity, of course, has a considerable modern tradition, and has been discussed by such writers as Camus as a function of man's spiritual homelessness and inability to find any meaning in traditional belief systems. But absurdity and mockery have taken much more extreme form in the post-World War II world, and have in fact become a prominent part of a universal life style.

In American life, absurdity and mockery are everywhere. Perhaps their most vivid expression can be found in such areas as Pop Art and the more general burgeoning of "pop culture." Important here is the complex stance of the pop artist toward the objects he depicts. On the one hand he embraces the materials of the everyday world, celebrates and even exalts them—boldly asserting his creative return to representational art (in active rebellion against the previously reigning nonobjective school), and his psychological return to the "real world" of *things*. On the other hand, everything he touches he mocks. "Thingness" is pressed to the point of caricature. He is indeed artistically reborn as he moves freely among the physical and symbolic materials of his environment, but mockery is his birth certificate and his passport. This kind of duality of approach is formalized in the stated "duplicity" of Camp, a poorly-defined aesthetic in which (among other things) all varieties of mockery converge under the guiding influence of the homosexual's subversion of a heterosexual world.

Also relevant are a group of expressions in current slang, some of them derived originally from jazz. The "dry mock" has replaced the dry wit; one refers to a segment of life experience as a "bit," "bag," "caper," "game" (or "con game"), "scene," "show" or "scenario"; and one seeks to "make the scene" (or "make it"), "beat the system" or "pull it off"—or else one "cools it" ("plays it cool") or "cops out." The thing to be experienced, in other words, is too absurd to be taken at its face value; one must either keep most of the self aloof from it, or if not one must lubricate the encounter with mockery.

A similar spirit seems to pervade literature and social action alike. What is best termed a "literature of mockery" has come to dominate fiction and other forms of writing on an international scale. Again Günter Grass's *The Tin Drum* comes to mind, and is probably the greatest single example of this literature—a work, I believe, which will eventually be appreciated as much as a general evocation of contemporary man as of the particular German experience with Nazism. In this country the divergent group of novelists known as "black humorists" also fit into the general category—related as they are to a trend in the American literary consciousness which R. W. B. Lewis has called a "savagely comical apocalypse" or a "new kind of ironic literary form and disturbing vision, the joining of the dark thread of apocalypse with the nervous detonations of satiric laughter." For it is precisely death itself, and particularly threats of the contemporary apocalypse, that protean man ultimately mocks.

The relationship of mockery to political and social action has been less apparent, but is, I would claim, equally significant. There is more than coincidence in the fact that [one of] the largest American student uprising[s] of recent decades, the Berkeley Free Speech Movement of 1965, was followed immediately by a "Dirty Speech Movement." While the object of the Dirty Speech Movement—achieving free expression of forbidden language, particularly of four-letter words—can be viewed as a serious one, the predominant effect, even in the matter of names, was that of a mocking caricature of the movement which preceded it. But if mockery can undermine protest, it can also enliven it. There have been signs of craving for it in major American expressions of protest such as the Negro movement and the opposition to the war in Vietnam. In the former a certain chord can be struck by the comedian Dick Gregory, and in the latter by the use of satirical skits and parodies, that revives the flagging attention of protestors becoming gradually bored with the repetition of their "straight" slogans and goals. And on an international scale, I would say that, during the past decade, Russian intellectual life has been enriched by a leavening spirit of mockery—against which the Chinese leaders are now, in the extremes of their "Cultural Revolution," fighting a vigorous but ultimately losing battle.

Closely related to the sense of absurdity and the spirit of mockery is another characteristic of protean man which can be called "suspicion of counterfeit nurturance." Involved here is a severe conflict of dependency, a core problem of protean man. I first began to think of the concept several years ago while working with survivors of the atomic bomb in Hiroshima. I found that these survivors both felt themselves in need of special help, and resented whatever help was offered them because they equated it with weakness and inferiority. In considering the matter more generally, I found this equation of nurturance with a threat to autonomy a major theme of contemporary life. The increased dependency needs resulting from the breakdown of traditional institutions lead protean man to seek out replacements wherever he can find them. The large organizations (government, business, academic, etc.) to which he turns, and which contemporary society more and more holds out as a substitute for traditional institutions, present an ambivalent threat to his autonomy in one way; and the intense individual relationships in which he seeks to anchor himself in another. Both are therefore likely to be perceived as counterfeit. But the obverse side of this tendency is an expanding sensitivity to the unauthentic, which may be just beginning to exert its general creative force on man's behalf.

Technology (and technique in general), together with science, have special significance for protean man. Technical achievement of any kind can be strongly embraced to combat inner tendencies toward diffusion, and to transcend feelings of absurdity and conflicts over counterfeit nurturance. The image of science itself, however, as the ultimate power behind technology and, to a considerable extent, behind contemporary thought in general, becomes much more difficult to cope with. Only in certain underdeveloped countries can one find, in relatively pure form, those expectations of scientific-utopian deliverance from all human want and conflict which were characteristic of eighteenth- and nineteenth-century Western thought. Protean man retains much of this utopian imagery, but he finds it increasingly undermined by massive disillusionment. More and more he calls forth the other side of the God-devil polarity generally applied to science, and sees it as a purveyor of total destructiveness. This kind of profound ambivalence creates for him the most extreme psychic paradox: the very force he still feels to be his liberator from the heavy burdens of past irrationality also threatens him with absolute annihilation, even extinction. But this paradox may well be—in fact, I believe, already has been—the source of imaginative efforts to achieve new relationships between science and man, and indeed, new visions of science itself.

I suggested before that protean man was not free of guilt. He indeed suffers from it considerably, but often without awareness of what is causing his suffering. For his is a form of hidden guilt: a vague but persistent kind of self-condemnation related to the symbolic disharmonies I have described, a sense of having no outlet for his loyalties and no symbolic structure for his achievements. This is the guilt of social breakdown, and it includes various forms of historical and racial guilt experienced by whole nations and peoples, both by the privileged and the abused. Rather than a clear feeling of evil or sinfulness, it takes the form of a nagging sense of unworthiness all the more troublesome for its lack of clear origin.

Protean man experiences similarly vague constellations of anxiety and resentment. These too have origin in symbolic impairments and are particularly tied-in with suspicion of counterfeit nurturance. Often feeling himself uncared for, even abandoned, protean man responds with diffuse fear and anger. But he can neither find a good cause for the former, nor a consistent target for the latter. He nonetheless cultivates his anger because he finds it more serviceable than anxiety, because there are plenty of targets of one kind or another beckoning, and because even moving targets are better than none. His difficulty is that focused indignation is as hard for him to sustain as is any single identification or conviction.

Involved in all of these patterns is a profound psychic struggle with the idea of change itself. For here too protean man finds himself ambivalent in the extreme. He is profoundly attracted to the idea of making all things, including himself, totally new—to the "mode of transformation." But he is equally drawn to an image of a mythical past of perfect harmony and prescientific wholeness, to the "mode of restoration." Moreover, beneath his transformationism is nostalgia, and beneath his restorationism is his fascinated attraction to contemporary forms and symbols. Constantly balancing these elements midst the extraordinarily rapid change surrounding his own life, the nostalgia is pervasive, and can be one of his most explosive and dangerous emotions. This longing for a "Golden Age" of absolute oneness, prior to individual and cultural separation or delineation, not only sets the tone for the restorationism of the politically Rightist antagonists of history: the still-extant Emperor-worshipping assassins in Japan, the Colons in France and the John Birchites and Ku Klux Klanners in this country. It also, in more disguised form, energizes that transformationist totalism of the Left which courts violence, and is even willing to risk nuclear violence, in a similarly elusive quest.

Following upon all that I have said are radical impairments to the symbolism of transition within the life cycle—the *rites de passage* surrounding birth, entry into adulthood, marriage and death. Whatever rites remain seem shallow, inappropriate, fragmentary. Protean man cannot take them seriously, and often seeks to improvise new ones with whatever contemporary materials he has available, including cars and drugs. Perhaps the central impairment here is that of symbolic immortality—of the universal need for imagery of connection predating and extending beyond the individual life span, whether the idiom of this immortality is biological (living on through children and grandchildren), theological (through a life after death), natural (*in* nature itself which outlasts all) or creative (through what man makes and does). I have suggested elsewhere that this sense of immortality is a fundamental component of ordinary psychic life, and that it is now being profoundly threatened: by simple historical velocity, which subverts the idioms (notably the theological) in which it has traditionally been maintained; and, of particular importance to protean man, by the existence of nuclear weapons, which, even without being used, call into question all modes of immortality. (Who can be certain of living on through children and grandchildren, through teachings or kindnesses?)

Protean man is left with two paths to symbolic immortality which he tries to cultivate, sometimes pleasurably and sometimes desperately. One is the natural mode we have mentioned. His attraction to nature and concern at its desecration has to do with an unconscious sense that, in whatever holocaust, at least nature will endure—though such are the dimensions of our present weapons that he cannot be absolutely certain even of this. His second path may be termed that of "experiential transcendence"— of seeking a sense of immortality in the way that mystics always have, through psychic experience of such great intensity that time and death are, in effect, eliminated. This, I believe, is the larger meaning of the "drug revolution," of protean man's hunger for chemical aids to "expanded consciousness." And indeed all revolutions may be thought of, at bottom, as innovations in the struggle for immortality, as new combinations of old modes.

We have seen that young adults individually, and youth movements collectively, express most vividly the psychological themes of protean man. And although it is true that these themes make contact with what we sometimes call the "psychology of adolescence," we err badly if we overlook their expression in all age groups and dismiss them as "mere adolescent phenomena." Rather, protean man's affinity for the young—his being metaphorically and psychologically so young in spirit—has to do with his never-ceasing quest for imagery of rebirth. He seeks such imagery from all sources: from ideas, techniques, religious and political systems, mass movements and drugs; or from special individuals of his own kind whom he sees as possessing that problematic gift of his namesake, the gift of prophecy. The dangers inherent in the quest seem hardly to require emphasis. What perhaps needs most to be kept in mind is the general principle that renewal on a large scale is impossible to achieve without forays into danger, destruction and negativity. The principle of "death and rebirth" is as valid psychohistorically as it is mythologically. However misguided many of his forays may be, protean man also carries with him an extraordinary range of possibility for man's betterment, or more important, for his survival.

II
The Nature
of Politics

Underlying the various images of the public situation are fundamental conceptions of the nature of the political process. As soon as one begins to think seriously about politics, one finds that it is not easy even to define it. Rather than being a quest for knowledge about political activity, political science frequently seems to be a debate over how to define the scope of a subject to be investigated. This situation stems from the fact that people use definitions of politics to *justify* the activities they favor as well as to *describe* those activities. For example, those in favor of preserving established practices often define politics in terms of cooperation, while those in favor of changing institutions frequently define politics in terms of conflict. Thus, thought about politics, and perhaps even politics itself, appears to be a process most adequately described as an interplay between diverse forces and perspectives.

The articles in this section reflect the important debates about the nature of politics. Herbert J. Spiro contends that politics is a process of debate over the nature of the good life. Thus, political science is the master science which describes and evaluates alternative designs for living. In contrast to Spiro, Hans Morgenthau argues that politics is a matter of power relations, and that political science is the study of how some groups and individuals are able to get their ways, even at the expense of others.

Another debate is illustrated by the contrasting positions of Haring and Nieburg. For Haring, politics is care of the community, or the process through which human beings come to recognize their interdependence and to arrange reciprocal relations with one another. Opposed to this interpretation is Nieburg, who holds that politics is a process in which groups and individuals enter into conflict with one another to realize the policies that they favor. This conflict can take on a multitude of forms ranging from discussion to violence.

Summing up both debates is Maurice Duverger, who notes that politics is Janus-faced, an interplay of opposites. For Duverger, there are political scientists who stress the integration of communities and political scientists who emphasize the conflict among groups. He argues that both viewpoints must be taken into account by those who want a comprehensive understanding of political activity.

While Duverger is undoubtedly correct that both political thought and political action have always been an interplay of opposites, it is perhaps possible to go one step further and note that all of the participants in the debates seem to be united on a single fundamental view of political activity. This view would hold that politics is active reflection on the human condition, or on the process of proposing, deciding, executing, and evaluating plans for the future public situation. Active reflection involves dialogue and power as well as cooperation and conflict.

Politics As
the Master Science

HERBERT J. SPIRO

If then, there is some end to the things we do, which we desire for its own sake (everything else being desired for the sake of this), and if we do not choose everything for the sake of something else (for at that rate the process would go on to infinity, so that our desire would be empty and vain), clearly this must be *the* good and the chief good. Will not the knowledge of it, then, have a great influence on life? Shall we not, like archers who have a mark to aim at, be more likely to hit upon what is right? If so we must try, in outline at least, to determine what it is, and of which of the sciences or faculties it is the object. It would seem to belong to the most authoritative science and to that which is most truly the master science. And politics appears to be of this nature; for it is politics that ordains which of the sciences should be studied in a state, and which each class of citizens should learn and up to what point they should learn them; and we see even the most highly esteemed of faculties to fall under this, e.g., strategy, economics, rhetoric; now since politics uses the rest of the sciences, and since again it legislates as to what we are to do and what we are to abstain from doing, the goal of this science must include those of the others, so that this end must be *the* good for man. For even if the end is the same for a single man and for a state, that of the state seems at all events something greater and more complete whether to attain or to preserve; though it is worthwhile to attain the end merely for one man, it is finer and more god-like to obtain it for a nation or for city-states. These, then, are the goals at which our inquiry aims, since it is political science, in one sense of that term.[1]

CLASSICAL ATHENS AND THE UNITED STATES TODAY

Politics is the master science, in the Aristotelian sense of the term, as much today as it was in classical Greece more than two thousand years ago. That is the thesis which we will try to demonstrate and whose meaning we will try to explore.

If politics is the master science now, its position at the pinnacle of human activities and as the most important discipline that can be a subject of systematic study has a much wider impact today than it could have had in classical Greece. Plato and Aristotle, for example, would have excluded from the politics of Athens the majority of the population: slaves, resident foreigners, women, and of course children. Aristotle would not even have admitted most of the readers of this book to the study of politics:

Now each man judges well the things he knows, and of these he is a good judge. And so the man who has been educated in a subject is a good judge

1. Aristotle, *Nicomachean Ethics*, book I, 2.

of that subject, and the man who has received an all-around education is a good judge in general. Hence a young man is not a proper hearer of lectures on political science; for he is inexperienced in the actions that occur in life, but its discussions start from these and are about these; and further, since he tends to follow his passions, his study will be vain and unprofitable, because the end aimed at is not knowledge but action. And it makes no difference whether he is young in years or youthful in character; the defect does not depend on time, but on his living, and pursuing each successive object, as passion directs. For to such persons, as to the incontinent, knowledge brings no profit; but to those who desire and act in accordance with a rational principle, knowledge about such matters will be of great benefit.[2]

Aristotle thought that young men should be excluded from the study of politics, because they lack the maturity of judgment that can be gained only from experience. He would have had men study politics only *after* they had studied all the other subjects. Today, by contrast, it is becoming existentially impossible to exclude any human being who has reached the age of reason from an awareness of politics or from some thought of participation, however passive, in politics. Everyone, everywhere on earth, belongs not only to the political system of his immediate local community but also to the complex, interdependent, emergent global political system. And it is only through the politics of this most comprehensive of communities, the community of mankind, that either progress or stagnation or the extermination of humanity will be brought about.

Politics was the queen of the sciences and the most important of human activities in the days of Plato and Aristotle, the founders of political science. Today it has become that again, in a very concrete sense. The most important events in the lives of individuals and of communities, whatever their scope or location, are all shaped more by politics than by anything else, even so-called acts of nature or of God, such as earthquakes or epidemics. Science, whose development is certainly shaped by politics, cannot yet prevent earthquakes, though it has gone far toward preventing epidemics. However, both the issuance of warnings about and the control of the effects of such natural disasters are almost wholly within the realm of the political. The same is true of all the other activities cited by Aristotle in the passage that opens this [selection]. This selection, characteristically, is taken not from the first book of his *Politics* but from the first book of his *Nicomachean Ethics*.

Some of our own contemporaries deny this ubiquity and primacy of politics. Others admit but bemoan it, and some try to reverse, or at least to reduce, the dominance of politics in our lives. In this respect, our own period differs from the age in which political science was born, for at that time, everyone accepted the supremacy of politics. (The philosophers known as the Cynics were a possible exception, because they rejected politics in its conventional meaning; that is, they rejected the politics of the *polis*, or city-state, for they considered it too restricted a community to be capable of providing generally valid norms of behavior. However,

2. Aristotle, *Nicomachean Ethics*, book I, 2.

while they rejected conventional politics, they at the same time laid the foundations for the cosmopolitanism of the Stoic philosophers who followed them. According to the Stoics, the universe was governed by one law, and all human beings were members of the great cosmopolitan community.) Politics in the classic age of Hellas was self-evidently more important than anything else.

This obviousness of the primacy of politics was due to the one crucial difference, among many important ones, between ancient Athens and contemporary United States. The Athenian community, life within it, and people's perception of this life were almost wholly undifferentiated in comparison with the contemporary American community, life within it, and our perceptions of this life. All of us today are members of (we say that we "belong to") a whole welter of functionally differentiated associations, organizations, and other formal and informal groupings. We belong to economic interest groups, each of us usually to several of them; to cultural groupings, including religious and educational ones; to the partly biological association of the family; and to other organizations that are politically defined. Some of the groups of which we are members—that is, some of the systems of which we are components or sub-systems—are understood to have geographical boundaries, like the state and the nation-state; others cut across geographical boundaries in a complex pattern of crisscrossing affinities and affiliations.

CLAIMS TO LOYALTY

None of these groupings to which we belong either claims, or is normally permitted to claim, our whole person or being: neither the nation-state, which in the United States operates under fairly strict constitutional restraints, safeguarding, for example, the individual's religious personality or his right not to be forced to incriminate himself; nor the various churches, since even priests can and do leave the most tightly disciplined religious orders; nor economic organizations, including both powerful business corporations and trade unions; nor professional associations or universities; nor even "political organizations" (in the strict sense of the term) that model themselves on fascist or communist movements outside the United States. None of these groupings is permitted to claim all of any one of us. And each of us normally feels that he belongs to several, and usually to many, of these groups.

This more or less institutionalized pluralism was lacking in ancient Athens and the other city-states of classical Greece. And if it was not wholly absent, it was at best only incipient. In Athens, the citizen belonged to the city. (The English words for *citizen* and *city* are derived from the Latin. In Greek as in Latin, the words for *citizen, politics,* and— as we will see later—*constitution* were derived from the master word, *polis,* which is usually inadequately translated into English as *city-state.*) A citizen belonged to the *polis* in his entirety, as Socrates makes clear in the *Crito.* (He had been condemned to death by a court consisting of about five hundred of his fellow-citizens of Athens. When his friends offered him an easy opportunity to flee Athens in order to seek refuge in another city, he refused. His whole being had been nourished by the *polis* and its laws and he could not picture living in another community after his own had condemned him, though unjustly, according to the procedures provided by its laws.)

In comparison with our view of the state and of ourselves, the Platonic and Aristotelian view was much less differentiated, much less mechanistic, much more holist, and much more organic. This was true of the classical view of both the *polis* and the individual: Socrates felt that he belonged to Athens, not to a party in Athens, not to the ruling class of Athens, not to what he thought was best in Athens, but simply to Athens. And he thought that it was all of Socrates that belonged in this way, not the best in him; not only his rational portion, or merely his emotional self, or the body that had been given sustenance by this *polis*, but all of Socrates belonged as one undifferentiated personality. It would have been impossible for Socrates, his disciples, or their contemporaries to "divide themselves up" intellectually into functional components, or "roles," as we frequently, and indeed usually, do. Nowadays, men identify themselves with the particular function they are performing, the role they are playing, at the time: as businessman, as husband or father, as part-time soldier, as the enjoyer of entertainment or the viewer of art, as motorist, as pedestrian, as member of an ethnic minority engaged in politics, as taxpayer, as voter, and so forth. This capacity to compartmentalize oneself was taken to its logical conclusion by some of Hitler's concentration camp commandants, who were efficient executors of Nazi terror, but at the same time loving family fathers, who after putting in a hard day's work at the gas ovens played Mozart sonatas on their violins at home.

THE CHANGE IN POLITICAL VOCABULARY

The lack of differentiation perceived in both *polis* and individual by the ancient Greeks is revealed in many ways, one of them the vocabulary of politics. As the Western political tradition grew it became increasingly differentiated, and this is shown by changes in the vocabulary of political philosophy. St. Thomas Aquinas revived Aristotelian thought in the thirteenth century and quoted "The Philosopher," as he referred to Aristotle, saying man is a "social and political animal" or being. Aristotle of course had said no such thing. His term was *zoon politikon,* "political being," his vocabulary providing no equivalent word for what St. Thomas meant by *social*.

In the nineteenth century, some philosophers began to speak of "economic man" to distinguish or differentiate the economic aspects, or functions, of the human being from the political, social, religious, and psychological ones. The word *economics* is of Greek origin, and Aristotle was one of the first authors to use it to denote the science of managing a household. But Aristotle would have found it inconceivable to compartmentalize or to segregate man's economic activities from his other functions or to deny that politics shaped and controlled economics, just as it shaped and controlled strategy, rhetoric, and all other lesser human activities.

The difference in degree of differentiation and in its perception by men between the classic past and our own day is very profound. Some readers may conclude from it that we can really learn little or nothing from the political thought of Plato, Aristotle, and their contemporaries in the comparatively undifferentiated *polis*. This conclusion would have to be based on the assumption that there is a qualitative difference between politics in classical Athens and politics in the modern world. This conclusion is erroneous, but it does point to one important cautionary imperative that students of politics must always bear in mind: Beware of false analogies!

At this point, one citation may serve to illustrate this danger. . . . There is a book in which some distinguished scholars have discussed whether Plato was a totalitarian or a democrat.[3] This is a senseless question. Since the end of World War II both scholars and politicians have referred to a number of political systems as "totalitarian." Among these are Hitler's Germany, Stalin's Soviet Union, and Mao Tse-tung's China. But these so-called totalitarian systems were brought into being *after* differentiation and, equally important, after awareness of differentiation, or at least an awareness of its possibility, had become universal facts. Plato's Athens was neither the Soviet Union or China nor, at the other end of the spectrum of differentiation, Barotseland in Zambia. It is therefore a waste of time, except possibly for propaganda purposes, to ask whether Plato favored or contributed to the development of totalitarianism in this sense.

However, the basic processes of politics as the quintessential human activities were the same in Plato's time as they are in ours, and they will remain the same until men exterminate themselves or breed themselves out of existence. (In the future there are good possibilities for either of these alternatives.) That is why there is a great deal we can learn today from the political philosophizing of both ancient and modern thinkers. Political theory has been called "The Great Conversation," and it is the greatest, most important, and longest-lasting conversation ever held on earth. It is a conversation in which we can all participate, in which, indeed, we are all being constantly compelled to participate, almost on a day-to-day basis. It is a dialectic in which you can talk back to the greatest thinkers of all times and in which they will talk back to you; it is a debate from which you can try to withdraw at the cost of surrendering the most vital portion of your humanity, but from which there is really no effective withdrawal.

3. T. L. Thomson, ed., *Plato: Totalitarian or Democrat?*, (Englewood Cliffs, N.J.: Prentice-Hall, 1963.)

Political Power

HANS J. MORGENTHAU

1. WHAT IS POLITICAL POWER?[1]

A. ITS RELATION TO THE NATION AS A WHOLE

International politics, like all politics, is a struggle for power. Whatever the ultimate aims of international politics, power is always the immediate aim. Statesmen and peoples may ultimately seek freedom, security, prosperity, or power itself. They may define their goals in terms of a religious, philosophic, economic, or social ideal. They may hope that this ideal will materialize through its own inner force, through divine intervention, or through the natural development of human affairs. They may also try to further its realization through nonpolitical means, such as technical co-operation with other nations or international organizations. But whenever they strive to realize their goal by means of international politics, they do so by striving for power. The Crusaders wanted to free the holy places from domination by the Infidels; Woodrow Wilson wanted to make the world safe for democracy; the National Socialists wanted to open Eastern Europe to German colonization, to dominate Europe, and to conquer the world. Since they all chose power to achieve these ends, they were actors on the scene of international politics.[2]

Two conclusions follow from this concept of international politics. First, not every action that a nation performs with respect to another nation is of a political nature. Many such activities are normally undertaken without any consideration of power, nor do they normally affect the power of the nation undertaking them. Many legal, economic, humanitarian, and cultural activities are of this kind. Thus a nation is not normally engaged in international politics when it concludes an extradition treaty with another nation, when it exchanges goods and services with other nations, when it co-operates with other nations in providing relief from natural catastrophes, and when it promotes the distribution of cultural achievements throughout the world. In other words, the involve-

1. The concept of political power poses one of the most difficult and controversial problems of political science. The value of any concept used in political science is determined by its ability to explain a maximum of the phenomena that are conventionally considered to belong to a certain sphere of political activity. Thus the coverage of a concept of political power, to be useful for the understanding of international politics, must be broader than the coverage of one adopted to operate in the field of municipal politics. The political means employed in the latter are much more narrowly circumscribed than are those employed in international politics.

2. For some significant remarks on power in relation to international politics, see Lionel Robbins, *The Economic Causes of War* (London: Jonathan Cape, 1939), pp. 63 ff.

ment of a nation in international politics is but one among many types of activities in which a nation can participate on the international scene.

Second, not all nations are at all times to the same extent involved in international politics. The degree of their involvement may run all the way from the maximum involvement that at present has been attained by the United States and the Soviet Union, through the minimum involvement of such countries as Switzerland, Luxembourg, or Venezuela, to the noninvolvement of Liechtenstein and Monaco. Similar extremes can be noticed in the history of particular countries. Spain in the sixteenth and seventeenth centuries was one of the main active participants in the struggle for power on the international scene, but plays today only a marginal role in it. The same is true of such countries as Austria, Sweden, and Switzerland. On the other hand, nations like the United States, the Soviet Union, and China are today much more deeply involved in international politics than they were fifty or even twenty years ago. In short, the relation of nations to international politics has a dynamic quality. It changes with the vicissitudes of power, which may push a nation into the forefront of the power struggle, or may deprive a nation of the ability to participate actively in it. It may also change under the impact of cultural transformations, which may make a nation prefer other pursuits, for instance commerce, to those of power.

B. ITS NATURE

When we speak of power in [this context], we have in mind not man's power over nature, or over an artistic medium, such as language, speech, sound, or color, or over the means of production or consumption, or over himself in the sense of self-control. When we speak of power, we mean man's control over the minds and actions of other men. By political power we refer to the mutual relations of control among the holders of public authority and between the latter and the people at large.

Political power, however, must be distinguished from force in the sense of the actual exercise of physical violence. The threat of physical violence in the form of police action, imprisonment, capital punishment, or war is an intrinsic element of politics. When violence becomes an actuality, it signifies the abdication of political power in favor of military or pseudo-military power. In international politics in particular, armed strength as a threat or a potentiality is the most important material factor making for the political power of a nation. If it becomes an actuality in war, it signifies the substitution of military for political power. The actual exercise of physical violence substitutes for the psychological relation between two minds, which is of the essence of political power, the physical relation between two bodies, one of which is strong enough to dominate the other's movements. It is for this reason that in the exercise of physical violence the psychological element of the political relationship is lost, and that we must distinguish between military and political power.

Political power is a psychological relation between those who exercise it and those over whom it is exercised. It gives the former control over certain actions of the latter through the influence which the former exert over the latter's minds. That influence may be exerted through orders, threats, persuasion, or a combination of any of these. The President of the United States, for instance, exerts political power over the executive branch of the government so long as his orders are obeyed by the members of that branch. The leader of a party has political power so long as he is able to mold the actions of the members of the party according to his will. We refer to the political power of an industrialist, labor leader, or lobby-ist in so far as his preferences influence the actions of other men. The United States exerts political power over Puerto Rico so long as the laws of the United States are observed by the citizens of that island. When we speak of the political power of the United States in Central America, we have in mind the conformity of the actions of Central American govern-ments with the wishes of the government of the United States. Thus the statement that A has or wants political power over B signifies always that A is able, or wants to be able, to control certain actions of B through influencing B's mind.

Whatever the material objectives of a foreign policy, such as the acquisition of sources of raw materials, the control of sea lanes, or terri-torial changes, they always entail control of the actions of others through influence over their minds. The Rhine frontier as a century-old objective of French foreign policy points to the political objective to destroy the desire of Germany to attack France by making it physically difficult or impossible for Germany to do so. Great Britain owed its predominant position in world politics throughout the nineteenth century to the cal-culated policy of making it either too dangerous (because Great Britain was too strong) or unnecessary (because its strength was used with mod-eration) for other nations to oppose it.

The political objective of military preparations of any kind is to deter other nations from using military force by making it too risky for them to do so. The political aim of military preparations is, in other words, to make the actual application of military force unnecessary by inducing the prospective enemy to desist from the use of military force. The political objective of war itself is not *per se* the conquest of territory and the annihilation of enemy armies, but a change in the mind of the enemy which will make him yield to the will of the victor.

Therefore, whenever economic, financial, territorial, or military policies are under discussion in international affairs, it is necessary to distinguish between, say, economic policies that are undertaken for their own sake and economic policies that are the instruments of a political policy—a policy, that is, whose economic purpose is but the means to the end of controlling the policies of another nation. The export policy of Switzerland with regard to the United States falls into the first category. The economic policies of the Soviet Union with regard to the nations of Eastern Europe fall into the latter category. So do many economic policies of the United States in Latin America, Asia, and Europe. The distinction is of great practical importance, and the failure to make it has led to much confusion in policy and public opinion.

An economic, financial, territorial, or military policy undertaken for its own sake is subject to evaluation in its own terms. Is it economically or financially advantageous? What effects has acquisition of territory upon the population and economy of the nation acquiring it? What are the consequences of a change in a military policy for education, population, and the domestic political system? The decisions with respect to these policies are made exclusively in terms of such intrinsic considerations.

When, however, the objectives of these policies serve to increase the power of the nation pursuing them with regard to other nations, these policies and their objectives must be judged primarily from the point of view of their contribution to national power. An economic policy that cannot be justified in purely economic terms might nevertheless be undertaken in view of the political policy pursued. The insecure and unprofitable character of a loan to a foreign nation may be a valid argument against it on purely financial grounds. But the argument is irrelevant if the loan, however unwise it may be from a banker's point of view, serves the political policies of the nation. It may of course be that the economic or financial losses involved in such policies will weaken the nation in its international position to such an extent as to outweigh the political advantages to be expected. On these grounds such policies might be rejected. In such a case, what decides the issue is not purely economic and financial considerations but a comparison of the political changes and risks involved; that is, the probable effect of these policies upon the power of the nation.

2. THE DEPRECIATION OF POLITICAL POWER

The aspiration for power being the distinguishing element of international politics, as of all politics, international politics is of necessity power politics. While this fact is generally recognized in the practice of international affairs, it is frequently denied in the pronouncements of scholars, publicists, and even statesmen. Since the end of the Napoleonic Wars, ever larger groups in the Western world have been persuaded that the struggle for power on the international scene is a temporary phenomenon, a historical accident that is bound to disappear once the peculiar historic conditions that have given rise to it have been eliminated. Thus Jeremy Bentham believed that the competition for colonies was at the root of all international conflicts. "Emancipate your colonies!" was his advice to the governments, and international conflict and war would of necessity disappear. Adherents of free trade, such as Cobden and Proudhon, were convinced that the removal of trade barriers was the only condition for the establishment of permanent harmony among nations, and might even lead to the disappearance of international politics altogether. "At some future election," said Cobden, "we may probably see the test 'no foreign politics' applied to those who offer to become the representatives of free constituencies."[3] For Marx and his followers, capitalism is at

3. Quoted in A. C. F. Beales, *A Short History of English Liberalism*, p. 195.

the root of international discord and war. They maintain that international socialism will do away with the struggle for power on the international scene and will bring about permanent peace. During the nineteenth century, liberals everywhere shared the conviction that power politics and war were residues of an obsolete system of government, and that with the victory of democracy and constitutional government over absolutism and autocracy international harmony and permanent peace would win out over power politics and war. Of this liberal school of thought, Woodrow Wilson was the most eloquent and most influential spokesman.

In recent times, the conviction that the struggle for power can be eliminated from the international scene has been connected with the great attempts at organizing the world, such as the League of Nations and the United Nations. Thus Cordell Hull, then U.S. Secretary of State, declared in 1943 on his return from the Moscow Conference, which laid the groundwork for the United Nations, that the new international organization would mean the end of power politics and usher in a new era of international collaboration. Mr. Philip Noel-Baker, then British Minister of State, declared in 1946 in the House of Commons that the British government was "determined to use the institutions of the United Nations to kill power politics, in order that, by the methods of democracy, the will of the people shall prevail."[4]

While we [could say more] about these theories and the expectations derived from them, it is sufficient to state that the struggle for power is universal in time and space and is an undeniable fact of experience. It cannot be denied that throughout historic time, regardless of social, economic, and political conditions, states have met each other in contests for power. Even though anthropologists have shown that certain primitive peoples seem to be free from the desire for power, nobody has yet shown how their state of mind and the conditions under which they live can be recreated on a worldwide scale so as to eliminate the struggle for power from the international scene.[5] It would be useless and even self-destructive to free one or the other of the peoples of the earth from the desire for power while leaving it extant in others. If the desire for power cannot be abolished everywhere in the world, those who might be cured would simply fall victims to the power of others.

The position taken here might be criticized on the ground that conclusions drawn from the past are unconvincing, and that to draw such conclusions has always been the main stock in trade of the enemies of progress and reform. Though it is true that certain social arrangements and institutions have always existed in the past, it does not necessarily follow that they must always exist in the future. The situation is, however, different when we deal not with social arrangements and institutions created by man but with those elemental biopsychological drives by which

4. *House of Commons Debates* (Fifth Series, 1946), Vol. 419, p. 1262.
5. For an illuminating discussion of this problem, see Malcolm Sharp, "Aggression: A Study of Values and Law," *Ethics*, Vol. 57, No. 4, Part II (July 1947).

in turn society is created. The drives to live, to propagate, and to dominate are common to all men.[6] Their relative strength is dependent upon social conditions that may favor one drive and tend to repress another, or that may withhold social approval from certain manifestations of these drives, while they encourage others. Thus, to take examples only from the sphere of power, most societies condemn killing as a means of attaining power within the society, but all societies encourage the killing of enemies in that struggle for power which is called war. Dictators look askance at the aspirations for political power among their fellow citizens, but democracies consider active participation in the competition for political power a civic duty. Where a monopolistic organization of economic activities exists, competition for economic power is absent, and in competitive economic systems certain manifestations of the struggle for economic power are outlawed, while others are encouraged.

Regardless of particular social conditions, the decisive argument against the opinion that the struggle for power on the international scene is a mere historic accident must be derived from the nature of domestic politics. The essence of international politics is identical with its domestic counterpart. Both domestic and international politics are a struggle for power, modified only by the different conditions under which this struggle takes place in the domestic and in the international spheres.

The tendency to dominate, in particular, is an element of all human associations, from the family through fraternal and professional associations and local political organizations, to the state. On the family level, the typical conflict between the mother-in-law and her child's spouse is in its essence a struggle for power, the defense of an established power position against the attempt to establish a new one. As such it foreshadows the conflict on the international scene between the policies of the status quo and the policies of imperialism. Social clubs, fraternities, faculties, and business organizations are scenes of continuous struggles for power between groups that either want to keep what power they already have or seek to attain greater power. Competitive contests between business enterprises as well as labor disputes between employers and employees are frequently fought not only, and sometimes not even primarily, for economic advantages, but for influence over each other and over others; that is, for power. Finally, the whole political life of a nation, particularly of a democratic nation, from the local to the national level, is a continuous struggle for power. In periodic elections, in voting in legislative assemblies, in lawsuits before courts, in administrative decisions and executive measures—in all these activities men try to maintain or to establish their power over other men. The processes by which legislative, judicial, execu-

6. Zoologists have tried to show that the drive to dominate is found even in animals, such as chickens and monkeys, who create social hierarchies on the basis of the will and the ability to dominate. See, *e.g.,* Warder Allee, *Animal Life and Social Growth* (Baltimore: The Williams and Wilkins Company, 1932), and *The Social Life of Animals* (New York: W. W. Norton and Company, Inc., 1938).

tive, and administrative decisions are reached are subject to pressures and counterpressures by "pressure groups" trying to defend and expand their positions of power. In the words of John of Salisbury:

Though it is not given to all men to seize princely or royal power, yet the man who is wholly untainted by tyranny is rare or nonexistent. In common speech the tyrant is one who oppresses a whole people by a rulership based on force; and yet it is not over a people as a whole that a man can play the tyrant, but he can do so if he will even in the meanest station. For if not over the whole body of the people, still each man will lord it as far as his power extends.[7]

In view of this ubiquity of the struggle for power in all social relations and on all levels of social organization, is it surprising that international politics is of necessity power politics? And would it not be rather surprising if the struggle for power were but an accidental and ephemeral attribute of international politics when it is a permanent and necessary element of all branches of domestic politics?

3. TWO ROOTS OF THE DEPRECIATION OF POLITICAL POWER

The depreciation of the role power plays on the international scene grows from two roots. One is the philosophy of international relations which dominated the better part of the nineteenth century and still holds sway over much of our thinking on international affairs. The other is the particular political and intellectual circumstances that have determined the relations of the United States of America to the rest of the world.

A. NINETEENTH-CENTURY PHILOSOPHY

The nineteenth century was led to its depreciation of power politics by its domestic experience. The distinctive characteristic of this experience was the domination of the middle classes by the aristocracy. By identifying this domination with political domination of any kind, the political philosophy of the nineteenth century came to identify the opposition to aristocratic politics with hostility to any kind of politics. After the defeat of aristocratic government, the middle classes developed a system of indirect domination. They replaced the traditional division into the governing and governed classes, and the military method of open violence, characteristic of aristocratic rule, with the invisible chains of economic dependence. This economic system operated through a network of seemingly equalitarian legal rules which concealed the very existence of power relations. The nineteenth century was unable to see the political nature of these legalized relations. They seemed to be essentially different

7. John of Salisbury, *Policraticus,* translated by John Dickinson (New York: Alfred A. Knopf, 1927), VII, 17.

from what had gone, so far, under the name of politics. Therefore, politics in its aristocratic—that is, open and violent—form was identified with politics as such. The struggle, then, for political power—in domestic as well as in international affairs—appeared to be only a historic accident, coincident with autocratic government and bound to disappear with the disappearance of autocratic government.

B. THE AMERICAN EXPERIENCE

This identification of power politics with aristocratic government found support in the American experience. It can be traced to three elements in that experience: the uniqueness of the American experiment, the actual isolation of the American continent from the centers of world conflict during the nineteenth century, and the humanitarian pacifism and anti-imperialism of American political ideology.

That the severance of constitutional ties with the British crown was meant to signify the initiation of an American foreign policy distinct from what went under the name of foreign policy in Europe is clearly stated in Washington's Farewell Address. "Europe has a set of primary interests, which to us have none, or a very remote relation. Hence she must be engaged in frequent controversies, the causes of which are essentially foreign to our concerns. Hence, therefore, it must be unwise in us to implicate ourselves, by artificial ties, in the ordinary vicissitudes of her politics, or the ordinary combinations and collisions of her friendships or enmities." In 1796, European politics and power politics were identical; there was no other power politics but the one engaged in by the princes of Europe. "The toils of European ambition, rivalship, interest, humor or caprice" were the only manifestations of the international struggle for power before the American eye. The retreat from European politics, as proclaimed by Washington, could, therefore, be taken to mean retreat from power politics as such.

Yet American aloofness from the European tradition of power politics was more than a political program. Certain sporadic exceptions notwithstanding, it was an established political fact until the end of the nineteenth century. This fact was a result of deliberate choice as well as of the objective conditions of geography. Popular writers might see in the uniqueness of America's geographic position the hand of God which had unalterably prescribed the course of American expansion as well as isolation. But more responsible observers, from Washington on, have been careful to emphasize the conjunction of geographic conditions and of a foreign policy choosing its ends in the light of geography, using geographic conditions to attain those ends. Washington referred to "our detached and distant situation" and asked: "Why forego the advantages of so peculiar a situation?" When this period of American foreign policy drew to a close, John Bright wrote to Alfred Love: "On your continent we may hope your growing millions may henceforth know nothing of war. None can assail you; and you are anxious to abstain from mingling with the quarrels of other nations."[8]

From the shores of the North American continent, the citizens of the new world watched the strange spectacle of the international struggle for power unfolding on the distant shores of Europe, Africa, and Asia. Since for the better part of the nineteenth century their foreign policy enabled them to retain the role of spectators, what was actually the result of a passing historic constellation appeared to Americans as a permanent condition, self-chosen as well as naturally ordained. At worst they would continue to watch the game of power politics played by others. At best the time was close at hand when, with democracy established everywhere, the final curtain would fall and the game of power politics would no longer be played.

To aid in the achievement of this goal was conceived to be part of America's mission. Throughout the nation's history, the national destiny of the United States has been understood in antimilitaristic, libertarian terms. Where that national mission finds a nonaggressive, abstentionist formulation, as in the political philosophy of John C. Calhoun, it is conceived as the promotion of domestic liberty. Thus we may "do more to extend liberty by our example over this continent and the world generally, than would be done by a thousand victories." When the United States, in the wake of the Spanish-American War, seemed to desert this anti-imperialist and democratic ideal, William Graham Sumner restated its essence: "Expansion and imperialism are a grand onslaught on democracy . . . expansion and imperialism are at war with the best traditions, principles, and interests of the American people."[9] Comparing the tendencies of European power politics with the ideals of the American tradition, Sumner thought with George Washington that they were incompatible. Yet, as a prophet of things to come, he saw that with the conclusion of the Spanish-American War America was irrevocably committed to the same course that was engulfing Europe in revolution and war.

Thus the general conception the nineteenth century had formed of the nature of foreign affairs combined with specific elements in the American experience to create the belief that involvement in power politics is not inevitable but only a historic accident, and that nations have a choice between power politics and other kinds of foreign policy not tainted by the desire for power.

8. Merle Curti, *Peace and War: The American Struggle 1636-1936* (New York: W. W. Norton and Company, 1936), p. 122.

9. "The Conquest of the United States by Spain," *Essays of William Graham Sumner* (New Haven: Yale University Press, 1940), II, 295.

The General Problem
of Human Existence

PHILIP S. HARING

> True politics I look on as a part of moral philosophy, which is nothing but
> the art of conducting men right in society and supporting a community among
> its neighbors.
>
> —John Locke to Lady Mordaunt

> For though in all places of the world men should lay the foundation of their
> houses on the sand, it could not thence be inferred that so it ought to be.
>
> —Thomas Hobbes, *Leviathan,* Bk. II, Ch. 20

> . . . under the present circumstances of human society both the structure and
> form of governments as well as the power which public authority wields in
> all the nations of the world, must be considered inadequate to promote the
> universal common good.
>
> —Pope John XXIII, *Pacem in Terris,* Sect. 135

Humanity forever hesitates on the brink of its next step forward. There
are more than enough ideas of how to accomplish our objectives. Yet we
hesitate to trust ourselves and each other to move ahead and reach those
objectives. We distrust our capacities to make our lives over, to improve
our lot. Part of this hesitancy must have arisen in childhood when repeatedly our parents proved us wrong as now we prove our children
wrong. Those scars from our vulnerability to error were bandaged over
with pride and truculence that in turn we offset with renewed caution.
At school and later, having once distrusted ourselves, we cling to whatever formulas for living and behaving that teachers pump-prime into us.
Mankind has always been the victim of its own ideas about itself as put
forth in each generation in each town and city on the earth's surface, in
every culture by teachers of that culture, its perpetuators. Teachers are a
hapless lot. They hand along what they were taught plus some reflections
of the day's mood which hopefully will be useful for getting forward in
the world. Nearly everything that they say is found in a textbook. Nor
could it be otherwise if a whole society of persons is to be offered some
common basis for behavior toward one another. Absence of such en-
culturation would make cooperation impossible and prevent the maintenance of any societies anywhere.

 The contents of a textbook are not wholly the author's fault. He
must satisfy parents, school officials, even the government which licenses
and often subsidizes education, and anyway has an interest in the new
generation's view of the society which that government is administering—
the author must satisfy everyone that he is not corrupting youth. It is a
very serious matter. It is not a question of truth or of science, the science
of how to train minds most efficiently or the science of how to conduct

social affairs most effectively. It is a matter of moral choice: of what youth ought to hear, of what is good for them, of how well they may fare in the world after imbibing this or that doctrine of social behavior. The textbook writer has to play it safe. He cannot condemn too critically the ways and thoughts of his students' elders lest students disdain their heritage, or read too closely and precisely what past philosophers actually taught lest the pitiful shallowness of contemporary interpretations equally engender students' disdain. These instructions would corrupt youth. No human society can withstand such corruption—because disdainful superciliousness erects no alternative foundation of hope on which to risk further behavior. Unless elders endorse new hopes and thus establish a new orthodoxy, old hopes however hollow cannot reasonably be discarded. The old might yet succeed. Less hesitancy and more trust might rescue the day. Civilization is no more than belief that we have transcended a brutish existence. Undermining that belief, or failing to sustain it, corrupts not only the means by which human affairs are improved but by which they survive.

People are deficient instruments for furthering their own welfare. Though their goals have failed them a thousand times, people need to reaffirm these guides or perish. This necessary disingenuousness inhibits youth as much as it formerly did their parents, who now are merely accustomed to it. For this reason, social goals are less questioned than insistently propounded. They are, for us, the attainment of peace, prosperity, health, and the end of exploitation. We have not trained our children to live in a world already peaceful or prosperous, healthy or non-exploitative. We dare not because we do not understand what peaceableness entails, and fear what would happen to them cast out defenseless in the bellicose world of their elders. Better that they hope for a peace not yet attained than be corrupted into supposing that we would tolerate its actual occurrence. And yet we would not disillusion them toward ourselves since we need their trust in us to support our self-confidence. In these ways the blind lead the blind in every time and place.

I have noted this phenomenon at some length because it lies at the center of human deficiency, explains why we fail to remake our behavior all in a day. We are bound not by a dispensable past but by the indispensable present of justifiable hesitation. I also note this phenomenon's universality to demonstrate that there are universal human experiences. Yet this and other universals are differently presented by every generation of scholars, each using its own language of concepts to sustain and explore parallel insights. The alteration of images from one language of concepts to another suggests that there is an endless flux of irreconcilable cultures independent of one another, though successive and foreshadowed in their predecessors. Awareness of this difficulty persuades many people that it is hopeless to seek certainty about anything trans-cultural. Yet differing conceptual languages merely disguise rather than refute what has been clearly universal, such as hesitancy to act and to trust ourselves, and our fear of corrupting youth. I seek those universals in this book. If they exist, they are the stuff from which any reliable philosophy would be deduced. And if they do not, my various theses are not destroyed; each can stand alone.

I assume that implicit in all these universals is a concern for personal and social survival. This is necessarily a constant concern. In primitive economies it derived from the fear that if the next generation should fail to maintain those economies, the old would starve, unable to labor. In our own time the fear is of societal changes making the world of our old age impossible for us to accept, so unfamiliar as to unnerve us. Moreover, the means of our survival need to be rationalized or we lose all élan to go forward in our daily tasks; why should we struggle? Rationalizations of capacity to surmount particular and purely contemporary threats to survival must embrace more than just those threats or else new ones will find us disarmed and vulnerable. Rationalizations must have the character of universal solutions to our dilemmas. For this reason a social theory is hardly persuasive which does not at least attempt to stand on universal grounds.

Among these rationalizations or beliefs I cite two that appear to me untrustworthy although they were carried around the globe by eighteenth and nineteenth century propagators of our culture and have become common sense if not self-evident truths for humanity as a whole. The first belief is an assumption that when any human good, material or otherwise, is scarce it will acquire value in human eyes, and that anything of value will be sought, will have market value. The result is supposed to be that somehow, somewhere a few or many people will be inspired to supply more of this rarity, make it more commonly available, thus bringing down its price in whatever coinage it is traded, and finally in this way fulfill human desires. An idea invented by early economists to explain the supposed fact of gradual material betterment in their time, it is a magnificent formula. If there is not enough of something, such as peace or prosperity, it is assumed in this model that no one yet has had time to supply it or has not yet found ways to supply it. But all will be well in the end. Negligence will be overcome by the pressures of demand. It is only a matter of political scientists discovering the way of peace, or of psychologists finding the true dynamics of marital bliss, or of economists prescribing for the ills of the poor. I may seem sarcastic and yet I believe a bit of this myself, at least to some extent. And I write this book partly to correct my own views of our folklore. Governments everywhere are expending billions through universities and in aid-to-the-unfortunate upon this very assumption—that scarcities of all good things exist, that governments should not oppose the inevitable trend of this inevitable law of scarcity-fulfillment, that by encouraging ever greater activity the most glaring of contemporary scarcities are bound to be overcome. The implication of this first belief is that mankind's difficulties have centered wholly upon scarcity. Where there is not enough of something, people suffer the lack of it. When they have enough of what they lack, they will be able to enjoy themselves. Anyone can understand this simple conclusion. It is not that people stupidly refuse to recognize good fortune, or that good fortune is an elusive concept; the formula for successful living plainly states that of course a starving man wants food and will know when his stomach is full. Nor is there a problem in fulfilling all human goods since, whenever a need appears, someone will turn to filling it.

Though we all believe this formula to some extent, we all know that it is nonsense. Any other answer, nevertheless, is hard to imagine. We know that the securely rich, famous, or otherwise replete have seldom if ever confessed themselves fulfilled. Their former poverty often seems to them a time of greater happiness than their present wealth. Certainly no vastly learned man confesses satisfaction with his knowledge. Is it merely that earlier scarcities are replaced by others at a later time? To some extent this is true. And yet must there not be some lacks whose fulfillment would complete existence for us, the rest being unimportant or peripheral? Or is the human condition such that we must be perpetually dissatisfied, all dreams of fulfillment an empty folly? The last answer has often been given, though without dampening our anticipations. Or is the trouble at the very center of this scarcity-fulfillment formula: that instead of there being someone, somewhere capable of meeting demands for a scarcity, very few and often no one is able to think past the mental blocks which originally created the scarcity? Most ills are accepted as unavoidable because no one has thought of a way around them. It is therefore untrue that absence or scarcity of a solution to some human ill inspires its discovery. Mankind's difficulties do not center upon scarcity but upon lack of imagination, initiative, and of willingness to reshape the culture toward mankind's vague desire for a better existence. Scarcity exists but it is primarily one of talents for living intelligently rather than any absence of time and resources for using talents already available. Were this not true statesmen would long ago have given us international peace and we would have welcomed it without hesitation.

The means to peace are obvious: to declare it, to disarm, to reap the benefits. Anyone supposing that whole peoples wish conflict and thus force statesmen to make war misreads all the evidence. How does any child come to know even the presence of other nations except through textbooks written as I have described? How does any citizen of one nation come to suppose another nation hostile except through press reports of what government leaders surmise? And how does a statesmen surmise another's hostility? Through reports of his ambassadors and secret agents, and through conversation with his enemy. Perhaps it is true after all that peace waits upon the genius of these statesmen and their associates to discover and supply the ingredients of peaceful rule for which a market has long existed. It is a much more difficult question whether during peacetimes people have consumed or appreciated peace with sufficient satisfaction to convince statesmen that there is no market for war.

The scarcity-fulfillment model is breaking down. Contrary to the model we have to admit that markets are created; they have no spontaneous existence even in the case of food for the starving. A man may well starve for being told that he must diet. Markets for peace and war are both engineered. Scarcities of trust between people are created; for example, an incredulous public is told that its friends of yesterday are today's enemies or that it has demanded unanimously what it had not even thought of until this moment. But are there limits to our being victims of propaganda? No doubt, but as for our more sophisticated beliefs and rationalizations like that about scarcity, I know no limits to credulity. Our problems, then, are not simple, to be solved through a self-generating process of knowing our lacks and fulfilling them, but are far more difficult.

A second very local and historically parochial belief about human behavior is that humans require only to be freed from interference by one another, by constraints of any kind, to become truly themselves—which is assumed to be a blissful state of freedom in expressing and acting upon all their potentialities. However limited are those potentialities, they presumably would fully occupy and delight their possessor if only they could be exercised. A perfect world would be frictionless; a unique psyche within each person would bloom like a desert flower. It is upon this assumption that statesmen have conceived the need or market for expansion of influence or national boundaries; those remaining alive after a war of defense-against-constriction would presumably be able to move about and fulfill potentialities previously inhibited. The supposition that all other statesmen must necessarily follow the same reasoning leads to preventive wars, or wars to prevent preventive wars. But shortcomings of the model are obvious. Were everyone free from others' interference, they would reveal not their inhibited potentialities but their own immense deficiencies of talent for conceiving or doing very much of anything. Better that people deceive themselves about their creative capacities than that they be humiliated by the vacuous stretches of their pitiful inadequacies. We are not self-sufficient. Everything that I have said about our need for rationalization, for reassurance, and about our deficiencies of talent confirms our interdependence. Freedom from interference is the last burden that we should be asked to bear. What talents we have are no doubt developed in response to others' needs, although mere response to challenge is not enough or else peace and prosperity would long ago have superseded war and poverty.

Rather, it is because of our interdependence and our aid of one another, through application of our very unequal and varied talents, that awareness and expressions of our unique selves arise, and that we grow into human beings able to survive together. This point cannot be over-stressed. At least it is the rock on which this book is erected. Models of automatic scarcity-fulfillment, or of an inherent requirement to live independently of one another, alike suppose a population of rational, self-sufficient, self-disciplined persons whom I have never met. Human existence remains for me a problem of finding means to the end of beneficial interdependence.

That is the problem. But solutions of human existence concern only individuals, not humanity at large. Solutions are for each individual to seek throughout his life and attain at this or that turning of it; there is no general solution of the whole human dilemma for everyone collectively. A state of war may provide one man with opportunities that solve pressing problems of his life; he may learn enough about how people die, about fear, bravery, and the capacity for bearing pain to enrich his understanding for the rest of his days. But that personal solution raises the problem of others' welfare, their good versus his, for which there is no over-all solution. Solutions to human problems are always personal, culture-bound, relative to particular situations. In contrast to these is the general problem of human existence to which all such particular solutions are subsidiary and upon which they depend. This collective social problem hangs without conclusion or resolution; it extends backward throughout history and forward to the end of the human race. This problem is essentially political. It is the integration and management of people's diverse talents in order to make possible (without guaranteeing) everyone's working out his own evolving situation, including even his awareness of it.

This perpetual problem of mankind's existence is the care of the human community. Care of community lies at the base of everything else ascribable to humans and is, therefore, primary over all other human phenomena. It could not be otherwise. Coming upon each other with our needs, unable to do without each other, we have to find some means of integrating, perhaps reconciling, certainly arranging and managing all our scattered lacks and capacities in order to achieve individual goals without damaging our ability to live together. Care of these relationships is the political function. Politics could not have been invented as a form of social behavior before there were human relationships needing integration and management. Human relationships as we know them require the purpose and definition which political action alone provides. Politics and political organization are thus inherent in the human enterprise; before there was politics there was no mankind as we understand mankind to be. It is plausible that the border between persons and other animals lies precisely at this point where conscious integration and management of social relationships supersede genetically determined associative behavior.

I seem to say that politics is independent of particular forms of social organization, that it is as necessary for a family as for a nation. I mean just that. Moreover I find no evidence or suggestion of differences of kind between the most simple and complex institutions. Leadership may pass from one to another member of a family and back again, and be more formalized in larger social organizations; but such differences do not alter the function served. There is thus no need to construct a typology of political organizations. The elements of politics appear to me to originate in the general human condition of mutual dependence (true also of other creatures, though for many possible reasons other creatures have not adopted political behavior comparable to ours). These elements did not arise from historical events such as the development of Roman law or of Anglo-American constitutionalism or, within a different perspective, from the genius of Plato or Confucius; political and intellectual history embodies only particular expressions of these elements. The human condition allows so little variation in the means of governing that differences between the constitutional structure of various regimes are largely deceptive; they hardly affect the capacity of those regimes to integrate or manage social relationships, or to achieve justice. I will therefore devote only minor attention to the delusion that one or another so-called "form of government" is superior.

Arising from a general human condition and independent of particular forms of social organization, is politics, as I conceive it, the integration and management of every human relationship or only of certain relationships? Our human condition is interdependence, and politics concerns only the care of that interdependence, of the community or potential community implied thereby. Politics is unconcerned with relationships irrelevant to some community. But since almost every community is interdependent with others, what we call "government" includes authority over sub-communities such as families, commercial enterprises, professions (as well as over its own self-regulation). "Government" is therefore superior in authority over all regulative activities; the integration and management of all economic and social endeavor must be governmentally initiated or at least sanctioned. For this reason whatever is essential for governing a community as a whole will be found true of governing any part of the community, although not everything done in order to govern all of a community's activities is needed to govern each of them. This being so, my interest in political morality does not require examining lesser instances of it than exist in an entire community or polity; nor did anyone living before the present age of discrete social science disciplines imagine otherwise. Only recently have we lost perspective upon the unity and simplicity of human affairs.

Process and Polity

H. L. NIEBURG

We Westerners tend to be blinded by words like rationality, reason, objectivity, truth, and to think of them as unique to our own values. This we have in common with untutored and primitive men who seek to control nature by word manipulation in prayers and incantations. Words are important because they carry an operational code about what reality is and what to do about it. To give a thing a right name is to imply the proper and prescribed reaction to it. Words imply a frame of reference based upon values shared by others.

Rationality is not a value. Technically, it is merely the structure of language—a set of rules governing a sequence of propositions based upon irreducible axioms, principles, and definitions. "Rational" merely means uniform, continuous, sequential, capable of being weighed or measured, following certain logical rules of language. The syllogism is the basic unit of rationality; through it anything can be "rationalized," that is, made to appear rationally sequential. Some entirely absurd descriptions of reality can be thoroughly rational even though we may quarrel with underlying assumptions and selection of relevant facts. There is no difference in rationality between a description of reality based upon demons and devils and one based upon impersonal physical forces. The difference lies in the choice of irreducible assumptions about reality, working hypotheses which are validated by their success in achieving values. Such conflicting perceptions of reality do coexist in societies and in individuals because there is a wide variety of values to be served.

In the political realm, where pluralistic value systems are common, the value-relative basis of rationality becomes evident. A *coherent* communication is rational whether you agree with its tendency or not. Although *reasoning* and *rational discourse* are interchangeable terms, the common tendency is to load them with other meanings; *rational* is transformed into reasonable, moderate, constructive, and amenable to resolution through negotiation, conciliation, and compromise. The difference between violent and nonviolent modes of conflict resolution is not a matter of rationality or reason, unless one equates these terms with his own preferences for moderation and abstract talk.

Any prescriptive syllogism is meaningless except in terms of the emotional force which is attached to the first principle. The infinite regress of syllogistic reasoning ends somewhere with a commitment of self. Such commitments cannot be explained or understood by reasoning alone. Efforts to adduce rational principles for explaining social and political change are futile unless one grapples with the often illogical (more correctly, "inarticulate" or "incoherent," "excited") intensity of self-commitment which marks social movements.

In political terms, one may define rationality, as does the economist, in terms of optimizing choices and rewards. Such a concept is value-neutral and can be mated to any given set of values. Obviously, this use of the word "rationality" has little to do with its use in formal logic. One can be completely rational, in the sense of maximizing ones' bargaining position, without relying on a web of logical symbols and verbal discourse. This is surely the case with animals, children, and inarticulate persons. Much that passes for rationality on the part of the articulate person is merely post hoc rationalization or part of the bargaining process itself (not necessarily the most important part).

It is not unusual for behavioral rationality (optimizing choices and rewards) to constitute a distinct and separate dimension quite apart from symbolic rationality (logical consistency). To achieve the latter, it is often necessary constantly to refine and qualify a verbal bargaining position in order to make it accord with the contradictions and reversals that are inherent in behavioral rationality under conditions of bargaining.

Reasoning, favored by lawyers, writers, and others who live by words, is not indispensable to the action-reaction patterns of behavior used as a means of maximizing self-evident values. In the context of bargaining, rationality is a synonym for pragmatic success: rational behavior is behavior that works; irrational behavior doesn't work. As students of political behavior, we must avoid the fallacy that "my values, which work for me, are rational; yours, *which do not work for me,* are irrational!" A distinction so obvious as this perhaps need not be stated, except that it tends to be blurred, in a self-serving and tendentious way, as part of the verbal dimension of social bargaining.

In real bargaining relationships, rationality is existential and universal. One may postulate a kind of thermodynamic law of human behavior. Drawing a comparison with the law of conservation of energy, we may assume that men seek to conserve energy and values. Keeping in mind the law of entropy (the tendency in nature toward disorder and energy decay), one may assume that social disorder and decay are constant threats which human energy and values must overcome. In any specific bargaining engagement, one party's order becomes another's entropy. All parties at all times seek to maximize the former and to manage and overcome whatever amount of the latter is forced upon them by particular bargaining outcomes.

THE NEW POLITICAL SCIENCE

Political scientists have traditionally been interested in constitutional and legal forms, structures, and systems. With the rise of the behavioral sciences in the 1930s, the emphasis has shifted. New tools and approaches provided by the sister disciplines, and increased awareness that formal systems did not tell the whole story, have brought attention to underlying, often informal, processes and relationships. It is now generally recognized that formal systems are something of a fiction whose real content depends upon other kinds of factors than formal rules. Emphasis upon individual and group behavior has moved toward study of the dynamics of authority relationships and bargaining. Just as the sociologist has moved from thinking about culture as an abstract structure of values to thinking about culture as a set of behavior patterns and society as a structure of relationships, so political science has moved toward sociology. Authority and bargaining relationships, both formal and informal, are discovered to be the substratum of formal policymaking, legislation, law enforcement. In the behavioral sciences, the distinction between social and political has become so blurred that the concepts are almost, but not quite, interchangeable.

Empirical study focuses on "behavior units" which are seen as parts of a whole hierarchy of systems, including the composite of individual personality, membership in large and small groups, both formal and informal, clusters and coalitions of groups organized in different patterns for different purposes, and so on. At the heart of research interest and theory development is the role of informal structures in performing the functions of socializing, recruiting, articulating, aggregating, structuring, and communicating the boundaries of conflict and accommodation, values, and behavior among groups and individuals.

The uncritical notion that values determine behavior through an abstract intellectual process is a vestige of the old doctrine of free will and the mind-body duality. Contemporary psychological and sociological studies have tended to reverse the principle, assuming that behavior arises from experience, trial-and-error, bargaining relationships, action-reaction conditioning. It is then rationalized and generalized in terms of attitudes, preferences, verbal formulations, and so on, which in their abstract and subjective form we call "values." Psychologist B. F. Skinner has played a leading role in this reversal. Both individuals and groups adjust symbolic value systems constantly to make their parts consistent and compatible. The form and content of ideologies reflect such rationalized values. However, working independently of these values, behavior continues to react to fresh experience and to the rewards and punishments of the bargaining process, with appropriate reinterpretations of old value systems to give apparent continuity and consistency to behavior. From this point of view, for example, a landlord who is forced by open housing laws to rent apartments to members of minority groups will eventually tend to rationalize his behavior in terms of values, becoming a genuinely open-minded egalitarian in the process and taking great pride in his conversion. If this be true, then it should indeed be possible to "legislate morality"— provided that the real bargaining relations of the informal polity reinforce the new norm.

Values are explanations of social situations and standards of appropriate action designed to produce desired goals and successful management. As social gestalts or paradigms held in common by large groups, values reflect group experience and bargaining positions. Insofar as they limit or predispose behavior in new situations, they also tend to stabilize and structure existing relationships.

A high degree of order and predictability is essential for the conduct of human affairs and the achievement of universal high-priority human values (such as manipulating and controlling the physical environment for sustenance, comfort, and convenience). The options available for internal organization are infinite. Furthermore, whatever the system of order prevailing, it is always subject to stress arising from its own dynamics as well as those from the physical environment. The most important and most typically human quality is *generalized adaptability*. Ashley Montagu says that man differs from his evolutionary antecedents because "he moved from a dimension of limited capacity for learning into an increasing, enlarging zone of adaptation in which he became entirely dependent upon learning from the man-made part of the environment, culture, for his development as a functioning human being." Far from being "phylogenetically programmed," man's behavior is characterized by a supremely developed nonspecific capacity for learning. "He has to learn his human nature from the human environment, from the culture that humanizes him. . . ."

Because human behavior appears to be dominated by learned responses within a largely man-made environment, the options for social order are at once infinite and changeable. Any given system is orderly only in relation to certain given human values. Slavery may be an orderly state of affairs for the slave owner but at the same time make personal order impossible for the slave. The natural and inevitable process of growth and change is one of conflict, that is, relative disorder. The definition of order for any given relationship of social groups tends to reflect the values, interests, and behavior of those who dominate the hierarchical structure of bargaining relationships.

The history of crime reflects the history of law, which in turn reflects the normative systems of prevailing power groups, that is, the social and economic conditions with which their emergence is identified and by which it is perpetuated. In the words of W. H. Auden: "Law is only crimes / Punished by places and by times. . . ." Crimes against property reflect laws which make property a built-in power advantage for certain individuals and groups, laws which developed during the commercial and industrial revolutions. The social values which receive the protection of a criminal code are those treasured by the dominant interest groups. The values of dominant groups are modified by shifts in the locus of power brought about by the emergence of new groups. A process of social bargaining forces modification, accommodation, and even revolutionary changes in the hierarchies of power.

In the process of shifting, integrating, and reintegrating the formal and informal hierarchies there is a strain toward humanizing power and conserving both energy and values. Organized groups are essential to human survival, and hierarchy itself is essential to the practical functioning of group life. But there is no absolute arbiter to determine among the options of changing order available to social systems and concretely represented by the conflicts of individuals and groups. In the midst of uncertainty, there must be a process of choice and provisional consensus. This process, the unremitting struggle for influence and authority, whose tide at any given moment is fixed by the formal authority structures of government and economic decision-making, is properly called "politics."

All individuals and groups seek to impose their own order around them. When a set of norms form a framework for the deliberate achievement of human purposes, they become part of a social institution. This term refers to the established forms or conditions of procedure characteristic of group activity. In the course of doing something, the members of a society repeat actions often enough to cause a pattern to emerge and become recognized, institutionalized, and internalized as a self-enforced norm.

The boundaries of conflicting systems of order overlap, creating arenas of social entropy (relative disorder) and competition. One set of values may become hierarchically dominant over those of other men and groups. The formal institutions of state authority reinforce them through socialization, consensus, and, ultimately, a monopoly on legal violence. This enables dominant groups to determine the choices available to the lower orders of the hierarchy. They organize and manage social policy, resources, and the environment in such a way as to reflect their own values of order, which limits the choices that remain open to conflicting value systems in ordering their own proximate environments. If the whole multileveled and differentiated hierarchy retains legitimacy (that is, achieves values for at least those groups capable of challenging its authority), the social system will remain stable, its power and negative reinforcement mostly passive, and the processes of collaboration and accommodation relatively successful. Such an integrated social order minimizes disruption, destruction, and potential schism.

LEGITIMACY AND LEGALITY

Legitimacy and legality of state or group authority are by no means synonomous. The procedural-structural aspect of the social order generally enjoys the broadest consensus of values. However, the substantive norms of social relationships, the matter of rights and duties, leadership and policies, carry no such broad agreement; they are the common grist of interest-group politics. Legality is an attribute of sovereignty. It is an abstraction which confers the authority of the state upon the acts, records, elections, and so on of those who conduct the offices of state power, and upon the code of law which regulates behavior. Legality is the technicality of formal consistency and adequate authority.

Legitimacy, on the other hand, reflects the vitality of the underlying consensus which endows the state and its officers with whatever authority and power they actually possess, not by virtue of legality, but by the reality of the respect which the citizens pay to the institutions and behavior norms. Legitimacy is earned by the ability of those who conduct the power of the state to represent and reflect a broad consensus. This is the familiar doctrine enunciated in the Declaration of Independence. Legitimacy cannot be claimed or granted by mere technicality of law; it must be won by the success of state institutions in cultivating and meeting expectations, in mediating interests and aiding the process by which the values of individuals and groups are allocated in the making, enforcement, adjudication, and general observance of law. Not all law is legitimate in this sense, whether because it is unenforced, unenforceable, or responsive only to sporadic and arbitrary enforcement by this or that police chief, policeman, judge, or jury. Laws that were once legitimate may still retain legality after losing legitimacy.

The complex components of the informal polity which vest the formal institutional structure with legitimacy are indispensable to the working of the political and social systems. Law enforcement and court and correctional activities are particular aspects of the system of social control, and probably the least important ones. They will not work when the informal systems by which individual behavior is integrated into a social order break down or suffer the cleavages of internal warfare. A criminologist [E. H. Johnson] claims that imprisonment is less punitive than, and dependent upon, its informal effects: "Stigmatization of [the prisoner] and his family; economic effects on his dependents; the mortification process instigated by a status inferior to that of policemen, court functionaries and correctional personnel; and restriction of social and economic privileges. . . ." Hannah Arendt writes that "authority excludes the use of external means of coercion; where force is used, authority itself has failed. The authoritarian relation between the one who commands and the one who obeys rests neither on common reason nor on the power of the one who commands; what they have in common is the hierarchy itself, whose rightness and legitimacy both recognize. . . ."

Most of the controls that exist within the informal polity are not perceived because they are right under our noses and taken for granted.

They function within the context of personality development and all the commonplace activities of daily life and human relations. When they work well, they are overlooked or considered to be simply "normal" or "just human nature." The newspapers do not report the performances of good fathers, obedient children, honest cashiers, and so on.

We become aware of the informal polity only when the fragile web begins to tear, partly because of the sense of danger, the irrepressible demand for attention, the evangelical energy liberated in those individuals who themselves are torn by the rough edges of the cleavage.

Whatever the historical, logical, or illogical culmination of events that unifies a population under central state sovereignty, the subjective aspect of its unity—its legitimacy—makes it a nation. The objective aspects, territorial boundaries, the letter of the law, the monopoly of legality and police power do not in themselves make a nation; in fact, they may generate more violence than collaboration unless a nation is built in the minds and hearts of the people. It is the consensus that supports the informal polity that constitutes the nation. Those who occupy the offices of state power face each day the continuing task of validating the legitimacy of the state by the way they manage and shape the life of the nation. This must be done because of and in spite of divided regional loyalties, economic rivalry, ideological and religious conflict, cultural variety, and the like.

The tension of normal social life is alive with ambivalence, conflicting loyalties, and shifting alliances of convenience. Competition and cooperation are by no means incompatible; they are poles of a continuum in a working social order. All individuals and groups are torn between conflicting interests and impulses and struggles for leadership and influence. Hostility and cooperation are intertwined in a complex maze whose day-to-day movements and adjustments are never conclusive. Ambivalence is the nature of the bargaining relationship, and all social relationships in the informal polity are a form of exchange of values, accommodation out of conflict, and conflict out of old accommodation. New states concocted from old colonies face a more difficult task, but even well-established, advanced nations must continuously prove and improve their legitimacy. The means of force are essential to maintain a threshold of deterrence against separatism, but such means are not a substitute for the positive achievement of values which can win legitimacy and create self-enforcing informal and formal processes of unity. There is always danger that the prevailing minority which holds power will use legality and force to deter pluralistic politics and opposition. In the swiftly changing human and physical environment of modern technology and international relations, such a mood can quickly dislocate a nation, destroy legitimacy, escalate violence, and endanger the peace of the world. A state system whose central and primary values become the negative and costly ones of internal security and repression is soon riddled by subversion, interventions, assassinations, and extremist fits and seizures of all sorts.

The Two Faces of Janus

MAURICE DUVERGER

Littré in his 1870 dictionary defined politics as "the science of government of states." Robert in 1962 defined it as "the art and practice of government of human societies." The comparison between the two definitions, given almost a century apart, is not without interest. Both make government the object of politics. Today, however, the government of states is related to that of other human societies, the term government thus meaning, in any society, organized power, the institutions of command and control. The issue is the subject of debate among specialists: some still consider politics as the science of the state, of organized power in the national community; the majority see it as the science of organized power in all communities.

This difference of opinion is unimportant. In fact, even those who define politics as the science of power in general recognize that it is in the state that power finds its most developed and most highly organized form, and hence it is in this context that it should mainly be studied; in other human societies it remains embryonic. However, the concept of politics as the science of power has one basic superiority: it is more operational because it alone allows verification of the hypothesis on which it is based. A comparative study of power in every kind of community may reveal the existence of differences between power in the state and power in other communities. On the other hand, to study power only within the framework of the state without comparing it with power elsewhere is restrictive, making it impossible to verify whether the difference of kind posited *a priori* exists or not.

It has been suggested that a distinction be made between large and small communities. In the latter, competition for power is between individuals, power itself being weakly organized; the situation roughly corresponds to the elementary distinction between the "rulers" and "ruled," between leaders and members. In large communities, on the other hand, political conflict involves social categories, intermediate groups set up within the total society, as well as individuals; power is organized structurally and hierarchically. Some sociologists limit politics to the study of this complex power which operates in large communities and exclude the analysis of leadership in small groupings.

The two phenomena are too closely linked to be studied separately. In ministerial committees, in administrative committees, in the executive committees of political parties, at every level of government in large communities, there are to be found small groups in which the political nature of authority is indisputable. The more valid distinction is between two levels of analysis: the micropolitical dealing with relations on the individual plane, based upon personal contact; the macropolitical dealing with group relationships where direct contact does not exist or is replaced by indirect contract between intermediaries, by administrative relationships or by artificial, theatrical contacts (the minister's handshake, the television appearance of the head of state). Research must be pursued simultaneously on both levels, but the passage from one to the other, the change in scale, raises an important problem.

The definitions of Littré and Robert differ on another point: the first speaks of politics as a science, the latter considers it simply as an art and an activity. *A priori,* the inverse would appear more natural. Today political science is recognized in almost every university in the world; it has its chairs, its professors and teachers, its students and its research funds. Every year several thousand books and articles are published in the field. A century ago it was scarcely being talked of. It was only between 1859 and 1872 that Paul Janet changed the title of his great work *Histoire de la philosophie politique dans ses rapports avec la morale,* replacing *philosophie politique* by *science politique.* At that time no university post catered for the subject; it had no official place in the Pantheon of knowledge. Linguistic development seems here to have run counter to scientific development.

Yet the two really go hand in hand. Littré was writing at the end of the nineteenth century, when it was thought that science would make possible the study of all human relations and not physical or biological phenomena only, when the coming of the "Positive age" announced by Auguste Comte was expected. The very development of the social sciences has led to a restriction of these ambitions. Today we have at our disposal very many much improved modes of investigation of social and political life, but at the same time we are more conscious of the narrowness of the limits within which they can be used. Politics is much more scientific in 1964 than in Littré's day. Statesmen can and do effectively use statistics, electronic computers, public opinion polls, techniques for the manipulation of the masses, and so on. However, we now know that the area covered by this scientific kind of politics is much smaller than that of politics as an art, based upon imprecise material that is not measurable but is intuitive and irrational.

It would be vain to hope that the two will ever entirely coincide, that politics can become entirely scientific. Political decisions bring into play not only objective data but also value-judgments about man and society. The fact that these value-judgments are not unrelated to the situation of those who formulate them, that indeed they in part reflect social class and personal interests, makes no difference. Liberty never exists *in vacuo;* it is always exercised by men who are conditioned by their experience. The disparity between the aims stated and those actually pursued, the masking of the one by the other, does not change the fact that political choice is dominated by aims. Political science is of major importance because it removes the masks, it demystifies. It can make clear the real terms of choice, but it cannot choose.

In so far as politics is based, then, on choices and commitments, its concepts are relative; definable in relation to particular sets of values and differing in significance. We can describe the Marxist, the Liberal, the Conservative, the Fascist view of politics, but there is no totally "objective" view of politics, because there is no totally objective politics. Political science can separate the objective elements from those which are not so, and thus critically assess each view. It is capable of determining the depth to which at a given period the particular view has penetrated, as well as its evolution. It is capable also, by confronting those views, of complementing them and of assessing them one against the others, in just the same way as different photographs of the same object taken from different points of view may be brought together in order to give a more complete picture of the object which cannot be seen directly in the round.

Behind all the systems of values and all individual judgments there are generally to be found two basic attitudes. Ever since men have been reflecting on politics they have oscillated between two dramatically opposed interpretations. According to one, politics is conflict, a struggle in which power allows those who possess it to ensure their hold on society and to profit by it. According to the other view, politics is an effort to bring about the rule of order and justice, in which power guarantees the general interest and the common good against the pressures of private interests. In the first case, politics serves to maintain the privileges of a minority against the majority. In the second, it is a means of realizing the integration of all citizens into the community and of creating the just state of which Aristotle spoke so long ago.

The acceptance of one or other of these theses is in part determined by social situation. The oppressed, the unsatisfied, the poor, the wretched, whether as individuals or as a class, cannot see power as assuring a real order, but only a caricature of it behind which is hidden the domination of privilege; for them politics means conflict. Those who are rich, well provided for, satisfied, find society harmonious and see power as maintaining an authentic order; for them politics means integration. It often happens that the latter succeed to some extent in persuading the former that political strife is dishonest, unhealthy, sordid, and that those who engage in it seek their own selfish interests by dubious means. To disarm opponents in such a way is to secure a considerable personal advantage. "Depolitization" always favors the established order, immobility and conservatism.

The two attitudes express only a part of the truth, of course. The most optimistic of Conservatives cannot deny that even if the aim of politics is to bring about social integration it rarely achieves it in a satisfactory way. They describe politics idealistically, as it ought to be. Their opponents describe it more realistically, as it is. But in their turn they can scarcely deny that they paint too black a picture. The most oppressive and unjust of governments fulfill some functions that are in the general interest, if only in the technical field, in regulating motor traffic, for example, in running the postal services or in arranging for the collection of household refuse.

In the last resort, the essence of politics, its real nature and true significance, is to be found in the fact that it is always and at all times ambivalent. The statue of Janus, the two-faced god, is the true image of the state and expresses the most profound of political realities. The state—and in a more general way, organized power in any society—is always and at all times both the instrument by which certain groups dominate others, an instrument used in the interest of the rulers and to the disadvantage of the ruled, and also a means of ensuring a particular social order, of achieving some integration of the individual into the collectivity for the general good. The two elements always co-exist, though the importance of each varies with the period, the circumstances and the country concerned. The relations between conflict and integration are, moreover, complex. Every attack on the existing social order implies the image and anticipation of a superior, more authentic order. Every conflict implies a dream of integration and represents an effort to bring it into being. Many thinkers maintain that conflict and integration are not two opposed faces but one and the same overall process in which conflict naturally produces integration, and divisions, by their development, tend naturally towards their own suppression leading to the coming of the city of harmony.

For classical liberal thinkers integration is produced by conflict as this develops, the two phenomena being concomitant. Competition produces the maximum increase in production and the best division of its proceeds, thus leading at any given moment to the best possible economic situation. Political competition is said to produce similar effects: as a result of it, the best, the most fitted, the *élite*, govern for the benefit of all. Political harmony, disturbed only by those who are abnormal, perverse or sick, thus parallels economic harmony. Marxist thinkers also see conflict as the driving force in the evolution of societies, leading necessarily to an ending of divisions and the coming of a society without conflict. However, this integration appears only as the last phase in a very long-term process, only in the distant future. A partial integration or synthesis is achieved at each stage and this immediately becomes a new source of contradiction and strife. Political harmony, it is said, will develop rhythmically until that end point in history which is the "higher phase of Communism."

III
Studying
Politics:
Approaches

Along with the various ways of defining politics have gone many approaches to studying political activity. It was noted earlier that descriptions of political activity could be evaluated by at least five general standards: factual accuracy, logical consistency, comprehensiveness, felt adequacy, and fruitfulness for further action. Most approaches to studying politics go even further than such general standards by providing goals for inquiry and general methods.

The articles in this section provide a sampling of some of the most widely discussed approaches in current American political science. They do not, however, exhaust all the approaches that have appeared in the past and certainly do not close off future possibilities. It is important to note that approaches and methods should be adapted to problems that one would like to solve, rather than the other way around. Thus, as human problems change, the approaches to studying them and solving them are likely to alter as well.

One current approach to the study of politics can best be called *classical*. Its foremost exponent, Leo Strauss, holds that the goal of political inquiry is knowledge of the good life, and that such knowledge can best be obtained through a dialogue in which competing conceptions of the good are criticized and clarified. Strauss objects strongly to the position that there can be no knowledge of good and evil, and holds that the majority of contemporary American political scientists have abandoned their proper vocation in favor of studying the shifting concentrations of power that appear in daily political activity. This leads him to take a position against positivism, the idea that human behavior can be explained through the methods of natural science. Similarly, he opposes historicism, the idea that human behavior is completely determined by historical processes, and that nothing in the human condition stands above history.

A second approach, represented here by E. H. Carr, is the *historical* approach. For Carr, the historical approach demands that the investigator study human activity as a continuous cumulation of experience over time. Unlike mere physical or biological existence, human existence adds novelty to the present because man can evaluate the past and imagine the future. It is this characteristic that makes human beings historical creatures. Carr holds that political historians are continuously reinterpreting the past in terms of a desired future and an image of the present. He argues that they cannot avoid this situation but can strive to become aware of their desires and judgments. Thus, while Strauss holds that the aim of political inquiry is knowledge of human good, Carr maintains that the goal is fruitful and plausible images of the public situation. This difference reflects a debate between those who believe that there is a single standard of human good applicable across historical periods and those who hold that human beings continually redefine good and evil as they engage in the historical process.

A third approach, represented here by Don Bowen, is the *behavioral* approach. For behavioralists, the goal of political inquiry is a science of politics that establishes invariant relations between political activities and allows the prediction of future occurrences. According to this approach, only those parts of human activity that can be observed publicly can be included in a science of politics. Opposed to behavioralism is a fourth approach, *phenomenology*. Two types of phenomenology are represented here, by Marvin Surkin and Henry Kariel, respectively. Surkin maintains that political scientists —rather than concentrating on behavior—should study the meanings that people attach to their own political activities. He would urge greater attention to understanding the frames of reference used by different groups and individuals to interpret their political experience. Henry Kariel would go one step farther than Surkin and attempt to convey the very quality of political experience as lived by diverse groups and individuals. He encourages political scientists to engage actively in political life with the aim of expanding their own and others' understanding of the varieties of political experience. Despite the differences between the two types of phenomenology, however, both Kariel and Surkin would agree that political scientists should study a far wider range of experience than merely publicly observable activity.

The debates over these various approaches reflect important splits in current political science which may not be capable of reconciliation. Between the classical and historical approaches is the issue of whether human good is knowable and changeless or whether human beings continually redefine the notion of good to fit new possibilities that appear in the historical process. Between the phenomenologists and the behavioralists is the issue of whether political scientists should study feelings, meanings, and behaviors, or just publicly observable behaviors. It is only fair to point out that the present book is inspired by an historical and a phenomenological approach.

What Is Political Philosophy?

LEO STRAUSS

The rejection of political philosophy as unscientific is characteristic of present-day positivism. Positivism is no longer what it desired to be when Auguste Comte originated it. It still agrees with Comte by maintaining that modern science is the highest form of knowledge, precisely because it aims no longer, as theology and metaphysics did, at absolute knowledge of the Why, but only at relative knowledge of the How. But after having been modified by utilitarianism, evolutionism, and neo-Kantianism, it has abandoned completely Comte's hope that a social science modeled on modern natural science would be able to overcome the intellectual anarchy of modern society. In about the last decade of the 19th century, social science positivism reached its final form by realizing or decreeing that there is a fundamental difference between facts and values, and that only factual judgments are within the competence of science: scientific social science is incompetent to pronounce value judgments, and must avoid value judgments altogether. As for the meaning of the term "value" in statements of this kind, we can hardly say more than that "values" mean both things preferred and principles of preference.

A discussion of the tenets of social science positivism is today indispensable for explaining the meaning of political philosophy. We reconsider especially the practical consequences of this positivism. Positivistic social science is "value-free" or "ethically neutral": it is neutral in the conflict between good and evil, however good and evil may be understood. This means that the ground which is common to all social scientists, the ground on which they carry on their investigations and discussions, can only be reached through a process of emancipation from moral judgments, or of abstracting from moral judgments: moral obtuseness is the necessary condition for scientific analysis. For to the extent to which we are not yet completely insensitive to moral distinctions, we are forced to make value judgments. The habit of looking at social or human phenomena without making value judgments has a corroding influence on any preferences. The more serious we are as social scientists, the more completely we develop within ourselves a state of indifference to any goal, or of aimlessness and drifting, a state which may be called nihilism. The social scientist is not immune to preferences; his activity is a constant fight against the preferences he has as a human being and a citizen and which threaten to overcome his scientific detachment. He derives the power to counteract these dangerous influences by his dedication to one and only one value—to truth. But according to his principles, truth is not a value which it is necessary to choose: one may reject it as well as choose it. The scientist as scientist must indeed have chosen it. But neither scientists nor science are simply necessary. Social science cannot pronounce

119

on the question of whether social science itself is good. It is then compelled to teach that society can with equal right and with equal reason favor social science as well as suppress it as disturbing, subversive, corrosive, nihilistic. But strangely enough we find social scientists very anxious to "sell" social science, i.e., to prove that social science is necessary. They will argue as follows. Regardless of what our preferences or ends may be, we wish to achieve our ends; to achieve our ends, we must know which means are conducive to our ends; but adequate knowledge of the means conducive to any social ends is the sole function of social science and only of social science; hence social science is necessary for any society or any social movement; social science is then simply necessary; it is a value from every point of view. But once we grant this we are seriously tempted to wonder if there are not a few other things which must be values from every point of view or for every thinking human being. To avoid this inconvenience the social scientist will scorn all considerations of public relations or of private advancement, and take refuge in the virtuous contention that he does not know, but merely believes that quest for truth is good: other men may believe with equal right that quest for truth is bad. But what does he mean by this contention? Either he makes a distinction between noble and ignoble objectives or he refuses to make such a distinction. If he makes a distinction between noble and ignoble objectives he will say there is a variety of noble objectives or of ideals, and that there is no ideal which is compatible with all other ideals: if one chooses truth as one's ideal, one necessarily rejects other ideals; this being the case, there cannot be a necessity, an evident necessity for noble men to choose truth in preference to other ideals. But as long as the social scientist speaks of ideals, and thus makes a distinction between noble and not noble objectives, or between idealistic integrity and petty egoism, he makes a value judgment which according to his fundamental contention is, as such, no longer necessary. He must then say that it is as legitimate to make the pursuit of safety, income, deference one's sole aim in life as it is to make the quest for truth one's chief aim. He thus lays himself open to the suspicion that his activity as a social scientist serves no other purpose than to increase his safety, his income, and his prestige, or that his competence as a social scientist is a skill which he is prepared to sell to the highest bidder. Honest citizens will begin to wonder whether such a man can be trusted, or whether he can be loyal, especially since he must maintain that it is as defensible to choose loyalty as one's value as it is to reject it. In a word, he will get entangled in the predicament which leads to the downfall of Thrasymachus and his taming by Socrates in the first book of Plato's *Republic*.

It goes without saying that while our social scientist may be confused, he is very far from being disloyal and from lacking integrity. His assertion that integrity and quest for truth are values which one can with equal right choose or reject is a mere movement of his lips and his tongue, to which nothing corresponds in his heart or mind. I have never met any scientific social scientist who apart from being dedicated to truth and integrity was not also wholeheartedly devoted to democracy. When he says that democracy is a value which is not evidently superior to the opposite value, he does not mean that he is impressed by the alternative which he rejects, or that his heart or his mind is torn between alternatives which in themselves are equally attractive. His "ethical neutrality" is so far from being nihilism or a road to nihilism that it is not more than an alibi for thoughtlessness and vulgarity: by saying that democracy and truth are values, he says in effect that one does not have to think about the reasons why these things are good, and that he may bow as well as anyone else to the values that are adopted and respected by his society. Social science positivism fosters not so much nihilism as conformism and philistinism.

It is not necessary to enter here and now into a discussion of the theoretical weaknesses of social science positivism. It suffices to allude to the considerations which speak decisively against this school. (1) It is impossible to study social phenomena, i.e., all important social phenomena, without making value judgments. A man who sees no reason for not despising people whose horizon is limited to their consumption of food and their digestion may be a tolerable econometrist; he cannot say anything relevant about the character of a human society. A man who refuses to distinguish between great statesmen, mediocrities, and insane impostors may be a good bibliographer; he cannot say anything relevant about politics and political history. A man who cannot distinguish between a profound religious thought and a languishing superstition may be a good statistician; he cannot say anything relevant about the sociology of religion. Generally speaking, it is impossible to understand thought or action or work without evaluating it. If we are unable to evaluate adequately, as we very frequently are, we have not yet succeeded in understanding adequately. The value judgments which are forbidden to enter through the front door of political science, sociology or economics, enter these disciplines through the back door; they come from that annex of present-day social science which is called psychopathology. Social scientists see themselves compelled to speak of unbalanced, neurotic, maladjusted people. But these value judgments are distinguished from those used by the great historians, not by greater clarity or certainty, but merely by their poverty: a slick operator is as well adjusted as, he may be better adjusted than, a good man or a good citizen. Finally, we must not overlook the invisible value judgments which are concealed from undiscerning eyes but nevertheless most powerfully present in allegedly purely descriptive concepts. For example, when social scientists distinguish between democratic and authoritarian habits or types of human beings, what they call "authoritarian" is in all cases known to me a caricature of everything of which they, as good democrats of a certain kind, disapprove. Or when they speak of three principles of legitimacy, rational, traditional, and charismatic, their very expression "routinization of charisma" betrays a Protestant or liberal preference which no conservative Jew and no Catholic would accept: in the light of the notion of "routinization of charisma," the genesis of the Halakah out of Biblical prophesy on the one hand, and the genesis of the Catholic Church out of the New Testament teaching, necessarily appear as cases of "routinization of charisma." If the objection should be made that value judgments are indeed inevitable in social science but have a merely conditional character, I would reply as follows: are the conditions in question not necessarily fulfilled when we are interested in social phenomena? must the social scientist not necessarily make the assumption that a healthy social life in this world is good, just as medicine necessarily makes the assumption that health and a healthy long life are good? And also are not all factual assertions based on conditions, or assumptions, which however do not become questionable as long as we deal with facts qua facts (e.g., that there are "facts," that events have causes)?

The impossibility of a "value-free" political science can be shown most simply as follows. Political science presupposes a distinction between political things and things which are not political; it presupposes therefore some answer to the question "what is political?" In order to be truly scientific, political science would have to raise this question and to answer it explicitly and adequately. But it is impossible to define the political, i.e., that which is related in a relevant way to the *polis*, the "country" or the "state," without answering the question of what constitutes this kind of society. Now, a society cannot be defined without reference to its purpose. The most well known attempt to define "the state" without regard to its purpose admittedly led to a definition which was derived from "the modern type of state" and which is fully applicable only to that type; it was an attempt to define the modern state without having first defined the state. But by defining the state, or rather civil society, with reference to its purpose, one admits a standard in the light of which one must judge political actions and institutions: the purpose of civil society necessarily functions as a standard for judging of civil societies.

(2) The rejection of value judgments is based on the assumption that the conflicts between different values or value-systems are essentially insoluble for human reason. But this assumption, while generally taken to be sufficiently established, has never been proven. Its proof would require an effort of the magnitude of that which went into the conception and elaboration of the *Critique of Pure Reason;* it would require a comprehensive critique of evaluating reason. What we find in fact are sketchy observations which pretend to prove that this or that specific value conflict is insoluble. It is prudent to grant that there are value conflicts which cannot in fact be settled by human reason. But if we cannot decide which of two mountains whose peaks are hidden by clouds is higher than the other, cannot we decide that a mountain is higher than a molehill? If we cannot decide, regarding a war between two neighboring nations which have been fighting each other for centuries, which nation's cause is more just, cannot we decide that Jezebel's action against Naboth was inexcusable? The greatest representative of social science positivism, Max Weber, has postulated the insolubility of all value conflicts, because his soul craved a universe in which failure, that bastard of forceful sinning accompanied by still more forceful faith, instead of felicity and serenity, was to be the mark of human nobility. The belief that value judgments are not subject, in the last analysis, to rational control, encourages the

inclination to make irresponsible assertions regarding right and wrong or good and bad. One evades serious discussion of serious issues by the simple device of passing them off as value problems. One even creates the impression that all important human conflicts are value conflicts, whereas, to say the least, many of these conflicts arise out of men's very agreement regarding values.

(3) The belief that scientific knowledge, i.e., the kind of knowledge possessed or aspired to by modern science, is the highest form of human knowledge, implies a depreciation of pre-scientific knowledge. If one takes into consideration the contrast between scientific knowledge of the world and pre-scientific knowledge of the world, one realizes that positivism preserves in a scarcely disguised manner Descartes' universal doubt of pre-scientific knowledge and his radical break with it. It certainly distrusts pre-scientific knowledge, which it likes to compare to folklore. This superstition fosters all sorts of sterile investigations or complicated idiocies. Things which every ten-year-old child of normal intelligence knows are regarded as being in need of scientific proof in order to become acceptable as facts. And this scientific proof, which is not only not necessary, is not even possible. To illustrate this by the simplest example: all studies in social science presuppose that its devotees can tell human beings from other beings; this most fundamental knowledge was not acquired by them in classrooms; and this knowledge is not transformed by social science into scientific knowledge, but retains its initial status without any modification throughout. If this pre-scientific knowledge is not knowledge, all scientific studies, which stand or fall with it, lack the character of knowledge. The preoccupation with scientific proof of things which everyone knows well enough, and better, without scientific proof, leads to the neglect of that thinking, or that reflection, which must precede all scientific studies if these studies are to be relevant. The scientific study of politics is often presented as ascending from the ascertainment of political "facts," i.e., of what has happened hitherto in politics, to the formulation of "laws" whose knowledge would permit the prediction of future political events. This goal is taken as a matter of course without a previous investigation as to whether the subject matter with which political science deals admits of adequate understanding in terms of "laws" or whether the universals through which political things can be understood as what they are must not be conceived of in entirely different terms. Scientific concern with political facts, relations of political facts, recurrent relations of political facts, or laws of political behavior, requires isolation of the phenomena which it is studying. But if this isolation is not to lead to irrelevant or misleading results, one must see the phenomena in question within the whole to which they belong, and one must clarify that whole, i.e., the whole political or politico-social order. One cannot arrive, e.g., at a kind of knowledge of "group politics" which deserves to be called scientific if one does not reflect on what genus of political orders is presupposed if there is to be "group politics" at all, and what kind of political order is presupposed by the specific "group politics" which one

is studying. But one cannot clarify the character of a specific democracy, e.g., or of democracy in general, without having a clear understanding of the alternatives to democracy. Scientific political scientists are inclined to leave it at the distinction between democracy and authoritarianism, i.e., they absolutize the given political order by remaining within a horizon which is defined by the given political order and its opposite. The scientific approach tends to lead to the neglect of the primary or fundamental questions and therewith to thoughtless acceptance of received opinion. As regards these fundamental questions our friends of scientific exactness are strangely unexacting. To refer again to the most simple and at the same time decisive example, political science requires clarification of what distinguishes political things from things which are not political; it requires that the question be raised and answered "what is political?" This question cannot be dealt with scientifically but only dialectically. And dialectical treatment necessarily begins from pre-scientific knowledge and takes it most seriously. Pre-scientific knowledge, or "common sense" knowledge, is thought to be discredited by Copernicus and the succeeding natural science. But the fact that what we may call telescopic-microscopic knowledge is very fruitful in certain areas does not entitle one to deny that there are things which can only be seen as what they are if they are seen with the unarmed eye; or, more precisely, if they are seen in the perspective of the citizen, as distinguished from the perspective of the scientific observer. If one denies this, one will repeat the experience of Gulliver with the nurse in Brobdingnag and become entangled in the kind of research projects by which he was amazed in Laputa.

(4) Positivism necessarily transforms itself into historicism. By virtue of its orientation by the model of natural science, social science is in danger of mistaking peculiarities of, say, mid-twentieth-century United States, or more generally of modern western society, for the essential character of human society. To avoid this danger, it is compelled to engage in "cross-cultural research," in the study of other cultures, both present and past. But in making this effort, it misses the meaning of those other cultures, because it interprets them through a conceptual scheme which originates in modern western society, which reflects that particular society, and which fits at best only that particular society. To avoid this danger, social science must attempt to understand those cultures as they understand or understood themselves: the understanding primarily required of the social scientist is historical understanding. Historical understanding becomes the basis of a truly empirical science of society. But if one considers the infinity of the task of historical understanding, one begins to wonder whether historical understanding does not take the place of the scientific study of society. Furthermore, social science is said to be a body of true propositions about social phenomena. The propositions are answers to questions. What valid answers, objectively valid answers, are, may be determined by the rules or principles of logic. But the questions depend on one's direction of interest, and hence on one's values, i.e., on subjective principles. Now it is the direction of interests, and not logic, which supplies the fundamental concepts. It is therefore

not possible to divorce from each other the subjective and objective elements of social science: the objective answers receive their meaning from the subjective questions. If one does not relapse into the decayed Platonism which is underlying the notion of timeless values, one must conceive of the values embodied in a given social science as dependent on the society to which the social science in question belongs, i.e., on history. Not only is social science superseded by historical studies; social science itself proves to be "historical." Reflection on social science as a historical phenomenon leads to the relativization of social science and ultimately of modern science generally. As a consequence, modern science comes to be viewed as one historically relative way of understanding things which is not in principle superior to alternative ways of understanding.

It is only at this point that we come face to face with the serious antagonist of political philosophy: historicism. After having reached its full growth historicism is distinguished from positivism by the following characteristics. (1) It abandons the distinction between facts and values, because every understanding, however theoretical, implies specific evaluations. (2) It denies the authoritative character of modern science, which appears as only one form among many of man's thinking orientation in the world. (3) It refuses to regard the historical process as fundamentally progressive, or, more generally stated, as reasonable. (4) It denies the relevance of the evolutionist thesis by contending that the evolution of man out of non-man cannot make intelligible man's humanity. Historicism rejects the question of the good society, that is to say, of *the* good society, because of the essentially historical character of society and of human thought: there is no essential necessity for raising the question of the good society; this question is not in principle coeval with man; its very possibility is the outcome of a mysterious dispensation of fate. The crucial issue concerns the status of those permanent characteristics of humanity, such as the distinction between the noble and the base, which are admitted by the thoughtful historicists: can these permanencies be used as criteria for distinguishing between good and bad dispensations of fate? The historicist answers this question in the negative. He looks down on the permanencies in question because of their objective, common, superficial and rudimentary character: to become relevant, they would have to be completed, and their completion is no longer common but historical. It was the contempt for these permanencies which permitted the most radical historicist in 1933[1] to submit to, or rather to welcome, as a dispensation of fate, the verdict of the least wise and least moderate part of his nation while it was in its least wise and least moderate mood, and at the same time to speak of wisdom and moderation. The biggest event of 1933 would rather seem to have proved, if such proof was necessary, that man cannot abandon the question of the good society, and that he cannot free himself from the responsibility for answering it by deferring to History or to any other power different from his own reason.

1. Ed. note: a reference to Paul von Hindenburg.

The Historical Approach

EDWARD HALLETT CARR

The birth of modern history was bound up with the belief that the path to knowledge is the discovery of certain laws and principles whose operation is exemplified in particular phenomena. This belief had its origin in the metaphysical rationalism of Descartes and the scientific rationalism of Newton. Its application to the processes of history began in France about 1750, when Montesquieu wrote in the preface to *L'Esprit des Lois:* "I have set forth the principles, I have seen particular cases conform to them as of their own accord, I have seen how the histories of all nations are nothing but their results." In the nineteenth century, belief became general in a principle of progress whose laws were exemplified in the events of history; the study of history was the key to an understanding of these laws. The laws of history were thus strictly analogous to the laws of science. After Darwin it was even thought that they were substantially the same laws: Darwin had proved that evolution proceeded through the struggle for existence, the elimination of the unfit and the survival of the fittest. It suddenly became obvious that these forces were also at work in the advance of mankind through history. Progress in history and progress in the natural world were different facets of the same process. As late as 1920 J. B. Bury, in the preface to his book *The Idea of Progress,* called progress "the animating and controlling idea of western civilization."

Intellectual fashions change rapidly (which proves that intellectuals are also human); and, in the thirty years since Bury wrote these words, theories of progress in history have disappeared as completely as last year's snows. They have been replaced by theories of a natural process of decay inherent in all mature civilizations and manifested by Western civilization at the present time. In 1918 Oswald Spengler published in Germany his massive work which was translated into English a few years later under the title *The Decline of the West.* In 1934 Professor Arnold Toynbee began his still unfinished *Study of History,* of which six volumes were published in the 1930's. Side by side with these, though resting on a different hypothesis, may be placed the view propounded by Professor Butterfield in his broadcast lectures on *Christianity and History* in 1949. This view also represents a reaction against the theory of progress and has pessimistic implications. Here we are at the heart of our subject—the fundamental character of the changes of the past 150 years out of which the new society of today is emerging; and in order to clear the ground I should like to begin by joining issue on certain points with these three writers whom I have chosen as the outstanding representatives of a large and miscellaneous school.

Spengler is the easiest; that is to say, he is always clear—perhaps clearer than any profound thinker has a right to be on so difficult a subject. Spengler believes in certain historical "organisms" called civilizations obeying laws of causation which he calls destiny and which infallibly determine their cause. Spengler's system is a powerful and consistent construction which cannot be refuted within the limit of its presuppositions. It can be rejected only by denying Spengler's initial belief in the existence of civilizations as objective entities, obeying fixed laws of development and decay. Since no important thinker, at any rate outside Germany, now accepts this belief, I need spend no more time on Spengler. But he deserves a place in the record as the first begetter of the fashionable current thesis of historical decadence.

From Spengler's heady, intoxicating, enervating brew one turns with relief to Toynbee's long, cool, sparkling drink of Spengler-and-splash. In *A Study of History* Toynbee takes over Spengler's general conclusions about the course of civilizations in general and of contemporary Western civilization in particular, but tries to reach them by less Germanic paths. He stems from the English empirical tradition, and refers to what he calls on one occasion "our trusty and well-beloved method of making an empirical survey." This presumably means that he seeks to establish the laws of behavior of civilizations by studying how they in fact behave; and this would be legitimate enough if he shared Spengler's view of civilizations as objective entities or organisms. But this view he explicitly abandons. For Toynbee, so far as can be judged from what he has published up to the present, civilizations are merely the name for bundles of phenomena which the historian finds it convenient to lump together; and a subjective definition of this kind, which would be perfectly satisfactory from my point of view, seems fatal to any attempt—such as I understand Toynbee to be making—to discover laws of behavior of civilizations. Spengler's conclusions follow logically from unsound premises. Toynbee's premises, however sound in themselves, fail to support either his main Spenglerian edifice or the sparkling cascade of historical generalizations which come so trippingly from his pen. My difference with Toynbee is that he regards history as repetitive, whereas I think of it as continuous. For him history consists of the same things happening over and over again with minor variations in different contexts; for me history is a procession of events about which almost the only thing that can be said with certainty is that it moves constantly on and never returns to the same place. And this difference naturally affects one's view of the lessons that history can teach.

The difference turns on fundamental conceptions of the nature of history. Toynbee's view, like Spengler's, rests on the analogy between history and science in which historical thought has been enmeshed for nearly two centuries. The analogy is false. In science the drama repeats itself over and over again because the *dramatis personae* are creatures unconscious of the past or inanimate objects. In history the drama cannot repeat itself because the *dramatis personae* at the second performance are already conscious of the prospective *dénouement;* the essential condition of the first performance can never be reconstituted. Between the two world wars a well-known military critic, having studied the conditions of land warfare between 1914 and 1918 and decided that these conditions still held, predicted that in the next war the defensive would once more triumph over the offensive. His objective reasoning may have been perfectly correct. But he omitted one factor. The German generals were determined not to repeat the unfortunate *dénouement* of 1918 at the second performance. They were thus enabled to introduce new elements into the chain of causation and to produce in 1940 directly opposite results to those predicted. Human consciousness of the past prevented history from repeating itself. Before the middle of the nineteenth century so-called bourgeois revolutions had put the middle class into power in most countries of western Europe. One result of this was a rapid expansion of the ruling middle class, and, as a result, an equally rapid expansion of the proletariat, so that Marx was emboldened to predict a proletarian revolution as the natural corollary of the bourgeois revolution. But, once this sequence of events had penetrated human consciousness, history could not repeat itself. The German middle class was by this time so frightened of the potential *dénouement* that it refused to perform the drama of the bourgeois revolution in Germany and preferred to come to terms with Bismarck. In history the presumption is not that the same thing will happen again, but that the same thing will not happen again. All analogies between history and science, all cyclical theories of history, are tainted with the fundamental error of neglecting human consciousness of the past. You cannot look forward intelligently into the future unless you also are prepared to look back attentively into the past. But this does not mean that you will find there either laws to obey or precedents to guide you. If I am deeply concerned [here] with the history of the last 150 years, this is not because I expect anything that happened then to happen again (this is the kind of lesson which history does not teach), but because history deals with a line or procession of events, half of which lies in the past and half in the future, and you cannot have an intelligent appreciation of one half unless you also concern yourself with the other half.

Butterfield has reacted just as strongly as Spengler and Toynbee from the doctrine of progress in history, and with more far-reaching results. Spengler and Toynbee take the doctrine of progress in the form in which it was held at the end of the nineteenth century, metaphysically in Germany, empirically in Britain, and turn it without much effort and without much fundamental change into a doctrine of decline. Butterfield jumps over the nineteenth century and the Age of the Enlightenment and lands us right back into providential history. (It seems to me fairer to call it the providential rather than the Christian view of history; for, just as most Christians today would not believe in the intervention of God to alter the courses of the stars, so many Christians would not believe in the intervention of God in the course of current history.) Butterfield is not unwilling, like Acton before him, to identify nineteenth-century progress with the hand of providence. But the present age appears to him rather as the age of judgment in history. "The hardest strokes of heaven in history," he writes, "fall on those who imagine that they can control things in a sovereign manner, as though they were kings of the earth playing providence not only for themselves, but for the far future"; and this goes not only for the Napoleons and the Hitlers but for makers of the League of Nations and such-like panacea-mongers who think to build a heaven on earth.

But on this I would venture two remarks. In the first place, I do not know why judgment in history, which fell so heavily on Napoleon and which has fallen so heavily on recent sinners, fell so lightly on those who committed similar sins between 1815 and 1914. Secondly, while these things cannot really be measured, I should have thought that the hardest stroke of all in recent history fell on the 6,000,000 or 8,000,000 Jews who were exterminated in the camps and in the gas-chambers; and, if I am told that this was not a stroke of judgment, but a case of unmerited suffering, then I find this conception of strokes of heaven in history still more difficult. It seems to me that belief in the intervention of providence in historical events is as hard to reconcile with serious history as belief in intervention in the movements of the stars would be with serious astronomy. History in the modern sense came into being precisely when belief in providential intervention was discarded.

This brings me to another red herring which both Toynbee and Butterfield seem to me to have dragged across the path. Both write eloquently on the theme of human wickedness. Butterfield is particularly anxious that nobody should think too well of human nature, and has some pertinent and penetrating comments on the admixture of evil in most seemingly good human actions. It would not occur to me to deny that human beings are often very wicked. Evil as well as good is of the stuff of almost everything that men do, and especially, perhaps, of everything that they do in their capacity as political animals. But this does not help us here. Our problem is to discover why, between 1815 and 1914, men succeeded in conducting their political affairs with a reasonable show of decency and without large-scale mutual destruction, and why, since 1914, hatred, intolerance, cruelty and mutual extermination have once more become the staple of political action over a large part of the world. It seems to me contrary to anything we know or anything that is plausible to suppose that individual men and women today are more wicked or specifically more cruel or more aggressive than they were a hundred years ago. If they are not, we must clearly look for some different explanation of what has happened in the last forty years. Let me use an illustration suggested by Marc Bloch's admirable but unfinished *Apologie pour l'histoire*. Scientists say that there can be no fire without oxygen in the air. When my house burns down, I shall call on Professors Toynbee and Butterfield to investigate the cause, and they will explain that the fire was due to the presence of oxygen in the air. The explanation will be cogent and correct, but will not satisfy the fire assessor. The attribution of recent calamities to human wickedness equally fails to satisfy the historian.

The views which I have so far discussed all postulate the existence of objective facts of history, broadly corresponding to the objective data of science. Even Butterfield, who knows that we all approach history with our own presuppositions, still speaks of "what can be established by concrete external evidence" and of "things which must be valid whether one

is a Jesuit or a Marxist." Such things do undoubtedly exist: the exact date
and place of William the Conqueror's landing in England, the number
and fire-power of the ships that fought at Trafalgar or at Jutland, the
statistics of population or industry or trade for a given country at a given
period. These things have the same relation to history as bricks or steel
or concrete have to architecture. They are facts which need to be established, tested and verified; the historian must not be caught out using
shoddy material. But they are not in themselves "facts of history." It is
only the decision of the historian to use them, the conviction of the historian that they are significant for his purpose, which makes them into
the "facts of history." That the Jesuit and the Marxist historian should
agree about certain facts is of small importance. What matters is their
agreement or disagreement on the question which facts are significant,
which facts are the "facts of history." "The facts of history," says the
American writer Carl Becker, "do not exist for any historian until he
creates them." His choice and arrangement of these facts, and the juxta-
positions of them which indicate his view of cause and effect, must be
dictated by presuppositions; and these presuppositions, whether he is
conscious of them or not, will be closely related to the conclusion which
he is seeking to establish. The Christian historian of the decline and fall
of the Roman Empire will select different facts, and arrange them in a
different way, from the historian who seeks to establish an equation
between barbarism and religion. The historian who believes in the primacy of the economic factor will isolate as significant a commercial or
financial transaction which, for another historian, may be as irrelevant
to history as a street accident. The notion that it is possible to determine
the nature of the historical process through a study of the "facts of history" is tainted with this unavoidable vice of circularity. The facts of
history come into being simultaneously with your diagnosis of the historical process and as an intrinsic part of it. They cannot precede it as
independent entities.

History is therefore a process of interaction between the historian
and the past of which he is writing. The facts help to mould the mind
of the historian. But the mind of the historian also, and just as essentially,
helps to mould the facts. History is a dialogue between past and present,
not between dead past and living present, but between living present and
a past which the historian makes live again by establishing its continuity
with the present; and, among recent writers on the subject, I find myself
most indebted to Collingwood, who has insisted most strongly on this
continuity and on this process of interaction. It is an old trouble that the
word "history," which by its derivation and in its proper use signifies the
enquiry conducted by the historian, should have been transferred by
popular usage to the material in which he works—the series of events
themselves; for this transferred usage encourages the fallacy that history
is something that exists outside the mind of the historian and independently of it. This popular usage has also encouraged confusion of thought
about the so-called "pattern" in history. Needless to say, I should reject
absolutely the conception once put forward by H. A. L. Fisher (and tacitly
held, I suspect, by some other modern historians) of a "patternless" his-

tory, that is to say of history as an inconsequential narration having no coherence and therefore no meaning for the present. But this does not commit me to the view of a pattern inherent in the events themselves—the view of Spengler and Toynbee; or of a pattern woven by an inscrutable providence—the view of Butterfield. For me the pattern in history is what is put there by the historian. History is itself the pattern into which the historian weaves his material; without pattern there can be no history. Pattern can only be the product of mind—the mind of the historian working on the events of the past.

The view that the pattern of history takes shape in the brain of the historian, and is fashioned not only by the events he is describing but also by the world in which he is living, is supported by an overwhelming weight of experience; and, although professional historians still sometimes put forward unguarded professions of objectivity, the "conditioned" character of all historical writing has now become almost a commonplace. Creators of historical systems are not exempt from this rule. The idea of progress which inspired nineteenth-century systems and the idea of cyclical movement and decline which inspires more recent systems have been transparently derived not so much from a dispassionate analysis of the past as from the emotional impact of the current situation. Even in detail those systems reflect the particular bias of those who construct them. Hegel found the culmination of the historical process in the Prussian State, Spencer in the free trade, free competition and free contract of mid-Victorian England. Spengler owed the immense popularity of his work to the occasion which it provided for his compatriots to treat the downfall of Germany in 1918 as an integral part of the predestined "decline of the west." The deepening pessimism about the future of Western civilization which marks successive volumes of Professor Toynbee's *Study of History* reflects the increasing solicitude of the 1930's about the weaknesses and failures of British policy. Articulate human groups share a natural human inclination to attach universal significance to their own experiences. The pattern is not inherent in the events themselves; it is imposed upon them out of the consciousness and experience of the historian. The pattern is, however, determined not so much by the historian's view of the present as by his view of the future. Past and future are the two essential time dimensions; the present is an infinitesimally small moving point on a continuous line consisting of past and future. It is thus the future prospect even more than the present reality which shapes the historian's view of the past. Macaulay and his nineteenth-century successors were influenced not so much by their satisfaction with what they saw around them as by their conviction that things would be even better in the future. Current theories of decline in history are prompted not so much by contemplation of our present difficulties as by the belief that things are going from bad to worse. It is the sense of direction which counts.

Moreover, this insistence on the future as the criterion of judgment on the past is perfectly logical. There is point in the story of the Chinese historian who, when asked what he thought about the French revolution, replied that no serious historian could yet be expected to have an opinion about so recent an event. Macaulay regarded the nineteenth century as a century of progress, Spengler and Toynbee as a century of decay. Even if we are content with a common-sense general view of progress and do not attempt a precise definition, we have today frankly no means of deciding which view is right. Will our posterity judge the nineteenth century as the beginning of a great new period of human achievement or as the beginning of the end of our civilization? We do not know what to think about the nineteenth century for the simple reason that the history of the twentieth century is still in the making. The historian of A.D. 2000 will be in a better case to pronounce judgment. But need we accept even his verdict—especially as it may easily be reversed by the historian of A.D. 2500? In modern times the shape of Roman history has changed almost from generation to generation. Gibbon found his hero in Marcus Aurelius, a philosopher-king. The age of the French revolution, which hated tyrants and liked rhetoric, saw in Cato and Brutus the pinnacles of Roman greatness; the later nineteenth century, which had discovered the survival of the fittest, preferred Caesar; a more recent epoch, keenly alive to the problems of planning and large-scale organization, has discerned the merits of Augustus. The question when the decline of Roman civilization began—quite apart from the more exciting question why—is still undecided by history. Two thousand years hence the final verdict on the nineteenth century may still be as uncertain as it is today. The historian is like an observer watching a moving procession from an aeroplane; since there is no constant or ascertainable relation between the speed, height and direction of the aircraft and the movement of the procession, changing and unfamiliar perspectives are juxtaposed in rapid succession, as in a cubist picture, none of them wholly false, none wholly true. Any static view of history purporting to be recorded from a fixed point by a stationary observer is fallacious.

Let me sum up, in the light of these reflections, what I mean by the historical approach and how I think it applicable to the problems which we have to face. History seeks to link the past with the future in a continuous line along which the historian himself is constantly moving. It is clear that we should not expect to extract from history any absolute judgments, either on the past or on the future. Such judgments it is not in its nature to give. All human judgment, like all human action, is involved in the logical dilemma of determinism and free will. The human being is indissolubly bound, in both his actions and his judgments, by a chain of causation reaching far back into the past; yet he has a qualified power to break the chain at a given point—the present—and so alter the future. In common-sense language, he can decide and judge for himself, but only up to a certain point; for the past limits and determines his decision and his judgment in innumerable ways. To admit that our judgments are wholly and irrevocably conditioned is to plead moral and intellectual bankruptcy. But to recognize the conditioned element in them is the best way to put us on our guard against too readily yielding to intellectual fashions—of which the nineteenth-century belief in progress and the twentieth-century belief in decadence are excellent examples.

The Origins of
the Behavioral Movement

DON R. BOWEN

In the two decades following World War II political science was racked by a fundamental conflict concerning its conceptual foundations. Much of the content and most of the procedures of the discipline were subjected to a searching, at times searing, criticism. The immediate cause of this controversy was the behavioral movement, whose members included alike those who perceived inadequacies in the substantive content and in the methods of inquiry of traditional political science. Today that controversy has largely dissipated. What was once a revolutionary approach to the study of political phenomena has been incorporated into the whole body of the discipline. Criticisms once received as daring or outrageous are now commonplace, even platitudinous. Political behavior is now treated as a subfield of inquiry within the general discipline.

The present harmony has many advantages, not the least of which is the end of intradisciplinary infighting. But it tends to obscure the distinctive contributions and pitfalls of the behavioral movement. This section includes, therefore, a short history of the genesis and development of the behavioral movement in the social sciences and its impact on political science. The intent is not to revive controversy but to study it, for an understanding of the behavioral movement is important as a foundation for the study of political behavior. With this background it will be possible to specify the impact the movement has had and to attach some coherence to the many forms of inquiry which today are labeled part of political behavior.

The behavioral movement in political science grew out of two, not unrelated, intellectual developments of the twentieth century; one in philosophy, the other in psychology. The second current was, and is, known as behavioral psychology, and the names associated with it primarily are those of the great Russian physiologist, Pavlov, and two American psychologists, John Watson[1] and B. F. Skinner. The central thread common to all three men is the development and employment of the stimulus-response model to explain behavior. Briefly, the model posits that the behavior of any organism can be adequately explained as a set of responses to prior stimuli. Therefore, by knowing the natural history of the organism in question (the total stimuli to which it has been subjected) it is possible to explain present and to predict future responses.

The implications of the model go far beyond its immediate applications, but in the hands of the behavioral psychologists it was directed

---

1. Watson himself was responsible for the term, "behaviorism." See his *Behaviorism* (New York: W. W. Norton & Company, Inc., 1925).

against two fronts. It first aimed at an older idealist tradition which sought to explain human behavior in terms of minds or souls; second, and more important, at the then recent Freudian psychology which sought an explanation of human behavior as a result of the interaction of ego, superego, and id. Despite vast differences, both the idealist and Freudian explanations have something in common. Both seek the causes of human behavior in non-observable constructs. Whether one works with souls or ids, one thing is certain—nobody ever observed either one of them.

Thus behavioral psychology turned away from the clinical problems and practices of Freudian psychopathology and stressed the observable stimuli which humans experience as the root causes of behavior. Being observable, stimuli can be classified, counted, correlated, and manipulated. They therefore have certain methodological advantages over that which cannot be observed. But Watson and his followers went much further. In the pursuit of what they perceived to be a truly scientific behavioral science they argued that only observable or "hard" data constituted admissible evidence. In their view one should disregard not only the constructs of other psychological explanations but any discourse whatsoever concerning such things as attitudes, values, preferences, or ideas. The basic message of behavioral psychology was a brute, hard-nosed empiricism.

The concurrent developments in philosophy have come collectively to be called "non-normative"—philosophy of science, theory of knowledge, linguistic analysis, and, above all, logical positivism. The central thread running through these developments in philosophy has been the separation of facts and values. The very title, "non-normative," conveys this notion exactly. The logical positivists argued that it was necessary to distinguish factual propositions (which are observable and objectively verifiable) from value propositions which indicate the subjective preferences of the speaker (and cannot therefore be objectively verified).

The distinction between facts on the one hand and values on the other can be traced back to David Hume who in the middle of the eighteenth century argued that it is impossible to derive a normative judgment from any set of judgments or statements which did not include that norm as a premise. For example, one cannot conclude that universal suffrage is good simply by knowing that in a given political system very nearly all citizens can and do vote. Hume would have said that by examining the effects of the suffrage it might be *judged* to be good. It might possibly give the citizens a sense of psychological well-being or it might make rulers responsive to citizen desires. Technically this position is known as naturalism because it holds that the value (in this case, goodness) is a property of the phenomena in question.

The positivist position, however, goes further than Hume. The modern position developed and sharpened by the non-normative philosophers holds that goodness or rectitude or whatever other value is in question cannot be shown to be a property of the phenomena at all without making further and equally untenable assumptions. To revert to the example above, universal suffrage cannot be judged good because it gives citizens a sense of well-being without further assuming that well-being is desirable. Obviously this thesis can be extended until the ethical naturalist is involved in an infinite regress. The positivist solution to this problem has been to view value judgments simply as the expression of the feelings of the individual making them. And while such statements may be a more or less accurate clue to the inner state of the speaker they can in no way be accepted as objective truth.

In the hands of the logical positivists then, ethical or normative propositions were reduced to individual preferences. As such, they are of course phenomena of the behavioral world. It may be a fact that a certain individual prefers a certain state of affairs. But this is cold comfort, for ethical propositions reduced to data lose their claim to universality and obligation which is the very essence of a normative proposition. The basis for the split between facts and values rested on the proposition that only statements which contained empirical referents had meaning. All other statements were "metaphysical," i.e., meaningless noise. Since normative statements are cast in the form that something ought to be the case (but not necessarily is) and because they involve, however minimally, a set of premises concerning what is right and good, they obviously contain components which have no empirical referents. Normative statements are therefore, according to the positivist view, "meaningless noise."[2]

Both of these powerful contemporary intellectual currents converged on political science. The messages which they conveyed reinforced each other. Scientific discourse was the only language in which meaningful communication was possible, and every symbol in this universe of discourse was meaningful precisely because each was unequivocally grounded in empirical fact. Hence, if political science was to deserve its name, a thorough purge was necessary. Traditional inquiry into the form and content of the "good life" was useless because the question posed was scientifically unanswerable. One man's social heaven is another's hell. Traditional categories of explanation had to be reformulated or cast aside because they were based on non-observable constructs. "Ghosts" was Arthur Bentley's contemptuous summation of the concepts of political science in his day (1908).[3]

Of course, the developments in philosophy and psychology were not the only influences working in the social sciences. Long before logical positivism grew out of the philosophies associated with the Vienna circle of the 1920's, the famous German sociologist Max Weber had formulated the distinction between facts and values and argued for a "value-free" social science. And long before John Watson had called for "hard" data, Lord Bryce had told the American Political Science Association, "Gentlemen, we must have facts, facts, facts."[4] The currents which culminated in the behavioral movement were abroad in the land and their antecedents extend far back into the intellectual history of the West. Be-

2. For a clear and forceful treatment of the fact-value dichotomy and its impact on political science, see Arnold Brecht, *Political Theory* (Princeton: Princeton University Press, 1957).

3. *The Process of Government* (Indianapolis: The Principia Press, 1963).

4. "Presidential Address," American Political Science Association Convention, 1909. *APSR*, Vol. III (1909).

havioral psychology and logical positivism represent the high water mark of these trends of thought but they are by no means the only sources.

The behavioral movement in political science became apparent after World War II. This is not to say that there were no behavioralists before that date. Almost anyone who has some knowledge of political behavior would point to the ground-breaking work of Arthur Bentley, Charles Merriam, George E. G. Catlin, Stuart Rice, and Harold Lasswell. It is only to note that the innovations these men had pressed did not become general ferment until after the second war. As the movement emerged it carried with it the signs of its intellectual paternity—a thoroughgoing commitment to empirical data as the only verifiable source of objective knowledge, and an even more thoroughgoing commitment to a reconstruction of the categories of explanation describing political phenomena.

Despite these commitments, however, political behavioralists have never restricted their scope of admissible evidence in the manner of the Watsonian psychologists. The major reason is probably simply convenience or laziness. To talk about politics in terms of "hard" data only is indeed difficult and most political scientists have never made the attempt. Most of what today is called "political behavior" continues to speak of motives, emotional states, goals, and calculations of political actors. Indeed, some of the most fruitful of all concepts in political science rest on the non-observable attitudes and psychic structures which cannot in any sense be called hard data. The "ghosts," then, have not been entirely exorcised.

In addition to convenience there are more fundamental theoretical reasons for the rejection of brute empiricism. Inquiry into the conceptual foundations of science has made it clear that a restriction of evidence to observable hard data is not only impossible, but disastrous. In the first place, "facts' 'have not the clear and unambiguous status that the empiricists assigned to them. For the most part, the empirical world strikes the sensory apparatus of the observer as a "blooming, buzzing confusion." It is inescapably necessary for the observer to select and order this factual universe in some kind of conceptual framework. As N.R. Hansen has put it, "there is more to seeing than meets the eyeball."[5] Facts take their place and their meaning only after they have been selected and organized—not before. Therefore one man's fact is another's fiction. Bhuddists, for example, do not "see" right angles and Western intimations that such angles are part of the warp and woof of reality may well strike the average Southeast Asian as more than a little impious.[6]

Even if agreement can be reached on what constitutes a fact there still arises the problem that there is potentially a whole universe of such facts and, since human attention can only be riveted on a very small section of that universe at any given time, one must somehow choose

5. Hansen, *Patterns of Discovery* (Cambridge: Cambridge University Press, 1961), p. 21.

6. F. S. C. Northrop has reduced the empiricists' argument to a virtual absurdity by examining closely the character and meaning of the concept of a fact. See his *Logic of the Sciences and Humanities* (New York: Meridian Books, 1959), especially pp. 40-49. The example given here is Northrop's.

what that section is to be. Perception, in short, is inescapably selective. This selection demands that observers should have some kind of criteria of relevance and, unfortunately, the empirical world does not tell us what facts are important or relevant to any given situation. Human observers abstract a small section of the factual world to concentrate upon and, as A. N. Whitehead has noted, therein "lies the possibility of error."[7] One must somehow select the piece of the universe to examine, and undue absorption in Aristotle, for example, may lead to regretfully erroneous criteria of relevance in heavy traffic.

In addition to the ambiguous status of the factual world, an even more formidable problem confronts those who seek to base all knowledge on "observables," for a very great number of highly fruitful scientific concepts are not, and never will be, observable. One thinks, for example, of electrons or neutrinos. Moreover, it can be shown that every mature science begins with a set of primitive axioms from which hypotheses are deduced which are then verified against empirical reality. This, of course, is a highly simplistic and rationalized description of a complex process. The point is, however, that verification by observation takes place at the end, not the beginning, of this process and that the primitive axioms of any conceptual scheme are only verified indirectly and only insofar as the hypotheses deduced from them are logically, but not necessarily empirically, required.

Finally it may be noted that so far as any science speaks in terms of laws which purport to hold universally, then this language, too, goes far beyond what is immediately observable. If a law or generalization is asserted to be universally true, then it is true in the future, and what lies in the future cannot, even in principle, be observable. In fact, as Hume long ago pointed out, if admissible evidence is restricted to observables than there can be no such thing as a causal law, or any kind of law for that matter.[8]

Any theory, whether in physics or political science, posits non-observable constructs. Otherwise it would not be a theory. The objection to Freudian psychoanalysis from a scientific standpoint is not that it employs concepts like ids or superegos which cannot be observed, but that the hypotheses derived from these concepts are sometimes used in such a manner that they cannot be disproved. Heuristically there is little difference between a subatomic particle and an oedipus complex. Both are non-observable constructs. From both, predictions are made about events which can be observed. But if the prediction does not bear out, the physicist is generally driven to conclude that his theory is at fault while some psychoanalysts, confronted with behavior which does not conform to the predicted oedipal pattern, are prone to exclaim, "Ah, but that just proves the point," and to rationalize the evidence as "really" meaning what they want it to mean.

There are, then, good and sufficient reasons for not following the trail of radical empiricism even though these reasons may have been

7. *Process and Reality* (New York: Harper & Row, Publishers, 1960).
8. *Treatise of Human Nature,* Book I, Sec. III.

dimly realized at the beginning. But if political behavioralists have not restricted themselves to observable facts, what then is the difference between the behavioral movement and the traditionalists? To answer this question it is necessary to examine the underlying commonalities which seem to characterize a vastly diverse set of inquiries, all of which go under the label "political behavior."

There seem to be at least four characteristics common to all behavioral inquiry. In the first place most behavioralists reject the institution as the basic unit of analysis in political science. This is most clearly evident when one examines the definitions of politics which have emerged from the hands of those who identify themselves with the behavioral movement. Politics has been variously defined as "the shaping and sharing of power,"[9] or "the authoritative allocation of values."[10] Each of these definitions—and most others—seek to preserve within political science formal institutions as objects of study but also to go beyond institutions and encompass other modes of behavior which seem political but are not generally included in the more traditional type of analysis.

The behavioral movement is itself divided as to whether the group or the individual political actor is the basic building block of political analysis, but it is at one on the proposition that the traditional study of "state" and "sovereignty" is an unnecessary, and misleading, restriction of the scope of political science. There are several reasons for this position. For one thing, the terms "state" and "sovereignty" are badly culture-bound. It can be shown that the origins of these concepts is intimately tied up with the rise of a centralized monarchy and a territorial national state in the West. In their recent discovery of the non-Western world, the social sciences generally, and political science particularly, have learned that there are numerous societies which have nothing remotely resembling a "sovereign." Hence a dilemma arises. Either one is forced to say these societies have no politics, or the definition of politics employed is inadequate. The behavioral movement argued the latter course.

Another compelling reason for a more inclusive definition of the term concerns the international arena. Clearly there is no institution or set of institutions which corresponds to the modern nation-state on the international scene. The United Nations, whatever else it may be, is certainly not a sovereign. Are we therefore to conclude that there is no international politics? Most political scientists would reject such a conclusion out of hand. Nevertheless, the traditional concepts have been, and remain, very influential. It is perhaps noteworthy that most American statesmen responsible for foreign affairs are trained as lawyers, which means that they learn firsthand the juridicial concept of the sovereign state as lawmaker (a concept stemming ultimately from Thomas Hobbes, but more immediately from the English legal thinker John Austin). Therefore, when speculating on an ideal solution to the world's political ills the best

9. Harold Lasswell and Abraham Kaplan, *Power and Society* (New Haven: Yale University Press, 1953).

10. David Easton, *The Political System* (New York: Alfred A. Knopf, Inc., 1953).

they can normally produce is to recommend a world government, usually one which closely parallels the United States Constitution. That cooperative and beneficial political interaction is even possible without benefit of a world sovereign is a perception which apparently escapes them.

A final major reason for the rejection of institutions as the basic unit of analysis is that strictly speaking some of the most interesting phenomena with which political scientists deal cannot be classified as institutions. Interest groups and political parties, for example, are not part of the formal institutions of government, although it can certainly be persuasively argued that they have become institutionalized over time. Similarly, such areas of inquiry as public opinion or political socialization have little to do with formal institutions. Yet both constitute part of the relevant social environment in which these institutions perform. Attitudes and underlying dimensions of human personality systems both condition and are conditioned by the more overt acts of government.

Most political behavioralists argue, then, that there is more to governing than government. They disagree on where to draw the line. Some, like Harold Lasswell, would apparently argue that any act which involves the use of power is a political act and therefore is properly defined as part of the province of political science. Presumably this would include the uses of power in even the smallest, most informal groups. Others, like David Easton, would restrict the scope of political science to those issues whose resolution is regarded as authoritative for the whole society and reserve the term "parapolitical" for the phenomena popularly known as "office politics" or "faculty politics." But both are in agreement that the older understanding of politics as the study of state and law is inadequate.

The controversy over the "boundaries" of political science is highly relevant to a second underlying characteristic of the behavioral movement in general; namely, a belief in the unity of the social sciences. Historically, the split between sociology, economics, political science, psychology, and history was relatively recent. For Thomas Hobbes all of what we now term the social sciences were unified in moral philosophy. But without pursuing the reasons for this division it is possible to specify why the behavioral movement argued their essential unity. They all have a common subject matter—human behavior. Very likely the proliferation of knowledge has made the current division of labor among the social sciences impossible to eliminate, even if it were thought desirable. Doubtless we shall have no more moral philosophers in Hobbes's sense of the word. But the behavioralists argue that the divisions among the social sciences are matters of analytic and practical convenience only. They are not, as it were, an eternal configuration of social reality.

The boundary lines among the social sciences are based on the concept of a role. Individuals may play many different roles, such as parent, consumer, or voter. The business of the political scientist is to study that segment of total human behavior which constitutes a *political* role. To be sure, a person's self-conception of that role, or his actions in an altogether different role such as producer, vitally affect the way he plays his political role; but for the political scientist these considerations, although important, are secondary. While a psychologist may be predominantly interested in self-conceptions of one's role in life, including political life, the political scientist is predominantly interested in the political role itself. The controversy over the boundaries of political science is relevant here because some political scientists have charged that too great an enlargement of the definition of a political role has expanded political science into the legitimate and necessary concerns of other social sciences.

The most important point to stress is the general agreement among all the social sciences that these role divisions, and the boundaries among the social sciences which flow from them, are analytic distinctions only. Human behavior is in a sense a seamless web. Few if any parents, for example, as they go about the business of rearing children in a family, stop to consider that the patterns of authority or the decision rules which they teach are part of a political role. More to the point, the role of parent and the role of agent of political socialization are bound together in a complex and indivisible set of actions. If one empirically attempted to separate these roles it would probably destroy the efficacy of both. Sociology, psychology, and political science do separate them but only for their own convenience and only at the level of abstract analysis.

The realization that every human act is intricately bound up with every other act in the life history of an individual is the basis for arguing the unity of the social sciences. Theoretically this implies that in order to understand a political act the political scientist should know how all of the other social roles an individual plays affect his political role. Practically speaking, what this belief has led to is the borrowing by political scientists of models and research techniques from other social scientists. Much has been done, for example, with models borrowed from economics such as game theory or exchange. A whole series of subdisciplines such as political psychology, political sociology, or political anthropology, have grown up at the points where the boundaries between these sciences break down and adequate explanation seems to demand a fusion of skills and resources of both. On a more mundane level, research into such things as political attitudes has relied heavily on techniques of interviewing, scaling, and questionnaire design first developed in other social sciences.

The behavioral movement in political science has been in large part the impetus for these developments. The belief in the unity of the subject matter of the social sciences has led to an immense cross-fertilization of theories and techniques. In good part, political science has been the beneficiary, not the source, of these trends. Perhaps this is a measure of the fact that the complex of outlooks which is here called "the behavioral movement" came later in time to political science than to almost any other social science. The unabashed borrowing from other disciplines by political scientists has not, however, been confined exclusively to the social sciences. Of late, mathematics has been the target of an envious eye.

The third general characteristic of the behavioral movement is its advocacy of the development and utilization of more precise techniques of observing, classifying, and measuring data and the employment of the most sophisticated available means of mathematical analysis. As one observer has pointed out, probably the most outstanding immediate characteristic of the work of the political behavioralists is that their writings are studded with charts, tables, formulae, and mathematical symbols. And it is probably safe to say that few things exasperate the critics of the behavioral movement more than their tendency to employ mathematical notation for that which "could be more easily and simply described in ordinary language."

Behavioralists would reply that the reason for the employment of jargon and beyond that of mathematical notation is that the ordinary language of politics is fraught with ambiguities. For the politician this may be a very great boon, but for the political scientist it is an insuperable block to clarity of thought and communication. For example, in the United States the language of politics is English. Spoken English also happens to be the language of a great and venerable poetic tradition. In part it is a rich poetic heritage because of the rich associative levels of meaning possible in the language. Any single word may be invested with literally hundreds of different symbolic contents. This makes for great poetry but for poor social science. Clarity, not ambiguity, is the goal of a science.

In addition, English and all other Western languages are subject-predicate languages. This is, in fact, the definition of a complete sentence. But the structure of language reflects the structure of thought; and the subject-predicate sentence structure is tied in with the philosophic view that phenomena are composed of essences, which are the given constituents of reality, and their attributes, which may be accidental or necessary. Thus the sentence, "Grass is green," implies that there is a thing called "grass," which has an attribute (adjective) "green," and that this combination is really given in the empirical world.

Needless to say, modern science left this view behind some time ago. The philosophic point about subatomic particles, for example, is that they have no essence which is stable over all time. They may be interpreted as either wave or particle phenomena depending on the context of the observation. Similarly, one cannot meaningfully describe an N-dimensional space-time continuum in ordinary language because the language is too hopelessly Euclidean in its assumptions. Likewise in social science, the reason for the employment of a difficult and obscure jargon and of mathematical notation is that the ordinary language describing human interaction is fraught with too many additional meanings, and carries with it philosophic assumptions to which the social scientist is not necessarily committed.

Beyond the invention and use of new ways of symbolizing political phenomena, there lies an even more significant development in the utilization of mathematical techniques. The political behavioralists have discovered that much, if not all, of the content of political science can be subjected to various sorts of statistical analyses. Most of this work has been extremely simple from a mathematical point of view. Usually it has been the discovery of simple correlations between variables which are unlikely to have occurred by chance. An example would be the correlation between formal education and political participation or between economic development and governmental stability.

Most important, the acceptance of these techniques implies a change in the thinking of political scientists. In the first place, political scientists have come to realize as never before the absolute necessity of classification schemes which are stable and unambiguous. At bottom, classification means simply differentiating one thing from another, but it is a prelude to any sort of analysis. And adequate schemes of classification for political phenomena are sometimes very hard to come by. One thinks, for example, of the difficulty of separating democratic, semi-democratic, and non-democratic governments.

Related to this has been the introduction of the idea of a scale or a continuum. Mathematical language, unlike the subject-predicate of ordinary language, allows political scientists to speak of degrees of political phenomena. If, for example, it could be specified exactly what was meant by "sovereignty," then an appropriate scale of "more or less sovereign" could be constructed. Such a notion would have been unthinkable to a scholarly tradition raised to search for the essence of a state in its sovereignty. It may be that sovereignty, like pregnancy, has a threshold level. Possibly a government cannot be just a little bit sovereign. But the demonstration of that proposition could only be made after the notions of scaling and ranking are generally accepted.

There are, of course, different sorts of scales corresponding to the level of measurement which is possible with the kind of data one has on hand. The example given above would probably be an ordinal scale in which one attempts to show simply that one government is more or less sovereign than others. If sovereignty were defined in certain ways, it might be possible to rise to a more demanding level of measurement such as an interval scale in which governments would be ranked and we would know the exact number of units of sovereignty between each two or more. If our definition of sovereignty were such that there was a zero point (no sovereignty at all) it would be possible to construct a ratio scale whereby a given government could not only be ranked and the distance between it and another government specified, but it would also become possible to note that the first government is, say, one-half as sovereign as the second.

The changes in the level of measurement employed are all dependent on how the term sovereignty is operationally defined. This concern with operational definitions has been another development of the behavioral movement. Briefly, such a definition is simply the specification of the procedures or operations that are employed to describe a certain phenomena. If sovereignty were defined as economic self-sufficiency, then no nation in the world could be described as completely sovereign, but it would be possible to attain at least an interval scale of sovereignty by examining, for example, the ratio of imports to total consumption. The point stressed by the behavioral movement, however, is that definitions are specifications of how something is measured, they are not specifications of its essence.

It is from this latter viewpoint that the behavioralists also approach the problem of quantitative and qualitative judgments. It has very often been argued that political science contains an area of "qualitative" judgments unsusceptible to measurement and other "quantitative" techniques. For example, the judgment as to whether a certain political system is or is not democratic is often asserted to be of a "qualitative" nature. Strictly speaking, this problem turns on the operational definition of democracy. If a set of political systems can be located which contain a characteristic called "democratic," and if this set is exhaustive (contains all systems that have it) and exclusive (excludes all systems that don't have it), then our qualitative judgment turns out to be a simple nominal scale composed of two categories, democratic and non-democratic political systems. By counting the number of cases in each we may be able to turn this into an ordinal scale with the observation that there are "more" or "less" democratic than non-democratic systems. Similarly, by carefully defining in advance what is meant, one can make nominal and ordinal scale statements such as x country is more socialist than y, or policy A is more conservative than policy B. On analysis it turns out that most "qualitative" statements are those which do not legitimately lend themselves to measurement above the ordinal level. To be sure, this is an important limitation on the mathematical analysis of political data since many very sophisticated techniques normally require at least an interval scale level of measurement. But it decidedly does not mean that all of political analysis is divided into two utterly distinct realms of "qualitative" and "quantitative" judgments which never meet in this world.

The fourth common thread running through the various phases of the behavioral movement has been the definition of the goal of political science as the construction of a systematic empirical theory of politics. In part this goal arises from a paradox. Despite the empiricist origins of the behavioral movement, one of the charges made by the behavioralists against their more traditional colleagues was that their epistemology was too grossly and naively empirical. Traditional political science, like any other sort of scholarly discipline, employed data or facts to support its analyses. And it assumed that the facts open to observation were real, clear, and unambiguous. But as indicated earlier . . . that is not necessarily or even usually the case. A fact is a complex, complicated construct. A fact, in Hansen's happy phrase, is "a theory-loaded concept."[11]

The instant the ancient distinction between facts and theory breaks down it becomes necessary to build what Robert Dahl has called an "empirical theory."[12] In essence, empirical theory is a science of what constitutes reliable knowledge. In political science this development has meant that the data available for analysis have come under increasingly sharp scrutiny. Ideally, the theory should specify criteria of relevance in such a manner that the facts selected and those excluded are clear to all; it should specify canons of acceptability in such a way that the hypothesis in question can be rejected; and it should define research procedures

11. Hansen, *op. cit.*, p. 19.
12. *Modern Political Analysis* (Englewood Cliffs, N.J.: Prentice-Hall, Inc., 1963).

which are stable throughout the whole course of the inquiry at hand. These standards are perhaps rarely met in practice but there is an increasing realization in political science that inquiry undertaken independent of them cannot, in the nature of things, yield reliable generalizations.

A systematic empirical theory of politics has meant, on the one hand, a critique of the traditional methods of gathering and analyzing information. On the other hand, empirical theory has been used as a term of distinction—a way to separate the kinds of theory in which behavioralists are interested from the traditional study of political philosophy. Traditional political philosophy had two primary components. The first, and by far the most extensively pursued, was the study of the history of past thought. This, of course, is not truly theory but a branch of intellectual history.[13] The second component was inquiry into the form and conditions of the good or proper political order.

It is with traditional political philosophy in this latter form that the behavioral movement has effected its most visible break. The behavioralists maintain that there is a clear and realizable distinction between judgments of fact and judgments of value. They have thus remained true to the origins of the behavioral movement in the philosophy of the logical positivists and the behavioral psychology of John Watson. The *empirical* side of theory is a way of emphasizing that the conceptual scheme being employed concerns itself only with the type of judgment which is objective—that which can in principle be agreed to by all men. Empirical theory seeks to formulate theoretical structures that relate observable phenomena in a meaningful fashion. In the physical sciences this is the sum total of inquiry; there is nothing further to be done when one has reached this happy stage.

Many political behavioralists have argued that political science must also end at this point. Value judgments, which go beyond the realm of objectivity, and therefore cannot be tested by criteria open to all, are not the proper concern of a political science. This position is perhaps not as restrictive as it appears. It does not mean that political scientists are prohibited from inquiry concerning the origin, meaning, consistency, and distribution of values or preferences. Indeed, some of the most fruitful data with which political science deals concern the distribution of value positions within a given population and the correlation of these value positions with other aspects of political behavior. What the position does say is that inquiry into the validity of the values in question cannot be pursued because of the absence of universal standards to judge them.

The systematic part of the goal of building a systematic empirical theory has been the search for a single or at least a small number of overarching theories which are able to account for most of the known phenomena of politics. Theories of this fruitfulness and economy occur more frequently in the natural sciences; e.g., relativity theory in physics.

---

13. I do not mean to downgrade the study of the history of political thought. Indeed, it is an indispensable requisite for the student of theory. My only point is that it is not theory, per se.

No theory that achieves this goal has as yet been formulated in political science although there are a number—such as systems theory, group theory, and game theory—which do order and explain a great deal of political phenomena. The difficulty thus far seems to be that none of these are logically or empirically cohesive enough that their value can either be proved or disproved by a small number of key observations or experiments. Yet there can be little doubt that among the greatest effects of the behavioral movement has been the stimulation of the search for grand theory.

At the opening of this [selection] it was noted that intellectual warfare between the behavioralists and the traditionalists has, for the most part, ceased. Each school has generally come to accept the approaches, training, and biases of the other, and each has generally profited from it. But this harmony obscures the fundamental changes in outlook which the behavioral movement effected in the whole of political science. Outwardly, this is most apparent in the techniques of research and inquiry. The employment of models borrowed from other disciplines, the use of statistical analyses, the growing number of computer studies are all signs of changes in techniques for understanding and describing the political process.

But in political science, as in any other areas of inquiry, there is an intimate link between theory and method. These new techniques of research reflect not just an increasing technical competence but a fundamental rethinking of the conceptual foundations of the field. The behavioral movement forced a change in the definition of politics and in the criteria of relevant and reliable knowledge about politics. Once this change had been accepted, the invention of new techniques of inquiry necessarily followed. This change did not, of course, take place in political science alone. It was part of a much broader movement in the intellectual history of the West and its impact was felt in many directions. And, as in political science, new ways of gathering knowledge were preceded by a new understanding of what constituted knowledge.

Sense and Non-Sense in Politics

MARVIN SURKIN

I take my cue for the title of this chapter from Merleau-Ponty, the French phenomenologist, who wrote in 1948 that "the political experiences of the past thirty years oblige us to evoke the background of non-sense against which every universal undertaking is silhouetted and by which it is threatened with failure."[1] Merleau-Ponty refers to the experience of that generation of intellectuals for whom Marxism was a "mistaken hope" because it lost "confidence in its own daring when it was successful in only one country."[2] But this criticism is equally relevant for a new generation of intellectuals in America who have witnessed the ideals of liberalism become little more than a superrational mystique for the Cold War, a counterrevolutionary reflex in the third world, and a narrow-range policy of social welfare at home. Merleau-Ponty argues that Marxism "abandoned its own proletarian methods and resumed the classical ones of history: hierarchy, obedience, myth, inequality, diplomacy, and police."[3] Today intellectuals in America are making the same critique with equal fervor about their own lost illusions.

As we search for new ways to comprehend the social realities of American life and new modes of social thought and political action to reconstruct "the American dream," Merleau-Ponty's notion of sense and non-sense is useful in determining the historical relationship between ideologies and practice, between thought and action, between man and the world he creates. The dialectic of sense and non-sense dramatizes that recurrent fact in history whereby reason parades as unreason, where even "the highest form of reason borders on unreason."[4] We must learn from recent history that "the experience of unreason cannot simply be forgotten";[5] that the most noble claims to universal truth, the most rational modes of philosophical or social inquiry, the most convincing declarations of political leaders are all contingent, and should be subject to revision and open to criticism and change. Marx and Kierkegaard, it should be recalled, shared in their revolt against Hegel's "Reason" insofar as the latter claimed to have attained through reason that universal truth in which history realizes itself, the real becomes rational, and the rational becomes real. The significance of this revolt against Hegelian rationalism is not its renunciation of reason itself, but rather the extent to which in Hegel's philosophical system reason is exalted and sanctified over and against the historical, human, and irrational in history.

Our primary task is therefore twofold: to recognize the historical linkage between the present social forces of reason and unreason, sense and nonsense; and unmask the guise by which the most prevalent modes of thought, their institutional expression, and their ideologies keep us from grasping their real social meaning.

My purpose in this essay is to show that the rigorous adherence to social science methodology adopted from the natural sciences and its claim to objectivity and value neutrality function as a guise for what is in fact becoming an increasingly ideological, nonobjective role for social science knowledge in the service of the dominant institutions in American society. And further, I will attempt to support the claim that the pre-

1. Maurice Merleau-Ponty, *Sense and Non-sense* (Evanston: Northwestern University Press, 1964) , p. 4.
2. *Ibid.*
3. *Ibid.*
4. *Ibid.*
5. *Ibid.*, p. 5.

vailing modes of inquiry in the social sciences in no way counter these recent developments in the uses of knowledge, but rather tend to reinforce them, that is, reinforce their "irrational" or, in this context, ideological uses. Moreover, I will examine what Noam Chomsky has called the double myth of the social sciences: the myth of political benevolence and the myth of scientific omniscience;[6] the view, in other words, that since we have arrived at the end of ideology, knowledge and technology are free—neutral or nonideological—to serve the interests and powers of the "benevolent" American state and corporate elite both at home and abroad.

Finally, I will outline an alternative methodology for the social sciences based on existential phenomenology the theoretical foundations of which are consistent with the position that for a social scientist to be empirical is not to assume that he must be value-free or nonideological. In fact, existential phenomenology is well suited to the view that an empirical analysis of reality is not only a way of understanding the social world, but that it is also a way of criticizing society and of changing it as well. For when one ruminates in the realm of ideas, questions of ideology or social goals need not arise, even though they may be applicable; but in the world of social reality in which ideas are always related to institutions and social practice, questions of the social use of knowledge and ideology cannot be avoided. In short, while this chapter deals with methodology in the social sciences, its primary concern is with ideology.

THE NEW ROLE OF THE SOCIAL SCIENCES

In recent years, the burgeoning critique of behavioralism has put forward the claims that its proponents are guilty of "implicit and unrecognized conservative values," "fearful of popular democracy," and tend to "avoid political issues" in their research.[7] It is argued, therefore, that the study of power as the observable exercise of power is conservative because it fails to consider the nonobservable, non-decision-making process; that to assume that elites are the guardians of liberal democratic values and succeed in satisfying most demands made on the American polity is to demonstrate a fear of popular democracy, especially when this view is coupled with the presumption that the masses tend to be undemocratic; and that the increasing trend to build mathematical models based on the criteria of the physical sciences abstracts political science from political reality and renders such research pseudo-political or apolitical by reducing it to a sophisticated numerology.

To the contrary, however, in a recent countercritique, Bert Rockman has developed the view that these troubles of social science methodology are due to the shortcomings of the researcher, his failure to understand the role his ideology plays in his research, and the limitations of the

6. Noam Chomsky, *American Power and the New Mandarins* (New York: Pantheon Books, 1969).
7. See Charles McCoy and John Playford, eds., *Apolitical Politics: A Critique of Behavioralism* (New York: Thomas Y. Crowell, 1967).

present level of knowledge; but not to the methodology itself.[8] Although this view is in many ways persuasive, it does not fully contend with the critique since it is obvious that one must judge social science on the basis of what it *knows* and what it *does*, not on the basis of what it *ought* to know or what it *ought* to do. For, to the extent that knowledge, including methods of inquiry and techniques of data collection, is socially determined, the social scientist's assertion of the purity of his methodology, "the quality of (his) operationalizations," his "resourceful utilization of technique," or the high moral virtue of his ideological biases are in themselves insufficient grounds for judging the results of empirical research. Bert Rockman's view, for example, is that "the only real issue is how well we are able to operationalize," which "is dependent upon what we define as reality."[9] But the point is that what we define as reality is also dependent on preconceived knowledge, and that the validity or relevance of methods of inquiry and the utilization of technique are also implicated in the social determination of knowledge. Therefore, the limitations of behavioral methodology are to be found even in Rockman's convincing paper because while on the one hand he puts forward a view, with which I fully agree,[10] that "our 'science' will consist of developing interpretations of the political universe, based partly on data and partly on ideology"; on the other, he concludes that "the data should enable us to test for the invalidity of clearly defined propositions on their own terms."[11] The latter point is questioned by even some positivists, who, like Moritz Schlick, assert that there is an important distinction between verified knowledge and verifiable knowledge. The former is subject to tests for validity or invalidity; but the latter, according to Schlick, cannot be verified here and now. For example in order to prove the proposition that God exists one must wait and see. This suggests that at least there are classes of knowledge for which the data will not enable us to test for validity or invalidity merely on the basis of clearly defined propositions taken on their own terms. Does social knowledge not fall into this class of knowledge? Moreover, there is no reason to conclude that because we have clearly defined propositions, they will necessarily be consistent with socially defined knowledge or socially acquired street knowledge. The point was well made by Murray Kempton, who recently noted:

I think there is a change now in our view of life; we know more than we ever knew before, but we know it instinctively, and not from the sources of public information we get. What do we know, exactly? We know now that Walt Whitman Rostow is a fool. We know that Dean Rusk is a clerk. We know that Mr. Nixon is not really very much worse than the people who preceded him (which

8. Bert Rockman, "A 'Behavioral' Evaluation of the Critique of Behavioralism" (Presented for the Caucus for a New Political Science, American Political Science Convention, September 1969).

9. *Ibid.*, p. 40.

10. Though I agree, I am not at all sure how one goes about determining the point at which science begins and ideology leaves off.

11. Rockman, *op. cit.*, p. 41.

is a sufficient judgement on them), and so on. We know all these things not because anyone told us but because events have explained them to us. And it is this explanation that people are looking for.[12]

To criticize social science methodology and its criteria of verification, operationalization, or objectivity is not to denigrate the relevance of scientific inquiry. It is rather to analyze the social and political nature of this methodology, and to see the extent to which knowledge is socially determined, the extent to which social forces decide *what* knowledge is relevant and *how* (and for what purposes) it is to be used. I will attempt to delineate three methodological approaches to social science with a view toward analyzing the linkage between scientific method and ideology or the ideological implications of research. These are (1) The New Mandarin; (2) The Public Advocate; (3) The Persuasive Neutralist.

The New Mandarin is best characterized by Ithiel de Sola Pool whose view it is that the social sciences should be devoted to the service of the mandarins of the future because psychology, sociology, systems analysis, and political science provide the knowledge by which "men of power are humanized and civilized." In order to keep the actions of the men of power from being "brutal, stupid, bureaucratic, they need a way of perceiving the consequences of what they do."[13] To perceive the consequences of public policy, that is, to describe the facts, is the primary contribution of the empirical social sciences to the uses of American power. As an example of this approach, Pool informs us of what we have learned in the past thirty years of intensive empirical study of contemporary societies by formulating the central issues of order and reform in this way:

In the Congo, in Vietnam, in the Dominican Republic, it is clear that order depends on somehow compelling newly mobilized strata to return to a measure of passivity and defeatism from which they have been recently aroused by the process of modernization. At least temporarily, the maintenance of order requires a lowering of newly acquired aspirations and levels of political activity.[14]

The meaning of this analysis for American policy is clearly in accord with counterrevolutionary American policies such as recent pacification programs, counterinsurgency and the like. But the social scientist denies that this sort of analysis is ideological, claiming instead that these studies conform to the scholarly, objective rigor of his discipline.

This is sheer non-sense. Take for example the following proposition by Professor Pool on "restructuring" government as an "empirical" formulation: "I rule out of consideration here a large range of viable political settlements" for restructuring government in South Vietnam, namely, those that involve "the inclusion of the Viet Cong in a coalition govern-

12. David Gelman and Beverly Kempton, "The Trouble with Newspapers: An Interview with Murray Kempton," *The Washington Monthly*, 1, no. 3 (April 1969) : 26.

13. Ithiel de Sola Pool, "The Necessity for Social Scientists Doing Research for Governments," *Background*, 10 (August 1966) : 111.

14. Cited in Chomsky, *op. cit.*, p. 36, *ibid.*, p. 49.

ment or even the persistence of the Viet Cong as a legal organization in South Vietnam." Such arrangements "are not acceptable" since the only acceptable settlement is one "imposed by the GVN despite the persisting great political power of the Viet Cong."[15] While it may argued, as Pool puts it, that "the only hope for humane government in the future is through the extensive use of the social sciences by government,"[16] the precise ideological nature of this new role, all claims of objectivity to the contrary, is not to be denied. In effect, intellectual detachment and the disinterested quest for truth—the professed essence of the value-free, neutral social scientist—are replaced by the new elite role of the masters of knowledge[17] whose knowledge is placed at the disposal of the "benevolent" political interests of the masters of power. Accordingly, social scientists become, in essence, "house-ideologues for those in power."[18]

The Public Advocate appears to be a more selfless servant of the people who is concerned primarily with reforming public policy to better the lot of the poor, disfranchised, or underdeveloped. His professed mission is to serve the public good rather than the government or the corporation. In response to the plight of the poor and black in America, Daniel P. Moynihan adopts the stance of the Public Advocate. He decries the failures of the War on Poverty to contend with the "problem."[19] His view is that the problem of poverty cannot be solved either by discouraging the rigorous inquiry into the social process that keeps men in poverty (or leads them out of it), or by falling back on the guilt complex of the white society which concludes that "white racism is essentially responsible for the explosive mixture which has been accumulating in our cities since the end of World War II."[20] Rather, for Moynihan, "American social science can do better, and so it ought."[21] This requires commitment on the part of the social scientist—the War on Poverty was such a commitment—and an honorable desire to be helpful. Therefore, even though there were many failures in the War on Poverty program, the commitment by social scientists and the government for which they worked was made, and "that commitment stands, and intellectuals, having played a major role in its establishment, now have a special responsibility both for keeping it alive and for keeping it on the proper track."[22]

The Public Advocate uses his social science knowledge to influence public policy, but he is not, so it is claimed, the servant of government since his primary objective is "to get public policy to react to unmet

15. Cited in *ibid.*, p. 49.

16. Pool, *op. cit.*

17. Daniel Bell, "Notes on the Post-Industrial Society: Part I," *The Public Interest*, No. 6 (1967): 24-35.

18. Zbigniew Brzezinski, "America in the Technetronic Age," *Encounter*, 30 (January 1968) : 16-26.

19. Daniel P. Moynihan, *Maximum Feasible Misunderstanding* (New York: Free Press, 1969) .

20. Daniel P. Moynihan, "The Professors and the Poor," *Commentary*, 46, no. 2 (August 1968) : 28.

21. *Ibid.*

22. *Ibid.*

social demands. . . ."[23] However, the research design, the questions posed, and the general framework of the analysis are all circumscribed by the Public Advocate's desire to do something *for* the poor and black people insofar as that "something" is possible within the known or assumed limits of the existing institutions. For the Public Advocate, "simply to blame the system is . . . obscurantism"[24] and best left out of consideration. He prefers to limit his research to influencing policy within the system—to make the system work better. The Public Advocate assumes, therefore, the values of the system and its operationality as given; he does not question it. Whatever the case may be, he has obviously not arrived at this analysis by empirical, objective, or neutral investigation.

In the Moynihan Report on the Negro family, "doing something for these people" was described in a special research report for the internal use of the government. The report revealed a pattern of instability in the Negro family structure which represented a "tangle of pathology . . . capable of perpetuating itself without assistance from the white world."[25] In addition, Moynihan adduced evidence to show that illegitimacy, crime and juvenile delinquency, drop-out rates and unemployment were "causally" connected to family structure.[26] The social scientist has here uncovered a case of deviant social pathology, the cure for which is to change the deviants, not the system. Christopher Jencks criticizes Moynihan's conservative analysis because "the guiding assumption is that social pathology is caused less by basic defects in the social system than by defects in particular individuals and groups which prevent their adjusting to the system."[27]

The major concern of the Public Advocate is not knowledge in itself but the policy relevance of his research findings. When he writes "a polemic which makes use of social science techniques and findings to convince others," it should be clear that he expects that "the social science data he could bring to bear would have a persuasive effect."[28] Therefore, the scholarly or "scientific" quality of his research or its political relevance for those whom he wants to help would seem to be of only secondary importance. The Public Advocate is committed primarily to advocating ways by which the existing social institutions can be made to function better. However broad a range of research or policy this may include, it is nonetheless limited to the established parameters of the system, and thus it appears that the Public Advocate always tends to tell the govern-

---

23. Lee Rainwater and William Yancey, eds., *The Moynihan Report and the Politics of Controversy* (Cambridge: M.I.T. Press, 1967) , p. 24.
24. Moynihan, *op. cit.,* p. 28.
25. *Ibid.,* p. 42.
26. In a perceptive article, William Ryan criticizes the Moynihan Report for drawing inexact conclusions from weak and insufficient data; encouraging a new form of subtle racism which he calls "Savage Discovery," i.e., the belief that it is the weakness and defects of the Negro himself that account for the present status of inequality between Negro and white; and for interpreting statistical relationships in cause-and-effect terms. See "Savage Discovery: The Moynihan Report," in *ibid.,* p. 458.
27. "The Moynihan Report," in *ibid.,* p. 443.
28. *Ibid.*

ment what it wants to hear, i.e., to constantly reinforce existing myths and ideologies or create "a new set of myths to justify the *status quo*."[29] In no way does this qualify the Public Advocate as an objective or value-free social scientist.

The only remaining question is whether and to what extent this sort of policy science is defined by and serves the interests of governmental agencies at the expense of the public. Herein lies the background of nonsense characterized by the Public Advocate's desire to do something *for* those poor, black people while knowing that in a very real sense his commitments are elsewhere. Julius Lester has correctly perceived the social and political function of the Public Advocate when he says, "Bang! Bang! Mr. Moynihan," because

somehow . . . nothing is true for a white man until a white man says it. Let the black say the same thing, and it will not be heard, or, if heard, ignored. Let a white man say it, and it becomes truth. It should be obvious why it will be the Moynihans we go after first rather than the southern sheriff.[30]

On the surface, the case of the *Persuasive Neutralist* seems to be altogether different from the first two types, for while the New Mandarin and the Public Advocate are ideologues for the existing social system, the Persuasive Neutralist appears as a professional methodologist who is concerned "strictly" with the techniques and knowledge brought forth by the scientific or "behavioral" revolution in the social sciences. His studies are generally not policy-oriented, though he claims that policy studies may also be "objective,"[31] and he carefully eschews any sign of ideological intent in his research. The Persuasive Neutralist, not unlike the other types, may have a calling, but it is to science, not polemics, dogma, or ideology. His main function is to cumulate knowledge about the social world, *to describe, understand and interpret reality, not change it.*[32]

In my view, however, the Persuasive Neutralist is equally subject to the claim of nonobjectivity, of ideology and non-sense stated above. The view, for instance, that one's research objective is to describe reality but *not* to change or criticize it is, I would argue, fundamentally conservative and will generally tend to reinforce existing institutions and social patterns. But I think the critique can be extended further than I have thus far suggested.

First, behavioral social scientists make the basic claim that the world of thought and knowledge is objective and rational. The social scientist so oriented adapts the intellectual posture of the physical scientist whose main function is to observe the phenomena of his chosen sphere of social reality and organize his data in such a way that he will be able to under-

29. Ryan, *op. cit.*, p. 465.
30. Julius Lester, *Look Out, Whitey: Black Power's Gon' Get Your Mama* (New York: Grove Press, 1968) , p. 54.
31. Heinz Eulau, *The Behavioral Persuasion in Politics* (New York: Grove Press, 1968) , p. 54.
32. *Ibid.*, p. 9.

stand, interpret and, hopefully, explain that segment of the world under observation. His work is piecemeal; he theorizes and hypothesizes and later, by employing the techniques of modern technology and science, cumulates data, replicates experiments, and amasses evidence for his propositions. In all events, his research is the work of the rational thinker, the "scientist," but one who is constrained by the self-imposed rules of the physical sciences to see the world from the outside, as a neutral observer. Naturally, he is also constrained in his view of social reality because for him the world is what "I think," not what "I live through." This world of science is the natural or physical world which reason alone (scientific or conceptual knowledge) can harness; but it is not the world of man and society which is always composed of reason and unreason, preconceptual knowledge and conceptual knowledge, thought and action, objective and external phenomena as well as subjective and internal phenomena. In short, for the behavioral scientist, "scientific" knowledge can overcome irrationality, contingency, and subjectivity. However, by its very nature, this knowledge has definite limitations, which William James clearly perceived when he distinguished "knowledge-about" or thought knowledge from "knowledge by acquaintance" or felt knowledge. To be empirical, according to James and contemporary phenomenologists, requires the distinction and elucidation of these different levels of knowing and meaning construction if the object of inquiry in social science is the social and human world itself. For James, "feelings are the germ and starting point of cognition, thoughts the developed tree,"[33] and therefore, a genuine empiricism "cannot simply construct experience as a logical patterning tailored to the convenience of this or that analysis of what valid propositions require."[34] Rather, "we must inquire into the ways in which logical order can relate to the concretely felt experience."[35]

Moreover, the claim of objectivity in behavioral social science is not warranted by the facts. Since objectivity refers to only external, observable, physical phenomena—the things of the world—it fails to recognize precisely those human and social experiences which also include internal, subjective, and psychical phenomena. What is essential for social science is the recognition that:

Human behavior is neither a series of blind reactions to external "stimuli," nor the project of acts which are motivated by the pure ideas of disembodied, wordless mind. It is neither exclusively subjective nor exclusively objective, but a dialectical interchange between man and the world, which cannot be adequately expressed in traditional causal terms.[36]

33. William James, *Principles of Psychology*, 1 (New York: Dover Publications, 1950), 222.
34. Eugene T. Gendlin, *Experiencing and The Creation of Meaning* (Glencoe: Free Press, 1962), pp. 9 and 139. Cited by H. Y. Jung, "Existential Phenomenology and Political Theory" (unpublished paper).
35. *Ibid.*
36. "Foreword," in Maurice Merleau-Ponty, *The Structure of Behavior* (Boston: Beacon Press, 1963), pp. xv-xvi.

To put it in other words, human behavior and human knowledge are neither exclusively rational nor exclusively irrational. The quest for exclusivity from either side simply has no scientific foundation when applied to men and society. To the contrary, behavioral science is primarily concerned with theory construction and scientific *testability* rather than social *tenability*. Models tend to be viewed as theories (provable or disprovable cause-effect propositions) which purport to forecast practical results, i.e., game theory or the domino theory.[37] The replicability of experiments or the uniformity of data are given the status of causal explanation. In contrast, Max Weber asserted that

. . . If adequacy in respect to meaning is lacking, then no matter how high the degree of uniformity and how precisely its probability can be numerically determined, it is still an incomprehensible statistical probability whether dealing with overt or subjective processes.[38]

In order to avoid the objectivism and intellectualism of science, one must recognize this dependence of conceptualization on the preconceptual life-world, which Husserl called the *Lebenswelt,* because:

The whole universe of science is built upon the world as directly experienced, and if we want to subject science itself to rigorous scrutiny and arrive at a precise awareness of its meaning and scope, we must begin by reawakening the basic experience of the world of which science is the second-order expression. . . . To return to things themselves is to return to that world which precedes knowledge, of which knowledge *speaks,* and in relation to which every scientific schematization is an abstract and derivative sign-language, as is geography in relation to the countryside in which we have learnt beforehand what a forest, a prairie or a river is.[39]

Insofar as behavioral scientists ignore this social "reality," insofar as they fail to distinguish scientific facts or natural reality from world facts or social reality, their research tends to objectify or reify human and social meanings. There can be no doubt that behavioral social science has amassed "knowledge-about," but the capacity for this knowledge to reconcile its theoretical understanding of social problems with the experienced reality of, say, the black power advocates, and employ it in the quest for free, creative social activity and responsive social institutions is today indeed questionable.

Second, it is becoming more evident with recent trends in the uses of technical and social science knowledge by large-scale institutions that science and technology are not necessarily progressive, as it was once thought. As John McDermott has recently noted:

37. Francis Wormuth, "Matched-Dependent Behavioralism: The Cargo Cult in Political Science," *Western Political Quarterly,* 20 (December 1967) : 809-840.

38. Max Weber, *The Theory of Social and Economic Organization* (New York: Free Press, 1966) , p. 88.

39. Maurice Merleau-Ponty, *Phenomenology of Perception* (London: Routledge and Kegan Paul, 1962) , pp. viii and ix.

Segments of knowledge still belong to technical specialists and pieces of knowledge to the well educated, but only the very largest organizations are able to integrate these proliferating segments and pieces into systems of productive, effective, or more likely, profitable information. That is the meaning of technological progress: the systematic application of new knowledge to practical purposes. And it dictates a continual increase in the size, wealth and managerial capacity of the organizations which seek thus to apply knowledge. Corporations, government agencies, universities, and foundations have been quick to respond.[40]

In the face of this technological explosion and increasing institutionalization and professionalization of knowledge, to claim a neutral or "objective" role for social science is clearly to fall under the onus of what Merleau-Ponty called "non-sense." Briefly put, the full thrust of reason and knowledge is being turned against itself—against truth and humanity, in favor of the dominant institutions and power-centers which are now tending to the *manipulation,* rather than the *liberation* of mankind, especially its underclasses. In short, the Persuasive Neutralist who inveighs against the ideologies and utopias that want to change the world in favor of a scientific or "objective" description or interpretation of social reality turns objective knowledge upside down: a fundamentally apolitical posture becomes highly political or ideological insofar as that knowledge serves entrenched institutions and power interests, whether these be pacification programs in South Vietnam or funneling of the energies of black youth into the established channels of American society.[41] To put it another way, the meaning and social significance of rational inquiry is inverted—sense is turned into nonsense. (From this perspective it could be argued that the Wallaceites and the New Left and other so-called social deviants have correctly perceived the insane world of reason against which they rebel.)

The serious limitations of even the most sophisticated methods and techniques of social science were underscored in a recent report by the Center for the Study of Conflict Resolution at the University of Michigan which noted that, after eleven years of research using the most proficient methods and techniques, they had gotten no closer to resolving conflict in the world or explaining the causes of violence. In fact, the report suggested, the situation requires all conceivable efforts to search for radically new methods of inquiry.

Finally, in terms of the ideological implications of social science, some behavioral scientists have taken the position that the recognition and clarification of their own biases will be sufficient to place such biases in perspective, enable them to then get on with the pursuit of science. This view is rightly attacked by Heinz Eulau, a well-known behavioralist. Eulau's argument is that one's science is either value-free or it is not. It "is a problem of fact," exhorts Eulau, "that can be answered only through empirical research into the nature of science as a form of human activity."

40. "Knowledge Is Power," *The Nation* (April 14, 1969), p. 458.

41. Elinor Graham, "The Politics of Poverty," in H. Gettleman and D. Mermelstein, eds., *The Great Society Reader* (New York: Random House, 1967) , p. 230.

The only quibble I have with Eulau, whose view is representative of most behavioral thought, is the assumption about the value-free study of politics he makes. In reference to policy science, Eulau writes: "The policy science approach does not assume that a value-free scientific study of politics is impossible because men pursue values through politics. Indeed, it sharply distinguishes between propositions of fact that are believed to be subject to scientific-empirical inquiry, and propositions of value for which empirical science has as yet no answer." Accordingly, the policy scientist can avoid violating the canons of scientific method by recognizing the existence of both facts and values and keeping a subtle balance or distance between them. Therefore, Eulau concludes, this approach "does not deny that scientific research on propositions of fact cannot serve policy objectives; indeed, it asserts that political science, as all science, should be put in the service of whatever goals men pursue in politics." But the keynote of Eulau's position gives a telling commentary on all three approaches when he asserts that science is still value-free even if "there is nothing in his science that prevents its being used for ends of which he disapproves."[42]

Despite his claims of value-neutrality, Heinz Eulau's conclusions could not be more insightful. Social science is always used by societies which generally determine what knowledge will be used and how knowledge will be used. The purity of knowledge is meaningless as long as that knowledge is used by social institutions for certain prescribed purposes. Hence, social knowledge, whether it be scientific or not, has a value for that society and plays a function which can most often be called ideological. Alas, we have come full circle back from the Persuasive Neutralist to the New Mandarin and Public Advocate. The differences could not have been very significant from the start.

TOWARD A RADICAL SOCIAL SCIENCE

American society is in need of a radical reorganization of social priorities. To achieve that end may call for a reconstruction of its dominant institutions, but at the least requires a redistribution of power and wealth as well as a redistribution of knowledge.[43] The need for radical change grows as America's institutions find it increasingly difficult to meet the rising social demands of its most needy, most powerless, most alienated members. The vision of a white, liberal power structure bent on exploiting and repressing the poor and black at home and fighting counterrevolutionary, imperialist wars abroad is becoming more evident to the underclasses, left intellectuals, and students. What they envisage is the rationalization of bureaucracy, the monopolization of power and wealth, the tailoring of knowledge and technology, and the manipulation and control of the people in the interests of self-serving elites—managerial, corporate, political, and intellectual. To argue to the contrary is of no avail since this generation has experienced (and is becoming more con-

42. Eulau, op. cit., pp. 135-137.
43. McDermott, op. cit.

scious of) its own poverty, powerlessness, alienation, and knows how these feelings relate to the reality of American power and ideology in Vietnam and Santo Domingo, Watts and Detroit, Chicago and Columbia University. To plead for reason, detachment, objectivity or patience in the face of abject poverty, political repression, and napalmed women and children is absurd. Along with the power structure, reason, they will tell you, is what gets us into Vietnam and keeps us there, produces a war on poverty but curtails funding, calls for "law and order" instead of freedom and justice. Moreover, what I have argued in this essay is that in spite of all claims to objectivity, rational, intellectual output, whether in the form of policy programs at home or pacification programs abroad, tends to reinforce the established order. That this may occur was underscored even by Heinz Eulau. In fact, the meaning of so much rational model-building, statistical data, theorizing, planning and programming can be viewed—as it is viewed by many of those most affected—as an elaboration of new, sophisticated techniques for "keeping the people down." This is the ideological significance of so-called "objective" or "scientific" knowledge as many have come to know it or experience its results.

Of course, this undercurrent in American society is merely the "knowledge by acquaintance" or felt knowledge of some Americans, certainly not the prevailing viewpoint, or the majority opinion. It is no wonder, then, that the rulers of both power and knowledge with their pluralistic, empiricist traditions find it so difficult to respond. For each of these two worlds of reality the other is incomprehensible, alien, quixotic. The situation is becoming more chaotic as these two worlds move farther and farther apart, demands become intolerable, and each side appears to be increasingly intransigent.

While the methods and uses of social science criticized in this chapter demonstrate behavioralism's intellectual and political incapacity to come to terms with this social reality, recent developments in existentialism and phenomenology have provided a radical alternative, one which, I contend, is more conducive to a critique of existing social institutions as well as to a theory of social change. At the same time, existential phenomenology provides a methodology for the social sciences which is no less rigorous, no less concerned with the verifiability of knowledge, and no less concerned with empirical inquiry.

The primary concern of existential phenomenology is the description of the life world (*Lebenswelt*) of everyday, common-sense reality. It is a way of looking at the world, or describing its social reality, and disclosing, therefore, its human and social meaning. Starting with the human situation, the primordial condition of man's being-in-the-world (*in-der-Welt-sein*), phenomenology sets out to explore the different regions of human existence, the foundations of which are to be discovered in the everydayness of existence itself as it is experienced. In the language of phenomenology, the primacy of human existence is in the perception of the lived body (*corps vecu*) which is thrown into existence (Heidegger) with others and the world. According to phenomenology, human existence is projective and intentional: through man's course of action new meaning is given to the world, history is made, and a new human and social *praxis* becomes possible. Man is condemned to history, said Merleau-Ponty; man, therefore, is condemned to be that being through whose actions the meaning construction of the world and of social relations is formed, deformed, reformed or transformed. Phenomenology, in short, is nothing less than a bold attempt to recover the primacy of human social existence, to reestablish human action as the motor of social forces and social relations, to reassert the social value and meaning of what William James called "the world of the street" in which every man and woman's actions have meaning in themselves as well as for others (*pour autrui*).[44]

In regard to its methodological approach to social reality, phenomenology conforms to neither classical modes of subjectivism (irrationalism, solipsism) nor to classical modes of objectivism (rationalism, behavioralism). Phenomenology transcends both by establishing what Husserl, and later Merleau-Ponty and Alfred Schutz, called *intersubjectivity*, by which is meant the fundamental interconnection between the external, objective world including other people (*être-en-soi*) and the internal, subjective world of consciousness (*être-pour-soi*). This philosophy denies neither the world nor man, neither social structures and ideas nor human action, but rather attempts to describe the ineradicable link between the two, and establish thereby the primacy of coexistence or *human* sociality. Hence the importance of phenomenology rests on its radical approach to social reality, its ability to describe the existential presence of man and his actions within the objective conditions of the world which are already established prior to his existence (i.e., man is thrown into the world). But equally important is the concept of *intersubjectivity* which lays the foundation for a new socialism based on its claim that all existence is coexistence and consequently all action is coaction, and a new humanism since ". . . a society is not the temple of value-idols that figure on the front of its monuments or in its constitutional scrolls; the value of a society is the value it places upon man's relations to man."[45]

44. A brief bibliography of the relevant major works of these authors is listed below. I omit Soren Kierkegaard for obvious reasons. Where available, English editions are cited. Martin Heidegger: *Being and Time* (New York: Harper and Row, 1962). Edmund Husserl: *Ideas* (New York: Collier Books, 1962), *The Crisis of European Sciences and Transcendental Phenomenology* (Evanston, Ill.: Northwestern University Press, 1970). Maurice Merleau-Ponty: *Les Aventures de la dialectique* (Paris: Gallimard, 1955), *Humanism and Terror* (Boston: Beacon Press, 1969), *Phenomenology of Perception* (London: Routledge and Kegan Paul, 1962), *In Praise of Philosophy* (Evanston: Northwestern University Press, 1963), *The Primacy of Perception* (Evanston: Northwestern University Press, 1964), *Sense and Non-sense* (Evanston: Northwestern University Press, 1964), *Signs* (Evanston: Northwestern University Press, 1964), and *The Structure of Behavior* (Boston: Beacon Press, 1963). Jean-Paul Sartre: *Being and Nothingness* (New York: Philosophical Library, 1956), *Critique de la raison dialectique* (Paris: Gallimard, 1960), *Literary and Philosophical Essays* (New York: Collier Books, 1955), and *Search for a Method* (New York: Alfred Knopf, 1963). Alfred Schutz: *Collected papers*, 3 vols. (The Hague: Martinus Nijhoff, 1962, 1964, 1966) and *The Phenomenology of the Social World* (Evanston: Northwestern University Press, 1967). John Wild: *Existence and the World of Freedom* (Englewood Cliffs, N. J.: Prentice-Hall, 1963).

45. Merleau-Ponty, *Humanism and Terror*, p. xiv.

Phenomenologists and existentialists, moreover, such as Merleau-Ponty, Schutz, and Sartre argue for a dialectical unity of thought and action which seeks the meaning of *praxis* for social existence. Thus, following Marx, existence is meaningful only insofar as we "connect ourselves with history instead of contemplating it."[46] For, what Marx calls *praxis* "is the meaning which works itself out spontaneously in the intercrossing of those activities by which man organizes his relations with nature and other men."[47] In other words, the root of existence is consciousness; yet consciousness is always consciousness of something, i.e., involved consciousness, or a way of organizing projects of action based on the intentions of men or social classes in order to give meaning to their concrete, historical situation.

This concern for social *praxis*, for the unity of thought and action, establishes existential phenomenology as a critical theory of radical political action, and represents a significant step toward reconciling Marxian socialism and existential humanism. These two movements share an awareness of the importance of a critical, humanistic, and existential attitude toward those petrified social forces and their ideological justifications which deny human existence, enforce patterns of social injustice, and alienate man from society itself. However, the key to the synthesis of these theoretical movements is the recognition of what Merleau-Ponty called the "dialectics of ambiguity." Briefly put, man is the motor of world historical forces, the being through whose actions social meaning, social change, and freedom are possible, but at the same time man is born into a world which he did not create and is always subject to others (co-actors) as well as to the existing ideas, institutions, and social processes which dominate his milieu. The dialectic, therefore, is an open-minded process, never restricted to either human action in itself or the social order in itself.

Finally, this approach to social science eschews value neutrality. It agrees with Marx that "philosophers have only interpreted the world in different ways; the point is to *change* it." While recognizing the central role of value and ideology in the quest for a free, open, and humane society and culture, existential phenomenologists and Marxists alike invite a sense of social commitment on the part of intellectuals, informed by a critical vision of the existing social world as well as a critical view toward transforming it. This approach is ideological in its quest for that historical truth by which man becomes the motor of the dialectic, enabling him to create the conditions under which he can make history and overcome both the resistance of the world and the institutional predilections of the political status quo to his projects for action.[48]

In conclusion, existential phenomenology aligned with a humanistic vision of social change is a radical alternative to behavioralism. First, because its vision of the world comprises the whole of social reality, including the common-sense reality of the man in the street, which the

46. Merleau-Ponty, *Sense and Non-sense*, p. 79.
47. Merleau-Ponty, *In Praise of Philosophy*, p. 50.
48. This formulation was suggested to me by Robin Blackburn.

rationalistic universe of behavioralism tends to overlook. Second, because its vision of the social world is based on a critical attitude toward the status quo rather than the apolitical description of and compliance with established political power so predominant among behavioralists. This radical methodology of social science offers some hope that from the seemingly mindless rationalism of America's political and intellectual elites and the seemingly mindless irrationalism of America's underclasses might emerge a new sense of reason and social purpose.[49]

49. A more thorough analysis of the theoretical and practical aspects of this approach to social reality has not been possible to include for publication in this volume. However, there are encouraging signs that a new direction in social theory is developing that combines many aspects of existential phenomenology and Marxism. See the sociological studies of Peter Berger and Thomas Luckman, *The Social Construction of Reality* (Garden City, 1967), Erving Goffman, *The Presentation of Self in Everyday Life* (Garden City, 1959), and Harold Garfinkel, *Studies in Ethnomethodology* (Englewood Cliffs, 1967); the works of R. D. Laing and his associates in phenomenological psychology and psychiatry; recent developments in public administration theory and communications theory including Frank Marini, ed., *Toward a New Public Administration* (Scranton, 1971), and Jurgen Habermas, *Toward a Rational Society* (Boston, 1970) and *Knowledge and Human Interests* (Boston, 1971). Also of considerable interest are Henri Lefebvre, *Everyday Life in the Modern World* (New York, 1971), and some recent interpretations of Herbert Marcuse in Paul Brienes, ed., *Critical Interruptions* (New York, 1970). In journal literature see especially recent issues of *Liberation, Radical Therapist* and *Telos*.

Creating Political Reality

HENRY S. KARIEL

"Suit yourself."—American colloquialism

Currently fashionable modes of political analysis deserve acclaim today for at least two reasons: they provide opportunities for participating in a pleasurable if strenuous activity (regardless of the value of the end results) and they effectively come to terms with the surface facts of political reality. Our posterity, too, may find it easy to esteem the contemporary products of the profession of political science should it ever look back and see how an affection for craftsmanship is combined with the ability to please. Moreover, the reward system of the profession should appear as having been nicely designed to promote the present display of talent, ingenuity, variety, and success. There is evidence, in any case, that the prevailing inclination to work hard and to develop ever more powerful analytical tools is welcomed and reinforced within the discipline. All would seem to be well.

Yet doubts continue to be expressed today even by those who govern the profession and engage in what Thomas Kuhn has called normal science. Partially, there is a petulant resentment among older practitioners, scholars who are made fretful and irritable by the entrepreneurial opportunism of the *nouveau riche,* by the feeling that mindless industriousness rather than scholarly contemplation is now rewarded by tenure as well as by space in journals, time on panels, positions on editorial boards, and cash for projects. It does not pain me, however, to disregard the indictment that comes from this source—not because I suspect its patrician origins but because I believe it is blind to the underlying impulse of empiricism, because it ignores the subversive, liberating thrust of empirical science. I am also prepared to disregard the assorted indictments which come from *within* the dominant paradigm of the profession: intramural critiques, letters to the editor blown up into articles, manuals by technicians more critical of one another's techniques than of their shared assumptions. It is a third kind of indictment—sometimes little more than an angry, incoherent expression of uneasiness—which I would like to take more seriously.

What has become annoying to political scientists of diverse methodological persuasions is the profession's inability to frame and illuminate the major events of recent times, events which, because they have run counter to expectations, are perceived as critical. And what makes this doubly annoying is that only unaccredited prophets, poets, seers, preachers, and metaphysicians would seem to have foreseen anything like the contemporary crisis in authority. Who within the profession has made our incapacity to govern ourselves—to control the most brutal and the most generous of our impulses at home and abroad—rationally manageable, subject to disciplined statement? One need not turn to the major catastrophes of the age to become uneasy about the way our professional activities are disconnected from our concerns, seemingly trivial matters close at hand having proved sufficient to provoke questions. Previously unseen (or irrelevant) parts of reality have suddenly had the nerve to make themselves visible. Pushing their way into camera range, unrecognized and unrepresented men have fought to be perceived as significant, becoming relevant if not to professional social scientists, then at least to administrators and legislators worried about the possibility of revolution. Submerged groups (students, blacks, women, construction workers, stockholders, homosexuals, clergymen, cops, and even Army recruits, though not yet patients, prisoners, teachers, coal miners, or bureaucrats) have crashed into the mass media and thereby into the arena of politics.

Their emergence (inevitably characterized as an emergency by those within the consensus) has of course been made comprehensible enough on one level: causal analysis has revealed, for example, that the longer and hotter the summer, as one article has solemnly concluded, the more likely the outbreaks of the lower orders.[1] But while causal analysis allows political scientists to cope with new data even in the city of New Haven, while it allows them to explain the appearance of previously eclipsed men or to demonstrate how to engineer their disappearance, the available scientific explanations nonetheless fail to satisfy. Somehow the prevailing modes of explanation do not enable political scientists to comprehend phenomena as fully as the forms used by some novelists, journalists, poets, or film directors. Political scientists—certainly those who have recently turned out in considerable numbers for the special convention panels set up by the Caucus for a New Political Science—vaguely sense that their approach does not permit them to see their subject matter as comprehensively as they might. They do perceive people in motion, but primarily as reflexes and outputs, as effects of causes. Convinced that men must be respected as agents capable of engaging in goal-oriented action, they nonetheless can see little which exhibits purpose, meaning, dignity, and integrity. As political scientists, they are directed to perceive manipulated and manipulatable data; as men with larger concerns and a greater range of compassion, they aspire to perceive something more, namely the public significance of others who happen to be outside the prevailing balance of manifest interests. Professionally, they are impelled—whether by memories of scope-and-methods courses or by the innuendos of their colleagues—to confuse science with an edifice of positivist theory and to identify explanations with unambiguous generalizations about neatly assorted variables. As nonprofessionals, however, they are sensitive to the need to challenge what are alleged to be the real attributes of functional systems.

To what extent is it possible to provide professional tools and rewards for such political scientists, for those whose generous moral sensibilities are betrayed by the astringency of their science?

A MODEL OF POLITICAL MAN

It is not likely, I believe, that we can expand the focus of political science unless we permit our vision and action to be directed by a model of human nature which allows us not only to account for man's private, economic interests but also to recognize his currently less apparent political possibilities. Unless we learn to acknowledge that more may be present than we have yet experienced, the best political scientists—those most torn between the demands of the discipline and their own moral perceptions, those who bear the greatest strains—will drop out of the profession, becoming increasingly unprofessional and undisciplined. They are apt to follow sentiment, ultimately identifying with their subject

1. David C. Schwartz, "On the Ecology of Political Violence: 'The Long Hot Summer' as a Hypothesis," *American Behavioral Scientist,* 11 (July-August 1968), 24-28. In his critique of the Kerner Commission report on civil disorders, Robert M. Fogelson has noted that the Commission, like social scientists who served it, viewed riots as mere reactions to ills manageable within the prevailing system of liberalism, that is, manageable without redistributing political power: see "Review Symposium," *American Political Science Review,* 63 (December 1969), 1269-1275.

matter, arrested and absorbed by its sheer presence, surrendering their critical capacities, becoming so thoroughly engaged by aggregated data that they will finally disdain efforts to bestow structure and form on their experience. If they do not go all the way, they will remain as cynics and opportunists who market the products of normal science in order to be at least free enough for occasional undisciplined, unprofessional forays into the ghettos of our cities and our minds.

To enable them to move coherently—that is, to make it possible for political science to integrate norms and facts, theory and practice, morality and science, ends and means—we will have to ask ourselves whether in our battle against metaphysics, superstition, prejudice, and ideology, we might not have won too large a victory. Frankly accepting the idealist overtones of model building, we will have to reconsider the pathetic directive that scientific models are merely to be checked against the common denominator of present experience and inquire how, instead, we might derive a model of political man from barely recorded, ill-articulated, marginal intimations of human possibilities.

Whatever the difficulties today in accepting the discursive styles generally employed for constructing such a model, it certainly has been recurrently envisaged and formulated. I have had previous occasion to identify its outlines by noting what is shared by Rousseau's self-governed individual, Marx's unalienated man, Nietzsche's self-activated hero, Dewey's educated person, Sartre's man of good faith, Fromm's autonomous individual, and Lifton's protean man. We can give further resonance to these available images of human nature by considering the nonauthoritarian personality of social psychology, the Hermes-like figures appearing in the various myths of the trickster, the picaresque nonhero of modern fiction, or Gordon Allport's portrait of man as a creature in continuous process of becoming. If the result of such an exploration should seem to resemble an unsorted collection of color slides, there is nothing to keep us from carefully sorting them, inquiring how they came to be, and speaking firmly about them with a measure of precision. This would in any case help make vivid a plausible ideal of the healthy personality and might encourage us to inquire into ways for reducing illness.

There is of course a reluctance to permit metaphors borrowed from medicine to orient political life. Won't citizens, unlike physicians, properly disagree on the ends of action? The application of the concept of health to political situations is questioned, in other words, because it would falsely imply agreement on some final ideal, on some static condition. But there is no need to entertain such a simplistic notion of "health." A healthy system may well be the *end* of medical practice; yet there are good empirical grounds for treating biopsychological systems—including the body politic—precisely as physicians or psychiatrists do, namely as open-ended ones, as systems which are healthy as long as they remain in process. And what is characteristic of human beings in process, of men engaged in political action, is their continuous resolve to display themselves, to express their determination to remain purposefully in motion, to defy necessity and assert as much of themselves as they dare.

That political scientists are actually not innocent of this self-exhibit-ing, self-promoting aspect of political action is shown by Murray Edelman's current work on poverty as well as by voting studies which allow that voters might conceivably be actors who can be understood in social settings which reveal the expressive character of their behavior.[2] Moreover, there may be an increasing readiness to concede that studies of attitudes and of participation do in practice incorporate unobservable intentions—something more than overt behavior.

The ground for such a perspective, given its classic definition by Aristotle, has been characterized as "political space" by Hannah Arendt. In terms echoing George Herbert Mead no less than Aristotle, she has tellingly identified it as

the space of appearance in the widest sense of the word, namely, the space where I appear to others as others appear to me, where men exist not merely like other living or inanimate things but make their appearance explicitly. . . . To be deprived of it means to be deprived of reality, which, humanly and politically speaking, is the same as appearance. To men the reality of the world is guaranteed by the presence of others, by its appearing to all; "for what appears to all, this we call Being," and whatever lacks this appearance comes and passes away like a dream, intimately and exclusively our own but without reality.[3]

Man's natural "need," in this view, is the opportunity to *be,* to gain recognition by making witnessed and comprehended appearances and thereby becoming significant to others.

That precisely this—nothing less *and nothing more*—is man's universal need is still hard to acknowledge. It does find implicit support in statements such as the epilogue of Amitai Etzioni's *Active Society,* a thoroughly lucid discussion of human inauthenticity, a term given meaning by his review of authentic basic needs.[4]

Yet whatever the appeal of such essays, they still respond to the essentialist question of what human needs "really" are. Needs continue to be specified as if some ontological heaven had to be decked out with an assortment of reifications.

To accept the spirit of Etzioni's discussion but avoid its residual Platonism, it should be useful to recall the tradition of empiricism and see it exemplified by Herbert Marcuse's work. His approach is at once far less idiosyncratic than his critics claim and far less complicated than his prose allows. Derived from Hegel, it gives rise to that "unhappy con-

2. See Murray Edelman, "Public Policy and Political Violence," discussion paper, Institute in Research on Poverty, University of Wisconsin, 1968; and Arthur S. Goldberg, "Social Determinism and Rationality as Bases of Party Identification," *American Political Science Review,* 63 (March 1969) , 5-25.

3. Hannah Arendt, *The Human Condition* (Chicago: University of Chicago Press, 1958) , pp. 198-199; the quotation is said to come from Aristotle, *Nicomachaen Ethics,* 1172b36 ff.

4. Amitai Etzioni, *The Active Society: A Theory of Societal and Political Processes* (New York: Free Press, 1968) , Chap. 21. See also Christian Bay, "Needs, Wants, and Political Legitimacy," *Canadian Journal of Political Science,* 1 (September 1968), 241-260; and Peter A. Corning, "The Biological Bases of Behavior and Their Implications for Political Theory," paper delivered at the American Political Science Association meeting, September 2-6, 1969.

sciousness" generated by the tension between the reality we know all too well and the reality which remains unconfirmed and unrealized—those unacknowledged intimations of life which the prevailing organization of society continues to repress, those unspeakable dimensions of ourselves from which we are kept alienated. Our needs, Marcuse argues with a good deal more fuss than necessary, will make themselves known to us when surplus repression—repression in excess of what men need—is eliminated.

To be sure, we feel that this argument begs the question: just how much repression *do* men need? But the kind of conclusive answer we tend to look for cannot be had within the empirical tradition. We want abstract, unconditional answers whereas Marcuse will rightly provide us only with hypothetical, conditional ones: *if* you reduce repression, his hypothesis states conditionally, *then* the ability of men to harmonize their conflicting drives is likely to be enhanced. Put differently: if reality were changed, men would be more apt to bring diverse experiences into relationships.

But, we might persist in asking, how valid is this proposition? For those empiricists not aligned with the established present, there is only one way to find out. We must proceed by acting as if it were valid: we must be prepared to invest in it, to try. The procedure is of course the familiar pragmatic one. Taking risks, we must attempt to *violate* whatever is alleged to be reality, whatever equilibrium positivists certify to be real. We will then either lose our wager or else compel reality to yield, learning (by doing) that, to the extent that we succeeded in pushing back the coercive forces of the wilderness, we will have gained in manageable experience, in political space. If we win, we will have learned that we did not *need* the prevailing degree of postponed gratification. We will know that there was, in Marcuse's phrase, surplus repression. We had felt we needed to live more amply—and we found out (if we survived) that, yes, we *could.* Clearly, to accept this experimentalism for discovering one's needs is to see how diversionary it is to draw up an abstract inventory of human needs, how such academic exercises function ideologically to keep us in line.

What we need—not what we want—we will only discover in practice, only by treating present systems of domination and necessity as if they used greater violence and more discipline than necessary. Because the surplus benefits elites, only non-elites, outcasts, or unattached outsiders are likely to be motivated to engage in testing, that is, probing in ways not yet legitimated, acting violently.

It cannot quite go without saying that a commitment to testing, to political life as an on-going, self-consciously conducted experiment, poses troublesome practical questions which no abstract theory can presume to answer. Experiments may be so intoxicating or exhausting that they make us frantic or listless, diminishing us in the very process of conducting them. Of course, we can advise (and compel) men to make only such choices which are likely to make their *continuous* action possible; we can direct them *not* to violate others whom they may yet need as irritants for promoting personal growth. The difficulty, we know, is that every course of action forecloses some future options. In short, it is not helpful merely to instruct men to avoid self-destruction and seek self-enhancement. Forced to make specific choices while unable to see far ahead and yet responsible for the *totality* of ourselves (including a future self which includes our present enemies), we are confronted by the most practical problems of priorities and tactics. To reduce the risks of self-destruction while promoting self-enhancement in practice, we surely need all the positive knowledge we can accumulate—whether by drawing on the conditional conclusions of cost-benefit analysis or comparative research. We must seek to know with a measure of certainty what will keep us from violating both our potential self—our present enemies—and those institutions required to realize it.

This pragmatic approach—implicit in Etzioni, radicalized by Marcuse who follows Dewey as much as Marx—also sustains Ernest Becker's case for making need satisfaction the test of existing regimes.[5] Though in many ways exasperatingly eccentric, Becker's work seems to me a useful attempt to define alienation in naturalistic terms, moving us beyond institutions and roles that prescribe *needless* destructions of the self. Further, there is Michael Shapiro's current effort to construct a model of man which would be responsive, as he has written,

to changing needs, values, and interpersonal orientations. Reacting against the way in which conceptions of man have been oriented toward justifying various institutional arrangements, this model of man-the-theorist will be oriented toward exploring man's potential for creating political orders to accommodate changing individual attributes. Such a model, unlike many current formulations, facilitates thinking about directions for changing institutions rather than individual therapy. Empirically, the model focusses on two basic aspects of individual decision-making, information gathering and information structuring. In this way individuals can be assessed in terms of the nature of their decisional postulates. Self-control (the ability to choose) is viewed as dependent upon the extent to which an individual entertains his decisional postulates in an experimental fashion. In this way man can be viewed not only in terms of the closures and reifications he imposes upon his conceptions but also in terms of his potential for learning and development toward forms of social and political organization that are yet unrealized.[6]

Scholarly essays such as these make it possible to see a drive to provide an empirical basis for a conception of man as an open-ended, multi-faceted being, as an actor resisting every certified truth, naturally given to posturing, simulating, performing, playing, equivocating, innovating, testing, improvising—in sum, acting.

Were we to welcome such a view of political man and permit it to work on us at least as an analytical construct, our attention would be drawn toward those presently unknown elements of experience which the newly formulated model would integrate but not assimilate, which it would esteem for being what they are. No doubt, we might hesitate to confront those elements in their fullness, not wishing to see and discuss

5. Ernest Becker, *The Structure of Evil: An Essay on the Unification of the Science of Man* (New York: George Braziller, 1968) .
6. Personal communication.

them publicly. After all, they are still private and taboo, only to be felt and fondled (as Norman O. Brown has insinuated). At best they may be related, like Portnoy's elaborate complaint, to one's analyst in private sessions as privileged communications. Yet if we should find the economic and psychological resources to expand our political consciousness by learning to speak up, we would expose repressed dimensions, gradually becoming aware of those eclipsed parts of life which still fail to live up to our model, which remain in repose, waiting to be exhibited, stimulated, and activated.

Our model, in other words, would serve to alert us to the gap between what we might be and what we are, between political possibilities and the present reality. When this gap makes us sufficiently uneasy, we will unavoidably feel impelled to close it. Our model would therefore do more than create awareness and direct attention: it would induce us to act, to test environments in order to make them yield. To use it would enable us to implement the Kantian view that society is not something "out there" to be studied, but rather, as Etzioni has written, "a human grouping we collectively organize and are free to restructure, within certain limits we seek to understand and untighten."[7]

When we compel reality to accommodate our model of political man—when we are successful both in pretending to *be* such men in sheltered laboratory settings and in extending our laboratories—at least some of the practices and institutions which are commonly alleged to be real will emerge as changeable. As our environments then turn out to be less intractable than we thought (or have been instructed to think) our action will defy and jeopardize the prevailing order of commitments: a functional division of labor, the distinction between private and public sectors, the system of fixed social and biological roles within hierarchical organizations, government by a plurality of elites, the market economy, the identification of security with military power, the separation of means from ends, and finally the organized repression—whether in the family, private associations, or public institutions—of action and pleasure, of politics and play.

Basically, such an approach follows Melvin Tumin by challenging existing captor-captive, superior-subordinate relationships. It questions the structures of power established in schools, prisons, hospitals, political parties, industrial plants, academic departments, professional associations, and nation-states.[8] Postulating political realities dialectically opposed to manifest ones, it negates empirically confirmed experience.[9] The

7. Preface to November-December, 1968 issue of *The American Behavioral Scientist.*

8. See Melvin Tumin, "Captives, Consensus and Conflict: Implications for New Roles in Social Change," in Herman D. Stein (ed.), *Social Theory and Social Invention* (Cleveland: Case Western Reserve University Press, 1968), pp. 93-113.

9. See Warren G. Bennis and Philip E. Slater, *The Temporary Society* (New York: Harper & Row, 1968) ; Orion F. White, "The Dialectical Organization: An Alternative to Bureaucracy," *Public Administration Review*, 29 (January-February 1969), 32-42; Theodor W. Adorno, *Negative Dialektik* (Frankfurt: Suhrkamp, 1966).

imposing social structures which have been discovered by a non-experimental, non-pragmatic, positivistic social science are thus treated as targets for a political science determined to test their value—their value always in the relation to the structure of human needs. Political science thereby comes to terms with whatever men in power insist is given—given by providence or merely by the process of history, the wisdom of the founding fathers, the necessities of industrialism, the iron law of oligarchy, the immutable nature of man, or the disoveries of a half-hearted empiricism more intent on finding answers "out there" than on honoring its own critical, negativistic, reality-defying spirit.

IV
Alternative
Futures:
Policy

The first phase of the political process is policy, in which individuals and groups advocate alternative definitions of the future with means ranging from violence to discussion. General notions of desired futures are frequently associated with major social groupings. Such general notions are called ideologies and are the most basic policy alternatives in competition at a given period and place. The articles in this section reflect current debates about the structure of ideology and policy, rather than conflicts over particular policies.

In his article, Seymour Martin Lipset argues that ideological divisions are no longer important in the West. Echoing to some extent Kenneth Melvin, Lipset holds that the construction of the welfare state since the 1930's has given rise to a broad agreement on the proper direction of political life. With the welfare state setting minimum limits of economic security, conflicts take place on a narrow basis and revolve around how much of the "pie" different interest groups shall receive. Thus, the great debates over whether production should be controlled by private interests or the state are no longer significant. Only small groups on the fringes of social life wish to dismantle the welfare state, while the vast majority are content to lead the "good life" provided by established institutions.

While not challenging Lipset's notion that battles over the public and private ownership of property have decreased in importance, David Apter holds that new ideological divisions may be appearing in the West between the skilled and the educated, and the unskilled. He anticipates a future of conflict between an emerging elite of technicians and those who are not experts. While Apter has begun to penetrate the emergent ideologies of the contemporary world, his account seems oversimplified. He has included the specialists and the "middle Americans," but he has not adequately considered the directors of the conglomerates and the dispossessed, both of which make contemporary conflicts far more complex.

Another important issue in the policy phase of the political process is discussed by Murray Edelman, who shows how the political attitudes of large masses of people are often manipulated by skillful propaganda. He notes that the visions of the future and the judgments of the present held by many people are manufactured for them and may have very little relation to events that are actually taking place. This adds an important complicating factor to the discussion of ideology above. Those who have the greatest access to the mass media of communication are in a favorable position to impose their ideologies on others.

Theodore Lowi discusses another way in which political attitudes are manipulated. By combining divergent opinions into vague statements of policy, politicians are able to create the illusion that there is broad agreement on major issues. Bringing the discussion of policy back to its beginnings, Hazel Henderson challenges Lowi to go beyond electoral politics and look at the important decisions being made by corporations and other large organizations. Henderson's argument is an implicit refutation of Lipset's idea that economic ideologies are dead. Lipset, it should be noted, wrote his article before the major conflicts of the late 1960's had fully surfaced.

The End of Ideology?

SEYMOUR MARTIN LIPSET

The problem of conformity which so troubles many Americans today has been noted as a major aspect of American culture from Tocqueville in the 1830s to Riesman in the 1950s. Analysts have repeatedly stressed the extent to which Americans (as compared to other peoples) are sensitive to the judgments of others. Never secure in their own status, they are concerned with "public opinion" in a way that elites in a more aristocratic and status-bound society do not have to be. As early as the nineteenth century foreign observers were struck by the "other-directedness" of Americans and accounted for it by the nature of the class system. This image of the American as "other-directed" can, as Riesman notes, be found in the writing of "Tocqueville and other curious and astonished visitors from Europe."[1] Harriet Martineau almost seems to be paraphrasing Riesman's own description of today's "other-directed" man in her picture of the early nineteenth-century American:

Americans may travel over the world, and find no society but their own which will submit [as much] to the restraint of perpetual caution, and reference to the opinions of others. They may travel over the whole world, and find no country but their own where the very children beware of getting into scrapes, and talk of the effect of actions on people's minds: where the youth of society determines in silence what opinions they shall bring forward, and what avow only in the family circle; where women write miserable letters, almost universally, because it is a settled matter that it is unsafe to commit oneself on paper; and where elderly people seem to lack almost universally that faith in principles which inspires a free expression of them at any time, and under all circumstances.[2]

It may be argued that in an open democratic society in which people are encouraged to struggle upward, but where there are no clearly defined reference points to mark their arrival, and where their success in achieving status is determined by the good opinion of others, the kind of caution and intense study of other people's opinions described by Martineau is natural. Like Riesman today, she notes that this "other-directed" type is found most commonly in urban centers in the middle and upper classes, where people live in "perpetual caution." Nowhere does there exist "so much heart-eating care [about others' judgments], so much nervous anxiety, as among the dwellers in the towns of the northern states of America."[3] Similarly, Max Weber, who visited the United States in the

1. David Riesman *et al.*, *The Lonely Crowd: A Study of the Changing American Character* (New Haven: Yale University Press, 1950), pp. 19-20.
2. Harriet Martineau, *Society in America*, Vol. II (New York: Saunders and Otley, 1837), pp. 158-59.
3. *Ibid.*, pp. 160-61.

early 1900s, noted the high degree of "submission to fashion in America, to a degree unknown in Germany," and explained it as a natural attribute of a democratic society without inherited class status.[4]

A society which emphasizes achievement, which denies status based on ancestry or even long-past personal achievements, must necessarily be a society in which men are sensitively oriented toward others, in which, to use Riesman's analogy, they employ a radar to keep their social equilibrium. And precisely as we become more equalitarian, as the lower strata attain citizenship, as more people are able to take part in the status race, to that extent do we, and other peoples as well, become more concerned with the opinions of others, and therefore more democratic and more American in the Tocquevillian sense.

The politics of democracy are to some extent necessarily the politics of conformity for the elite of the society. As soon as the masses have access to the society's elite, as soon as they must consider mass reaction in determining their own actions, the freedom of the elite (whether political or artistic) is limited. As Tocqueville pointed out, the "most serious reproach which can be addressed" to democratic republics is that they "extend the practice of currying favor with the many and introduce it into all classes at once," and he attributed "the small number of distinguished men in political life to the ever increasing despotism of the majority in the United States."[5]

The same point has been made in regard to much of the discussion about the negative consequences of mass culture. Increased access by the mass of the population to the culture market necessarily means a limitation in cultural taste as compared to a time or a country in which culture is limited to the well to do and the well educated.

The current debates on education reflect the same dilemma—that many who believe in democracy and equalitarianism would also like to preserve some of the attributes of an elitist society. In England, where the integrated "comprehensive" school is seen as a progressive reform, the argument for it is based on the assumption that the health of the society is best served by what is best for the largest number. This argument was used in this country when liberal educators urged that special treatment for the gifted child served to perpetuate inequality and that it rewarded those from better home and class environments at the expense of those from poorer backgrounds. Educators in Britain today argue strongly that separate schools for brighter children (the so-called "grammar schools")

4. Max Weber, *Essays in Sociology* (New York: Oxford University Press, 1946), p. 188.

5. Alexis de Tocqueville, *Democracy in America*, Vol. I (New York: Vintage Books, 1954), pp. 276, 277. Of course, Plato made the same points 2500 years ago when he argued that in a democracy, the father "accustoms himself to become like his child and to fear his sons, and the son in his desire for freedom becomes like his father and has no fear or reverence for his parent. . . . The school master fears and flatters his pupils . . . while the old men condescend to the young and become triumphs of versatility. . . . The main result of all these things, taken together, is that it makes the souls of the citizens . . . sensitive." *The Republic of Plato*, ed. by Ernest Rhys (London: J. M. Dent and Co., 1935), pp. 200-26.

are a source of psychic punishment for the less gifted. Many of us have forgotten that liberals in this country shared similar sentiments not too long ago; that, for example, Fiorello La Guardia, as Mayor of New York, abolished Townsend Harris High School, a special school for gifted boys in which four years of school work were completed in three, on the ground that the very existence of such a school was undemocratic, that it gave special privileges to a minority.

What I am saying is simply that we cannot have our cake and eat it too. We cannot have the advantages of an aristocratic *and* a democratic society; we cannot have segregated elite schools in a society which stresses equality; we cannot have a cultural elite which produces without regard to mass taste in a society which emphasizes the value of popular judgment. By the same token we cannot have a low divorce rate and end differentiation in sex roles, and we cannot expect to have secure adolescents in a culture which offers no definitive path from adolescence to adulthood.

I do not mean to suggest that a democratic society can do nothing about reducing conformity or increasing creativity. There is considerable evidence to suggest that higher education, greater economic security, and higher standards of living strengthen the level of culture and democratic freedom. The market for good books, good paintings, and good music is at a high point in American history.[6] There is evidence that tolerance for ethnic minorities too is greater than in the past. More people are receiving a good education in America today than ever before, and regardless of the many weaknesses of that education, it is still true that the more of it one has, the better one's values and consumption patterns from the point of view of the liberal and culturally concerned intellectual.

There is a further point about the presumed growth of conformity and the decline in ideology which has been made by various analysts who rightly fear the inherent conformist aspects of populist democracy. They suggest that the growth of large bureaucratic organizations, an endemic aspect of modern industrial society, whether capitalist or socialist, is reducing the scope of individual freedom because "organization men" must conform to succeed. This point is sometimes linked to the decline in the intensity of political conflict, because politics is seen as changing into administration as the manager and expert take over in government as well as in business. From James Burnham's *Managerial Revolution* to more recent restatements of this thesis by Peter Drucker and others, this trend has been sometimes welcomed, but more often in recent years deplored.

The growth of large organizations may, however, actually have the more important consequences of providing new sources of continued freedom and more opportunity to innovate. Bureaucratization means (among other things) a decline of the arbitrary power of those in authority. By establishing norms of fair and equal treatment, and by reducing the unlimited power possessed by the leaders of many nonbureaucratic or-

6. See Daniel Bell, "The Theory of Mass Society," *Commentary,* 22 (1956), p. 82, and Clyde Kluckhohn, "Shifts in American Values," *World Politics,* 11 (1959), pp. 250-61, for evidence concerning the growth rather than the decline of "genuine individuality in the United States."

ganizations, bureaucracy may mean less rather than greater need to conform to superiors. In spite of the emergence of security tests, I think that
there is little doubt that men are much less likely to be fired from their
jobs for their opinions and behavior today than they were fifty or even
twenty-five years ago. Anyone who compares the position of a worker or
an executive in a family-owned corporation like the Ford Motor Company when its founder was running it to that of comparably placed people in General Motors or today's Ford Motor Company can hardly argue
that bureaucratization has meant greater pressure to conform on any level
of industry. Trade unions accurately reflect their members' desires when
they move in the direction of greater bureaucratization by winning, for
example, seniority rules in hiring, firing, and promotion, or a stable
three-year contract with detailed provisions for grievance procedures.
Unionization, of both manual and white-collar workers, increases under
conditions of large-scale organization and serves to free the worker or
employee from subjection to relatively uncontrolled power. Those who
fear the subjection of the workers to the organizational power of unionism ignore for the most part the alternative of arbitrary management
power. In many ways the employee of a large corporation who is the
subject of controversy between two giant organizations—the company and
the union—has a much higher degree of freedom than one not in a large
organization.

Although the pressures toward conformity within democratic and
bureaucratic society are an appropriate source of serious concern for
Western intellectuals, my reading of the historical evidence suggests that
the problem is less acute or threatening today than it has been in the past,
if we limit our analysis to domestic threats to the system. There is reason
to expect that stable democratic institutions in which individual political
freedom is great and even increasing (as it is, say, in Britain or Sweden)
will continue to characterize the mature industrialized Western societies.

The controversies about cultural creativity and conformity reflect
the general trend discussed at the beginning of the chapter—the shift
away from ideology towards sociology. The very growth of sociology as
an intellectual force outside the academy in many Western nations is a
tribute, not primarily to the power of sociological analysis but to the loss
of interest in political inquiry. It may seem curious, therefore, for a sociologist to end on a note of concern about this trend. But I believe that
there is still a real need for political analysis, ideology, and controversy
within the world community, if not within the Western democracies. In
a larger sense, the domestic controversies within the advanced democratic
countries have become comparable to struggles within American party
primary elections. Like all nomination contests, they are fought to determine who will lead the party, in this case the democratic camp, in the
larger political struggle in the world as a whole with its marginal constituencies, the underdeveloped states. The horizon of intellectual political concerns must turn from the new version of local elections—those
which determine who will run national administrations—to this larger
contest.

This larger fight makes politics much more complex in the various underdeveloped countries than it appears within Western democracies. In these states there is still a need for intense political controversy and ideology. The problems of industrialization, of the place of religion, of the character of political institutions are still unsettled, and the arguments about them have become intertwined with the international struggle. The past political relations between former colonial countries and the West, between colored and white peoples, make the task even more difficult. It is necessary for us to recognize that our allies in the underdeveloped countries must be radicals, probably socialists, because only parties which promise to improve the situation of the masses through widespread reform, and which are transvaluational and equalitarian, can hope to compete with the Communists. Asian and African socialist movements, even where they are committed to political democracy (and unfortunately not all of them are, or can be even if they want to), must often express hostility to many of the economic, political, and religious institutions of the West.

Where radicals are in power—in India, Ghana, Ceylon, Burma, and other countries—they must take responsibility for the economic development of the country, and hence must suffer the brunt of the resentments caused by industrialization, rapid urbanization, bad housing, and extreme poverty. The democratic leftist leader must find a scapegoat to blame for these ills—domestic capitalists, foreign investors, or the machinations of the departed imperialists. If he does not, he will lose his hold on the masses who need the hope implicit in revolutionary chiliastic doctrine—a hope the Communists are ready to supply. The socialist in power in an underdeveloped country must continue, therefore, to lead a revolutionary struggle against capitalism, the Western imperialists, and, increasingly, against Christianity as the dominant remaining foreign institution. If he accepts the arguments of Western socialists that the West has changed, that complete socialism is dangerous, that Marxism is an outmoded doctrine, he becomes a conservative within his own society, a role he cannot play and still retain a popular following.

The leftist intellectual, the trade-union leader, and the socialist politician in the West have an important role to play in this political struggle. By virtue of the fact that they still represent the tradition of socialism and equalitarianism within their own countries, they can find an audience among the leaders of the non-Communist left in those nations where socialism and trade unionism cannot be conservative or even gradualist. To demand that such leaders adapt their politics to Western images of responsible behavior is to forget that many Western unions, socialist parties, and intellectuals were similarly "irresponsible and demagogic" in the early stages of their development. Today Western leaders must communicate and work with non-Communist revolutionaries in the Orient and Africa at the same time that they accept the fact that serious ideological controversies have ended at home.

[My] concern with making explicit the conditions of the democratic order reflects my perhaps overrationalistic belief that a fuller understanding of the various conditions under which democracy has existed may help men to develop it where it does not now exist. Although we have concluded that Aristotle's basic hypothesis of the relationship of democracy to a class structure bulging toward the middle . . . is still valid, this does not encourage political optimism, since it implies that political activity should be directed primarily toward assuring economic development. Yet we must not be unduly pessimistic. Democracy has existed in a variety of circumstances, even if it is most commonly sustained by a limited set of conditions. It cannot be achieved by acts of will alone, of course, but men's wills expressed in action can shape institutions and events in directions that reduce or increase the chances for democracy's development and survival. Ideology and passion may no longer be necessary to sustain the class struggle within stable and affluent democracies, but they are clearly needed in the international effort to develop free political and economic institutions in the rest of the world. It is only the ideological class struggle within the West which is ending. Ideological conflicts linked to levels and problems of economic development and of appropriate political institutions among different nations will last far beyond our lifetime, and men committed to democracy can abstain from them only at their peril. To aid men's actions in furthering democracy in then absolutist Europe was in some measure Tocqueville's purpose in studying the operation of American society in 1830. To clarify the operation of Western democracy in the mid-twentieth century may contribute to the political battle in Asia and Africa.

The New American Dilemma

DAVID E. APTER

The United States has clearly opted for science, and precisely because it has done so it must take the consequences. One of these consequences is that power and prestige will be based on functional roles germane to modern industrial society, in which science and efficiency go hand in hand. Equality of opportunity means that social life is a continuous screening process that begins with education. Parental status is no guarantee of future success. Ours is a system of downward, as well as of upward, mobility—but a special kind of downward mobility. The "downwardness" is a measure of inability, while "upwardness" is a measure of ability and proficiency. The criteria are based on natural talent.

This phenomenon is as yet only dimly understood and only beginning to emerge in our society. Luck, fortune, special advantages—these excuses could always be used to explain personal failure or success. Increasingly they cannot and an individual of the future will have to confront himself with some agonizing questions. Can the less gifted accept the fact? We have developed an elaborate rhetoric to disguise low status and to give it false dignity through titles, euphemistic job descriptions, and other accommodations that the "establishment" uses to salve its conscience. This rhetoric does not help to prepare us for the bifurcation that is occurring in our country—in which society divides into two mutually antagonistic and, in many ways, lonely groups. One is composed of ideologues who devoutly defend unreason because they are afraid that, in the face of reason, their orientation to the world around them will fall apart and that in the process their world will disappear. Ideology becomes a protection for people alienated from their society—a protection against the final alienation. They therefore stubbornly hang on to their ideologies in the hope that, by sheer persistence, they will prevail against other ideologies or even against reason itself. They represent the "disestablishment."

The second group is also alienated. Theirs is an alienation brought about by "superior wisdom," that is, by the ability to penetrate the ideologies of others and thereby to emancipate themselves. In this group is the social scientist, who is the objective observer. He penetrates all the disguises created by the untrained mind or the ideological mind and attaches himself to the image of the wise. He represents the "establishment."

The social scientist and the ideologue represent two increasingly antagonistic roles in modern society. The antagonism is all the sharper because, in an age of science, the nonrationality of the ideologue only makes him more defensive about his beliefs. More and more the social scientist is at the center of the society, and his probing and inevitably remorseless search for deeper levels of reality confuse the ideologue. The latter, more alienated, is therefore likely to engage in bold behavior calculated to inhibit the scientist and cause him to refrain from probing too deeply. To the disestablished, the language of social science is obscure and dangerous. The levels of reality probed by the social scientist are only dimly understood, if at all. Meanwhile, the universities controlled by the established set higher and higher standards of "quality." The insurance salesman, the bank clerk, the businessman, the retired army officer, and the other nonprofessional representatives of the middle class most often in possession of university degrees become the most concerned. They cannot find their places in the functionally unequal society.

The pattern of mutual alienation between these two groups is only intensified by the spread of quality education. With the increased dependence of the population on educational qualifications for positions that a generation ago did not require the same knowledge, the social scientist controls many of the main routes to power and prestige. The only recourse of the ideologue is intimidation of the social scientist by arousing the public against unorthodox or heretical views. And, episodically, he does so. So well entrenched are the universities, however, and so widely accepted is the norm of academic freedom that the ideologues as a group are rarely very successful, although individual ideologues may successfully enhance their personal careers by becoming professional witch-hunters.

Today's American ideologue is a middle-class man who objects to his dependence on science even when he accepts its norms. He is resentful of the superiority of the educated and antagonistic to knowldge. His ideology is characteristically not of the left but of the right. It is, in extreme cases, of the radical right, looking back to a more bucolic age of individuality and localism, in which parochial qualities of mind were precisely those most esteemed—to a simple democracy, in fact. Robbed of its individuality, the middle-class "disestablishment" forms loose associations with others who are escaping from the fate of superfluousness. Social hatred is directed against the Negro, the black enemy who can destroy the disestablished, and against the Negro's protector, the establishment man whose belief in rationality and equal opportunity has altered the system of power and prestige so that it is based on universalistic selection and talent. *Today, the radical right fights against the bifurcation of society on the basis of talent.* It is the resistance ideology of all those who hitherto were the *Stand* figures of our society in an earlier day; the models of once sober, industrious, and responsible citizens.

For the truly superfluous men, there is no ideology, only generalized hatred. Speed, violence, a frenetic round of petulant actions, or perhaps more simply despair, characterize these groups, which have been largely ignored by a prosperous society. Black or white, they are an embarrassment to the "establishment," which would like to take drastic remedial action—action that they find consistently blocked by the disestablished majority, which on the contrary, tries to preserve its superiority over those beneath it. And in the process, the disestablished look more and more alike. Violence, militancy, activism, in the name of a conservatism for which, especially in the United States, we have no traditional rhetoric— the result is seen in comical but dangerous extremist groups, which by their activities give to a nebulous conservatism greater appeal and mystique.

Mannheim argues that the discovery that much thought is ideological challenges the validity of thought itself.

Man's thought had from time immemorial appeared to him as a segment of his spiritual existence and not simply as a discrete objective fact. Reorientation had in the past frequently meant a change in man himself. In these earlier periods it was mostly a case of slow shifts in values and norms, of a gradual transformation of the frame of reference from which men's actions derived their ultimate orientation. But in modern times it is a much more profoundly disorganizing affair. The resort to the unconscious tended to dig up the soil out of which the varying points of view emerged. The roots from which human thought had hitherto derived its nourishment were exposed. Gradually it becomes clear to all of us that we cannot go on living in the same way once we know about our unconscious motives as we did when we were ignorant of them. What we now experience is more than a new idea, and the questions we raise constitute more than a new problem. What we are concerned with here is the elemental perplexity of our time, which can be epitomized in the symptomatic question, "How is it possible for man to continue to think and live in a time when the problems of ideology and utopia are being radically raised and thought through in all their implications?"

To expose the ideological aspects of human thinking does not, however, make ideological thought impossible. It divides it into new forms. One is that of dogma, which easily leads to violence and dissension. Those who see the world in stereotypes seek to protect their beliefs from those who would undermine them.

The more hopeful alternative is the spread of social science. It is in this sense that we can say that social science has become the ultimate ideology and science the ultimate talisman against cynicism. It defines its own purposes through the logic of enquiry. Some years ago, Michael Polanyi pointed out this process very clearly. What he said then of scientists in general applies more and more to the *social* scientist today:

Professional scientists form a very small minority in the community, perhaps one in ten thousand. The ideas and opinions of so small a group can be of importance only by virtue of the response which they evoke from the general public. This response is indispensable to science, which depends on it for the money to pay the costs of research and for recruits to replenish the ranks of the profession. Why do people decide to accept science as valid? Can they not see the limitations of scientific demonstrations—in the pre-selected evidence, the preconceived theories, the always basically deficient documentation? They may see these shortcomings, or at least they may be made to see them. The fact remains that they must make up their minds about their material surroundings in one way or another. Men must form ideas about the material universe and must embrace definite convictions on the subject. No part of the human race has ever been known to exist without a system of such convictions, and it is clear that their absence would mean intellectual annihilation. The public must choose, therefore, either to believe in science or else in Aristotle, the Bible, Astrology or Magic. Of all such alternatives, the public of our times has, in its majority, chosen science.

But the "Polanyi choice" . . . embodies some very troubling and universal problems. His statement shows a certain comfortableness about the majority choice. But what happens if, having chosen, the majority does not follow through on its choice and indeed rejects many aspects of it? What is the effect, too, upon the minority that has not made this choice—and by effect I mean particularly political consequences? Perhaps one illustration of what occurs is to be found in the United States at the present time.

What is happening in the United States may well be typical of other highly developed societies. In a functional and rationalistic universe, the scientists and social scientists are accorded an increasing monitor role in political life—though not because they possess a kind of Platonic predisposition that prepares them for the role of leaders. Quite the contrary, they share all the ambiguity about their roles that their fellow citizens have. By gaining a superior insight into the conduct of their fellows, however, they create a new role and an ideology that follows from it, a hierarchy of power and prestige based on intellectual ability, which, in its extreme form, is what Michael Young called the "meritocracy." Once the social scientist discovered that there is a discrepancy between behavior observed and behavior felt, between the act and the rationalization, between the conscious and the subconscious, and between virtue and conduct, he fashioned a new role for himself—the theoretically omniscient observer. Human mysteries have become technical problems. In the modern development communities, he is asked to apply his knowledge. He displaces the physician as a new symbol of aloofness. (The professional intellect is antiseptic.) He regards the layman as irresponsible or, at best, uninformed. It is therefore not surprising that the recourse of the disestablished is intimidation of the social scientist by arousing the public against unorthodox or heretical views.

The major propositions that emerge from this brief examination can now be indicated: (1) Science is a well defined ideology possessing norms of empiricism, predictability, and rationality as guides to conduct. (2) Social science is becoming accepted as scientific, and scientific norms are increasingly accepted as guides to social conduct. (3) There is a universal trend toward planning, calculation, and rationalistic goals concerned with the future in both the developing and developed areas. (4) In the developing areas, vulgar ideologies express the urge to science in some form of socialism associated with national independence movements (African socialism, Egyptian socialism, Indonesian socialism). (5) In the developed areas, the new ideology expresses itself in the "meritocracy." Recruitment of talent is on the basis of competitive school and university examinations, with increasingly close links between the educational "establishment" and the bureaucratic "establishment."

Durkheim remarked about the pioneering role of economics that

for two centuries economic life has taken on an expansion it never knew before. From being a secondary function, despised and left to inferior classes, it passed onto one of the first rank. We see the military, governmental and religious functions falling back more and more in the face of it. The scientific functions alone are in a position to dispute its ground. . . .

What was true for economics is increasingly true for the other social sciences. Both science and technology are, in application, intertwined with the social sciences. In modern scientific communities, governments are the greatest single consumers of social science. They not only stimulate policy research but consume the product as well.

It is in the political sphere that the battle between social scientists and ideologues will be the most intense. More and more political leaders rely on the social scientists, as we have suggested. This reliance is growing both in the early- and later-stage development communities. As long as social science cannot perform functions of identity and solidarity, recourse will be had to ideology in its more dogmatic forms. Certainly there will be antiscientific ideologies. Political leaders will need to learn how to tread lightly between the alienated ideologues and the desire to apply science to human affairs.

We have suggested . . . that the dialogue in the developing areas is between nationalism and socialism. In the more developed countries, it will be between social science and nonrational vulgar ideologies. The ideologue will manipulate the slogans. The social scientist will ignore him. Political leaders will learn to rely on the latter without unduly arousing the former. Perhaps the long-run trend in both types of development community is a drawing of the lines between idiocy and intellectual merit more sharply until the ideologues fall of their own weight. But this end is too much to hope for.

What is the antidote? We need to understand problems of solidarity and identity more clearly. A kind of settling-down process is in order. With respect to ideology, social science differs from all others in one respect. The only antidote for it is more of it, addressed to solidarity and identity problems. Both new and highly developed communities need to accept the openness of spirit, the attitudes of questioning that probe the innermost secrets of social and political life (without feeling threatened). Such a spirit, essential to democracy, will perhaps have a destructive effect on all other ideologies.

We need, too, to pay more attention to the total educational system. I do not mean simply to refer to education in a pious way and to argue that modifying it will solve all our problems when obviously it cannot. But more social science education, the early development of a questioning attitude toward human affairs, and attention to discovery as a means of identifying the self, will help to break down the growing dichotomy between layman and specialist. That this process will take place has always been part of our liberal faith. It will not occur, however, through the trickling-down of jargon and a few manipulative ideas (as advertising executives, for example, pick up psychological jargon). What is needed, in addition to the modesty and propriety inherent in the scientific enterprise, is an understanding of relevant criteria for the evaluation of conduct, our own as well as others'.

We have suggested that the main uses of ideology in the developing areas are to promote solidarity and identity. The one represents the linking up of institutions, some of which are old, some new, and most of which emerge at the interstices between them. The other is the assertion of self (identity) through the marking out of new roles and the fulfillment of personality through such roles. The survival of "vulgar" ideologies, which are programmatic and explanatory, depends on the effectiveness with which they perform these two functions.

The scientific ideology can do little to promote solidarity and identity. The obligations implied in either are not very relevant, and a scientific ideology tends to downgrade the beliefs and intimacies that the vulgar ideologies promote. On the other hand, the scientific ideology handles these matters through professionality. The key to the "establishment" is its professional status. Its authority derives from superior knowledge. It has a code of ethics that enshrines integrity. The integrity of the research worker is only slightly less entrenched than the code from which it derives, academic freedom. This code, in turn, is linked with the concept of free enquiry. And, in an area where free enquiry produces a superior range of technological social alternatives for decision-makers, its concrete advantages become manifest.

Professionalization creates a sense of obligation among individuals, which by becoming moral is therefore much more significant than a simple contract and more reliable. A feeling of custodianship derives from this professional form of obligation, for it is the profession, the body of theory, the set of ideas that contain universals and represent the human intellectual inheritance that need to be enlarged by the incumbents of professional roles. Older professional roles that cannot make this kind of contribution become more mechanical rather than professional; become trades rather than professions. A move into the "establishment" begins when a particular group adopts a code of ethics and tries to establish some theory for its work, some transmittable body of ideas that can be called "scientific." The public relations experts who run polls, do sample studies for private firms on a contract basis, and function between the universities proper and corporate business are an example. The Bureau of Applied Social Research at Columbia University, the National Opinion Research Center at the University of Chicago, and the Stanford Research Associates are other examples of bodies that, although clearly professional, are doing contract work. The next step is for the large-scale private firms to claim the same professional status, followed by the more skilled advertising technicians. By this means, relating the needed skills to transmittable theory and the theory to some opinion—professionalization occurs.

Professionalization then gives identity to the role and solidarity to the organization. Such organizational identity and solidarity link the professional to the "establishment." Once in the "establishment," the individual has "arrived."

In this respect, the long-term aspects of ideology in the developing areas are the same as for the developed countries. Subordinate but senior roles on the basis of technical ability are already associated with civil-service positions, planning positions, and fiscal and other technical roles associated with development in the new nations. The occupants of such roles are like their counterparts from abroad. They have been trained in more or less the same institutions, and similar professional standards obtain. To this degree, the vulgar ideologies decline, and the scientific ideology takes over. Perhaps the long-run basis of association between new nations and old ones will take place largely between members of the professional establishments; for the sense of shared solidarity and identity, like the canons of science themselves, are more or less universal for professionals.

What we have been saying has, of course, been said before—and better. I know of no more adequate summary of these remarks than Werner Jaeger's introductory paragraph in *Paideia*.

Every nation which has reached a certain stage of development is instinctively impelled to practice education. Education is the process by which a community preserves and transmits its physical and intellectual character. For the individual passes away, but the main type remains. The natural process of transmission from one generation to another ensures the perpetuation of the physical characteristics of animals and men; but men can transmit their social and intellectual nature only by exercising the qualities through which they created it—reason and conscious will. Through the exercise of these qualities man commands a freedom of development which is impossible to other living creatures. . . .

It is in this spirit that we examine ideology and discontent.

Mass Responses
to Political Symbols

MURRAY EDELMAN

1

. . . [My] basic thesis is that mass publics respond to currently conspicuous political symbols: not to "facts," and not to moral codes embedded in the character or soul, but to the gestures and speeches that make up the drama of the state.

The mass public does not study and analyze detailed data about secondary boycotts, provisions for stock ownership and control in a proposed space communications corporation, or missile installations in Cuba. It ignores these things until political actions and speeches make them symbolically threatening or reassuring, and it then responds to the cues furnished by the actions and the speeches, not to direct knowledge of the facts.

It is therefore political actions that chiefly shape men's political wants and "knowledge," not the other way around. The common assumption that what democratic government does is somehow always a response to the moral codes, desires, and knowledge embedded inside people is as inverted as it is reassuring. This model, avidly taught and ritualistically repeated, cannot explain what happens; but it may persist in our folklore because it so effectively sanctifies prevailing policies and permits us to avoid worrying about them.

Values, it is true, are persistent. . . . Fundamental norms as created by reference groups persist, leading interested groups to claim increasing increments of the values the norms embody. How fast successive levels of benefit are sought or how intensely deprivations are resisted hinges upon what is legitimized and upon what is made to appear possible. Political acts and settings, leadership, and language all influence legitimations and assumptions about possibility.

A reversal in mass political demands respecting American policy toward Germany occurred, for example, in the years immediately following World War II. At the end of the war there were widespread demands for stamping out religious persecution, genocide, and dictatorship, and for eliminating those who had been associated with these German practices. The Nuremberg trials reflected this political configuration. A series of governmental actions rather swiftly replaced the assumption that the threat to be guarded against was Hitlerism, however, and replaced it with equally widespread fears of Russia. These actions included the creation of a new military alliance in NATO, jousting with Russia in the United Nations and elsewhere, and a series of other American and Russian acts dramatizing the emergence of a cold war, an iron curtain, and other symbols of a major new threat. The political acts to which the mass public responded may have been rational and effective or they may not. That question remains controversial and also irrelevant to this inquiry. That the response of spectators was to these acts, however, and not directly to exhaustive and dispassionate analysis of the military situation is central. The public is not in touch with the situation, and it "knows" the situation only through the symbols that engage it.

In view of the changed perceptual world created by the symbols of cold war, "Germany" quickly took on a new meaning. There were new sources of anxiety and a new view of the future and the possible. Germany became an ally against Russia; and if former Nazis in high military and political posts could help cope with the new dangers, they were welcomed and their past actions rewritten or ignored. It thus turned out that very intense mass concerns about denazification were not generators of public policy, but rather highly vulnerable victims of a changed perceptual world.

It is clear enough that whatever promises and hazards men see as possibilities on the political horizon depend upon the assumptions created for them by political acts and events. The possibilities they perceive influence their immediate political demands and actions in turn.

Changes in mass response of the kind just illustrated are, of course, neither instantaneous nor unanimous. They entail struggle and resistance among people with different interests. By the same token they involve struggle and resistance within a great many ambivalent individuals who experience a sometimes painful effort to find a new perceptual outlook that has more meaning than the one they have reason to abandon: a world that permits them to understand and to act with less tension. The political symbols that bring about the change do so, in one sense, by changing the tensions associated with the old and the new as they suggest altered possibilities.

2

Under what conditions are such changes in mass behavior likely and when will they be resisted? Because the factors involved are so closely dependent on each other, there is a danger that any analysis will distort by implying with undue certainty that some one social phenomenon is a cause or an independent variable. Let it be emphasized that we are dealing here with a total transaction. The theory that follows consists of a series of assumptions and inferences. Although we do not have adequate empirical observations to validate the entire theory, various segments are substantiated by findings in disparate fields of social science.

The degree of consensus or division in a society on issues that persist and arouse men emotionally is a useful starting point for the analysis of mass responses. Examples of such issues in the United States are: the status of minority religious, racial, and ethnic groups, restrictions on the economic activities of the wealthy, and willingness to compromise differences with other countries.

Mass responses depend upon whether public values with respect to strong norms of this kind are heavily concentrated (unimodal), polarized into two clearly defined adversary foci (bimodal), or dispersed rather widely along a scale (multimodal). The dispersion of values on one issue will often correspond in some measure with the dispersion on the other strong ones. In the United States, for example, people who oppose restrictions on economic activity may also be more likely than "welfare staters" to support racial, ethnic, or religious status distinctions and to be opposed to a "soft" line toward the Communist bloc. To the extent that such overlap exists, deep-seated cleavage or consensus is reinforced.

When, on the issues that arouse men emotionally, there is a bimodal value structuring, threat and insecurity are maximized. Those who hold the other value become the enemy. Under these circumstances condensation symbolism and mental rigidity become key factors in social interaction for reasons already considered, and it becomes relatively easy to shift men's assumptions about the future and therefore their responses to present conditions. Under this kind of value patterning, mass responses are more manipulable than under either of the other two to be considered because responses are chiefly to threat perceptions and can be readily changed by making it appear that new threats are now dominant. George Orwell dramatized the possibilities in his novel *1984* with accounts of overnight changes in the national enemy and in history books: reversals enthusiastically accepted by the public.

A multimodal scattering of values is the opposite extreme. In this situation a very large part of the population is likely to see some merit in both sides of the argument: to be ambivalent and at the same time free to explore the possibilities of alternative courses of action. Rather than fear of an enemy, there is stimulating tension. A minimal fraction of the population is frozen in a narrow class or other fixed grouping, and a major fraction is marginal and searching for a synthesis. Value structuring is therefore relatively slight. Rather than a fixed past and future, accepted with passion and carrying clear implications for present behavior, alternative possibilities can be recognized and pluralistic politics supported. The preconditions exist for cognitive planning, negotiation, and logrolling.

The unimodal value structure is the type to which the American population has most closely conformed through most of United States history. Here there is a wide measure of consensus on the fundamental policy directions of the state. In this kind of polity nongovernmental groups and organizations enjoy a maximum degree of maneuverability because they are not constantly opposed by adversary groupings, and most of the public remains uninvolved and uncritical.

At the same time the unimodal structure encourages a maximum of democratic procedures, forms, and structuring because political parties and private power groups will predictably move in the same direction. There can be open and dramatic appeals for public support, for the support is already great and the likelihood of massive opposition to basic policies slight. The creation and dramatic employment of democratic forms may therefore be not so much an indication of responsiveness to changing popular values as a sign that values are unimodal and that the mass public is uncritical. In a unimodal situation evocative political symbols are likely to have similar meanings and call forth similar responses in a larger proportion of the population than under other conditions. This result is likely because the people are more alike in respect to education, socioeconomic status, upbringing, experiences, and ambitions.

There is good reason to suspect that wide agreement on a centrist or "middle of the road" orientation offers a barrier to politically induced change. Nongovernmental organizations then become the foci of change in tangible resource allocations. There is a built-in depreciation of tension and criticism, so that responsiveness to suggestions for innovation is slight, leading to low viability, to great suspicion of critics of the status quo, and eventually to mass movements dedicated not to change but to the suppression of heretics. In this respect Aristotle's contention that popular government gives way eventually to tyranny jibes in some degree with the view of recent mass society theorists, such as Kornhauser, who believe they can record a movement from pluralism to mass society.

Tension levels play a key role in this theory. It suggests that a bimodal value structure creates such great tension that rational responses are held to a minimum and symbolic cues and assurances avidly grasped. A unimodal structure creates little tension regarding norms, leaving a clear field for organized group maneuvering but also creating the conditions for the emergence of mass society symptoms if deviants or "outsiders" appear to be threatening the consensus. A multimodal structure comes closest to establishing optimal tension for critical mass response to policy proposals. Harold Lasswell observed three decades ago that "the dynamic of politics is to be found in the tension level of the individuals in society."

Clearly the model deals with ideal types. A polity that is basically unimodal, for example, may become bimodal on a major issue for a period of years and begin to exhibit the characteristics of the latter form. Though pure examples of any type may be hard to find in the real world, this theory predicts what kinds of mass response are likely for a particular patterning of values.

The political party structure of a country offers a clue to the dispersal of fundamental values among its population. Anthony Downs has developed an "economic theory of democracy," which suggests, among other things, that a unimodal value structure gives rise to a two party system and a bimodal or multimodal structure to a multiple party system.

In Italy and France, where popular values are more clearly bimodal than in other democracies, in the Scandinavian countries, which conform most closely to the multimodal type, and in the United States his proposition fits well. The Downs theory would also lead one to expect the current trend toward a two party system in West Germany.

3

The constant involvement of private organizations and groups in actions that are essentially public in character has been a major theme of this discussion. We turn now to another sense in which private groups and public institutions are integrally related.

Man is constantly creating and responding to symbols, whether he is at any moment concerned with public affairs or not. Susanne Langer declares:

This basic need, which certainly is obvious only in man, is the need of symbolization. The symbol-making function is one of man's primary activities, like eating, looking, or moving about. It is the fundamental process of his mind, and goes on all the time. . . .
The material furnished by the senses is constantly wrought into symbols, which are our elementary ideas. Some of these ideas can be combined and manipulated in the manner we call "reasoning." Others do not lend themselves to this use, but are naturally telescoped into dreams, or vapor off in conscious fantasy; and a vast number of them build the most typical and fundamental edifice of the human mind—religion.

While men differ in the meanings symbols convey to them and in the manner of their reaction, no man can remain alive and avoid symbolic response. As has already been suggested, following Mead, this is what gives him a self and a mind.

Symbolic involvement with governmental acts, settings, and actors can therefore be recognized as one of various devices by which men engage themselves in a fashion that is symbolically necessary and satisfying. Religion, as Langer points out, is another such universal device, and work, together with the economic organizations in which it involves men, is a third major one. Family attachments and participation in social organizations also contribute to the richness or emptiness of man's symbolic life.

There is reason to believe that the style of men's symbolic engagements in these various associations is related and often contagious, and that they are sometimes complementary in the sense that needs not supplied by one of them may be sought in another. Generalizations must remain tentative.

Certainly a central dimension of involvement in all of them lies between the poles of identification and alienation. A great many people, particularly specialists, professionals, and managers in industry, develop a tie to their work that is relatively rational and efficient. Their effectiveness derives from their special ability to devise methods of accomplishing desired ends, and they experience deep satisfaction as they exercise such ability. . . . Such rational and effective manipulation of resources is in part a function of the opportunity to work with the concrete environment and to see the results of one's work. Nobody functions in this way in everything he does, and some people apparently never do so. It may be that only people who have learned through some such gratifying association how to deal effectively with men and objects are likely to respond to political leadership and movements in a way that serves their objective interests and brings them tangible resources. There is evidence in earlier chapters that business management and other organized elites are consistently most effective in gaining resources through government. This is not to say that most individual managers or specialists are effective at political tactics or even that they are directly involved, for survey research indicates that, "political participation to satisfy economic needs is unrelated to level of income in the American culture." The consistent success of organized elites in utilizing the governmental process to serve their material interests does suggest, however, both that some individual managers and specialists are effective at it and that their constituents have learned how to support them and how to avoid defeating their efforts through irrational actions.

People who are effective in some of their activities may nonetheless seek nonrational satisfactions from other pursuits. The highly effective specialist or manager may identify with his company or his profession in an emotional manner. His opinions on political matters unrelated to his economic interests may serve chiefly to project inner tensions or to aid in social adjustment. As an extreme example, Henry Ford, who epitomized rationality in organizing the production of automobiles, became transfixed with undemonstrable and unreal threats and distortions when behaving in other settings.

Ford was extreme, not typical. For most men who function well and effectively, condensation symbols evidently serve as a spur, catalyst, and complement to their work. If they are sure, without objective evidence, that what is good for General Motors is good for the country, the belief doubtless makes them work with greater zeal for General Motors, and the sense of harmony both their work and their beliefs confer may also make them work more effectively for their country if called to do so. The testing of work and its results remains a testing against tangible results, not satisfaction with pipedreams.

Similarly, effective workmanship in a man's occupation frequently occurs together with a high degree of identification with condensation symbols in his religious life, the two activities apparently complementing and enriching each other by reinforcing a feeling of usefulness and of being an important part of something larger than oneself. The key contrast in man's symbolic engagements with work, state, church, and other associations is not the difference between identification and hostility, but that between satisfying involvement and despairing noninvolvement.

For those whose identification with work, political party, and community is slight and unsatisfying, the yearning to escape from isolation and responsibility becomes very strong. The alienated man, who feels little sense of belonging to any group and cherishes no organization as an extension of his own personality, will, for reasons already explored, predictably become authoritarian. He will seek strong leadership, person-alize, stereotype and distort his environment, and will react to distortions and abstractions rather than to concrete people and things.

Lipset has called attention to the prevalence of "working class au-thoritarianism." Among unskilled workers ethnocentric and authori-tarian reactions are apparently more common than among those with higher socioeconomic status. This condition is understandable as in part at least a resultant of the working conditions for unskilled labor in mod-ern industry. Summing up the environmental influences contributing to mass authoritarian movements Frenkel-Brunswik has written:

In our society the increasing mental standardization accompanying the processes of mass production, the increasing difficulty of genuine identification with society due to the anonymity of the big organizations and the ensuing isolation of the individual, the unintelligibility of political and social forces, the decline of the individual's ability to decide and master his life rationally and autono-mously, and finally the power of propaganda machinery to manipulate—are among the most potent of the factors which might contribute to such mass sup-port in the foreseeable future.

To divide work in the factory to the point that the worker cannot have any feeling of satisfaction, accomplishment, or autonomy is to em-phasize to the worker throughout the day that he is being used as a machine and not as a man. Here is one facet of modern social organization that has clear implications for obsessive symbol seeking in the political and religious realms.

The Artificial Majority

THEODORE J. LOWI

The election of 1970 was an overwhelming bore. James Reston observed in *The New York Times* that "None have come forward," and he, like many others, had in mind such leaders as Humphrey, Muskie, Stevenson, Bayh, McGovern, Tunney, Kennedy, Mondale, Hart, and House members and gubernatorial candidates too numerous to mention. On the Republican side, many candidates stuck like barnacles to their Democratic opponents, and couldn't be pried loose to give voters a clear view of the difference. Humphrey ran a virtual law-and-order campaign; Stevenson absolutely avoided distinction until late in the campaign; Tunney seemed just younger, not better.

The only excitement was the uncertainty of outcome in a few states. But if politics is to be more than a winter replacement for night baseball, mere excitement is not enough.

There was only one surprise, and it was not the stridency of Spiro

Agnew. What he did was absolutely typical of Republicans, especially at the end of periods of war, when there is usually a Republican majority and a bit of panic in the air as to whether all the killing accomplished anything toward ridding the world of America's enemies. If it had not been Agnew, some other figure would have taken the lead that Nixon took during the 1950s. The surprise was the frailty of the liberals, liberal Democrats mainly, but Republican liberals as well. It was the unwillingness of these people to bring to the electorate the message that the country is in trouble; the reluctance of these usually thoughtful public men to define our problems in terms that might lead to meaningful public policies. The surprise lay in their willingness to let Agnew define the agenda and the terms of discourse. In politics, as in the courtroom, he who does that has gone a long way toward winning the debate.

Of course, it was not a matter of personal frailty. These men have all demonstrated courage upon occasion. There is something about the political system itself that explains their espousal of politics-as-usual at a time when everything else is unusual. So the question really is: what kind of electoral and party system do we have that it can be impervious to social change and disorder?

Part of the answer lies in the assumption of centrality, which goes back to Locke and passes to us through a host of American historians and political scientists. It supposes that the American spirit is, as the statistician would say, "normally distributed." Americans, it is argued, think very much alike about many fundamental things. And when they disagree, they do not clash with much passion. Only a very small percentage of the population feels intensely about issues, and they are best treated as exceptions, as intellectual outsiders. Extreme disagreement means unwillingness to compromise, and that violates one of the unwritten but sacred rules of American politics. The attitudes of Americans are assumed to distribute themselves like the model given in Diagram 1.

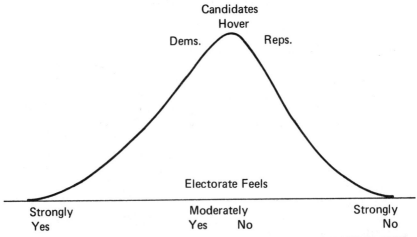

DIAGRAM 1   HOW THE ELECTORATE LOOKS TO THE CANDIDATES

That is not necessarily a true description of Americans. It is only a model, but it is the model that political personalities carry around in their heads. They did not need to be told by Scammon and Wattenberg. They might have been surprised to learn from *The Real Majority* that the electorate had moved a bit to the right; but no one could tell the candidates, and no one tried to tell them, that the mass of voters had ceased to hover around dead center.

This assumption is reinforced by the opinion polls, but in a peculiar way. It is doubtful that the polls influence people by reporting results with which the previously uncommitted align themselves. The more likely explanation is a "McLuhan effect"—the medium is indeed the message. Polling agencies, first of all, ask only certain questions; there is simply no room for everything on the questionnaire. Often the only issues touched upon are those that have been on the agenda for some time, and it is probable that for many of these, opinion hovers around the center.

A second important factor in polling is the way in which questions are asked and responses are structured. For example, the respondent may be asked how he feels about "the law-and-order issue," and he will have to pick a single response (either For or Against; or Strongly For, For, Against, Strongly Against—"Please check only one"). Or the question could be more specific: "Do you favor appropriating more money for the local police department?" In either case, the respondent on the usual opinion poll cannot expand on his response. Instead, he undertakes an inner dialogue, trying to balance all his plusses and minuses in order to give the interviewer his best accounting, which is really a complex response expressed in terribly simple terms. It is a "net response," a "Well, yes and no," or a "Well, I don't know," or, to be safe, a "moderate Yes" or "Maybe not."

The polling agency must then code these responses for entry on computer cards. These "net responses" have to be treated centrally, as moderate yesses and noes. At one level that is accurate; yet many of these middle-ground respondents may actually feel very intensely about certain aspects of the questions, but were given no opportunity on the questionnaire to express these intensities. The result is reaffirmation of the assumption of centrality. Reaffirmation is putting it too mildly. The polls lend Scientific Validation to the assumption of centrality.

Two most important results flow from this assumption of centrality. First, if candidates or parties believe that voters are overwhelmingly in the middle, it would be irrational of them to develop appeals and campaign strategies that were not center-oriented. Exactly the same problem arises in merchandising. Competing service stations occupy all four corners of a single intersection, where the traffic patterns are concentrated. To move slightly away from that center would be to move from the site of best exposure. Similarly, the candidates feel that, if they moved "away from center," they would be moving down the slope of the curve, where obviously there are fewer voters—if it is true that they are so distributed.

Over the years, a few major party candidates—Taft and Goldwater are the most important examples—have made a different assumption. They thought it more probable that voters were distinctly partisan and tended to distribute themselves "bi-modally," like a camel's hump, rather than in a single, central mode. In that case it would be rational to move to one or the other side of center, as suggested in Diagram 2. Only Goldwater got a Presidential nomination and the opportunity to test this theory. His defeat does not necessarily prove that there are no clearly divisive issues in the country, but it obviously convinced most candidates for all public offices that the centricity assumption was the safest.

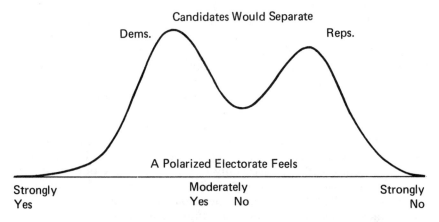

DIAGRAM 2 HOW THE ELECTORATE
ACTUALLY LOOKS ON SOME ISSUES

The second result of assuming centricity is the self-fulfilling prophecy. If candidates assume that voters are moderate and centrally distributed, and if they conduct their appeals accordingly, they help bring about that very situation.

This second consequence is not as simple as it sounds, because it does not happen merely because the politicians influence thousands of voters to be moderate by making moderate appeals. That may be the effect in a few cases, but more often something else happens, as we can see all too clearly in the 1970 campaigns.

Centricity prevails, first of all, because the candidates give the voters no choice but centricity. Even if the polls did not tilt the responses in favor of moderation, the candidates would. They hang together so closely around a mean that voters must vote for a middle-of-the-road position or stay home.

And even that is not the most important part of the process. How do candidates hang close together? They do it by "strategic obfuscation." In other words, they define the issues in terms so general that each candidate can virtually subsume the other. That is why the Democrats let the Agnew Republicans define the terms of discourse in 1970, why they so rapidly accepted "Law and Order" as the issue.

Law and Order is a generalized concept, a basket phrase that includes six, eight, even ten specific issues. Supporting this generalized form of law and order, the Democratic candidate could say, "I'm for Law and Order—with justice," as the Republicans were saying, "I'm for Law and Order—with safety." Thus they create the impression of debate, while in fact they agree to define as irrelevant to the campaign the specific issues that are part of the law-and-order basket.

At least two things follow from this. First, each voter goes through the same internal dialogue as does the respondent to an opinion poll. He has only one vote and must use it according to his own balancing of the various issues in the law-and-order package. This pulls him toward the center because, if he is to vote at all, he must vote "on net" as a Democrat or a Republican.

But a second, fascinating thing happens: the extremes are eliminated statistically! Let us say that six hard-core issues are hidden underneath the candidate's definition of law and order. Let us even propose that the electorate is polarized on all six of these, so that voter distributions on attitudes toward racial integration, student radicals, police powers and restraints, preventive detention, the Black Panthers and unilateral withdrawal are all bi-modal, like the camel's hump, with most voters intensely for or intensely against. See then what happens when the six are treated simultaneously under the law-and-order concept, rather than one issue at a time, as in a real debate.

Diagram 3 is the almost inevitable result of grouping issues in one basket, because the same people are not intensely for or against all the issues. Racial questions are salient to certain voters, who will feel intensely "yes" or "no" about questions in that field. But many of these people care little one way or another about preventive detention or students. Thus only a very few highly militant types will be consistent *and* intense on all six (or eight or ten) issues.

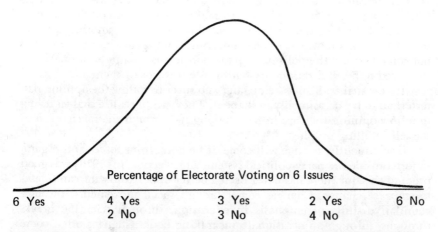

Percentage of Electorate Voting on 6 Issues

6 Yes	4 Yes	3 Yes	2 Yes	6 No
	2 No	3 No	4 No	

DIAGRAM 3 HOW THE ELECTORATE ACTUALLY LOOKS WHEN SIX (OR MORE) POLARIZED ISSUES ARE PRESENTED SIMULTANEOUSLY

You can be almost certain that when politicians advance conglomerate rather than specific definitions of issues they will produce, quite artificially, the impression of centrality. In effect, the Real Majority is an Artificial Majority, created by artifice, and in fact combining very unlike positions. As the great political scientist E. E. Schattschneider put it thirty years ago, "Persuasion is unnecessary or secondary. Politicians take people as they find them. The politician has a technical specialty based on a profitable discovery about the behavior of numbers."

This explains the paradox of political quiescence in the midst of social disorder. When they can, politicians avoid polarized issues; when avoidance becomes impossible, they lump controversies together and thus cancel out the extremes. This is probably the controlling reason why American electoral and party politics are so stable, and so isolated from the big issues of the day. It also suggests that, as the social turmoil increases, the separation between party politics and society becomes ever greater.

This pattern also suggests why there is rarely much to be gained from looking to party and electoral politics as agents of great changes. American party politics is designed to maintain the system. It maintains good things about the system, and it militates against removing bad things. And once change comes, usually through other channels, party politics adjusts and maintains the change as well. For example, a party politics all by itself would never have spread suffrage to Southern blacks; but once the suffrage was expanded, a party politics emerged to help realize a more effective participation.

Once in a great while political parties and elections do become channels of change. Students of these critical elections, particularly V. O. Key, Dean Burnham and Duncan MacRae, have located perhaps five national elections in 180 years that directly produced significant changes in the system. The last such "critical election" was probably 1928 (when Herbert Hoover defeated Alfred Smith), following which parties were for a brief while organized in ways relevant to making significant public policies. Students of these matters have probably been expecting another election for several years now, since the conditions again seem ripe. But one has not come because the polls have made politicians far more rational than they used to be, and rationality hath made cowards of them all.

It now strikes them as being safer and surer to follow the opinion pattern than to try occasionally to shape it. They fail to realize that in trying to follow opinion they are in fact shaping it—through the mechanism of the self-fulfilling prophecy.

Consequently, change will come, if he does, from forces and organizations outside the party-political system. The election [of 1970] was good proof of this, for there has never been a better opportunity for candidates to embrace change. Changes come through social movements, through cumulative shifts of emphasis in education, through scientific breakthroughs, through an occasional muckraking book. Changes often come through more aristocratic channels, such as Supreme Court decisions or capitalistic advancement of important new technologies.

We need to revise our outlook toward campaigns and elections. Party and electoral politics can be understood only if accepted as the way to buy stability—Law and Order in the broadest sense. When we want a little productive disorder, we must look elsewhere. And if in large numbers we were to turn away from party politics, treating elections as the great bore they have become, perhaps that would bring on a critical election, because politicians would try a little harder to get our attention.

Corporate Responsibility: Politics by Other Means

HAZEL HENDERSON

The current pessimism as to the ability of our political system to respond to change may reflect a narrow definition of "politics." [See the preceding article, "The Artificial Majority," by Theodore J. Lowi.] Especially today, we need to remember that politics covers a much broader area than merely those activities through which the citizens elect representatives to various national, state and local legislative bodies. The word also means "the total complex of relations between men and society." Whenever and wherever issues of power arise between people, "politics" occurs. Therefore, as some continue to fight on the electoral front—scuttling seniority rules and the Electoral College system, overhauling Congressional ethical standards, abolishing unrecorded teller votes, and tackling the serious abuses caused by unequal political access to television—it is as important for others to focus directly on the parallel and often unchecked power of those informal and private governments, the large American corporations.

This new "movement for corporate responsibility," whose goal is to politicize such corporations, could become the most significant political development of the 1970s. The extension of politics into what is nostalgically referred to as "private industry" will, in the view of many civic activists, open an almost untapped channel for organizing new constituencies. Many also believe that the corporation may prove more responsive to political pressure than has formal government—at least, the average age of its managers is considerably less than that of the leaders of Congress, and it depends on the brightest university graduates for its continued growth.

The movement began and will continue to draw its strength from the growing awareness of the enormous and often arbitrary social power wielded by these large corporations. A plaintive letter to *The New York Times* sums up this new awareness of corporate power, with its concomitant feeling of individual helplessness:

Dear Sirs:

I am disturbed and offended by your editorial statement that the Capitol Building belongs to the nation. This is a good example of the kind of muddled thinking that has led to the student revolt, riots and crime in the streets. In the interests of peace, plenty and the American Way of Life, you must print the truth:

> The Capitol Building belongs to Senator Eastland.
> The air belongs to General Motors.
> The mountains belong to Con Edison.
> The water belongs to U.S. Steel.
> The oil belongs to Secretary Hickel.
> The airwaves belong to NBC, CBS and ABC.
> The courts belong to the rich.
> The taxes belong to the working man, etc., etc.

Corporate power is encountered daily by millions of citizens who attempt to fight polluted air, oil-smeared beaches, plagues of nonreturnable cans and bottles, supersonic transports, rampant freeways, deceptive advertising, racial discrimination in employment, exploitation of natural resources, mushrooming shopping centers and housing developments, as well as huge military appropriations. In all such battles, sooner or later, they come up against some corporate Goliath, and find their slings unavailing. Newly radicalized, they learn that the 500 largest corporations not only control more than two-thirds of the country's manufacturing assets but also influence elections by carefully channeled campaign contributions that avoid legal restrictions. When, indeed, the law is observed. In a recent case, American President Lines and Pacific Far East Lines were fined $5,000 each under the Corrupt Practices Act for contributing to the campaign of members of Senate and House committees that control federal subsidies for the lines. No one knows how much money flows into the campaign coffers of compliant Congressmen, but ample channels are available—setting up special committees, "ear marking" a portion of a company officer's salary raise for political support, or dispensing the money through lobbyists or other intermediaries. Corporations also wield pervasive influence on government policies and regulatory agencies by tacitly holding out prize industry jobs to sympathetic officials on their retirement from government.

In addition, corporate lobbyists and Washington law firms regularly emasculate new legislation, in spite of the opposing efforts of underfinanced citizen groups. In recognition of this, John W. Gardner's new organization, Common Cause, is trying to rally a countervailing "citizens' lobby." Through extensive influence on the mass media, corporations can manage public opinion on a wide range of social issues and affect national priorities in resource allocation. With advertising, they can sell, along with their products, such underlying assumptions as approval of the homogeneous, suburban, two-car, artifact-filled way of life.

As this submerged iceberg of corporate power becomes increasingly visible, the new politics of corporate responsibility is rapidly gaining constituents and developing both theoretical content and strategy. Activists have already discovered serious fissures in the seemingly invulnerable corporate armor; notably its fear of "bad publicity," which can be exploited by "street theatre" tactics, and its slow reaction time and heavy-handedness, which can be used to abrade still more an outraged public opinion. The movement is becoming good electoral politics. Sen. Edmund S. Muskie, arguing for his National Air Quality Standards Act of 1970, asked rhetorically: "Are matters of the public health to be left to the decisions of the board of directors of these great motor companies?"

Much of the movement's initial impetus should be credited to Ralph Nader. It began defensively as "consumer protection," stressing full disclosure of information and legal redress of grievances; but as young recruits flocked to Nader's side and as other leaders emerged—among them John Banzhaf, whose test of the FCC's "Fairness Doctrine" released millions of dollars of free air time to anti-smoking advertisements—the movement turned to the offensive. Groups began actively seeking judicial tests of new tenets in consumer law; they began conducting such well-disciplined investigations as the now famous Nader's Raiders research studies of corruption and malfeasance in federal regulatory agencies.

As the young corporate crusaders became widely known and trusted, their exposés of corporate intransigence and disregard for consumer interests have brought the movement new recruits. Local civic activists found in the example of the Raiders a means to overcome their feeling of impotence when dealing with corporations and local governments. It was no plot; Nader's Center for the Study of Responsive Law, and the growing band of similar public advocate law firms (the Center for Law and Social Policy, the Citizens Advocate Center, the Environmental Defense Fund), as well as Saul Alinsky's Industrial Areas Foundation had simply confirmed the objective reality of the subjective experiences of millions of Americans. Local assaults against corporations were undertaken as early as 1967, when the militant black group, FIGHT, picketed the Eastman Kodak Company of Rochester to demand jobs. FIGHT won many concessions from the company at the annual meeting, where it came armed with proxies and with the support of local churches and civic groups. Other prototype corporate campaigns included the consumer boycott for minority jobs waged by Operation Breadbasket in Chicago; Project Equality, started in 1965 by the National Catholic Conference on Interracial Justice to withhold church purchases from companies which discriminate, and the diverse activities ranged against Dow Chemical Company's production of napalm.

In 1970, the movement to enforce corporate responsibility gained from the new public alarm over environmental pollution. Ecology produced new issues to add to the more familiar rallying points of Vietnam and racial discrimination. Environmentalists, enraged by huge corporate expenditures on apologist and often distorted advertising campaigns (they dubbed it "eco-pornography"), added regiments of potential activists to those willing to confront business in stock-proxy skirmishes at annual meetings. The most successful coalition of environmental, consumer and minority interests was the widely reported Campaign To Make General Motors Responsible, run by Philip Moore, Geoffrey Cowan, John Esposito and Joseph Onek. Campaign GM sought to add three public-interest directors to the auto maker's board and set up a shareholders' committee to report on the company's performance in consumer affairs, minority hiring and pollution control. Although it failed in its stated goals, it polled more than 5 million shares for each of its proposals and raised the issue of corporate accountability in a way understandable to millions of upper-income stockholders, as well as banks, mutual funds, insurance companies and other institutional investors.

Simultaneously, other proxy skirmishes were mounted, notably the Campaign Against Pollution's challenge to Commonwealth Edison of Chicago, which led to a strict new air pollution ordinance. This case illustrated the intertwining of business and government; pressure against the giant Chicago utility proving sufficient to lever action at City Hall. Other campaigns were conducted with varying degrees of success against Honeywell in Minneapolis, American Telephone and Telegraph in Cleveland, and United Aircraft in East Hartford. The Business Executives Move for Peace in Vietnam, with some 3,000 members, challenged corporate policies concerning Vietnam at the annual meetings of International Business Machines, Chase Manhattan Bank and the Bank of America.

Some groups went to court. The Scenic Hudson Preservation Conference, for example, established the right of citizen groups to participate in formerly narrow economic decisions, such as the siting of power plants. In another case, the United Church of Christ challenged the license of TV station WLBT in Jackson, Miss., for allegedly racist programming. This landmark decision established the right of civic groups to be party to FCC license-renewal hearings and reversed the FCC's decision to extend the station's license. The church group is now participating in an attack, on similar grounds, upon the license of WKRO in Cairo, Ill.

Still other groups have been testing the use of class action, which enables one or several plaintiffs to bring suit for damages against a corporation on behalf of a large number of injured parties. Using this device, two Chicago aldermen recently filed suit for $3 billion in damages against the big four auto makers in the name of all the citizens of Chicago injured by auto pollution. Class action is a powerful tool not only because it aims at the company's earnings but because judgments awarded are likely to be large enough to interest lawyers in working for a contingency fee.

The Medical Committee for Human Rights won an important victory in its suit against the Securities & Exchange Commission, brought after it sought, and was refused, permission to raise the issue of napalm production before the 1969 meeting of Dow Chemical. The July ruling by the U.S. Court of Appeals significantly broadened the scope of the corporate responsibility movement's future legal activities. Judge Edward Tamm stated: "We think there is a clear and compelling distinction between management's legitimate need for freedom to apply its expertise in matters of day-to-day business judgment, and management's patently illegitimate claim of power to treat modern corporations with their vast resources as personal satrapies implementing personal political or moral predilections." Prior to this broadened interpretation of shareholders' rights, the movement had relied largely on a ruling by the New Jersey

Supreme Court in the case of *A. P. Smith* vs. *Barlow* that "Modern conditions require that corporations discharge social as well as private responsibilities . . . to insure and strengthen the society which gives them existence."

In this way, a new body of legal doctrine of corporate responsibility is steadily emerging. Critics of the movement, whether corporate leaders such as AT&T's H. I. Rommes, institutional investor Lawrence Rubin, president of the Scudder Special Fund, or lawyers and traditional economists, argue that campaigns directed against particular corporations are unfair, and that only across-the-board legislative action can insure uniformity of constraint on all corporations. Legislative remedies should certainly be pursued as vigorously as possible, but given the near paralysis of normal legislative processes, outpaced by rapid technological change and dominated by the very corporate power they seek to control, the next best traditional avenue of redress is the courts, which can act only upon presentation of specific cases that embody the conflicts and issues requiring resolution.

Another argument often leveled by critics, as when Milton Friedman commented on Campaign GM in a recent *New York Times Magazine* article, is that in a free enterprise, private property system, the responsibility of business is to assure the shareholder the largest possible return on his investment; and that the corporate manager, as an agent of the stockholders, has no right to make social decisions that might adversely affect profits. On a practical level, it can be argued in reply that the manager of a giant corporation, performing his everyday duties to improve stockholders' profits, also makes *de facto* social decisions that are often experienced by the public as unpleasant side effects. Society can therefore legitimately seek redress by taking the issue of management's actions back to their stockholders in the form of a proxy contest. On a theoretical level, however, one can agree wholeheartedly with Professor Friedman, and a remarkably similar analysis is at the very basis of the corporate responsibility movement. Its proponents agree that traditional economics and corporate charters *are* still governed by such outmoded tenets, but their radically different conclusion is that only massive external pressures from consumers, stockholders, employees, fiduciaries and the affected general public can hope to produce a new formulation of the corporation's mandate and the needed overhaul of economic theory. The goal is to replace what Kenneth Boulding calls the "cowboy," consumption-oriented economy with a new closed-end, "husbandry" economy that is needed for man to survive on "Spaceship Earth."

As the corporate responsibility movement broadens and diversifies into unexplored aspects of unrestrained private industrial power, it is to be hoped that each new campaign will illuminate an emerging issue. These endeavors will seek to redefine the corporate mandate through all existing legal channels and in the light of current needs, to arrive at a new balance between the often conflicting interests of stockholders, employees, consumers and the public. The new campaigns will be as diverse as the issues and the groups involved. However, the overarching theory is remarkably uniform, and strategy appears to fall into two broad categories. First, there are those who would spend their energy on national campaigns that raise national issues, in the style of Campaign GM, so as to create public awareness of the range of options available for adapting corporations to new social needs. Such groups play on the corporation's turf, seeking openings through which to reinterpret its rules, using sophisticated arguments and tactics to organize the corporation's latent countervailing constituencies, including students, institutional investors, employees, customers and conservationists, as well as mobilizing stockholders themselves. Such campaigns are generally more educational than "experiential," on the theory that a sophisticated approach must be used to radicalize bankers and affluent stockholders, who might be repelled by more direct tactics.

But there are others, like Richard Harmon of Saul Alinsky's Industrial Areas Foundation Institute, who undertake to build real constituencies at the local level, which express themselves through hundreds of local actions ranging from boycotts, proxy fights and picketing, to tying up the local franchisers of national companies. The educational component of such campaigns is necessarily sacrificed in order to provide more direct experiences for participants, to raise consciousness of group needs and power relationships, and to identify common problems and targets on which leaders can build cohesive communities.

In fact, all successful volunteer organizations employ both concepts, and the full range of permutations can be seen in the movement's organizations. There are objective, conceptual research groups. Of these, the Council on Economic Priorities prepares detailed profiles of corporate and industry-wide performance in four social areas (pollution, minority hiring, military involvement and foreign investments) for concerned shareholders, fiduciaries, religious and civic groups and citizens. The Citizens Communications Center combines research and legal advocacy to champion citizens' rights in broadcasting; the *Chicago Journalism Review* keeps Chicago's establishment press on its toes with exposés of corporate and civil corruption. Still others, often college students, prefer direct action with high media appeal, such as burying internal combustion engines or dumping truckloads of cans on the pristine lawns of their manufacturer's headquarters.

New precedents in environmental law are being developed by such crusading lawyers as David Sive and Victor Yannacone and by the president of the Sierra Club, Philip S. Berry, who proposes enactment of a national corporations code and the amendment of all existing state corporations codes to specify that protection of the environment is one of the corporation's chartered purposes. The Lloyd Harbor Study Group on Long Island, in its current discussion with the Long Island Lighting Company, is negotiating for the company to finance an independent study group of technical and public health experts which would continuously monitor a proposed nuclear plant's radioactive effluent and thermal pollution. Dennis Farrar, of the volunteer Council of New York Law Associates, considers drafting model legislation to provide that all public contracts should include means for independent, affected groups to hire their own technical appraisers and legal advocates, and thus guard in advance against arbitrary or environmentally harmful planning decisions. Round Two of Campaign GM, announced recently, will elicit candidates for board membership in General Motors from various constituent groups, such as employees, dealers and stockholders. That is another attempt to restructure corporate decision-making patterns.

These and other efforts may eventually quantify "corporate responsibility" precisely enough to provide workable yardsticks for management to cite when facing stockholders. Managers will need such guides when the current doctrine of maximum profits gives way to new principles of recycling resources and absorbing all social costs in the price of the product. One of the "*Fortune* 500" list of companies, Eastern Gas & Fuel Associates, is studying all its operations with a view to setting up an internal social accounting system that will assess its relations with employees, customers, suppliers and the communities in which it operates. Henry Ford II believes that "the freedom of big business in the years ahead depends on how it responds to the changing spirit of the public."

It is entirely possible that future stockholders will have either to content themselves with reduced profits, or be prepared to accept higher taxes to pay for otherwise soaring social costs. There may also be a new definition of which vital functions—say, power generation, transportation or mail services—are best performed by public agencies and which by private enterprise. As J. Kenneth Galbraith is fond of pointing out, we have had a mixed economy for decades; it is the theory and the rhetoric that have become outmoded.

The corporate responsibility movement, this new "politics by other means," can be a useful tool to modify and adapt capitalism to changing needs. While Karl Marx was thundering that capitalism would destroy itself, his contemporary, John Stuart Mill, was predicting that it might evolve into something very like what we see emerging today, an equilibrium economy, no longer based on endless production and consumption but on mutual service.

Only the most determined idealist could view our current economy and its distorted priorities with any hope that Mill's prediction will be realized in the near future. And yet *Fortune* estimates that nearly all the increase in employment between now and 1980 will be in the service sector. At the same time, there is a glimmer of hope in the increasing flow of capital into the pollution-control and recycling industry, as well as into other public sector markets.

The new movement can help irrigate corporate decision making by exposing management to these new ideas, opening up board memberships to out-groups, such as minorities, women and environmentalists, thereby providing faster "feedback" on the social consequences of management decisions. It might even become analagous to the labor movement, which enabled capitalism to adapt and survive in spite of itself. Like unions, the politics of corporate responsibility is evolutionary and conservative in the Burkean sense of the term. It is a valid proposition that citizens, representing the broader values of the public interest, must use whatever political and economic means are necessary to achieve a countervailing force to business.

Private enterprise, with its narrowly conceived premises based on "value-free" economic criteria, will always be at odds with the broader public-interest values which are the nation's collective moral and ethical judgment as to what constitutes "the good society." Most economists would agree with both Kenneth Boulding and Milton Friedman that their discipline is not concerned with these metaphysical value judgments, but rather with quantifiable relative exchange values. This pervasive use of two-dimensional economic decision making, as if the country were a vast Monopoly game, is precisely the problem. We must learn a new game of three-dimensional Monopoly, where the player can't put his factory on "Atlantic Avenue" just because he happens to own the site. He must also overcome the objections of the other residents by spending additional sums on making the plant clean and socially acceptable. This, in turn, may cost so much that his product may be too expensive and buyers will decide they can do without it. The process will discipline capitalists' decisions and tend to keep socially and ecologically undesirable items from cluttering up the market and countryside. Until now, the power of the modern corporation has enabled it, through mass persuasion, to impose its narrow economic game on society. The new politics of corporate responsibility is an attempt to reimpose the higher values of the whole society—of the public interest over special interests. If successful, it will produce political results as tangible as any achieved by traditional electoral politics.

V
Commitment
to a Future:
Decision

Decision is that phase of the political process in which choices are made to attempt to put one or more visions of the future into effect. Two main issues are involved here. First, there is the question of how the choices are to be made. Second, there is the question of who is to make the choices. The articles in this section reflect different contemporary responses to these questions.

The articles by Robert A. Dahl and Peter Bachrach illustrate contrasting interpretations of how decisions are to be made. According to Dahl, political decisions in the United States are generally an outcome of competition between interest groups, and the competition is facilitated by professional politicians. Dahl not only states that this pattern of decision-making actually characterizes American politics, but also suggests that it has the benefit of maintaining political stability (through generally satisfying the demands of the most intense and powerful groups) and allowing most people to lead their own private lives in relative unconcern about politics (through narrowing the definition of policies so that only particular groups are interested in each outcome). In opposition to Dahl, Bachrach declares that separating the private from the public by making political activity a specialty only furthers exploitation of the majority by shifting minorities. He argues that greater participation in decisions should be encouraged and that democratic control be extended to the complex organizations that dominate contemporary life. Thus, the arguments of Dahl and Bachrach point up the alternatives of pluralism and participatory democracy, respectively.

C. Wright Mills, Milovan Djilas, and Jean Meynaud address themselves to the question of who makes decisions in the contemporary world. According to Mills, a "power elite" has grown up in the United States, and this elite is composed of an interlocking directorate of high officials in large corporations, top military leaders, and high-ranking government officials. Mills argues that this "power elite" determines such issues as whether there will be war or peace and whether there will be inflation or deflation. Those who make up the elite do not determine issues through a conscious conspiracy but as a result of their organizational position and common background. Djilas does the same thing for Communist Europe as Mills does for the United States. Djilas claims that decisions in the Communist countries are made by a "new class" of Communist Party officials, who take special privileges for themselves and ignore in practice the stated goal of speeding social equality. Finally, Meynaud presents a case for the emergence of an elite of technicians throughout the industrialized world. He fears domination by such an elite, because it has no principle of rule beyond mere efficiency.

The articles in this section show the tension between democracy and elitism in the contemporary world. As we have already noted, increased demands for participation are being accompanied by widespread fears of domination by various elites.

from **Who Governs?**

ROBERT A. DAHL

CONSENSUS AS A PROCESS

Most of us, I suppose, are ready to recognize long-run changes in the beliefs expressed by the more articulate segments of the political stratum and the intelligentsia, and we can infer from various kinds of evidence—all of it, alas, highly debatable—that changes of some sort take place over long periods of time in the attitudes about democracy held in the general population. We tend to assume, however, that except for these long-run shifts beliefs about democracy are more or less static. I want to propose an alternative explanation, namely that democratic beliefs, like other political beliefs, are influenced by a recurring *process* of interchange among political professionals, the political stratum, and the great bulk of the population. The process generates enough agreement on rules and norms so as to permit the system to operate, but agreement tends to be incomplete, and typically it decays. So the process is frequently repeated. "Consensus," then, is not at all a static and unchanging attribute of citizens. It is a variable element in a complex and more or less continuous process.

This process seems to me to have the following characteristics:

1. Over long periods of time the great bulk of the citizens possess a fairly stable set of democratic beliefs at a high level of abstraction. Let me call these beliefs the democratic creed. In Ann Arbor and Tallahassee, Prothro and Grigg found that very nearly everyone they interviewed agreed with five abstract democratic propositions.[1] We can, I think, confidently conclude that most Americans believe in democracy as the best form of government, in the desirability of rights and procedures insuring a goodly measure of majority rule and minority freedom, and in a wide but not necessarily comprehensive electorate. At a somewhat lower level of agreement, probably the great majority of citizens also believe in the essential legitimacy of certain specific American political institutions: the presidency, Congress, the Supreme Court, the states, the local governments, etc.

2. Most citizens assume that the American political system is consistent with the democratic creed. Indeed, the common view seems to be that our system is not only democratic but is perhaps the most perfect expression of democracy that exists anywhere; if deficiencies exist, either

---

1. "Democracy is the best form of government." "Public officials should be chosen by majority vote." "Every citizen should have an equal chance to influence government policy." "The minority should be free to criticize majority decisions." "People in the minority should be free to try to win majority support for their opinions." Prothro and Grigg, "Fundamental Principles of Democracy," 282, 284.

they can, and ultimately will, be remedied, or else they reflect the usual gap between ideal and reality that men of common sense take for granted. Moreover, because leading officials with key roles in the legitimate political institutions automatically acquire authority for their views on the proper functioning of the political institutions, as long as these various officials seem to agree, the ordinary citizen is inclined to assume that existing ways of carrying on the public business do not violate, at least in an important way, the democratic creed to which he is committed.

3. Widespread adherence to the democratic creed is produced and maintained by a variety of powerful social processes. Of these, probably formal schooling is the most important. The more formal education an American has, the more democratic formulas he knows, expresses, and presumably believes. But almost the entire adult population has been subjected to *some* degree of indoctrination through the schools. Beliefs acquired in school are reinforced in adult life through normal exposure to the democratic creed, particularly as the creed is articulated by leading political figures and transmitted through the mass media.

These social processes have an enormous impact on the citizen, partly because they begin early in life and partly because the very unanimity with which the creed is espoused makes rejection of it almost impossible. To reject the creed is infinitely more than a simple matter of disagreement. To reject the creed is to reject one's society and one's chances of full acceptance in it—in short, to be an outcast. (As a mental experiment, try to imagine the psychic and social burdens an American child in an American school would incur if he steadfastly denied to himself and others that democracy is the best form of government.)

To reject the democratic creed is in effect to refuse to be an American. As a nation we have taken great pains to insure that few citizens will ever want to do anything so rash, so preposterous—in fact, so wholly un-American. In New Haven, as in many other parts of the United States, vast social energies have been poured into the process of "Americanization," teaching citizens what is expected in the way of words, beliefs, and behavior if they are to earn acceptance as Americans, for it was obvious to the political stratum that unless the immigrants and their children quickly accepted American political norms, the flood of aliens, particularly from countries with few traditions of self-government, would disrupt the political system. In a characteristic response, the Board of Education of the city of New Haven created a supervisor for Americanization (a post, incidentally, that still exists). Something of the feeling of urgency and accomplishment that must have prevailed in many segments of the political stratum shines through these enthusiastic words in the annual report of the New Haven superintendent of schools in 1919:

The public school is the greatest and most effective of all Americanization agencies. This is the one place where all children in a community or district, regardless of nationality, religion, politics, or social status, meet and work together in a cooperative and harmonious spirit. . . . The children work and play together, they catch the school spirit, they live the democratic life, American heroes become their own, American history wins their loyalty, the Stars and

Stripes, always before their eyes in the school room, receives their daily salute. Not only are these immigrant children Americanized through the public school, but they, in turn, Americanize their parents carrying into the home many lessons of democracy learned at school.[2]

For their part, the immigrants and their children were highly motivated to learn how to be Americans, for they were desperately, sometimes pathetically, eager to win acceptance as true Americans.

In one form or another the process of Americanization has absorbed enormous social energies all over the United States. As a factor in shaping American behavior and attitudes, the process of Americanization must surely have been as important as the frontier, or industrialization, or urbanization. That regional, ethnic, racial, religious, or economic differences might disrupt the American political system has been a recurring fear among the political stratum of the United States from the very beginning of the republic. Doubtless this anxiety was painfully stimulated by the Civil War. It was aroused again by the influx of immigrants. Throughout the country then the political stratum has seen to it that new citizens, young and old, have been properly trained in "American" principles and beliefs. Everywhere, too, the pupils have been highly motivated to talk, look and believe as Americans should. The result was as astonishing an act of voluntary political and cultural assimilation and speedy elimination of regional, ethnic, and cultural dissimilarities as history can provide. The extent to which Americans agree today on the key propositions about democracy is a measure of the almost unbelievable success of this deliberate attempt to create a seemingly uncoerced nation-wide consensus.

4. Despite wide agreement on a general democratic creed, however, citizens frequently disagree on specific applications. Many citizens oppose what some political philosophers would regard as necessary implications of the creed. Many citizens also disagree with the way the creed is actually applied—or perhaps it would be more accurate to say, with the existing rules of the game, the prevailing political norms. Again and again, for example, surveys indicate that a large number of Americans, sometimes even a majority, do not approve of the extension of important rights, liberties, and privileges to individuals and groups that do in fact enjoy them.

A citizen is able to adhere to these seemingly inconsistent beliefs for a great variety of reasons. For one thing, he himself need not see any inconsistency in his beliefs. The creed is so vague (and incomplete) that strict deductions are difficult or impossible even for sophisticated logicians. Moreover, propositions stated in universal terms are rarely assumed by men of common sense to imply universality in practice; to the frequent dismay of logicians, a common tendency of mankind—and not least of Americans—is to qualify universals in application while leaving them intact in rhetoric. Then, too, the capacity for (or interest in) working out

2. "Report of the Superintendent of Schools," *Annual Report of the Board of Education of the New Haven City School District*, 1919.

a set of consistent political attitudes is rather limited. As the authors of *The American Voter* have shown, most voters seem to operate at a low level of ideological sophistication; even among intelligent (though not necessarily highy educated) citizens, conceptions of politics are often of a simplicity that the political philosopher might find it hard to comprehend.[3] In addition, most citizens operate with a very small fund of political information; often they lack the elementary information required even to be aware of inconsistencies between their views and what is actually happening in the political system, particularly if the subject is (as most questions of rights and procedures are) arcane and complex. Again, questions that bother theorists are often not interesting or salient to most voters; their attention and energies are diverted elsewhere, usually to activities that lie entirely outside the political arena. As long as a citizen believes that democracy is the best political system, that the United States is a democracy, and that the people in office can be trusted, by and large, to apply the abstract creed to specific cases, issues of democratic theory and practice hotly discussed by political philosophers, or even by publicists and columnists, are likely never to penetrate through the manifold barriers to abstract political thinking that are erected by the essentially apolitical culture in which he lives. Finally, even if the issues do manage to get through, many citizens feel themselves incompetent to decide them; this, after all, is what Supreme Court judges, presidents, and members of Congress are supposed to do. Worse yet, many citizens feel that no one in public office will care much about their opinions anyway.

5. Members of the political stratum (who live in a much more politicized culture) are more familiar with the "democratic" norms, more consistent, more ideological, more detailed and explicit in their political attitudes, and more completely in agreement on the norms. They are more in agreement not only on what norms are implied by the abstract democratic creed but also in supporting the norms currently operating. This relatively higher degree of support for the prevailing norms in the existing political system is generated and maintained by a variety of processes. Because members of the political stratum have on the average considerably more formal education than the population as a whole, they have been more thoroughly exposed to the creed and its implications. Because they are more involved in, concerned with, and articulate about politics, they invest more time and effort in elaborating a consistent ideology. Because they participate more extensively in politics, they more frequently express and defend their views, encounter criticism, and face the charge of inconsistency. They know more about politics, read more, experience more, see more.

Within the political stratum, the professionals tend to agree even more on what the norms should be, what they are, and the desirability of maintaining them substantially as they are. Agreement among the professionals is generated by all the factors that account for it among the rest

3. A. Campbell, P. E. Converse, W. E. Miller, D. D. Stokes, *The American Voter* (New York, Wiley, 1960), Chs. 9 and 10.

of the political stratum and even among the apolitical strata. Mastery over the existing norms of the political system represents the particular stockpile of skills peculiar to the professional's vocation. Norms also tend to legitimate his power and position in the political system, furnish an agreed-on method of getting on with the immediate tasks at hand, carry the authority of tradition, and help to reduce the baffling uncertainty that surrounds the professional's every choice. Finally, the professional is likely to support the existing norms because his own endorsement of existing norms was initially a criterion in his own recruitment and advancement; complex processes of political selection and rejection tend to exclude the deviant who challenges the prevailing norms of the existing political system. Most of the professionals might properly be called democratic "legitimists."

6. The professionals, of course, have access to extensive political resources which they employ at a high rate with superior efficiency. Consequently, a challenge to the existing norms is bound to be costly to the challenger, for legitimist professionals can quickly shift their skills and resources into the urgent task of doing in the dissenter. As long as the professionals remain substantially legitimist in outlook, therefore, the critic is likely to make a little headway. Indeed, the chances are that anyone who advocates extensive changes in the prevailing democratic norms is likely to be treated by the professionals, and even by a fair share of the political stratum, as an outsider, possibly even as a crackpot whose views need not be seriously debated. No worse fate can befall the dissenter, for unless he can gain the attention of the political stratum, it is difficult for him to gain space in the mass media; if he cannot win space in the mass media, it is difficult for him to win a large following; if he cannot win a large following, it is difficult for him to gain the attention of the political stratum.

7. Sometimes, of course, disagreements over the prevailing norms occur within the political stratum and among the professionals themselves. But these disagreements need not, and perhaps ordinarily do not, produce much effort to involve the general public in the dispute. The disagreements are not, to be sure, secret; the electorate is not *legally* barred from finding out about the conflict and becoming involved. It does not need to be. Given the low salience of politics in the life of the average citizen, most conflicts over the prevailing norms might attract more attention if they were held behind locked doors. Unless a professional is willing to invest very great resources in whipping up public interest, he is not likely to get much effective support. In any case, public involvement may seem undesirable to the legitimist, for alterations in the prevailing norms are often subtle matters, better obtained by negotiation than by the crudities and oversimplifications of public debate.

8. Among the rules and procedures supported strongly by the legitimists in the public stratum, and particularly by the professionals, are some that prescribe ways of settling disagreements as to rules and procedures. These involve appeals to authorities who give decisions widely accepted as binding, authoritative, and legitimate—though not necessarily as "good" or "correct." Typically these include appeals to courts or quasi-

judicial institutions that ostensibly arrive at their decisions by appeals to norms, codes, formulas, and beliefs that appear to transcend partisan and policy differences in the political stratum.

9. Ordinarily, then, it is not difficult for a stable system of rights and privileges to exist that, at least in important details, does not have widespread public support and occasionally even lacks majority approval. As long as the matter is not a salient public issue—and whether it is or not depends partly on how the political stratum handles it—the question is substantially determined within the political stratum itself. When disagreements arise, these are adjudicated by officials who share the beliefs of the political stratum rather than those of the populace; and even when these officials adopt positions that do not command the undivided support of the political stratum, members of the political stratum, and particularly the professionals, tend to accept a decision as binding until and unless it can be changed through the accepted procedures. This is the essence of their code of democratic legitimism.

10. Occasionally, however, a sizable segment of the political stratum develops doubts that it can ever achieve the changes it seeks through accepted procedures that are, in a sense, internal to the political stratum and the professionals. One or more of these dissenters may push his way into the professional group, or the dissenters may be numerous and vocal enough to acquire a spokesman or two among the professionals. The strategy of the dissenters may now begin to shift. Instead of adjudicating the matter according to the accepted procedures, the dissenters attempt to arouse public support for their proposals, hoping that when a sufficient number of voters are won over to their cause, other professionals—legitimist or not—will have to come around.

The professionals, as I have said, live in a world of uncertainty. They search for omens and portents. If the auguries indicate that the appeal to the populace has failed, then the legitimists may confidently close ranks against the dissenter. But if the auguries are uncertain or unfavorable, then the legitimists, too, are forced to make a counter-appeal to the populace. Since public opinion is often as difficult to interpret as the flights of birds or the entrails of a sheep, political professionals may and frequently do misread the auspices. In October 1954, the Survey Research Center discovered that only 12 per cent of their sample said they would be more likely to vote for a candidate who had the support of Senator McCarthy; 37 per cent said they would be less likely, and 43 per cent said it would make no difference.[4] In retrospect, these proportions do not look wildly off, but in 1954 belief in McCarthy's mass following was widespread throughout the whole political stratum and not least among the professionals. The legitimists could probably have ignored the late Senator with impunity—as they later did—but he followed a classic strategy—(required, I am suggesting, by the tendency of the legitimists to monopolize the internal devices for adjudicating disputes over norms)—

4. Angus Campbell and Homer C. Cooper, *Group Differences in Attitudes and Votes, A Study of the 1954 Congressional Election* (Ann Arbor, Mich., University of Michigan Survey Research Center, 1954) , p. 145.

by taking the issue out of the hands of the professionals, where the rules of the game were bound to run against him, and appealing instead to the populace.

If the dissenters succeed in forcing the issue out beyond the political stratum, and dissenters and legitimists begin making appeals to the populace, then the nature of the debate begins to change. Technical questions, subtle distinctions, fine matters of degree are shed. The appeal is now shaped to the simple democratic creed which nearly every citizen believes in. Because the creed does not constitute a tightly logical system, it is possible for the legitimists to demonstrate that existing norms are necessary consequences of the creed, and for the dissenters to show that existing norms run counter to the creed. Because the creed is deeply laden with tradition and sentiment, emotion rises and reasoned discussion declines.

11. Ordinary citizens who normally remain outside these debates now find their attention—and their votes—solicited by both sides. They become aware that the very officials who ordinarily decide these matters, to whom the citizen himself turns for his cues as to what is legitimate and consistent with the creed, are locked in deadly, heated battle. These citizens must now find ways of applying the creed to the issue. One way is to withdraw even more deeply into the political shadows; a citizen can simply refuse to choose. Many do. In March 1937, at the height of the debate over President Roosevelt's proposal to enlarge the Supreme Court, 50 per cent of the people interviewed in a Gallup poll had listened to neither of the President's two recent radio speeches defending his plan. A month later, one out of seven persons who were asked whether Congress should pass the President's bill expressed no opinion.[5] In New Haven, after several years of public discussion and debate over charter reform, when a sample of registered voters was asked in 1959 whether they personally would do anything if a revision of the charter was proposed that would make the mayor stronger, over 40 per cent of those who disapproved of such an idea said they would do nothing to oppose it, and nearly three-quarters of those who approved said they would do nothing to support it. (These seemed to be tolerably honest responses; in the preceding election, after wide discussion among the political stratum and hot debate among the professionals over a new charter, less than half the voters who went to the polls even bothered to vote on the charter.) Thus when dissenters and legitimists appeal to the populace to settle questions they ordinarily decide among themselves, they cannot be at all sure that they will actually produce much of a response no matter how much they try to stir up the public.

However, citizens who *do* make up their minds must find some ways for arriving at a choice. For many citizens the decision is eased by their existing loyalties to parties or political leaders. In April 1937, 68 per cent of the Democrats in a Gallup poll said that Congress should pass Roosevelt's court plan; 93 per cent of the Republicans said Congress should not.

5. Hadley Cantril, ed., *Public Opinion, 1935-1946* (Princeton, Princeton University Press, 1951) , p. 150.

Those who had no strong party identifications were, as one might expect, split—42 per cent in favor and 58 per cent against.[6] In 1954, attitudes toward McCarthy were closely related to party identifications. Among strong Democrats, those who said that McCarthy's support would make them *less* likely to vote for a candidate were six times as great as those who said his support would make them *more* likely; strong Republicans, by contrast, split about evenly. Among Catholics who were strong Democrats, the ratio was two to one against McCarthy; among Catholics who were strong Republicans it was nearly two to one in his favor.[7]

If the parties give no clear guidance, citizens may look to particular leaders or institutions. They may turn to spokesmen in their churches, for example, or trade unions, or regions. They often turn, of course, to attitudes prevalent in their own circle of intimates, friends, associates, acquaintances. If their search yields no consistent cues, they may give up. In the struggle over charter reform in New Haven in 1958, when Democratic leaders were split from the top down, judging from a sample of registered voters interviewed shortly after the election the proportion of people who went to the polls and voted on the general election but did not vote either for or against the charter was higher among Democrats than among either Republicans or independents.

12. An appeal to the populace may terminate in several ways. The appeal may simply fail to create a stir. Interest in political matters wanes rather quickly; since complex issues of democratic norms nearly always lack a direct relation to the on-going life of an individual, they have even less capacity for holding attention than many other issues. However passionately the dissenters feel about their case, life does move on, old questions become tiresome, and the newspapers begin to shove the conflict to the inside pages. Perhaps the legitimists, buoyed by their reading of the electorate, defeat the dissenters in a clear-cut trial of strength and, having done so, close ranks and go on to the next business. Perhaps the dissenters win, or a compromise is worked out; if so the dissenters, like as not, turn into the next generation of legitimists.

THE ROLE OF DEMOCRATIC BELIEFS

The specific beliefs of the average citizen thus have a rather limited though important function. Ordinarily, conflicts over democratic norms are resolved among the professionals, with perhaps some involvement by parts of the political stratum but little or no involvement by most citizens. Thus the fact that a large number of citizens do not believe in the political norms actually applied, particularly extending political liberties to unpopular individuals and groups, has slight effect on the outcome.

The beliefs of the ordinary citizen become relevant only when professionals engage in an intensive appeal to the populace. Even then, the

6. Ibid.
7. Campbell and Cooper, *Group Differences in Attitudes,* Tables VI-VIII (p. 92) and B-81 (p. 149). See also Nelson W. Polsby, "Towards an Explanation of McCarthyism," *Political Studies, 8,* No. 3 (1960), 250-71.

actual outcome of the appeal does not necessarily reflect majority attitudes at all accurately. These are not always known; they are guessed at in a variety of inaccurate ways, and they have to be filtered through the tighter mesh of the political stratum and the professionals before they can become public policy.

Nonetheless, wide consensus on the democratic creed does have two important kinds of consequences. On the one hand, this very consensus makes occasional appeal all but inevitable, for the creed itself gives legitimacy to an appeal to the populace. On the other hand, widespread adherence to the creed limits the character and the course of an appeal. It insures that no appeal is likely to succeed unless it is framed in terms consistent with the creed—which is perhaps not so small a constraint. Some solutions pretty evidently are *not* consistent. Because an appeal must take place in the face of criticism from legitimists and extensive appraisal by members of the political stratum, blatant inconsistencies are likely to be exposed. Moreover, because the appeal is legitimized by the creed, it provides an orderly way to conduct a dispute that exceeds the capacities of the professionals to resolve among themselves.

No one, I imagine, has ever supposed that the existence of the creed entails no risks. People can be deceived by appeals intended to destroy democracy in the name of democracy. Dissenters who believe in the democratic creed may unwittingly advocate or legitimists may insist on preserving rules of the game destined to have unforeseen and unintended consequences disastrous to the stability and perhaps the survival of the democracy.

Nonetheless, we can be reasonably sure of this: even if universal belief in a democratic creed does not guarantee the stability of a democratic system, a substantial decline in the popular consensus would greatly increase the chance of serious instability. How the professionals act, what they advocate, what they are likely to believe, are all constrained by the wide adherence to the creed that exists throughout the community. If a substantial segment of the electorate begins to doubt the creed, professionals will quickly come forth to fan that doubt. The nature and course of an appeal to the populace will change. What today is a question of applying the fundamental norms of democracy will become tomorrow an inquiry into the validity of these norms. If a substantial number of citizens begin to deny not merely to *some* minorities but to minorities *as such* the rights and powers prescribed in the creed, an appeal to the populace is likely to end sooner or later in a call to arms.

Thus consensus on political beliefs and practices has much in common with other aspects of a democratic system. Here, too, leaders lead— and often are led. Citizens are very far indeed from exerting equal influence over the content, application, and development of the political consensus. Yet widely held beliefs by Americans in a creed of democracy and political equality serve as a critical limit on the ways in which leaders can shape the consensus.

Neither the prevailing consensus, the creed, nor even the political system itself are immutable products of democratic ideas, beliefs, and institutions inherited from the past. For better or worse, they are always open, in some measure, to alteration through those complex processes of symbiosis and change that constitute the relations of leaders and citizens in a pluralistic democracy.

An Alternative Approach

PETER BACHRACH

While it is true that there are many theories of democracy, it is also true that there is a general theory of democracy which is supported by most leading theorists and which reflects the main currents of thought in social science today. It is a theory largely explanatory rather than normative in approach; directed toward clarifying on-going democratic systems rather than suggesting how they ought to operate. Yet it is a theory which reflects, on the one hand, a receptiveness toward the existing structure of power and elite decision-making in large industrial societies, and on the other, an impatience with old myths and sentiments associated with phrases such as "will of the people," "grass-roots democracy," and "the dignity of the common man."

This general theory purports to be above ideology but is in reality deeply rooted in an ideology, an ideology which is grounded upon a profound distrust of the majority of ordinary men and women, and a reliance upon the established elites to maintain the values of civility and the "rules of the game" of democracy. It is an ideology which is closely attached to and protective of the liberal principles embodied in the rule of law and in the rights of the individual to freedom of conscience, expression, and privacy. While embracing liberalism it rejects, in effect, the major tenet of classical democratic theory—belief and confidence in the people. The suspicion that liberalism and classical theory are fundamentally incompatible is manifested in the key explanatory concepts of democratic elitism.

Democracy conceived solely as a political method is one of these concepts. Since democracy is not seen as embodying an overriding objective, such as enhancing the self-esteem and development of the individual, the democratic-elite theorist frees himself from the charge that democratic means have failed to achieve democratic ends. He holds only that democracy must be self-perpetuating as method, and thus able to secure the open society through time. In focusing upon openness *qua* openness—avoiding the question of openness for whom—he is in a position to show that the system is in good health, while acknowledging at the same time that a large number of people are probably alienated from the social and political life around them.

While the concept of democracy as political method is not inherently elitist, it does serve as a formidable defense of the elite-mass structure of on-going democratic systems. The charge, for example, that the common man is not given sufficient opportunity to participate in meaningful decision-making and is therefore deprived of an essential means to develop his faculties and broaden his outlook is, under this concept, irrelevant. For, conceived as political method, the standard for judging democracy is not the degree of centralization or devolution in the decision-making process but rather the degree to which the system conforms to the basic principles of the democratic method: political equality (universal suffrage), freedom of discussion, majority rule, free periodic elections, and the like. When these principles are adhered to, the system is characterized by the accountability of political elites to non-elites. And in being held accountable, the former, owing to the phenomenon of anticipated reactions, normally rules in the interests of the latter. Thus, although democracy as a political method is defined in terms of procedural principles, it invariably is defended today on the basis of its service to the interests of the people.

This defense of democracy construes the interests of the people narrowly and the democratic elite theorist has little difficulty in accepting it. He posits that the value of the democratic system for ordinary individuals should be measured by the degree to which the "outputs" of the system, in the form of security, services, and material support, benefit them. On the basis of this reasoning, the less the individual has to participate in politics on the "input" and demand side of the system in order to gain his interests on the output side, the better off he is. With rare exception elites are available to represent his interest in the decision-making process, relegating to him the comparatively painless task of paying nominal dues and occasionally attending a meeting and casting a ballot. By assuming a one-dimensional view of political interest, the democratic elitist is led to the conclusion that there is a natural division of labor within a democratic system between elite rule and non-elite interest.

By conceiving of man's political interest solely in terms of that which accrues to him from government, the democratic elitist implicitly rejects the contention of classical theorists that interests also include the opportunity for development which accrues from participation in meaningful political decisions. This two-dimensional view of political interests—interests as end results and interest in the process of participation—is rejected by the democratic elitists on the ground that it has little relevance to the reality of political life in large-scale industrial societies, and that it is based on the concept of equality of power in decision-making which is completely at odds with existing practices in modern democracies, where key political decisions must of necessity be made by a small minority. The main thrust of the elitist argument is incontestable. However, although participation in key political decisions on the national level must remain extremely limited, is there any sound reason, within the context of democratic theory, why participation in political decisions by the constituencies of "private" bureaucratic institutions of power could not be widely extended on those issues which primarily affect their lives within these institutions?

The answer to the question turns on what constitutes "political." If private organizations, at least the more powerful among them, were considered political—on the ground that they are organs which regularly share in authoritatively allocating values for society—then there would be a compelling case, in terms of the democratic principle of equality of power, to expand participation in decision-making within these organizations. This could be achieved by radically altering their hierarchical structures to facilitate the devolution of the decision-making process. However, if one holds, as the democratic elite theorist does, to a narrow and institutional concept of political (when referring to political elites and political equality), this line of reasoning is effectively excluded from democratic theory. If "political" is confined to governmental decision-making and that which relates to it, the clearly nongovernmental institutions, irrespective of the power which they may wield and the impact of their decisions on society, are not political. And in being not political, they are exempt, as far as the reach of democratic theory goes, from democratization.

The importance to the theory of democratic elitism of interpreting narrowly the integral and key concept "political" cannot be overemphasized. First, on the basis of this interpretation, the argument for expanding democracy to encompass a portion of the economic sector can be discarded out of hand as irrelevant. Democracy is a *political* method, neither intended nor designed to operate beyond the political realm. Second, this narrow concept supports the legitimacy of the elite decision-making process within the corporations and other large private institutions. It is common knowledge that corporate elites, who regularly make decisions directly affecting social values, are accountable largely, if not solely, to themselves. But this is not considered to be an irresponsible exercise of political power since corporate managers act as private citizens on nonpolitical matters. Finally, and most important, by accepting a rigid and narrow concept of political, the elite theorist removes from consideration (within the context of democratic theory) the question of the feasibility of increasing participation in decision-making by enlarging the political scope to include the more powerful private institutions. The existing elite–non-elite relationship is consequently made immune to attack by democratic theorists loyal to the classical tradition.

If the area of politics is conceived narrowly for purposes of democratic theory, then it is understandable that the principle of equality of power, long identified as an ideal of democracy, must give way to the more realistic principle of equality of opportunity to obtain a position of power. For the former principle is only meaningful as an ideal to strive for in a society in which there is hope of obtaining a more equalitarian base for decision-making. The latter principle is suited to a political system in which power is highly stratified.

In sum, the explanatory side of democratic elite theory, in the form of its conceptualization of "method," "interest," "political," and "equality," unmistakably leads to a twofold conclusion: (a) on-going democratic systems, characterized by elite rule and mass passivity, handsomely meet the requirements of democratic theory; and (b) any suggestion that a departure from the system in the direction of obtaining a more equalitarian relationship between elites and non-elites is, on objective grounds, unrealistic.

These conclusions are in harmony with and support the normative judgment, as reflected in the writing of democratic elitists, that the illiberal propensity of the masses is the overriding threat to the free society, which, if it does survive, will do so because of the wisdom and courage of established elites. The theory of democratic elitism is not a theory of the status quo. For on the one hand it is completely in tune with the rapid change toward greater concentration of power in the hands of managerial elites, and on the other, it manifests an uneasiness that, in the absence of the creation of an elite consensus, the system is doomed.

2

Classical theory . . . is based on the supposition that man's dignity, and indeed his growth and development as a functioning and responsive individual in a free society, is dependent upon an opportunity to participate actively in decisions that significantly affect him. The psychological soundness of this supposition has in recent years been supported by the well-known experiments contrasting the impact of authoritarian and democratic leadership on group behavior, conducted by Kurt Lewin and associates in the late 1930's,[1] by the subsequent testing of the "participation hypothesis" by numerous small group researchers,[2] and in the more speculative writings of Eric Fromm and others.[3] But surely one does not have to rely upon hard data to share in the belief of Rousseau, Kant, Mill, Lindsay, and others, that man's development as a human being is closely dependent upon his opportunity to contribute to the solution of problems relating to his own actions.

Although firmly grounded on what I consider to be a sound ethical position, classical theory falls short of being a viable political theory for modern society. For in underscoring the importance of widespread participation in political decision-making, it offers no realistic guidelines as to how its prescription is to be filled in large urban societies.

On its face it would appear that the democrat is left with a Hobson's choice: a theory which is normatively sound but unrealistic, or a theory

1. For these experiments, see Kurt Lewin, Ronald Lippitt, and R. White, "Patterns of Aggressive Behavior in Experimentally Created Social Climates," *Journal of Social Psychology* (vol. 10, 1939), pp. 271-99.

2. For a review of these studies, see Sidney Verba, *Small Groups and Political Behavior* (Princeton, 1961), pp. 216-25.

3. See especially *Escape from Freedom* (New York, 1941); and *The Sane Society* (New York, 1955); also see A. H. Maslow, "Power Relationship and Patterns of Personal Development," and sources cited in A. Kornhauser (ed.), *Problems in Power* (Detroit, 1957), pp. 92-131; Christian Bay, *Structure of Freedom* (Stanford, 1958), pp. 155-240.

which is realistic but heavily skewed toward elitism. It is my contention that he should reject both and instead accept the challenge to create a democratic theory for the twentieth century; one that is founded on the self-developmental objective and one that at the same time firmly confronts the elite-mass structure characteristic of modern societies. This approach to democracy can perhaps best be understood by contrasting it with the position of the democratic elitists in reference to certain key concepts and empirical statements that closely relate to the role of elites in a democracy. Table 1 is, in summary form, an attempt to make this contrast.

At the outset the democratic theorist must abandon explanatory theory as an approach to his subject. By adhering to it he tends to accept as unalterable the configuration of society as shaped by impersonal forces. In accepting the growing concentration of elite power as given, he has been left with the task of pruning democratic theory in accord with changing conditions. Invariably this leads to support for an ideology that is strongly elitist in character. Instead, what we must acquire, as Richard Crossman has suggested, is a healthy dose of Promethean defiance against

TABLE 1. THE CONTRAST BETWEEN DEMOCRATIC ELITISM
AND SELF-DEVELOPMENTAL THEORY OF DEMOCRACY

Concepts & Empirical Statement	Democratic Elitism	Modern Self-Developmental
Democracy	political method	political method and ethical end
Interest	interest-as-end-results	interest-as-end-results and interest-as-process
Equality	equality of opportunity	equality of power
Political	governmental decision-making and that which relates to it	decision-making which significantly affects societal values
Elite-mass structure of modern industrial societies	unalterable	alterable
Anti-liberal propensity of a great number of non-elites	reliance upon elites to safeguard the system	reliance upon broadening and enriching the democratic process

the illiberal and impersonal forces which tend to devastate us. To submit to those forces which threaten to emasculate democracy, to adjust values eagerly to facts as the latter turn against us, is not the attitude of the scientist but of the defeatist.[4]

4. For as Mannheim argued, the determinist—and the positivist can be included—"overlooks the fact that every major phase of social change constitutes a choice between alternatives." *Essays on the Sociology of Culture* (London, 1956), p. 169.

Stripped of normative ends, political theory, including democratic theory, cannot perform the crucial function of providing direction to man's actions. To argue that we must be content to struggle modestly forward by combating social evil as it arises is to assume that a series of incremental moves to combat various evils will add up over time to a step forward. That need not be and often is not the case. In any event, the fundamental issue is not whether democracy should or should not have an overriding objective; it is rather whether its objective should be implicitly dedicated to the viability of a democratic elitist system or explicitly to the self-development of the individual.

In opting for the latter objective, I believe that a theory of democracy should be based upon the following assumptions and principles: the majority of individuals stand to gain in self-esteem and growth toward a fuller affirmation of their personalities by participating more actively in meaningful community decisions; people generally, therefore, have a twofold interest in politics—interest in end results and interest in the process of participation; benefits from the latter interest are closely related to the degree to which the principle of equality of power is realized; and progress toward the realization of this principle is initially dependent upon the acceptance by social scientists of a realistic concept of what constitutes the political sector of society.

The elite-mass structure of present-day society is very much a reality. But it is an unalterable structure only if political decision-making is viewed narrowly, as governmental decision-making. I have argued that such a view is untenable, that the evidence will simply not support a *twofold* definition of political. To define political broadly for general purposes and then, when concerned with the meaning of political elites or political equality, to retreat to a nineteenth-century notion of the concept is to remove an important area of politics from political research. If the political scientist is to be realistic, he must recognize that large areas within existing so-called private centers of power are political and therefore potentially open to a wide and democratic sharing in decision-making.

It is true that political scientists of all persuasions are very willing to analyze both the power structure of "private governments" and the interaction of these units with government policy. But these institutions are distinguished from government on the ground that they, unlike the latter, do not possess the exclusive and legitimate right to exercise force. Of course this is a valid distinction, but is it sufficient to exempt private governments from scrutiny within the context of the democratic norms of political equality, popular participation in the formulation of basic policy, and accountability of leaders to lead? I do not believe so. Obviously General Motors is not the United States government. However, there is a basic similarity between the two: they both authoritatively allocate values for the society. It is on the basis of this similarity that General Motors and other giant private governments should be considered a part of the political sector in which democratic norms apply. Within the context of constitutional law, a private firm which performs a public function is subject, like the government, to the limitations of the Constitution. The expansion of the concept of "state action" by the Supreme Court, which has had a significant effect in constitutionalizing private governments, reflects the Court's insistence that the Constitution will be a viable instrument to meet the needs of the present. It is time that democratic theorists emulate the spirit of their judicial brethren. They may begin by holding that when a private government performs a public function—such as authoritatively allocating values for society or a large part of it—that for purposes of democratic theory as well as constitutional law, it is considered a political institution and thus within the reach of the Constitution *and* democratic principles.

It might be asked, why is it necessary to politicize private centers of power in order to broaden the base for participation? Does not the argument erroneously assume that ordinary men and women actually desire a greater share in shaping policies which affect them? If this were the case, one would think that the people would have already exploited to the fullest every opportunity to engage in politics within existing political institutions. As one study after another has shown, a comparatively large portion of the public is indifferent to politics; they abstain from voting, they are virtually ignorant of public affairs, and they lack a strong commitment to the democratic process. Would not this same pattern of indifference exist within a broadened political area?

If the newly recognized political sector were the factory, the office, the enterprise, I do not believe this would be the case. For many individuals political issues and elections appear either trivial or remote and beyond the reach of their influence. Of a different magnitude are issues which directly affect them in their place of work, issues which are comparatively trivial, yet are overlaid with tensions and emotions that often infuriate and try men's souls. It is here—despite the legitimatizing effects of bureaucratic forms—that the ugliness of man's domination of man is fully revealed, and it is here, consequently, that democracy must become established and put to use. I am not suggesting that the average worker, for example, if given the opportunity to share in the making of factory decisions, would be magically transformed, in the fashion of Rousseau's common man, from an unimaginative, parochial, selfish human being to a broad-minded, intelligent, public-spirited citizen. I am saying that political education is most effective on a level which challenges the individual to engage cooperatively in the solution of concrete problems affecting himself and his immediate community. In the past this task was ideally performed in the New England town meeting; in twentieth-century America it can effectively be performed in the factory community.

Clearly the highly complex, mammoth industrial corporate structure of today has little resemblance to the town meetings of eighteenth-century America. This does not mean, however, that the modern corporation could not, to a significant extent, be democratized in line with the principles and objectives that I have outlined above. Admittedly at this point it is a matter of conjecture whether such an undertaking, from both a political and economic standpoint, is workable. However, in my view, it borders on dogmatism to reject this challenge out of hand, on the assertion, for example, that the principles of accountability and equality of power are irreconcilable, or that the devolution of decision-making is, without serious loss of efficiency, impossible within the modern industrial firm. We cannot, with any degree of confidence, extrapolate a democratic scheme for modern industry from on-going oligarchic institutions. It seems equally evident that we cannot, with any degree of confidence, conclude from observation of oligarchic practices that such a democratic scheme, if put into practice, would be doomed to failure. If democracy is to be taken seriously, we cannot remain on dead center on this issue. What is called for, at minimum, is discussion and debate on various aspects of the question with the view of possible experimentation with nationalization of one or a few corporate political giants. Serious consideration of such a proposal can no longer be left to socialists, nor should controversy centering on such a proposal be fought along traditional socialist-capitalist lines of argument. Today, argument along those lines would border on the irrelevant. For the fundamental issue no longer relates to the problem of production or distribution but to the problem of power.

The illiberal and anti-democratic propensity of the common man is an undeniable fact that must be faced. But to face it realistically is not, as I have attempted to show, to rely upon elites to sustain the system. For in the first place, there is little evidence that elites, any more than non-elites, are prepared to defend procedural rights at the risk of jeopardizing their own personal status, prestige, and power. Secondly, to assume a harmony between the vested interests of elites and the well-being of democracy is to sap the latter of the boldness and imaginativeness characteristic of democracies of the past. To do so would be to confine the expansion of democracy to an area where it does not threaten the basic substantive interests of dominant elites. Thirdly, it is difficult to understand how elites, who have conflicting substantive interests, can reach a consensus sufficiently effective to safeguard democracy from attack. Finally, assuming elites can reach such a consensus, it seems doubtful that they could generate sufficient power *democratically* to restrain the excessive demands and actions of the undemocratic mass and its leaders.

If it is time to abandon the myth of the common man's allegiance to democracy, it is also time that elites in general and political scientists in particular recognize that without the common man's active support, liberty cannot be preserved over the long run. The battle for freedom will be lost by default if elites insulate themselves from the people and rely on countervailing forces, institutional and social barriers, and their own colleagues to defend the system from the demagogic leader of the mob. Democracy can best be assured of survival by enlisting the people's support in a continual effort to make democracy meaningful in the lives of all men.

The Higher Circles

C. WRIGHT MILLS

The powers of ordinary men are circumscribed by the everyday worlds in which they live, yet even in these rounds of job, family, and neighborhood they often seem driven by forces they can neither understand nor govern. "Great changes" are beyond their control, but affect their conduct and outlook nonetheless. The very framework of modern society confines them to projects not their own, but from every side, such changes now press upon the men and women of the mass society, who accordingly feel that they are without purpose in an epoch in which they are without power.

But not all men are in this sense ordinary. As the means of information and of power are centralized, some men come to occupy positions in American society from which they can look down upon, so to speak, and by their decisions mightily affect, the everyday worlds of ordinary men and women. They are not made by their jobs; they set up and break down jobs for thousands of others; they are not confined by simple family responsibilities; they can escape. They may live in many hotels and houses, but they are bound by no one community. They need not merely "meet the demands of the day and hour"; in some part, they create these demands, and cause others to meet them. Whether or not they profess their power, their technical and political experience of it far transcends that of the underlying population. What Jacob Burckhardt said of "great men," most Americans might well say of their elite: "They are all that we are not."

The power elite is composed of men whose positions enable them to transcend the ordinary environments of ordinary men and women; they are in positions to make decisions having major consequences. Whether they do or do not make such decisions is less important than the fact that they do occupy such pivotal positions: their failure to act, their failure to make decisions, is itself an act that is often of greater consequence than the decisions they do make. For they are in command of the major hierarchies and organizations of modern society. They rule the big corporations. They run the machinery of the state and claim its prerogatives. They direct the military establishment. They occupy the strategic command posts of the social structure, in which are now centered the effective means of the power and the wealth and the celebrity which they enjoy.

The power elite are not solitary rulers. Advisers and consultants, spokesmen and opinion-makers are often the captains of their higher thought and decision. Immediately below the elite are the professional politicians of the middle levels of power, in the Congress and in the pressure groups, as well as among the new and old upper classes of town and city and region. Mingling with them, in curious ways which we shall explore, are those professional celebrities who live by being continually displayed but are never, so long as they remain celebrities, displayed enough. If such celebrities are not at the head of any dominating hierarchy, they do often have the power to distract the attention of the public or afford sensations to the masses, or, more directly, to gain the ear of those who do occupy positions of direct power. More or less unattached, as critics of morality and technicians of power, as spokesmen of God and creators of mass sensibility, such celebrities and consultants are part of the immediate scene in which the drama of the elite is enacted. But that drama itself is centered in the command posts of the major institutional hierarchies.

1

The truth about the nature and the power of the elite is not some secret which men of affairs know but will not tell. Such men hold quite various theories about their own roles in the sequence of event and decision. Often they are uncertain about their roles, and even more often they allow their fears and their hopes to affect their assessment of their own power. No matter how great their actual power, they tend to be less acutely aware of it than of the resistances of others to its use. Moreover, most American men of affairs have learned well the rhetoric of public relations, in some cases even to the point of using it when they are alone, and thus coming to believe it. The personal awareness of the actors is only one of the several sources one must examine in order to understand the higher circles. Yet many who believe that there is no elite, or at any rate none of any consequence, rest their argument upon what men of affairs believe about themselves, or at least assert in public.

There is, however, another view: those who feel, even if vaguely, that a compact and powerful elite of great importance does now prevail in America often base that feeling upon the historical trend of our time. They have felt, for example, the domination of the military event, and from this they infer that generals and admirals, as well as other men of decision influenced by them, must be enormously powerful. They hear that the Congress has again abdicated to a handful of men decisions clearly related to the issue of war or peace. They know that the bomb was dropped over Japan in the name of the United States of America, although they were at no time consulted about the matter. They feel that they live in a time of big decisions; they know that they are not making any. Accordingly, as they consider the present as history, they infer that at its center, making decisions or failing to make them, there must be an elite of power.

On the one hand, those who share this feeling about big historical events assume that there is an elite and that its power is great. On the other hand, those who listen carefully to the reports of men apparently involved in the great decisions often do not believe that there is an elite whose powers are of decisive consequence.

Both views must be taken into account, but neither is adequate. The way to understand the power of the American elite lies neither solely in recognizing the historic scale of events nor in accepting the personal awareness reported by men of apparent decision. Behind such men and behind the events of history, linking the two, are the major institutions of modern society. These hierarchies of state and corporation and army constitute the means of power; as such they are now of a consequence not before equaled in human history—and at their summits, there are now those command posts of modern society which offer us the sociological key to an understanding of the role of the higher circles in America.

Within American society, major national power now resides in the economic, the political, and the military domains. Other institutions seem off to the side of modern history, and, on occasion, duly subordinated to these. No family is as directly powerful in national affairs as any major corporation; no church is as directly powerful in the external biographies of young men in America today as the military establishments; no college is as powerful in the shaping of momentous events as the National Security Council. Religious, educational, and family institutions are not autonomous centers of national power; on the contrary, these decentralized areas are increasingly shaped by the big three, in which developments of decisive and immediate consequence now occur.

Families and churches and schools adapt to modern life; governments and armies and corporations shape it; and, as they do so, they turn these lesser institutions into means for their ends. Religious institutions provide chaplains to the armed forces where they are used as a means of increasing the effectiveness of its morale to kill. Schools select and train men for their jobs in corporations and their specialized tasks in the armed forces. The extended family has, of course, long been broken up by the industrial revolution, and now the son and the father are removed from the family, by compulsion if need be, whenever the army of the state sends out the call. And the symbols of all these lesser institutions are used to legitimate the power and the decisions of the big three.

The life-fate of the modern individual depends not only upon the family into which he was born or which he enters by marriage, but increasingly upon the corporation in which he spends the most alert hours of his best years; not only upon the school where he is educated as a child and adolescent, but also upon the state which touches him throughout his life; not only upon the church in which on occasion he hears the word of God, but also upon the army in which he is disciplined.

If the centralized state could not rely upon the inculcation of nationalist loyalties in public and private schools, its leaders would promptly seek to modify the decentralized educational system. If the bankruptcy rate among the top five hundred corporations were as high as the general divorce rate among the thirty-seven million married couples, there would be economic catastrophe on an international scale. If members of armies gave to them no more of their lives than do believers to the churches to which they belong, there would be a military crisis.

Within each of the big three, the typical institutional unit has be-

come enlarged, has become administrative, and, in the power of its decisions, has become centralized. Behind these developments there is a
fabulous technology, for as institutions, they have incorporated this technology and guide it, even as it shapes and paces their developments.

The economy—once a great scatter of small productive units in autonomous balance—has become dominated by two or three hundred giant
corporations, administratively and politically interrelated, which together hold the keys to economic decisions.

The political order, once a decentralized set of several dozen states
with a weak spinal cord, has become a centralized, executive establishment which has taken up into itself many powers previously scattered,
and now enters into each and every cranny of the social structure.

The military order, once a slim establishment in a context of distrust fed by state militia, has become the largest and most expensive feature of government, and, although well versed in smiling public relations, now has all the grim and clumsy efficiency of a sprawling bureaucratic domain.

In each of these institutional areas, the means of power at the disposal of decision makers have increased enormously; their central executive powers have been enhanced; within each of them modern administrative routines have been elaborated and tightened up.

As each of these domains becomes enlarged and centralized, the consequences of its activities become greater, and its traffic with the others
increases. The decisions of a handful of corporations bear upon military
and political as well as upon economic developments around the world.
The decisions of the military establishment rest upon and grievously
affect political life as well as the very level of economic activity. The decisions made within the political domain determine economic activities
and military programs. There is no longer, on the one hand, an economy,
and, on the other hand, a political order containing a military establishment unimportant to politics and to money-making. There is a political
economy linked, in a thousand ways, with military institutions and decisions. On each side of the world-split running through central Europe and
around the Asiatic rimlands, there is an ever-increasing interlocking of
economic, military, and political structures. If there is government intervention in the corporate economy, so is there corporate intervention in
the governmental process. In the structural sense, this triangle of power
is the source of the interlocking directorate that is most important for
the historical structure of the present.

The fact of the interlocking is clearly revealed at each of the points of
crisis of modern capitalist society—slump, war, and boom. In each, men
of decision are led to an awareness of the interdependence of the major
institutional orders. In the nineteenth century, when the scale of all institutions was smaller, their liberal integration was achieved in the automatic economy, by an autonomous play of market forces, and in the
automatic political domain, by the bargain and the vote. It was then
assumed that out of the imbalance and friction that followed the limited

decisions then possible a new equilibrium would in due course emerge. That can no longer be assumed, and it is not assumed by the men at the top of each of the three dominant hierarchies.

For given the scope of their consequences, decisions—and indecisions —in any one of these ramify into the others, and hence top decisions tend either to become co-ordinated or to lead to a commanding indecision. It has not always been like this. When numerous small entrepreneurs made up the economy, for example, many of them could fail and the consequences still remained local; political and military authorities did not intervene. But now, given political expectations and military commitments, can they afford to allow key units of the private corporate economy to break down in slump? Increasingly, they do intervene in economic affairs, and as they do so, the controlling decisions in each order are inspected by agents of the other two, and economic, military, and political structures are interlocked.

At the pinnacle of each of the three enlarged and centralized domains, there have arisen those higher circles which make up the economic, the political, and the military elites. At the top of the economy, among the corporate rich, there are the chief executives; at the top of the political order, the members of the political directorate; at the top of the military establishment, the elite of soldier-statesmen clustered in and around the Joint Chiefs of Staff and the upper echelon. As each of these domains has coincided with the others, as decisions tend to become total in their consequence, the leading men in each of the three domains of power—the warlords, the corporation chieftains, the political directorate— tend to come together, to form the power elite of America.

2

The higher circles in and around these command posts are often thought of in terms of what their members possess: they have a greater share than other people of the things and experiences that are most highly valued. From this point of view, the elite are simply those who have the most of what there is to have, which is generally held to include money, power, and prestige—as well as all the ways of life to which these lead. But the elite are not simply those who have the most, for they could not "have the most" were it not for their positions in the great institutions. For such institutions are the necessary bases of power, of wealth, and of prestige, and at the same time, the chief means of exercising power, of acquiring and retaining wealth, and of cashing in the higher claims for prestige.

By the powerful we mean, of course, those who are able to realize their will, even if others resist it. No one, accordingly, can be truly powerful unless he has access to the command of major institutions, for it is over these institutional means of power that the truly powerful are, in the first instance, powerful. Higher politicians and key officials of government command such institutional power; so do admirals and generals, and so do the major owners and executives of the larger corporations. Not all power, it is true, is anchored in and exercised by means of such institutions, but only within and through them can power be more or less continuous and important.

Wealth also is acquired and held in and through institutions. The pyramid of wealth cannot be understood merely in terms of the very rich; for the great inheriting families . . . are now supplemented by the corporate institutions of modern society: every one of the very rich families has been and is closely connected—always legally and frequently managerially as well—with one of the multi-million dollar corporations.

The modern corporation is the prime source of wealth, but, in latter-day capitalism, the political apparatus also opens and closes many avenues to wealth. The amount as well as the source of income, the power over consumer's goods as well as over productive capital, are determined by position within the political economy. If our interest in the very rich goes beyond their lavish or their miserly consumption, we must examine their relations to modern forms of corporate property as well as to the state; for such relations now determine the chances of men to secure big property and to receive high income.

Great prestige increasingly follows the major institutional units of the social structure. It is obvious that prestige depends, often quite decisively, upon access to the publicity machines that are now a central and normal feature of all the big institutions of modern America. Moreover, one feature of these hierarchies of corporation, state, and military establishment is that their top positions are increasingly interchangeable. One result of this is the accumulative nature of prestige. Claims for prestige, for example, may be initially based on military roles, then expressed in and augmented by an educational institution run by corporate executives, and cashed in, finally, in the political order, where, for General Eisenhower and those he represents, power and prestige finally meet at the very peak. Like wealth and power, prestige tends to be cumulative: the more of it you have, the more you can get. These values also tend to be translatable into one another: the wealthy find it easier than the poor to gain power; those with status find it easier than those without it to control opportunities for wealth.

If we took the one hundred most powerful men in America, the one hundred wealthiest, and the one hundred most celebrated away from the institutional positions they now occupy, away from their resources of men and women and money, away from the media of mass communication that are now focused upon them—then they would be powerless and poor and uncelebrated. For power is not of a man. Wealth does not center in the person of the wealthy. Celebrity is not inherent in any personality. To be celebrated, to be wealthy, to have power requires access to major institutions, for the institutional positions men occupy determine in large part their chances to have and to hold these valued experiences.

The New Class

MILOVAN DJILAS

1

Everything happened differently in the U.S.S.R. and other Communist countries from what the leaders—even such prominent ones as Lenin, Stalin, Trotsky, and Bukharin—anticipated. They expected that the state would rapidly wither away, that democracy would be strengthened. The reverse happened. They expected a rapid improvement in the standard of living—there has been scarcely any change in this respect and, in the subjugated East European countries, the standard has even declined. In every instance, the standard of living has failed to rise in proportion to the rate of industrialization, which was much more rapid. It was believed that the differences between cities and villages, between intellectual and physical labor, would slowly disappear; instead these differences have increased. Communist anticipations in other areas—including their expectations for developments in the non-Communist world—have also failed to materialize.

The greatest illusion was that industrialization and collectivization in the U.S.S.R., and destruction of capitalist ownership, would result in a classless society. In 1936, when the new Constitution was promulgated, Stalin announced that the "exploiting class" had ceased to exist. The capitalist and other classes of ancient origin had in fact been destroyed, but a new class, previously unknown to history, had been formed.

It is understandable that this class, like those before it, should believe that the establishment of its power would result in happiness and freedom for all men. The only difference between this and other classes was that it treated the delay in the realization of its illusions more crudely. It thus affirmed that its power was more complete than the power of any other class before in history, and its class illusions and prejudices were proportionally greater.

This new class, the bureaucracy, or more accurately the political bureaucracy, has all the characteristics of earlier ones as well as some new characteristics of its own. Its origin had its special characteristics also, even though in essence it was similar to the beginnings of other classes.

Other classes, too, obtained their strength and power by the revolutionary path, destroying the political, social, and other orders they met in their way. However, almost without exception, these classes attained power *after* new economic patterns had taken shape in the old society. The case was the reverse with new classes in the Communist systems. It did not come to power to *complete* a new economic order but to *establish* its own and, in so doing, to establish its power over society.

In earlier epochs the coming to power of some class, some part of a class, or of some party, was the final event resulting from its formation and its development. The reverse was true in the U.S.S.R. There the new

232

class was definitely formed after it attained power. Its consciousness had to develop before its economic and physical powers, because the class had not taken root in the life of the nation. This class viewed its role in relation to the world from an idealistic point of view. Its practical possibilities were not diminished by this. In spite of its illusions, it represented an objective tendency toward industrialization. Its practical bent emanated from this tendency. The promise of an ideal world increased the faith in the ranks of the new class and sowed illusions among the masses. At the same time it inspired gigantic physical undertakings.

Because this new class had not been formed as a part of the economic and social life before it came to power, it could only be created in an organization of a special type, distinguished by a special discipline based on identical philosophic and ideological views of its members. A unity of belief and iron discipline was necessary to overcome its weaknesses.

The roots of the new class were implanted in a special party, of the Bolshevik type. Lenin was right in his view that his party was an exception in the history of human society, although he did not suspect that it would be the beginning of a new class.

To be more precise, the initiators of the new class are not found in the party of the Bolshevik type as a whole but in that stratum of professional revolutionaries who made up its core even before it attained power. It was not by accident that Lenin asserted after the failure of the 1905 revolution that only professional revolutionaries—men whose sole profession was revolutionary work—could build a new party of the Bolshevik type. It was still less accidental that even Stalin, the future creator of a new class, was the most outstanding example of such a professional revolutionary. The new ruling class has been gradually developing from this very narrow stratum of revolutionaries. These revolutionaries composed its core for a long period. Trotsky noted that in pre-revolutionary professional revolutionaries was the origin of the future Stalinist bureaucrat. What he did not detect was the beginning of a new class of owners and exploiters.

This is not to say that the new party and the new class are identical. The party, however, is the core of that class, and its base. It is very difficult, perhaps impossible, to define the limits of the new class and to identify its members. The new class may be said to be made up of those who have special privileges and economic preference because of the administrative monopoly they hold.

Since administration is unavoidable in society, necessary administrative functions may be coexistent with parasitic functions in the same person. Not every member of the party is a member of the new class, any more than every artisan or member of the city party was a bourgeois.

In loose terms, as the new class becomes stronger and attains a more perceptible physiognomy, the role of the party diminishes. The core and the basis of the new class is created in the party and at its top, as well as in the state political organs. The once live, compact party, full of initiative, is disappearing to become transformed into the traditional oligarchy of the new class, irresistibly drawing into its ranks those who aspire to join the new class and repressing those who have any ideals.

The party makes the class, but the class grows as a result and uses the party as a basis. The class grows stronger, while the party grows weaker; this is the inescapable fate of every Communist party in power.

If it were not materially interested in production or if it did not have within itself the potentialities for the creation of a new class, no party could act in so morally and ideologically foolhardy a fashion, let alone stay in power for long. Stalin declared, after the end of the First Five-Year Plan: "If we had not created the apparatus, we would have failed!" He should have substituted "new class" for the word "apparatus," and everything would have been clearer.

It seems unusual that a political party could be the beginning of a new class. Parties are generally the product of classes and strata which have become intellectually and economically strong. However, if one grasps the actual conditions in pre-revolutionary Russia and in other countries in which Communism prevailed over national forces, it will be clear that a party of this type is the product of specific opportunities and that there is nothing unusual or accidental in this being so. Although the roots of Bolshevism reach far back into Russian history, the party is partly the product of the unique pattern of international relationships in which Russia found itself at the end of the nineteenth and the beginning of the twentieth century. Russia was no longer able to live in the modern world as an absolute monarchy, and Russia's capitalism was too weak and too dependent on the interests of foreign powers to make it possible to have an industrial revolution. This revolution could only be implemented by a new class, or by a change in the social order. As yet, there was no such class.

In history, it is not important who implements a process, it is only important that the process be implemented. Such was the case in Russia and other countries in which Communist revolutions took place. The revolution created forces, leaders, organizations, and ideas which were necessary to it. The new class came into existence for objective reasons, and by the wish, wits, and action of its leaders.

2

The social origin of the new class lies in the proletariat just as the aristocracy arose in a peasant society, and the bourgeoisie in a commercial and artisans' society. There are exceptions, depending on national conditions, but the proletariat in economically underdeveloped countries, being backward, constitutes the raw material from which the new class arises.

There are other reasons why the new class always acts as the champion of the working class. The new class is anti-capitalistic and, consequently, logically dependent upon the working strata. The new class is supported by the proletarian struggle and the traditional faith of the proletariat in a socialist, Communist society where there is no brutal exploitation. It is vitally important for the new class to assure a normal flow of production, hence it cannot ever lose its connection with the proletariat. Most important of all, the new class cannot achieve industrialization and consolidate its power without the help of the working class. On the other hand, the working class sees in expanded industry the salvation from its poverty and despair. Over a long period of time, the interests, ideas, faith, and hope of the new class, and of parts of the working class and of the poor peasants, coincide and unite. Such mergers have occurred in the past among other widely different classes. Did not the bourgeoisie represent the peasantry in the struggle against the feudal lords?

The movement of the new class toward power comes as a result of the efforts of the proletariat and the poor. These are the masses upon which the party or the new class must lean and with which its interests are most closely allied. This is true until the new class finally establishes its power and authority. Over and above this, the new class is interested in the proletariat and the poor only to the extent necessary for developing production and for maintaining in subjugation the most aggressive and rebellious social forces.

The monopoly which the new class establishes in the name of the working class over the whole of society is, primarily, a monopoly over the working class itself. This monopoly is first intellectual, over the so-called *avant-garde* proletariat, and then over the whole proletariat. This is the biggest deception the class must accomplish, but it shows that the power and interests of the new class lie primarily in industry. Without industry the new class cannot consolidate its position or authority.

Former sons of the working class are the most steadfast members of the new class. It has always been the fate of slaves to provide for their masters the most clever and gifted representatives. In this case a new exploiting and governing class is born from the exploited class.

3

When Communist systems are being critically analyzed, it is considered that their fundamental distinction lies in the fact that a bureaucracy, organized in a special stratum, rules over the people. This is generally true. However, a more detailed analysis will show that only a special stratum of bureaucrats, those who are not administrative officials, make up the core of the governing bureaucracy, or, in my terminology, of the new class. This is actually a party or political bureaucracy. Other officials are only the apparatus under the control of the new class; the apparatus may be clumsy and slow but, no matter what, it must exist in every socialist society. It is sociologically possible to draw the borderline between the different types of officials, but in practice they are practically indistinguishable. This is true not only because the Communist system by its very nature is bureaucratic, but because Communists handle the various important administrative functions. In addition, the stratum of political bureaucrats cannot enjoy their privileges if they do not give crumbs from their tables to other bureaucratic categories.

It is important to note the fundamental differences between the political bureaucracies mentioned here and those which arise with every centralization in modern economy—especially centralizations that lead to collective forms of ownership such as monopolies, companies, and state ownership. The number of white-collar workers is constantly increasing in capitalistic monopolies, and also in nationalized industries in the West. In *Human Relations in Administration,* R. Dubin says that state functionaries in the economy are being transformed into a special stratum of society.

> . . . Functionaries have the sense of a common destiny for all those who work together. They share the same interests, especially since there is relatively little competition insofar as promotion is in terms of seniority. In-group aggression is thus minimized and this arrangement is therefore conceived to be positively functional for the bureaucracy. However, the esprit de corps and informal social organization which typically develops in such situations often leads the personnel to defend their entrenched interests rather than to assist their clientele and elected higher officials.

While such functionaries have much in common with Communist bureaucrats, especially as regards "esprit de corps," they are not identical. Although state and other bureaucrats in non-Communist systems form a special stratum, they do not exercise authority as the Communists do. Bureaucrats in a non-Communist state have political masters, usually elected, or owners over them, while Communists have neither masters nor owners over them. The bureaucrats in a non-Communist state are officials in modern capitalist economy, while the Communists are something different and new: a new class.

As in other owning classes, the proof that it is a special class lies in its ownership and its special relations to other classes. In the same way, the class to which a member belongs is indicated by the material and other privileges which ownership brings to him.

As defined by Roman law, property constitutes the use, enjoyment, and disposition of material goods. The Communist political bureaucracy uses, enjoys, and disposes of nationalized property.

If we assume that membership in this bureaucracy or new owning class is predicated on the use of privileges inherent in ownership—in this instance nationalized material goods—then membership in the new party class, or political bureaucracy, is reflected in a larger income in material goods and privileges than society should normally grant for such functions. In practice, the ownership privilege of the new class manifests itself as an exclusive right, as a party monopoly, for the political bureaucracy to distribute the national income, to set wages, direct economic development, and dispose of nationalized and other property. This is the way it appears to the ordinary man who considers the Communist functionary as being very rich and as a man who does not have to work.

The ownership of private property has, for many reasons, proved to be unfavorable for the establishment of the new class's authority. Besides, the destruction of private ownership was necessary for the economic transformation of nations. The new class obtains its power, privileges, ideology, and its customs from one specific form of ownership—collective ownership—which the class administers and distributes in the name of the nation and society.

The new class maintains that ownership derives from a designated social relationship. This is the relationship between the monopolists of administration, who constitute a narrow and closed stratum, and the mass of producers (farmers, workers, and intelligentsia) who have no rights. However, this relationship is not valid since the Communist bureaucracy enjoys a monopoly over the distribution of material goods.

Every fundamental change in the social relationship between those who monopolize administration and those who work is inevitably reflected in the ownership relationship. Social and political relations and ownership—the totalitarianism of the government and the monopoly of authority—are being more fully brought into accord in Communism than in any other single system.

To divest Communists of their ownership rights would be to abolish them as a class. To compel them to relinquish their other social powers, so that workers may participate in sharing the profits of their work—which capitalists have had to permit as a result of strikes and parliamentary action—would mean that Communists were being deprived of their monopoly over property, ideology, and government. This would be the beginning of democracy and freedom in Communism, the end of Communist monopolism and totalitarianism. Until this happens, there can be no indication that important, fundamental changes are taking place in Communist systems, at least not in the eyes of men who think seriously about social progress.

The ownership privileges of the new class and membership in that class are the privileges of *administration*. This privilege extends from state administration and the administration of economic enterprises to that of sports and humanitarian organizations. Political, party, or so-called "general leadership" is executed by the core. This position of leadership carries privileges with it. In his *Stalin au pouvoir*, published in Paris in 1951, Orlov states that the average pay of a worker in the U.S.S.R. in 1935 was 1, 800 rubles annually, while the pay and allowances of the secretary of a rayon committee amounted to 45,000 rubles annually. The situation has changed since then for both workers and party functionaries, but the essence remains the same. Other authors have arrived at the same conclusions. Discrepancies between the pay of workers and party functionaries are extreme; this could not be hidden from persons visiting the U.S.S.R. or other Communist countries in the past few years.

Other systems, too, have their professional politicians. One can think well or ill of them, but they must exist. Society cannot live without a state or a government, and therefore it cannot live without those who fight for it.

However, there are fundamental differences between professional politicians in other systems and in the Communist system. In extreme cases, politicians in other systems use the government to secure privileges for themselves and their cohorts, or to favor the economic interests of one social stratum or another. The situation is different with the Communist system where the power and the government are identical with the use, enjoyment, and disposition of almost all the nation's goods. He who grabs power grabs privileges and indirectly grabs property. Consequently, in Communism, power or politics as a profession is the ideal of those who have the desire or the prospect of living as parasites at the expense of others.

Membership in the Communist Party before the Revolution meant sacrifice. Being a professional revolutionary was one of the highest honors. Now that the party has consolidated its power, party membership means that one belongs to a privileged class. And at the core of the party are the all-powerful exploiters and masters.

For a long time the Communist revolution and the Communist system have been concealing their real nature. The emergence of the new class has been concealed under socialist phraseology and, more important, under the new collective forms of property ownership. The so-called socialist ownership is a disguise for the real ownership by the political bureaucracy. And in the beginning this bureaucracy was in a hurry to complete industrialization, and hid its class composition under that guise.

from Technocracy

JEAN MEYNAUD

The advent of industrial civilization is far from being the cause of the disappearance or even the decline of political activity in human societies. The thesis that politics must inevitably be absorbed into technics cannot really be supported. The most knowledgeable thinkers always stress the impossibility of totally mechanizing human decisions. However, we must admit that the field in which electronic computers are employed is developing. The risk—the only one in fact—is that man will become a slave of those who feed these machines with information and make use of the results.

In other words, an examination of the foreseeable future reveals that there is no legitimate reason to assume that political relations will disappear: the important point is to ascertain who will be behind them and control them, and to whose advantage. These standard questions apply to technocratic forms of government as much as to any others.

In beginning this reappraisal, we must remember that the very existence of technocratic influence—resulting, at least in several cases, in technicians' acquisition of true decision-making powers—is not unanimously recognized by all sections of opinion. Marxists especially refute it: they regard attempts at highlighting technocracy as mere diversions or an attempt to confuse the issue. But apart from them, various other people also refuse to admit that patterns of behavior and practices which are ranked as technocratic constitute a real or new problem and point to the persistence throughout history of the constant endeavors of administrative power to gain autonomy. According to them, this invasion of politics by technics could find a qualified antedote in a spread of rational education throughout society. From the moment when, in contrast with the material means of production, technical competence is not the monopoly of some particular group, there is no reason to regard technocracy as a prime factor of political breakdown. In other words, extending technical ideals and methods to the government sector does not give rise to any problem or difficulty that a more general access to education or change in its content (two objectives which are still a long way off) would not be capable of resolving.

According to a very different and pessimistic body of thought, the factors which cause the increase in technicians' powers also create a state of mind in society, particularly among the workers, which facilitates political domination by a relatively closed group of men. Technical progress, giving government technicians control of a "totalitarian and dictatorial machinery" (G. Bernanos) which already governs the existence of every man, will ultimately result in a unification of industrial societies on the basis of collectivization, which could go as far as a total negation of individuals.

One of the essential aspects of this standardization, which is indifferent to juridical forms of social organization (especially the property system), would be the abolition of any direct relationship between individuals and the higher authorities and this would be to the benefit of groups. In this way, the technical factor, working through the social groups which inspire and direct national life, would lead ultimately, slowly but surely, to the domestication of the citizen. In such conditions, public or private endeavors against government by technicians would be nothing but vain agitations. Technical centralization would of necessity propel humanity towards the "best of all possible worlds."

Accepting this prospect, several people have no hesitation in forecasting the immediate advent of new masters with authority based not on any popular delegation, but on power derived from ability. If this happened, leaders of the tradition type would either be dispensed with or kept as figureheads with nominal powers only. In this latter situation, the public might not fully realize the modifications which had taken place.

I have analyzed . . . the mechanisms which could produce such a change. The starting point is the extension of the technical attitude, with its stress on efficiency, in the government system and bureaucratized management of large organizations. Deliberate restraint of this movement would have unfortunate consequences for the general good. Except when technical reasoning is mis-used by interest groups, it seems both desirable and inevitable that these tendencies be strengthened, to achieve greater co-ordination in the services responsible for state action, improvement in and greater use of methods of forecasting, and so on. There are some factors in opposition to these advantages: such changes strengthen the role of technicians who possess the knowledge and technical know-how and they are accompanied by a development of technocratic ideology, through a moral justification of government by technicians.

The result is a fresh decline of democracy, already weakened and circumscribed when compared with its ideal form. This is not so much the result of a clearly defined plot as of a progressive rise to power of forces exempt from all political connections, no longer ultimately responsible to the electorate. This movement goes along with the public's lack of interest in the conduct of the nation's affairs; the time he devotes to this is meagre in all respects. Technocratic intervention alone is not responsible for this minimal amount of participation which has deep roots in social structures and human attitudes, but it is a contributory factor, especially through the respect for ability upon which it is based.

Certain supporters of technocracy will doubtless protest at this view of it, and affirm their concern to safeguard the democratic ideal by breathing new life into it through calling on the help of technicians. A. Frisch, who sees technocracy as the way of saving our society, declares that it is necessary and believes that it is possible to protect technocracy from the "anti-democratic temptations." The integration of technocracy into a "democratically based" whole is conceivable. "It will be a question of . . . raising it in some degree to the level of a publicly recognized institution. This decision will automatically destroy its hidden power and oblige it to work as openly as the complexity of our modern mechanisms allows."

Frisch supplements his ideas with some institutional suggestions, but they are not very convincing. I have underlined the difficulty of organizing a balance and even more a conciliation between the power of the politician based on election and that of the technician founded on real or assumed ability. For obvious reasons, the politician cannot dream of ejecting the technician from the government machine, but the opposite is not true. Even when it is made in good faith, the aspiration towards a democratically inspired technocracy seems to stem from a mistaken analysis.

Today, the risk of a technocratic infiltration gathers strength from perfected techniques aimed at working on the minds and taming the wills of men without recourse to violence: because of the rate of progress in the field of psychological analysis, man runs the increasing risk of falling into the hands of the engineer of souls. We could add to this already ominous picture the prospects of automatic regulation opened up by cybernetics. Although it is not so sensational or terrifying in nature, as some of its experts suggest (G.-Th. Guilbaud, for example, calls it the "crossroad of science") this branch of knowledge seems capable of making a further contribution to "conditioning" human beings.

Let us remember that until now complete domination of politics by technics, or the theft of political office by technicians, is still fiction. There is no example of technicians being used throughout the whole of the government machine. Technocracy has not managed to gain a completely preponderant control of government action in any contemporary régime, supposing that this is in fact the true wish of technicians. Based on infiltrations in the sphere of supreme decision-making, and finding its substance in the accumulation of instances of partial dispossession, techno-cratic influence is not a completely autonomous and sovereign power. In short, André Molitor is correct in saying that, in most countries, the political machine can defend itself and defend itself well.

However, the process of transfer seems to me to be under way and many signs indicate that, unless some check is made . . . the expansion of technocracy will continue. The spirit of our day, directed towards the search for maximal productivity, is definitely favorable to technocratic ideology. At this point, it is essential to identify those who will benefit from the movement.

The great politico-economic structures erected by technicians them-selves generally fall into a distressing social void. All the important ques-tions of our time posed about man's destiny, social groups and nations receive replies which are simple professions of faith in the limitless virtues of science. In short, looking for and finding ever-increasing methods of efficiency would seem to constitute the solution to all our difficulties, for we could thus increase the amount of available wealth, like the well-known image of the cake which can only satisfy man by growing bigger. This is how the myth of the all-powerful technocrat is created—the technocrat who can bring peace to society by organizing and distributing fairly a growing prosperity, basing his actions on the analysis of electronic brains.

There is a whole school of thought today which proclaims that social conflicts are artificial and outmoded. The prime merit of technics would be to make this rivalry disappear from a humanity reconciled to the cult of efficiency and the enjoyment of the well-being which results from it. This idea that the technician revolution renders useless the programmes of modification of social structures and redistribution of power between social groups is in fact one of the elements of the theory of decline in ideologies, and it is, at least partly, an attempt at persuasion. The belief that social conflicts can be wiped out by technical progress is one of the gravest errors of this ragbag of ideas about social mechanics so much in vogue today in a number of "engineering" circles. Benefiting from the clamor of many propaganda voices and in the direct interests of the upper classes, this affirmation is dangerous in so far as it may convince people that the political struggle is useless, thereby strengthening the privileges of the propertied classes.

In the same way, manifestations of technocratic power usually result in bolstering up the existing socio-economic order. I should certainly hesitate to say that all technocrats are Conservative and at the command of the *haute bourgeoisie* (this observation is particularly true of the senior civil service today). This would be a gross misinterpretation of far more complex behavior and aspirations. It is fair to say that, as a general rule without taking account of the implications of *"pantouflage,"*[1] technicians do not reveal themselves as exclusively preoccupied with money-making,

1. Translator's Note: *"Pantouflage"*: The colloquial term given to the French Civil Service habit of "parachuting" into the private sector after a spell of government service.

and they have no personal stake in the measures they decide upon. Without believing that they have been the only element in the Fifth Republic capable and desirous of setting the general interest against that of particular groups, I accept Maurice Duverger's contention that they have formed a "very useful kind of counterweight" to a free-for-all of greedy groups.

The tendency I am examining here does not arise from public technicians' general propensity to defend a régime whose considerable and in many respects irremediable faults they know better than anyone. It results from the fact that the régime is now strong enough and sufficiently well-established to centralize to its own advantage initiatives taken on behalf of the common good. After the Liberation, French capitalism incurred a huge debt towards the higher civil servants, whose concern for productivity and preference for economic expansion certainly helped to modify the attitudes of directors in the private sector.

One can thus explain the contradiction . . . between recognition of the great services rendered by technicians and the criticism of the too high a place granted to them in the government system. . . . Whether they wish it or not, technicians are compelled to act and intervene according to the bias given to the régime by dominant forces. It is not true that the technical function, or in other words, efficiency, has a social significance in itself, it is an instrument the direction of whose use depends upon the stimulae which technicians receive or create.

In a society which tends toward agreement on the meaning of communal development, weak control from the political sector certainly opens up opportunities for technicians to make autonomous choices, but we can say that the solutions adopted by technicians will be likely to correspond with general aspirations: at all events, this tendency does not normally result in a radical alteration of government activity. Even if, in fact, technicians favor a certain group or social system, they are still bound to submit this preferential action to a consensus of opinion.

On the contrary, in the case of a society which is not or is no longer unanimous on its destiny, the incompetence or impotence of the political impetus, whatever the cause, acts in favor of the existing order. Whenever anyone draws attention to the decline or outdating of political ideologies (this touchstone of modern conservatism), we know full well that the object of the operation is to establish the futility, or more simply to sign the death certificate of socialism. A man who denounces the archaic character of political struggles is necessarily taking a stand in favor of maintaining the existing system of political control and domination.

For technocracy to cease being essentially conservative, technicians themselves would have to become inspired with the will to change. Their technical boldness is rarely accompanied by a deep concern for social change. But it is not rare for the technician to consider that the social system (one which manifests itself with continuity) is necessary to the realization of his designs. After all, the supporters of Saint-Simon were not lacking in human generosity, but they finally gave the best of themselves to the big industrial undertakings and commercial banks in the middle of the nineteenth century. It seems unreasonable to suppose that our technocrats, left to themselves, would be capable of acting otherwise.

To avoid falling into the trap of making slick interpretations, I must admit that a number of technicians are fully aware of the nature of their activity and the falsity of their claim to be outside politics. But long experience of these circles makes me unable to postulate that this behavior is the general rule. The conduct of a number of technicians would certainly change if the impetus given by government leaders was more vigorous and precise. We have now reached the heart of the discussion: there is no other way of placing the technical function once more at the service of the society as a whole, except by making it answerable for its actions to a democratic power.

While admitting that technicians often constitute a valuable and irreplaceable counterweight to particular interests, I believe that it is desirable that their actions be placed under the supervision of a higher authority. It seems to me that no exclusive coterie of technicians can be justified in imposing its views on the nation, even if they are concerned with highly technical matters like establishing an economic plan. This proposition requires no comment: it represents a moral choice which anyone is free to accept or reject. If we accept it, it seems to me that there is no other way of ensuring its implementation than by putting technicians under the control of elected authorities. What I call "rectifying the situation" consists simply of placing technicians once more in a position subordinate to that of elected representatives.

According to supporters of the "Q2 phase," the old ideologies have run their course. I would consider this proposition only if its authors could demonstrate that the technical revolution has brought about a change in human nature. If this is not so—in other words, if men in power are still ready to abuse it according to their own conceptions or interests—I believe that former experience valuable, and that we would be mad to throw overboard this wealth of ideas which sums up and gives voice to the sufferings and aspirations of men.

But this association, desired or suffered, of technical power with a particular form of social organization is not inevitable, and nothing except the wish to perpetuate the situation allows us to say that the present state of affairs is permanent. In this light, we might be tempted to consider technocracy as a false problem, the only serious difficulty being that of building a social base which could direct the ability of technicians and the results gained from technical progress in a different manner. In short, a political change adapted to such a purpose might suffice to prevent the technocratic peril from continuing.

Instant acceptance of these ideas entails a risk that might be overlooked. Technicians, completely freed from the old ruling classes, may take advantage of this to form a managerial category of their own, with the material privileges normally attached to such positions. Burnham, as we know, puts forward this possibility as an absolute certainty and Djilas, speaking of Communist societies, describes the birth of a "new class." These are not very impressive commentators, intellectually speaking, but sociologists of sound scientific integrity like G. Gurvitch have made disturbing observations on the propensity of technicians to organize themselves as a group within the framework of a collectivized society.

The action of technicians has an inevitable social dimension. It seems permissible to suggest that, on average, this activity, even if carried on in an autonomous manner, tends to work in favor of that part of the system benefitting the ruling classes. Paradoxically, this view is rather reassuring in the sense that it postulates that men will ultimately possess, through the means of that political action which a technical civilization does not have, the power to instil a social content in their choices. In the same way, I do not believe that the formation of a closed group of technicians governing society in accordance with their own conceptions and interests should be regarded as inevitable. But in order that such a peril should cease to be plausible, we have to believe that man is not the instrument causing his own abdication, and on the basis of contemporary social life this is an optimistic supposition.

The considerations I have just outlined are based on human experience. In this respect, do they not reflect, to quote Valéry, the inability to imagine or even to confront, "what has never been." In this case, of course, it is the role of science which is the large unknown quantity. Some people talk of a "scientific society" as the framework of the world of tomorrow, a society containing the majority of Western European countries, the United States, and the U.S.S.R., with Japan and some South American countries in a state of transition. One of the clearest signs of this evolution is the important place that the British Labour Government give to science in their programmes. It seems that their whole effort leads to bolstering the idea of socialism adapted to the "scientific revolution" of our time, in short, to socialism in the "managerial era."

The foremost trait of this social structure in the making is, according to G. Guéron, "to let oneself to be increasingly dominated by science and technique" in order to obtain increased output. Preferring to "refer to the future rather than to the past" (an attitude typical of "historical societies") the new type of societies "judge themselves by their measurable expansion and planned progress. Socially, they are urban societies with a residue of agricultural man-power." Because of increased productivity, these new societies are "the first which can conceive—on the horizon of their efforts—of a very general participation of all individuals in the wealth produced by collectivism."

On this basis, scientific societies, in which religious and traditional forces would no longer intervene in an active manner, would be profoundly democratic. But another trait distinguishes the scientific society: the ability or the tendency to transform knowledge into power. This society "embodies scientists in its organization of power, binds them together by the methods it gives them, the secrets it often imposes upon them and the purposes which it pursues, with or without them." From this point, as much in respect of themselves as of opinion, scientists cannot escape the consequences of their discoveries (a situation of which the "cosmic remorse" of certain atomic scientists is one aspect). This is responsible for the present fashion in many scientific circles (the Pugwash Conference, for example) to intervene in national and international politics in order to prevent scientific inventions from resulting in the destruction of humanity.

At this stage, we come up against the question of whether, in societies of the future, science runs the risk of becoming a permanent incitement to the conquest of power, something which is not yet true. On the basis of a thorough examination of all available literature, I would like to put forward the opinion that at the present time there is no scientific imperialism in the sense that scientists claim the right to govern men. However, we might wonder whether the determination to obtain maximal efficiency, combined with greater prosperity in larger sectors of society, is not likely to throw into gear a movement which will lead to progressive monopoly of power by "competence." Supposing that such an evolution occurs, the final end of the scientific society might perhaps be democratic, but its functioning would no longer be so. In the extreme case, a scientific technocracy, progressively taking power because of concern for maximum efficiency, would replace traditional political machinery, conserving the essential nature of the established order.

Many aspects of contemporary social life (alienation of men by the attractions of mass consumption and mechanized leisure) forbid us to neglect these suppositions. The writing on the wall is already too clear. I doubt whether the observation of social facts, when it is not biased towards the defense of a particular system of organization, can avoid giving rise *initially* to a pessimistic reaction. But such an attitude is a healthy one if it brings about the desire to join battle against those factors of enslavement and degradation which threaten our existence. This fight can only have meaning if we reject completely the theory that progress and technique alone have the ultimate ability to settle the latent tensions and open conflicts which its development has caused.

As an instrument of analysis, the notion of "scientific society" (an expression which will perhaps replace the very fashionable but highly contestable term "industrial society") has some plausible aspects: several of the traits chosen to characterize it correspond not to an anticipation of events but to tendencies that may be observed now. I cannot, however, come round to the opinion that science (or industry) can be made the sole principle for explanation and classification, taking no account of the social structures within which scientific or industrial progress are accomplished. On the contrary, it seems to me that the system of social organization introduces a fundamental element of difference between societies which have reached the same technical level, with only relative gaps between them which could be filled fairly quickly. In particular, I refuse to believe that how productive wealth is appropriated and the social consequences which stem from it are only of secondary importance compared with the powerful impetus of science.

The existence of several types of scientific or industrial societies, irreducible one to the other, seems to me to guarantee the survival of the political mechanisms of democracy for a foreseeable period except where the public surrenders its own rights. I believe that I am well aware of democracy's grave faults and inadequacies. Yet, having observed the behavior of technicians and read their works (whose often comic aspects—for example, Louis Armand's invitations to engineers to play in politics the role played by tetravalent carbon in nature—must not be allowed to mask the dangers) I admit that I feel some special sympathy for politicians.

My attitude then, of not underestimating nor ignoring the technocratic peril, or in other words, not making an absolute myth out of a partial and relative reality, is perhaps influenced by these value judgments. It is my hope that it owes enough to the analysis of contemporary political régimes to prove itself coherent and well-grounded.

VI
Shaping
the Future:
Administration

Administration is the phase of the political process in which policies that have been decided upon are put into effect with more or less success. Since the current public situation is dominated by complex organizations, administration has become an increasingly important part of the political process. Thinkers like Kenneth Melvin and Seymour Lipset view vast administrative conglomerates as essential parts of the welfare society, while thinkers like Friedrich Georg Junger and Kenneth A. Megill see these conglomerates as oppressive barriers to human fulfillment. Despite these differences, however, all are agreed on the importance of administration in the current public situation.

The articles in this section describe various aspects of the administrative phase of the political process. Peter M. Blau and W. Richard Scott hold that organizational life is characterized by dilemmas that can never be fully reconciled. For example, in an organization there is a choice between giving encouragement to individual initiative and stressing the predictable coordination of activities. There is no way of escaping this dilemma or of resolving it, though a balance between the two poles is always struck. The idea that organizational life is ridden by dilemmas takes some of the sting out of the nightmarish visions of mechanized administration. Perhaps organizations contain built-in limits to their effectiveness.

Victor A. Thompson adds another dimension to the complexity of organizational life. He shows how superiors in organizational positions indulge in theatrics and image-making to justify their authority. Such "dramaturgy" allows a great deal of incompetence to be hidden and, in Thompson's view, preserves the authority structure from the attacks that it might suffer if incompetence were unmasked. It is with Thompson's remarks in mind that John Kenneth Galbraith's article on the "technostructure" should be read. According to Galbraith, the most significant part of contemporary organizations is the specialist group, which alone has the expertise to determine whether or not projects are feasible. Thus, Galbraith argues that they, and not the directors, ultimately make organizational decisions. In evaluating Galbraith's argument it is important to remember that specialists are not unified into a cohesive group, do not make general policy decisions, and probably mask a great deal of their incompetence through dramaturgy.

Peter F. Drucker's discussion moves the ground from the dynamics of organizational behavior to the general question of how the other phases of the political process relate to administration. Drucker argues that the present "sickness of government" is due to the fact that governments have undertaken to administer particular activities directly. He believes that management of specific activities is best

249

done by private or non-profit organizations, while coordination and regulation is best done by government. Michael M. Harmon disputes the claim that phases of the political process can be sharply separated from one another. He states that administrators should be responsible for the actions they perform and that they may have to disobey commands they feel are immoral. Some of the problems involved in abandoning the traditional notion of the administrator as one who should follow orders unquestionably are discussed by John Paynter.

from Formal Organizations

PETER M. BLAU AND W. RICHARD SCOTT

DILEMMAS OF FORMAL ORGANIZATION

We shall review three dilemmas of formal organization: (1) coordination and communication; (2) bureaucratic discipline and professional expertness; (3) managerial planning and initiative.

COORDINATION AND COMMUNICATION

The experiments and field studies on communication and performance . . . lead to the conclusion that the free flow of communication contributes to problem-solving. There are three ways in which decisions are improved by the unrestricted exchange of ideas, criticisms, and advice. First, social support relieves the anxieties engendered by decision-making. In the discussion of problems with others, their social approval of the first step taken toward a solution mitigates the anxieties that might otherwise create a blocking of associations, and it thus facilitates reaching a solution. Once consultation patterns have become established, moreover, the very knowledge that advice is readily accessible makes it less disturbing to encounter a difficult problem, and the experience of being consulted by others strengthens self-confidence; both factors lessen anxieties that impede decision-making.

Second, communication processes provide an error-correction mechanism. Different persons are guided by different frameworks in their approach to a given problem, and the differences make it easier for them to detect the mistakes and blind spots in the suggestions of one another. Although social support and error correction are in some respects opposite processes, both of them are, nevertheless, important for problem-solving, as indicated by Pelz's finding that optimum research performance is associated with consulting some colleagues whose orientation differs from one's own (who challenge one's ideas) and some who share one's orientation (who support one's ideas).[1]

Third, the competition for respect that occurs in the course of discussing problems furnishes incentives for making good suggestions and for criticizing the apparently poor suggestions of others.

While the free flow of communication improves problem-solving, it impedes coordination. Unrestricted communication creates a battleground of ideas; the battle helps in selecting the only correct or best among several alternative suggestions, but makes it difficult to come to an agreement; and coordination always requires agreeing on *one* masterplan, even though different plans might do equally well. Processes of

---

1. Donald C. Pelz, "Some Social Factors Related to Performance in a Research Organization," *Administrative Science Quarterly*, 1 (1956), pp. 310-325.

social communication, consequently, make the performance of groups superior to that of individuals when the task is finding the best solution to a problem but inferior when the task is one of coordination.

Hierarchical differentiation is dysfunctional for decision-making because it interferes with the free flow of communication. Studies of experimental and work groups have shown that status differences restrict the participation of low-status members, channel a disproportionate amount of communication to high-status members, discourage criticism of the suggestions of the highs, encourage rejecting correct suggestions of the lows, and reduce the work satisfaction of the lows and their motivation to make contributions. All these factors are detrimental to effective problem-solving. If hierarchical differentiation does not block but frees the flow of communication, however, it improves decision-making; this observation indicates that the adverse effects that hierarchical differentiation typically has for problem-solving are specifically due to the obstacles to free communication it usually creates. But the very restriction of communication that makes hierarchical differentiation dysfunctional for problem-solving improves performance when the task is essentially one of coordination. Experiments with various communication networks show that differentiation, centralized direction, and restricted communication are necessary for efficient coordination. However, the achievement of such a differentiated organization—itself a problem-solving task—seems to have been easier for groups in which communication flowed freely than for those where it was experimentally restricted.

These conclusions point to a fundamental dilemma in formal organizations. Organizations require, of course, both effective coordination and effective problem-solving to discharge their functions. But the very mechanism through which hierarchical differentiation improves coordination—restricting and directing the flow of communications—is what impedes problem-solving. In peer groups, moreover, the free flow of communication that contributes to problem-solving also creates an informal differentiation of status as some members earn the respect and deference of others, and this differentiation, once established, creates obstacles to communication. This dilemma appears to be inherent in **the conflicting requirements** of coordination and problem-solving. To be sure, some types of centralized direction are more compatible with work on complex problems than others, but the fundamental dilemma posed by the need for unrestricted and for restricted communication cannot be resolved—it must be endured.

BUREAUCRATIC DISCIPLINE AND PROFESSIONAL EXPERTNESS

Weber's approach to the study of administration fails to distinguish the principles that govern bureaucratic organizations from professional principles, as both Parsons and Gouldner have emphasized.[2] To be sure,

2. Talcott Parsons, "Introduction" to Max Weber, *The Theory of Social and Economic Organization*, A. M. Henderson and Talcott Parsons (trans.) and Talcott Parsons (ed.), Glencoe, Ill.: Free Press and Falcon's Wing Press, 1947, pp. 58-60; and Gouldner, *Patterns of Industrial Bureaucracy*, pp. 22-24.

these two sets of principles have much in common. Both require that decisions be governed by universalistic standards independent of any personal considerations in the particular cases handled. The orientations of both professionals and bureaucrats are expected to be impersonal and detached, a principle designed to facilitate rational judgment. Both bureaucracy and professionalism are marked by specialized competence based on technical training and limit the official's or professional's authority to a specialized area of jurisdiction. Both professionals and bureaucrats occupy an achieved rather than ascribed status, with the selection of personnel governed by such performance criteria as competence and training. These are important similarities, but they should not be allowed to obscure the equally important differences between the two.

The first difference between the organizing principles of a profession and those of a bureaucracy is that the professional is bound by a norm of service and a code of ethics to represent the welfare and interests of his clients, whereas the bureaucrat's foremost responsibility is to represent and promote the interests of his organization. Only in the case of service organizations do the ultimate objectives of serving clients and serving the organization coincide, and even here the specific immediate objectives often conflict. For a service organization is oriented to serving the collective interests of its entire clientele, which demands that the interests of some clients may have to be sacrificed to further those of the majority or of future clients, while the distinctive feature of the professional orientation is that each client's interests reign supreme and must not be sacrificed for the sake of the welfare of other clients.

A second basic difference concerns the source of authority. The bureaucratic official's authority rests on a legal contract backed by formal sanctions, but the professional's authority is rooted in his acknowledged technical expertness. Although some technical competence may be required for performing the duties of a customs official, it is not this skill but his legal status that authorizes the customs inspector to decide whether goods can be imported duty-free or not. An individual is legally obligated to submit to the authority of the policeman, whatever he thinks of his decision, but the same person submits to the authority of his doctor because, and only if, he acknowledges that the doctor has the technical knowledge to determine whether he should have surgery, medicine, or neither.

A third difference, related to the foregoing, is that the bureaucrat's decisions are expected to be governed by disciplined compliance with directives from superiors, whereas the professional's are to be governed by internalized professional standards. To be sure, superiors may be more highly qualified in a field than their subordinates. The crucial problem, however, is that bureaucratic management must base its decisions in part on administrative considerations, which often conflict with purely professional considerations.

Finally, the differences between the two systems are reflected in the locus of the last court of appeal in case of disagreement. When a decision of a bureaucrat is questioned, the final judgment of whether he is right or not is a prerogative of management, but when a decision of a professional is questioned, the right of reviewing its correctness is reserved to his professional colleague group. The actions of the professional expert, therefore, are under the ultimate control of his peers who have the same specialized skills as he, whereas control over the bureaucrat's action is exercised by superiors in the organization whose technical skills tend to differ from his. One complains to the medical society or to the bar association about a physician's or a lawyer's actions, and there his professional colleagues will judge whether or not the complaint is justified; but one complains to a mechanic's boss about a mechanic's actions, and the boss who judges the mechanic is typically not an expert mechanic himself.

With increasing numbers of professionals being employed in bureaucratic settings, much attention has been directed toward examining conflicts between the demands of the administrative organization and those of professional standards. These conflicts usually find expression in contrasting orientations of employees; some adopt management as their major reference group, and others, their professional colleagues. The significance of this difference is indicated by the fact that studies of professionals or semiprofessionals in formal organizations have consistently found that the conflict between bureaucratic and professional orientation is a fundamental issue. Hughes reports conflicts between itinerants and the homeguard in numerous work settings;[3] Francis and Stone emphasize the distinction between a service and a procedure orientation in their study of a public employment agency;[4] and Gouldner focuses on the contrast between cosmopolitan and local orientations in his study of a college faculty.[5] Our research, too, found that semiprofessional workers in a public assistance agency could be differentiated on the basis of whether their orientation was confined to the organization or extended to the profession of social work. Those oriented to their profession tended to be less attached to the welfare agency, more critical of its operations—particularly of service to clients—and less confined by administrative procedure. Although a professional orientation motivates a person to do better work in terms of professional standards, it also gives him a basis for ignoring administrative considerations and thus may lead to poorer performance in terms of the standards of the organization. Thus, professionally oriented caseworkers were more apt than others to fail to visit their clients on schedule.

Research on production organizations in widely different social contexts indicates that a rational organization for the collective pursuit of formally established goals may exist whether or not the specific mechanism employed for this purpose is a bureaucratic structure. Stinch-

3. Everett C. Hughes, *Men and Their Work*, Glencoe, Ill.: Free Press, 1958, pp. 31, 129-130, 136.
4. Roy G. Francis and Robert C. Stone, *Service and Procedure in Bureaucracy*, Minneapolis: University of Minnesota Press, 1956.
5. Alvin W. Gouldner, "Cosmopolitans and Locals," *Administrative Science Quarterly*, 2 (1957), pp. 281-306.

combe presents a comparative analysis of construction and mass-production industries in our highly complex and industrialized society.[6] Udy reports a quantitative investigation of rudimentary production organizations in a large number of simple, non-Western societies.[7] Despite the great difference in source materials, the two studies arrive at essentially the same conclusion. The findings of both indicate that a rational formal organization may be but is not necessarily bureaucratic. Specifically, the fact that an organization is governed by such rational principles as specialization, rewards for performance, and contractual agreements is independent of the existence of a bureaucratic structure, that is, a hierarchy of authority and an administrative apparatus. Stinchcombe concludes that the professionalized labor force in the construction industry serves as an alternative to bureaucratization for assuring rational production, because seasonal fluctuations in this industry make it impractical to maintain continuous bureaucratic organizations. Seasonal variation, however, is not the only condition that encourages employment of a professional labor force; another is the complexity of the services to be performed. When the over-all responsibility of the organization cannot be broken down into fairly routine specialized tasks—as exemplified by organizations responsible for research, the care of the ill, and casework service—expert judgments of professionals rather than disciplined compliance with the commands of superiors must govern operations in the interest of efficiency.

Professional expertness and bureaucratic discipline may be viewed as alternative methods of coping with areas of uncertainty. Discipline does so by reducing the scope of uncertainty; expertness, by providing the knowledge and social support that enable individuals to cope with uncertainty and thus to assume more responsibility. The dilemma, however, remains and, indeed, affects wider and wider circles as the number of people subject to both these conflicting control mechanisms grows, since the work of professionals is increasingly carried out in bureaucratic organizations, and since operations in bureaucracies seem to become increasingly professionalized, modern warfare being a conspicuous example.

MANAGERIAL PLANNING AND INITIATIVE

The need for centralized planning and individual initiative poses a third dilemma for formal organizations—or, perhaps more correctly, a third manifestation of the basic dilemma between order and freedom.[8] Notwithstanding the importance of free communication, freedom to follow one's best professional judgment, and conditions permitting the

6. Arthur L. Stinchcombe, "Bureaucratic and Craft Administration of Production," *Administrative Science Quarterly*, 4 (1959), pp. 168-187.

7. Stanley H. Udy, Jr., " 'Bureaucracy' and 'Rationality' in Weber's Theory," *American Sociological Review*, 24 (1959), pp. 791-795.

8. See the discussion of the dilemma between bureaucracy and enterprise, as he calls it, by Marshall Dimock, *Administrative Vitality*, New York: Harper, 1959.

exercise of initiative, effective coordination in a large organization requires some centralized direction. But the assumption that managerial coordination necessitates control through a hierarchy of authority is questionable, since it can be and often is achieved by other methods, notably through various types of impersonal mechanisms of control designed by management.

The assembly line is such an impersonal mechanism through which managerial planning effects coordination of the production processes without the use of directives that are passed down the hierarchy. As a matter of fact, the impersonal constraints exerted on operators tend to reverse the flow of demand in the hierarchy. Since the moving line makes most of the demands on workers, the role of the foreman is changed from one who primarily makes demands on workers to one who responds to their demands for help and assistance, and similar changes occur on higher levels. There is centralized direction, but it is not attained through commands transmitted down the hierarchy.

Performance records are another impersonal mechanism of control, one suitable for controlling nonmanual as well as manual tasks. The regular evaluation of employee performance on the basis of quantitative records of accomplished results exerts constraints that obviate the need for routine supervisory checking. Performance records, like the assembly line, reverse the flow of demand in the organization and cast the supervisor in the role of advisor and helper to workers rather than in the role of a person who makes continual demands on them. This evaluation system also facilitates coordination, since it centralizes the direction of operations in the hands of the higher managers who design the records.

Both performance records and assembly lines minimize reliance on hierarchical authority and discipline to control operations and, therefore, improve relations between supervisors and subordinates. However, there is an important difference between these two mechanisms. Assembly-line production reduces the discretion workers can exercise and hence lowers their work satisfaction. In contrast, evaluation of performance on the basis of a quantitative record of results achieved increases the discretion employees are allowed to exercise and thus raises their work satisfaction.

We had expected that automation would be an impersonal control mechanism more similar in its consequences to performance records than to the assembly line. We further anticipated that most workers in automated plants, where routine tasks are performed by machines, would be technical experts engaged in maintenance and trouble-shooting, and that they, consequently, would enjoy more discretion and have higher work satisfaction. The surprising findings of studies conducted in automated organizations by Walker, Faunce, and Mann and Williams is that the average level of skill and responsibility of workers was not superior to the level that had existed prior to automation.[9] The discretion permitted

9. Walker, *op. cit.;* William A. Faunce, "Automation in the Automobile Industry," *American Sociological Review,* 23 (1958), pp. 401-407; and Floyd C. Mann and Lawrence K. Williams, "Observations of the Dynamics of a Change to Electronic Data-Processing Equipment," *Administrative Science Quarterly,* 5 (1960), pp. 217-256.

workers had not been increased. Indeed, in the automated factory studied by Faunce, supervision was closer than on the assembly line, because foremen were concerned with preventing costly machine breakdowns. Since automation removed some of the higher positions in the organization as well as some lower ones, it reduced chances for advancement, a situation which was a source of considerable dissatisfaction. It appears that automated plants have not yet reorganized their work processes to take full advantage of the technological innovations. This reorganization would require, in our opinion, the training or recruitment of expert mechanics and the redesigning of the division of labor to include minor machine maintenance in the duties of operators. Under these conditions, machine breakdowns, or the impending danger of them, would not lead to closer supervision as it did in the plants studied, and the highly technical operations would permit the exercise of considerable discretion.

It is conceivable that union pressure to increase wage rates on automated jobs will force management to institute such a reorganization. Higher labor costs constrain management to attempt to improve productivity, and one means for accomplishing this improvement is through further automation that eliminates routine jobs. The remaining highly paid workers could be held responsible for acquiring the skills needed for the maintenance functions now discharged by foremen or specialists. Such changes would give them more discretion, lessen the need for close supervision, and thus probably raise work satisfaction. These predictions are in line with Melman's conclusion that union pressures and high wages have induced management to introduce technological innovations more rapidly than would otherwise have been the case.[10] Such a professionalization of the labor force might also require a reorganization of the reward system, since piece rates do not furnish incentives suited for professionalized tasks. Even in the semiautomated department studied by Walker, where tasks were far from professionalized, and where workers were quite satisfied with their rate of pay, there was much dissatisfaction with the piece-rate system for failing to take mental work and judgment into account. A reward system that emphasizes advancement chances rather than immediate earnings and evaluation of results rather than sheer productivity would seem to furnish more effective incentives for professionalized tasks.

Managerial planning of the production process and a professionalized labor force that can exercise initiative and is motivated to do so by opportunities for advancement would sharply reduce the need for hierarchical supervision and control through directives passed down the pyramid of authority. Indeed, coordination appears to be achieved frequently through centralized planning and by means of direct communication between responsible managers . . . rather than through the cumbersome process of passing messages up and down the hierarchy. But our suggestion that managerial planning interferes less with the exercise of initiative than hierarchical authority is not meant to imply that the

10. See Seymour Melman, *Decision-making and Productivity*, Oxford, England: Basil Blackwell, 1958, pp. 105-106, 141-143.

dilemma between managerial control and initiative is resolved. The best that can be hoped for, as Bendix has suggested, is that

. . . the employees of all ranks in industry and government strike a balance between compliance and initiative, that they temper their adherence to formal rules by a judicious exercise of independent judgement and that they fit their initiative into the framework of the formal regulation.[11]

But even this best is too much to expect. For this balance is continually disrupted by the need for more order on the one hand and the need for more freedom on the other.

DIALECTICAL PROCESSES OF CHANGE

The conception of dilemma directs attention to the inevitability of conflict and change in organizations. Mary Parker Follett, an astute observer of administrative practice, has noted: "When we think that we have *solved* a problem, well, by the very process of solving, new elements or forces come into the situation and you have a new problem on your hands to be solved."[12] The innovations instituted to solve one problem often create others because effectiveness in an organization depends on many different factors, some of which are incompatible with others; hence, the dilemma. The very improvements in some conditions that further the achievement of the organization's objectives often interfere with other conditions equally important for this purpose. A by now familiar example is that hierarchical differentiation promotes coordination but simultaneously restricts the communication processes that benefit decision-making.

New problems are internally generated in organizations in the process of solving old ones. However, the experience gained in solving earlier problems is not lost but contributes to the search for solutions to later problems. These facts suggest that the process of organizational development is dialectical—problems appear, and while the process of solving them tends to give rise to new problems, learning has occurred which influences how the new challenges are met.[13] Consequently, effectiveness in an organization improves as a result of accumulated experience. These dialectical processes are illustrated by the introduction of assembly-line production. This new production method raised productivity and effected centralized control and coordination without the need for hierarchical

11. Reinhard Bendix, "Bureaucracy," *American Sociological Review*, 12 (1947), p. 503.

12. Mary Parker Follett, "The Process of Control," Luther Gulick and L. Urwick (eds.), *Papers on the Science of Administration*, New York: Institute of Public Administration, 1937, p. 166 (italics in original).

13. If we classify problems into dichotomies or other very broad categories, it inevitably seems as if the same ones recur, simply because all new ones are put into one of the few existing categories.

directives. However, by routinizing tasks and lowering work satisfaction, the assembly line created problems of absenteeism and turnover—problems that were particularly serious given the interdependence of operations on the assembly line. Management had succeeded in solving one set of problems, but the mechanism by which they were solved produced new problems which were quite different from those that had existed in earlier stages of mechanization. Contrary to our expectations, the introduction of automation has not yet met the problems created by monotonous tasks and low work satisfaction. But should these problems be solved through a reorganization of the work force that requires operators to assume more responsibility, as we have suggested, management would no doubt again be faced with new difficulties. For example, increased responsibility and discretion in performing complex, interdependent tasks might engender anxieties over decision-making which would impede effective performance, and these new problems would require management to devote attention to developing mechanisms that reduce such anxieties.

Conflicts of interest between various groups or persons in the organization are another source of dialectical change. What constitutes satisfactory adjustment for one group may be the opposite for another, since different interests serve as the criteria of adjustment. Thus, when the efforts of managers are judged by the results they achieve and they are given freedom to exercise responsibility and initiative in achieving them, conflicts between them are likely to ensue. For each manager will seek to promote the interests and expand the jurisdiction of his department, and his endeavors will bring him into conflict with others who have staked out the same claims. Compromises will be reached and coalitions will be formed, but since the responsibilities and interests of the managers continue to differ, new conflicts are apt to arise as changing conditions produce new challenges. Moreover, as various occupational subgroups in the organization try to improve their economic position, their interests may come into conflict, particularly if the success of one group upsets the existing status hierarchy and motivates the others it has displaced to recoup their advantage. Conflicts of interest are most conspicuous in the relation between union and management. The union is interested in obtaining higher wages and better working conditions, while management is interested in lowering costs and improving productivity. Collective bargaining furnishes mechanisms for resolving issues, but the conflicting interests generate new ones. Thus, management introduces new machines in an attempt to improve efficiency, disturbing the existing adjustment and producing a variety of difficulties with which the union has to deal. Similarly, once workers have attained the right to collective bargaining, they use it to fight for pensions and other fringe benefits, thereby creating new problems for management.

Another source of disruption and change is turnover in personnel. Valuable experience is lost as older workers are replaced by new trainees, and social ties are disrupted by transfers and loss of personnel. As we have seen, the methods available to a new manager in discharging his responsibilities are dependent in part on those of his predecessor. If the latter commanded the loyalty of subordinates, the successor will find it difficult to do so and be constrained to resort to bureaucratic methods, whereas the successor to an authoritarian bureaucrat will find it advantageous to use more informal managerial practices. Again we see that organizational developments alternate in direction in a dialectical pattern. The succession of goals leads to such an alternating pattern of change in the relations between organizations. Once earlier objectives are achieved, management seeks new objectives and by doing so disturbs the existing equilibrium in the network of organizations. The dominance of one organization in a sector restores order as former competitors become exchange partners, but further power struggles are stimulated by a further succession of goals as groups of sellers start to compete with groups of buyers for dominant power over a set of related markets.

In mutual-benefit associations, there is still another source of dialectical change. These organizations are subject to conflicts that arise from the dilemma posed by their twofold formal purpose. One purpose, just as in the case of other organizations, is the effective accomplishment of the specific objectives of the organization—for example, improving employment conditions in the case of unions. But another distinctive purpose of these associations is to provide their members with a mechanism for arriving at agreements on their common objectives. For to serve the interests of its members a mutual-benefit association must furnish mechanisms for ascertaining what their collective objectives are as well as mechanisms for implementing them, and the ascertaining of objectives requires democratic self-government and freedom of dissent. Endeavors to attain one of these purposes frequently impede the attainment of the other. In the interests of effective accomplishment of union objectives, as Michels has pointed out, democratic processes are often set aside. Conversely, preoccupation with democratic self-government and freedom of dissent may interfere with efforts to implement the common objectives. But the study by Lipset and his colleagues shows that a strong union which has accomplished some of its specific objectives can and sometimes does turn its attention and energy to maintaining internal democracy.

Democratic societies are in this respect organized like mutual-benefit associations. They have the double purpose of remaining strong enough to survive and yet maintaining the freedoms that permit the democratic establishment of common objectives. Under current conditions in the world, the issue of promoting national security and strength versus preserving civil liberties and freedom of dissent poses the dilemma most sharply. No final solution is possible for this dilemma. Indeed, attempts finally to resolve it tend to sacrifice one purpose for the other and thus endanger the very nature of democratic societies. For we surely need to survive in order to preserve our democratic institutions, but we just as surely do not want to survive at the cost of losing our freedom.

Dramaturgy

VICTOR A. THOMPSON

1. THE DRAMATURGICAL ASPECT OF ORGANIZATIONS

In a remarkable study, Erving Goffman has recently shown how the performance of their roles of various kinds involves people in impression management.[1] We must try to control the information or cues imparted to others in order to protect our representations of self and to control the impressions others form about us. We are all involved, therefore, in dramaturgy.

Although, for reasons given below, this [essay] is principally concerned with dramaturgy in the hierarchy, we should mention briefly that specialization also has its dramaturgical side. Specialist dramaturgy seems to be particularly related to the problem of accreditation. The ubiquitous white coat of the medical doctor suggests that here is a man of fastidious cleanliness, the stethoscope dangling from his pocket suggests the great and mysterious range of his knowledge. The engineer's slide rule performs a similar function. If a specialist role is only weakly established, we should expect a dramaturgy of insecurity, with pompous self-importance, lack of communicativeness, etc.

As Goffman points out, the dramaturgical side of formal organizations has been neglected. Students have in the past been interested in the technical, the political, the structural, and the cultural aspects, but not this.[2] We believe that dramaturgical behavior in the bureaucratic organization is structurally related to its other and more familiar characteristics. Perceptions of leadership, status, and power depend heavily upon communication. People will rate a position in a scale of leadership, status, or power at least partly in accordance with information they have about that position. The control of information, therefore, and the management of impressions become important techniques in the struggle for authority, status, and power.

2. LEGITIMATION OF AUTHORITY ROLES

. . . A number of developments are challenging the legitimacy of hierarchical authority in bureaucratic organization. Particularly crucial is the gap which advancing specialization and technical complexity are creating between the right to take a specific action and the knowledge

1. Erving Goffman: *The Presentation of Self in Everyday Life* (Garden City, New York: Doubleday & Company, Inc.; 1959).
2. Ibid., pp. 239-40.

needed to do so. Cultural definitions of hierarchical rights and expectations of hierarchical role performance are increasingly at war with reality. The greater the discrepancy between the self-image projected, on the one hand, and reality, on the other, the greater the load placed upon sheer play acting. Dramaturgical skill has become increasingly essential to the hierarchical role, and technical competence increasingly irrelevant.

Discrepancies between role expectations and the technical imperatives related to goal accomplishment are generally hidden or at least disguised by fictions, myths, and "just-pretend" behavior which are quite general throughout our bureaucratic organizations. For instance, the inability of the organization to live with the superior's right to control communication leads inevitably to the development of elaborate informal channels of communication. The existence of these informal channels is often officially denied, or the superior's signature is put on the communication by rubber stamp to pretend that it came from him. If these informal channels are depicted on organizational charts (they usually are not), dotted lines are used, indicating the taint of illegality about them. In general, any informal or unofficial arrangements are considered somewhat illegal and are undertaken surreptitiously.

The fact that those who are traditionally empowered to make all decisions cannot any longer have the range of knowledge necessary to do so brings about a good deal of pretense in organizational activities. In fact, much of the organization's work is done by surreptitious methods. Everyone is involved in "playing the game." Reality is hidden by "double talk." As Goffman points out,[3] "double-talk" communication may convey information between people inconsistent with their roles. One person in a relationship says one thing but means something else. The overt expression is consistent with the formal relationship, but the hidden meaning is not. The other person in the relationship may accept the hidden communication; or he may ignore it and accept the overt expression which is consistent with the relationship, which is "proper." A common example concerns breaking in a new boss. When an assistant must break in a new boss, he will have to convey instructions to his boss in a form which makes it appear overtly as though he were receiving these instructions from the boss. This kind of communication occurs in connection with matters outside a person's formal jurisdiction but depending upon him. It occurs when a subordinate tries to seize the direction of action or his superior tries to extend it to him. In this kind of situation, "double-talk" communication allows a subordinate to initiate lines of endeavor without giving explicit recognition to the implications this action has for the formal role relationship between him and his superior.

Discrepancies between actual authority and expected authority inevitably arise, because organizationally defined competencies of centralized specialties conflict with the culturally defined rights of hierarchical position. The attempt is universally made to hide these discrepancies by simply denying them. Thus it is alleged that the central specialists, the "staff," only advise; they have no authority. If their advice comes in the

3. Ibid., pp. 194-5.

form of a command, everyone is supposed to pretend that it comes from a higher executive, and sometimes provision is made to have his signature stamped on the more formal specialist commands. This "just-pretend" behavior also protects status-inflated self-images of those receiving specialist commands, a necessity since these commands are quite likely to come from lower-status people.

The dramaturgical management of impressions about hierarchical positions and roles is no longer a sporadic affair depending upon the accidents of personality. It appears to be institutionally organized. That is to say, opportunities for hierarchical success in modern bureaucracy depend to a very large extent upon the ability and willingness to engage in impression management. Our contention is that this kind of behavior is essential as a device for maintaining the legitimacy of hierarchical roles in the face of advancing specialization. Although no leadership traits have been discovered, a definite executive type seems to be emerging.[4]

3. DRAMATURGY OF THE SUPERIOR

What are the impressions fostered by hierarchical dramaturgy? As would be expected, they are the heroic and charismatic qualities—the same ones that leadership-trait studies have been seeking. The impression is fostered that occupants of hierarchical positions are, of all people in the organization, the ablest, the most industrious, the most indispensable, the most loyal, the most reliable, the most self-controlled, the most ethical, which is to say, the most honest, fair, and impartial. Technical skill is not among these fostered impressions. Modern bureaucracy derogates technical skill or any great learning. To "get ahead," a person must give up his technical specialty. By derogating the role of the specialist, the superior protects his own role in the hierarchy.

It is within this framework that the extreme busyness of persons in hierarchical positions is to be understood. Busyness suggests indispensability, as Riesman, Glazer, and Denney have noted. It also suggests that the very busy person is of unusual importance to the organization and takes its interests more to heart than do others. The very busy person is felt to be more dependable and loyal than the others. Consequently, it is advisable for those who want to get ahead to load their briefcases when they leave at night, and perhaps to come in for a few hours on the week end.

Impression management follows certain broad rules already supplied

4. It has been reported that employers now seem to look for an ideal "Hollywood type." Perrin Stryker, quoting Ann Hoff, the placement expert: "How Executives Get Jobs," *Fortune* (August 1953), p. 182. Shape of teeth and size of ears have disqualified men. (Ibid.) ". . . executives often project an air of competency and general grasp of the situation." Goffman: op. cit., p. 47. "More and more, the executive must act according to the role that he is cast for—the calm eye that never strays from the other's gaze, the easy, controlled laughter, the whole demeanor that tells onlookers that here certainly is a man without neurosis and inner rumblings." William H. Whyte, Jr., *The Organization Man* (Garden City, New York: Doubleday & Company, Inc., 1957), p. 172.

by the culture. Such audience rules as taking a person at his face value and not interfering with his performance when it is going on operate to everyone's advantage. Persons in high positions have some additional dramaturgical advantages in the form of hierarchical rights, especially their rights of deference. The status system is sustained by its own well worn dramaturgical apparatus, including familiar status symbols such as insignia, titles, and ceremonies; and office symbols such as private offices, rugs, and special furniture. "A name on the door rates a rug on the floor."

Impression management requires that some attention be paid to the preparation of the audience.[5] For hierarchical presentations, the audience has already been prepared by the status system. The audience is trained to take cues at their face value, to show the proper appreciation for the performance. Status behavior protects the backstage area by teaching people to "keep their place." Information inconsistent with fostered impressions is kept secret. Status training has prepared the audience to exercise tact, and the performers to exercise tact with respect to tact. Both sides "play the game," thus protecting the performances from miscues, bad acting, *faux pas,* "scenes," etc.

An act has a better chance of coming off well when the audience is not too large and when the interaction is of short duration. Superiors are therefore admonished to deal with subordinates individually and privately. The status system allows the hierarchical superior to choose his audience, the time, place, and duration of the performance, by giving the high-status person the initiative in interaction. He can usually begin and terminate the interview. This ability to control the timing of the interaction is particularly valuable in sustaining the impression of busyness and importance to the organization.

The more background information possessed by the audience, the less likely it is that the performance will have an important influence. The status system puts social distance between people so that the audience is not likely to have much background information about higher-status performers. Superiors are therefore advised not to become intimate with subordinates. "Don't go to lunch with the wrong person." The executive eats in an "executive dining room"; he has a private secretary disciplined in discretion; he has control of access to his office. Finally, the status system provides a more or less elaborate set of staging devices or props as background for the management of impressions about the character and activities of persons occupying hierarchical roles.

The point has been made that the general institutionalized system of deference, the "status system," provides a set of situational definitions of great value for the management of impressions on the part of persons in the hierarchy. Other general attitudes toward self-expression reinforce the status system in this respect. People generally believe there is a "sacred compatibility between the man and the job," a sacred connection between the right to play a part and the capacity to do so. Since the person in a hierarchical position has the right to make "decisions," he is assumed to have the ability to do so.

5. Goffman: op. cit., ch. vi.

Furthermore, since it is generally assumed that a person should be accepted as what he claims to be, should be taken at face value and given the benefit of the doubt, advantageous definitions of any situations based upon technical performance are more difficult to secure than those based upon dramaturgy, upon impression management. It is easier to be what you say you are than what you do. In this connection, people seem to be more concerned with the right to give a performance than with the performance itself. Even though the performance is outstanding, if the person did not have the right to perform, he is severely criticized, perhaps even jailed as an impostor. Conversely, even though the performance is of low quality, the right to give it will protect it from criticism. Here again the hierarchical role is fortunately situated, insofar as inability to perform will be masked by the undoubted right to do so. The same is true of well-established specialist roles, like that of the doctor, of the lawyer, or of the engineer.

The Technostructure

JOHN KENNETH GALBRAITH

". . . the prevalence of group, instead of individual, action is a striking characteristic of management organization in the large corporation."
—R. A. Gordon, *Business Leadership in the Large Corporation*

The individual has far more standing in our culture than the group. An individual has a presumption of accomplishment; a committee has a presumption of inaction. We react sympathetically to the individual who seeks to safeguard his personality from engulfment by the mass. We call for proof, at least in principle, before curbing his aggressions against society. Individuals have souls; corporations are notably soulless. The entrepreneur—individualistic, restless, with vision, guile and courage—has been the economists' only hero. The great business organization arouses no similar admiration. Admission to heaven is individually and by families; the top management even of an enterprise with an excellent corporate image cannot yet go in as a group. To have, in pursuit of truth, to assert the superiority of the organization over the individual for important social tasks is a taxing prospect.

Yet it is a necessary task. It is not to individuals but to organizations that power in the business enterprise and power in the society has passed. And modern economic society can only be understood as an effort, wholly successful, to synthesize by organization a group personality far superior *for its purposes* to a natural person and with the added advantage of immortality.

The need for such a group personality begins with the circumstance that in modern industry a large number of decisions, and *all* that are important, draw on information possessed by more than one man. Typically they draw on the specialized scientific and technical knowledge, the accumulated information or experience and the artistic or intuitive sense of many persons. And this is guided by further information which is assembled, analyzed and interpreted by professionals using highly technical equipment. The final decision will be informed only as it draws systematically on all those whose information is relevant. Nor, human beings what they are, can it take all of the information that is offered at face value. There must, additionally, be a mechanism for testing each person's contribution for its relevance and reliability as it is brought to bear on the decision.

2

The need to draw on, and appraise, the information of numerous individuals in modern industrial decision-making has three principal points of origin. It derives, first, from the technological requirements of modern industry. It is not that these are always inordinately sophisticated; a man of moderate genius could, quite conceivably, provide himself with the knowledge of the various branches of metallurgy and chemistry, and of engineering, procurement, production management, quality control, labor relations, styling and merchandising which are involved in the development of a modern motor car. But even moderate genius is in unpredictable supply, and to keep abreast of all these branches of science, engineering and art would be time-consuming even for a genius. The elementary solution, which allows of the use of far more common talent and with far greater predictability of result, is to have men who are appropriately qualified or experienced in each limited area of specialized knowledge or art. Their information is then combined for carrying out the design and production of the vehicle. It is a common public impression, not discouraged by scientists, engineers and industrialists, that modern scientific, engineering and industrial achievements are the work of a new and quite remarkable race of men. This is pure vanity; were it so, there would be few such achievements. The real accomplishment of modern science and technology consists in taking ordinary men, informing them narrowly and deeply and then, through appropriate organization, arranging to have their knowledge combined with that of other specialized but equally ordinary men. This dispenses with the need for genius. The resulting performance, though less inspiring, is far more predictable.

The second factor requiring the combination of specialized talent derives from advanced technology, the associated use of capital, and the resulting need for planning with its accompanying control of environment. The market is, in remarkable degree, an intellectually undemanding institution. The Wisconsin farmer . . . need not anticipate his requirements for fertilizers, pesticides or even machine parts; the market stocks and supplies them. The cost of these is substantially the same for the man of intelligence and for his neighbor who, under medical examination, shows daylight in either ear. And the farmer need have no price or selling strategy; the market takes all his milk at the ruling price. Much of the appeal of the market, to economists at least, has been from the way it seems to simplify life. Better orderly error than complex truth.

For complexity enters with planning and is endemic thereto. The manufacturer of missiles, space vehicles or modern aircraft must foresee the requirements for specialized plant, specialized manpower, exotic materials and intricate components and take steps to insure their availability when they are needed. For procuring such things, we have seen, the market is either unreliable or unavailable. And there is no open market for the finished product. Everything here depends on the care and skill with which contracts are sought and nurtured in Washington or in Whitehall or Paris.

The same foresight and responding action are required, in lesser degree, from manufacturers of automobiles, processed foods and detergents. They too must foresee requirements and manage markets. Planning, in short, requires a great variety of information. It requires variously informed men and men who are suitably specialized in obtaining the requisite information. There must be men whose knowledge allows them to foresee need and to insure a supply of labor, materials and other production requirements; those who have knowledge to plan price strategies and see that customers are suitably persuaded to buy at these prices; those who, at higher levels of technology, are so informed that they can work effectively with the state to see that it is suitably guided; and those who can organize the flow of information that the above tasks and many others require. Thus, to the requirements of technology for specialized technical and scientific talent are added the very large further requirements of the planning that technology makes necessary.

Finally, following from the need for this variety of specialized talent, is the need for its coordination. Talent must be brought to bear on the common purpose. More specifically, on large and small matters, information must be extracted from the various specialists, tested for its reliability and relevance, and made to yield a decision. This process, which is much misunderstood, requires a special word.

3

The modern business organization, or that part which has to do with guidance and direction, consists of numerous individuals who are engaged, at any given time, in obtaining, digesting or exchanging and testing information. A very large part of the exchange and testing of information is by word-of-mouth—a discussion in an office, at lunch or over the telephone. But the most typical procedure is through the committee and the committee meeting. One can do worse than think of a business organization as a hierarchy of committees. Coordination, in turn, consists in assigning the appropriate talent to committees, intervening on occasion to force a decision, and, as the case may be, announcing the decision or carrying it as information for a yet further decision by a yet higher committee.

Nor should it be supposed that this is an inefficient procedure. On the contrary it is, normally, the only efficient procedure. Association in a committee enables each member to come to know the intellectual resources and the reliability of his colleagues. Committee discussion enables members to pool information under circumstances which allow, also, of immediate probing to assess the relevance and reliability of the information offered. Uncertainty about one's information or error is revealed as in no other way. There is also, no doubt, considerable stimulus to mental effort from such association. One may enjoy the luxury of torpor in private but not so comfortably in public at least during working hours. Men who believe themselves deeply engaged in private thought are usually doing nothing. Committees are condemned by the cliché that individual effort is somehow superior to group effort; by those who guiltily suspect that since group effort is more congenial, it must be less productive; and by those who do not see that the process of extracting, and especially of testing, information has necessarily a somewhat undirected quality—briskly conducted meetings invariably decide matters previously decided; and by those who fail to realize that highly paid men, when sitting around a table as a committee, are not necessarily wasting more time than, in the aggregate, they would each waste in private by themselves. Forthright and determined administrators frequently react to belief in the superior capacity of individuals for decision by abolishing all committees. They then constitute working parties, task forces, assault teams or executive groups in order to avoid the one truly disastrous consequence of their action which would be that they should make the decisions themselves.

Thus decision in the modern business enterprise is the product not of individuals but of groups. The groups are numerous, as often informal as formal, and subject to constant change in composition. Each contains the men possessed of the information, or with access to the information, that bears on the particular decision together with those whose skill consists in extracting and testing this information and obtaining a conclusion. This is how men act successfully on matters where no single one, however exalted or intelligent, has more than a fraction of the necessary knowledge. It is what makes modern business possible, and in other contexts it is what makes modern government possible. It is fortunate that men of limited knowledge are so constituted that they can work together in this way. Were it otherwise, business and government, at any given moment, would be at a standstill awaiting the appearance of a man with the requisite breadth of knowledge to resolve the problem presently at hand. Some further characteristics of group decision-making must now be noticed.

4

Group decision-making extends deeply into the business enterprise. Effective participation is not closely related to rank in the formal hierarchy of the organization. This takes an effort of mind to grasp. Everyone is influenced by the stereotyped organization chart of the business enterprise. At its top is the Board of Directors and the Board Chairman; next comes the President; next comes the Executive Vice President; thereafter come the Department or Divisional heads—those who preside over the Chevrolet division, the large-generators division, the computer division. Power is assumed to pass down from the pinnacle. Those at the top give orders; those below relay them on or respond.

This happens, but only in very simple organizations—the peacetime drill of the National Guard or a troop of Boy Scouts moving out on Saturday maneuvers. Elsewhere the decision will require information. Some power will then pass to the person or persons who have this information. If this knowledge is highly particular to themselves then their power becomes very great. In Los Alamos, during the development of the atomic bomb, Enrico Fermi rode a bicycle up the hill to work; Major General Leslie R. Groves presided in grandeur over the entire Manhattan District. Fermi had the final word on numerous questions of feasibility and design. In association with a handful of others he could, at various early stages, have brought the entire enterprise to an end. No such power resided with Groves. At any moment he could have been replaced without loss and with possible benefit.

When power is exercised by a group, not only does it pass into the organization but it passes irrevocably. If an individual has taken a decision he can be called before another individual, who is his superior in the hierarchy, his information can be examined and his decision reversed by the greater wisdom or experience of the superior. But if the decision required the combined information of a group, it cannot be safely reversed by an individual. He will have to get the judgment of other specialists. This returns the power once more to organization.

No one should insist, in these matters, on pure cases. There will often be instances when an individual has the knowledge to modify or change the finding of a group. But the broad rule holds: If a decision requires the specialized knowledge of a group of men, it is subject to safe review only by the similar knowledge of a similar group. Group decision, unless acted upon by another group, tends to be absolute.[1]

1. I reached some of these conclusions during World War II when, in the early years, I was in charge of price control. Decisions on prices—to fix, raise, rearrange or, very rarely, to lower them—came to my office after an extensive exercise in group decision-making in which lawyers, economists, accountants, men knowledgeable of the product and industry, and specialists in public righteousness had all participated. Alone one was nearly helpless to alter such decisions; hours or days of investigation would be required and, in the meantime, a dozen other decisions would have been made. Given what is commonly called an "adequate" staff, one could have exercised control. But an adequate staff would be one that largely duplicated the decision-making group with adverse effect on the good nature and sense of responsibility of the latter and the time required for decision. To have responsibility for all of the prices in the United States was awesome; to discover how slight was one's power in face of group decision-making was sobering. President Kennedy enjoyed responding to proposals for public action of one sort or another by saying: "I agree but I don't know whether the government will agree."

5

Next, it must not be supposed that group decision is important only in such evident instances as nuclear technology or space mechanics. Simple products are made and packaged by sophisticated processes. And the most massive programs of market control, together with the most specialized marketing talent, are used on behalf of soap, detergents, cigarettes, aspirin, packaged cereals and gasoline. These, beyond others, are the valued advertising accounts. The simplicity and uniformity of these products require the investment of compensatingly elaborate science and art to suppress market influences and make prices and amounts sold subject to the largest possible measure of control. For these products too, decision passes to a group which combines specialized and esoteric knowledge. Here too power goes deeply and more or less irrevocably into the organization.

For purposes of pedagogy, I have sometimes illustrated these tendencies by reference to a technically uncomplicated product, which, unaccountably, neither General Electric nor Westinghouse has yet placed on the market. It is a toaster of standard performance, the pop-up kind, except that it etches on the surface of the toast, in darker carbon, one of a selection of standard messages or designs. For the elegant, an attractive monogram would be available or a coat of arms; for the devout, at breakfast there would be an appropriate devotional message from the Reverend Billy Graham; for the patriotic or worried, there would be an aphorism urging vigilance from Mr. J. Edgar Hoover; for modern painters and economists, there would be a purely abstract design. A restaurant version would sell advertising or urge the peaceful integration of public eating places.

Conceivably this is a vision that could come from the head of General Electric. But the systematic proliferation of such ideas is the designated function of much more lowly men who are charged with product development. At an early stage in the developing of the toaster the participation of specialists in engineering, production, styling and design and possibly philosophy, art and spelling would have to be sought. No one in position to authorize the product would do so without a judgment on how the problems of inscription were to be solved and at what cost. Nor, ordinarily, would an adverse finding on technical and economic feasibility be overridden. At some stage, further development would become contingent on the findings of market researchers and merchandise experts on whether the toaster could be sold and at what price. Nor, would an adverse decision by this group be overruled. In the end there would be a comprehensive finding on the feasibility of the innovation. If unfavorable this would not be overruled. Nor, given the notoriety that attaches to lost opportunity, would be the more plausible contingency of a favorable recommendation. It will be evident that nearly all powers—initiation, character of development, rejection or acceptance—are exercised deep in the company. It is not the managers who decide. Effective power of decision is lodged deeply in the technical, planning and other specialized staff.

6

We must notice next that this exercise of group power can be rendered unreliable or ineffective by external interference. Not only does power pass into the organization but the quality of decision can easily be impaired by efforts of an individual to retain control over the decision-making process.

Specifically the group reaches decisions by receiving and evaluating the specialized information of its members. If it is to act responsibly, it must be accorded responsibility. It cannot be arbitrarily or capriciously overruled. If it is, it will develop the same tendencies to irresponsibility as an individual similarly treated.

But the tendency will be far more damaging. The efficiency of the group and the quality of its decisions depend on the quality of the information provided and the precision with which it is tested. The last increases greatly as men work together. It comes to be known that some are reliable and that some though useful are at a tacit discount. All information offered must be so weighed. The sudden intervention of a superior introduces information, often of dubious quality, that is not subject to this testing. His reliability, as a newcomer, is unknown; his information, since he is boss, may be automatically exempt from the proper discount; or his intervention may take the form of an instruction and thus be outside the process of group decision in a matter where only group decision incorporating the required specialized judgments is reliable. In all cases the intrusion is damaging.

It follows both from the tendency for decision-making to pass down into organization and the need to protect the autonomy of the group that those who hold high formal rank in an organization—the President of General Motors or General Electric—exercise only modest powers of substantive decision. This does not mean that they are without power. This power is certainly less than conventional obeisance, professional public relations or, on occasion, personal vanity insist. Decision and ratification are often confused. The first is important; the second is not. Routine decisions, if they involve a good deal of money, are also invariably thought important. The nominal head of a large corporation, though with slight power and, perhaps, in the first stages of retirement, is visible, tangible and comprehensible. It is tempting and perhaps valuable for the corporate personality to attribute to him power of decision that, in fact, belongs to a dull and not easily comprehended collectivity. Nor is it a valid explanation that the boss, though impotent on specific questions, acts on broad issues of policy. Such issues of policy, if genuine, are preeminently the ones that require the specialized information of the group.

Leadership does cast the membership of the groups that make the decisions and it constitutes and reconstitutes these groups in accordance with changing need. This is its most important function. In an economy where organized intelligence is the decisive factor of production this is not unimportant. On the contrary. But it cannot be supposed that it can replace or even second-guess organized intelligence on substantive decisions.

7

In the past, leadership in business organization was identified with the entrepreneur—the individual who united ownership or control of capital with capacity for organizing the other factors of production and, in most contexts, with a further capacity for innovation. With the rise of the modern corporation, the emergence of the organization required by modern technology and planning and the divorce of the owner of the capital from control of the enterprise, the entrepreneur no longer exists as an individual person in the mature industrial enterprise. Everyday discourse, except in the economics textbooks, recognizes this change. It replaces the entrepreneur, as the directing force of the enterprise, with management. This is a collective and imperfectly defined entity; in the large corporation it embraces chairman, president, those vice presidents with important staff or departmental responsibility, occupants of other major staff positions and, perhaps, division or department heads not included above. It includes, however, only a small proportion of those who, as participants, contribute information to group decisions. This latter group is very large; it extends from the most senior officials of the corporation to where it meets, at the outer perimeter, the white and blue collar workers whose function is to conform more or less mechanically to instruction or routine. It embraces all who bring specialized knowledge, talent or experience to group decision-making. This, not the management, is the guiding intelligence—the brain—of the enterprise. There is no name for all who participate in group decision-making or the organization which they form. I propose to call this organization the Technostructure.

The Sickness of Government

PETER F. DRUCKER

The purpose of government is to make fundamental decisions, and to make them effectively. The purpose of government is to focus the political energies of society. It is to dramatize issues. It is to present fundamental choices.

The purpose of government, in other words, is to govern.

This, as we have learned in other institutions, is incompatible with "doing." Any attempt to combine governing with "doing" on a large scale paralyzes the decision-making capacity. Any attempt to have decision-making organs actually "do," also means very poor "doing." They are not focused on "doing." They are not equipped for it. They are not fundamentally concerned with it.

There is good reason today why soldiers, civil servants, and hospital administrators look to business management for concepts, principles, and practices. For business, during the last thirty years, has had to face, on a much smaller scale, the problem which modern government now faces: the incompatibility between "governing" and "doing." Business management learned that the two have to be separated, and that the top organ, the decision maker, has to be detached from "doing." Otherwise he does not make decisions, and the "doing" does not get done either.

In business this goes by the name of "decentralization." The term is misleading. It implies a weakening of the central organ, the top management of a business. The purpose of decentralization as a principle of structure and constitutional order is, however, to make the center, the top management of a business, strong and capable of performing the central, the top-management, task. The purpose is to make it possible for top management to concentrate on decision making and direction by sloughing off the "doing" to operating managements, each with its own mission and goals, and with its own sphere of action and autonomy.

If this lesson were applied to government, the other institutions of society would then rightly become the "doers." "Decentralization" applied to government would not be just another form of "federalism" in which local rather than central government discharges the "doing" tasks. It would rather be a systematic policy of using the other, the nongovernmental institutions of the society of organizations, for the actual "doing," i.e., for performance, operations, execution.

Such a policy might be called "reprivatization." The tasks which flowed to government in the last century because the original private institution of society, the family, could not discharge them, would be turned over to the new, nongovernmental institutions that have sprung up and grown these last sixty to seventy years.

Government would start out by asking the question: "How do these institutions work and what can they do?" It would then ask: "How can political and social objectives be formulated and organized in such a manner as to become opportunities for performance for these institutions?" It would also ask: "And what opportunities for accomplishment of political objectives do the abilities and capacities of these institutions offer to government?"

This would be a very different role for government from that it plays in traditional political theory. In all our theories government is *the* institution. If "reprivatization" were to be applied, however, government would become *one* institution albeit the central, the top, institution.

Reprivatization would give us a different society from any our social theories now assume. In these theories government does not exist. It is outside of society. Under reprivatization government would become the central social institution.

Political theory and social theory, for the last two hundred and fifty years, have been separate. If we applied to government and to society what we have learned about organization these last fifty years, the two would again come together. The nongovernmental institutions—university, business, and hospital, for instance—would be seen as organs for the

accomplishment of results. Government would be seen as society's resource for the determination of major objectives, and as the "conductor"
of social diversity.

I have deliberately used the term "conductor." It might not be too fanciful to
compare the situation today with the development of music two hundred years
ago. The dominant musical figure of the early eighteenth century was the great
organ virtuoso, especially in the Protestant north. In organ music, as a Buxtehude
or a Bach practiced it, one instrument with one performer expressed the total
range of music. But as a result, it required almost superhuman virtuosity to be
a musician.
    By the end of the century, the organ virtuoso had disappeared. In his
place was the modern orchestra. There each instrument played only one part,
and a conductor up front pulled together all these diverse and divergent instruments into one score and one performance. As a result, what had seemed to be
absolute limits to music suddenly disappeared. Even the small orchestra of
Haydn could express a musical range far beyond the reach of the greatest organ
virtuoso of a generation earlier.
    The conductor himself does not play an instrument. He need not even
know how to play an instrument. His job is to know the capacity of each instrument and to evoke optimal performance from each. Instead of being the "performer," he has become the "conductor." Instead of "doing," he leads.

The next major development in politics, and the one needed to make
this middle-aged failure—our tired, overextended, flabby, and impotent
government—effective again, might therefore be reprivatization of the
"doing," the performance of society's tasks. This need not mean "return
to private ownership." Indeed, what is going on in the Communist satellite countries of Eastern Europe today—especially in Yugoslavia—is reprivatization in which ownership is not involved at all. Instead, autonomous
businesses depend on the market for the sale of goods, the supply of labor,
and the supply of capital. That their "ownership" is in the hands of the
government is a legal rather than an economic fact—though, of course,
important. Yet to some Yugoslavs it does not appear to be incompatible
with that ultrabourgeois institution, a stock exchange.
    What matters, in other words, is that institutions not be *run* by
government but be autonomous. Cooperatives, for instance, are not
considered "capitalist" in the Anglo-American countries, although they
are "private" in that they are not run by government. And the same applies to "private" hospitals and the "private" universities. On the other
hand, the German university has traditionally been almost as autonomous
as the American "private" university, even though it is a state institution.
    Reprivatization, therefore, may create social structures that are
strikingly similar, though the laws in respect to ownership differ greatly
from one country to another and from one institution to another. What
they would have in common is a principle of performance rather than a
principle of authority. In all of them the autonomous institution created
for the performance of a major social task would be the "doer." Government would become increasingly the decision maker, the vision maker,

the political organ. It would try to figure out how to structure a given political objective so as to make it attractive to one of the autonomous institutions. It would, in other words, be the "conductor" who tries to think through what each instrument is best designed to do. And just as we praise a composer for his ability to write "playable" music, which best uses the specific performance characteristic of French horn, violin, or flute, we may come to praise the lawmaker who best structures a particular task so as to make it most congenial for this or that of the autonomous, self-governing, private institutions of pluralist society.

Business is likely to be only one, but a very important, institution in such a structure. Whether it be owned by the capitalist, that is, by the investor, or by a cooperative or a government, might even become a secondary consideration. For even if owned by government, it would have to be independent of government and autonomous—as the Yugoslavs show—not only in its day-to-day management, but, perhaps more important, in its position in the market, and especially in a competitive capital market.

What makes business particularly appropriate for reprivatization is that it is predominantly an organ of innovation; of all social institutions, it is the only one created for the express purpose of making and managing change. All other institutions were originally created to prevent, or at least to slow down, change. They become innovators only by necessity and most reluctantly.

Specifically business has two advantages where government has major weaknesses. Business can abandon an activity. Indeed, it is forced to do so if it operates in a market—and even more, if it depends on a market for its supply of capital. There is a point beyond which even the most stubborn businessman cannot argue with the market test, no matter how rich he may be himself. Even Henry Ford had to abandon the Model T when it no longer could be sold. Even his grandson had to abandon the Edsel.

What is more: of all our institutions, business is the only one that society will let disappear.

It takes a major catastrophe, a war, or a great revolution, to allow the disappearance of a university or of a hospital, no matter how superfluous and unproductive they might have become. Again and again, for instance, the Catholic Church in the United States attempts to close down hospitals that have ceased to be useful. In almost every case, a storm of community nostalgia forces the supposedly absolute bishop to retract his decision.

Only a foreigner, a Canadian, sent as a provincial from the outside, could force the English Jesuits to abandon their boarding school even though it had become an anomaly. And this provincial had then to be pulled out of England fast and moved back to Canada. The Russians had the same experience when they tried, in the late forties, to consolidate a number of provincial universities. Even Stalin had to give in and rescind the order.

But when the best-known airplane manufacturer in the United States, the Douglas Company, designer and producer of the DC-3 (or Dakota, as the military and the Europeans call it), was in difficulty in 1967, neither American public nor American government rushed to its rescue. If a competitor had not bought the company and merged it into his operations, we would have accepted the disappearance of Douglas—with regret, to be sure, and with a good deal of nostalgic rhetoric, but also with the feeling: "It's their own fault, after all."

Precisely because business can make a profit, it *must* run the risk of loss.

This risk, in turn, goes back to the second strength of business: alone among all institutions it has a test of performance. No matter how inadequate profitability is, it is a test for all to see. One can argue that this or that obsolete hospital is really needed in the community or that it will one day again be needed. One can argue that even the poorest university is better than none. The alumni or the community always has a "moral duty" to save "dear old Siwash."

The consumer, however, is unsentimental. It leaves him singularly unmoved to be told that he has a duty to buy the product of a company because it has been around a long time. The consumer always asks: "And what will the product do for me tomorrow?" If the answer is "Nothing," he will see its manufacturer disappear without the slightest regret. And so will the investor.

This is the strength of business as an institution. It is the best reason for keeping it in private ownership. The argument that the capitalist should not be allowed to make profits is a popular one. But the real role of the capitalist is to be expendable. His role is to take risks and to take losses as a result. This role the private investor is much better equipped to discharge than the public one. We want privately owned business precisely because we want institutions that can go bankrupt and can disappear. We want at least one institution that, from the beginning, is adapted to change, one institution that has to prove its right to survival again and again. This is what business is designed for, precisely because it is designed to make and to manage change.

If we want a really strong and effective government, therefore, we should want businesses that are not owned by government. We should want businesses in which private investors, motivated by their own self-interest and deciding on the basis of their own best judgment, take the risk of failure. The strongest argument for "private enterprise" is not the function of profit. The strongest argument is the function of loss. Because of it business is the most adaptable and the most flexible of the institutions around. It is the one that has a clear, even though limited, performance test. It is the one that has a yardstick.

Therefore, it is the one best equipped to manage. For if there is a yardstick for results, one can determine the efficiency and adequacy of efforts. One can say in a business: "Our greatest profits are at a level where we control 95 per cent of the costs rather than where we control 99 per cent. Controlling and auditing the last 4 per cent or 5 per cent costs us much more than the profits from these marginal activities could ever be." One cannot say this with respect to patient care in a hospital. One cannot say this with respect to instruction in a university. And one cannot say this in any government agency. There one has to guess, to judge, to have opinions. In a business one can measure. Business, therefore, is the most manageable of all these institutions, the one where we are most likely to find the right balance between results and the cost of efforts. It is the only institution where control need not be an emotional or a moral issue, where in talking "control" we discuss "value" and not "values."

Reprivatization is still heretical doctrine. But it is no longer heretical practice. Reprivatization is hardly a creed of "fat cat millionaires" when black-power advocates seriously propose making education in the slums "competitive" by turning it over to private enterprise, competing for the tax dollar on the basis of proven performance in teaching ghetto children. It may be argued that the problems of the black ghetto in the American city are very peculiar problems—and so they are. They are extreme malfunctions of modern government. But, if reprivatization works in the extreme case, it is likely to work even better in less desperate ones.

One instance of reprivatization in the international sphere is the World Bank. Though founded by governments, it is autonomous. It finances itself directly through selling its own securities on the capital markets. The International Monetary Fund, too, is reprivatization. Indeed, if we develop the money and credit system we need for the world economy, we will have effectively reprivatized creation and management of money and credit which have been considered for millennia attributes of sovereignty.

Again business is well equipped to become the "doer" in the international sphere. The multinational corporation, for instance, is our best organ for rapid social and economic development through the "contract growing" of people and of capital. In the Communications Satellite Corporation (COMSAT) we are organizing worldwide communications (another traditional prerogative of the sovereign) as a multinational corporation. A Socialist government, the Labour government of Britain, has used reprivatization to bring cheap energy to Britain—in contracts with the multinational oil companies for the exploration and development of the natural gas fields under the North Atlantic Ocean.

And the multinational corporation may be the only institution equipped to get performance where the fragmentation into tribal splinter units such as the "ministates" of Equatorial Africa makes performance by government impossible.

But domestically as well as internationally business is, of course, only one institution and equipped to do only one task, the economic one. Indeed it is important . . . to confine business—and every other institution—to its own task. Reprivatization will, therefore, entail using other nongovernmental institutions—the hospital, for instance, or the university—for other, noneconomic "doing" tasks. Indeed the design of new nongovernmental, autonomous institutions as agents of social performance under reprivatization may well become a central job for tomorrow's political architects.

We have the first beginnings of worldwide universities—with their roots probably in the "extramural accreditation" which London University extended gradually to new institutions in the last decades of the British Empire. Today

American universities are building more and more multinational institutions. There is also a group of aggressive new business schools throughout Latin America in which nine separate schools in nine different Latin countries run themselves increasingly as one institution with common goals, a common faculty, and interchanges of programs and students. Indeed the multinational university may be our best tool to stop, if not to reverse, the "brain drain."

We do not face a "withering away of the state." On the contrary, we need a vigorous, a strong, and a very active government. But we do face a choice between big but impotent government and a government that is strong because it confines itself to decision and direction and leaves the "doing" to others. We do not face a "return of laissez-faire" in which the economy is left alone. The economic sphere cannot and will not be considered to lie outside the public domain. But the choices for the economy—as well as for all other sectors—are no longer *either* complete governmental indifference or complete governmental control.

In all major areas we have a new choice in this pluralist society of organizations: an organic diversity in which institutions are used to do what they are best equipped to do. This is a society in which all sectors are "affected with the public interest," while in each sector a specific institution, under its own management and dedicated to its own job, emerges as the organ of action and performance.

This is a difficult and complex structure. Such symbiosis between institutions can work only if each disciplines itself to strict concentration on its own sphere, and to strict respect for the integrity of the other institutions. Each, to use again the analogy of the orchestra, must be content to play its own part. This will come hardest for government, especially after the last fifty years in which it had been encouraged in the belief of the eighteenth-century organ virtuoso that it could—and should—play all parts simultaneously. But every institution will have to learn the same lesson.

Reprivatization will not weaken government. Indeed, its main purpose is to restore strength and performance capacity to sick and incapacitated government. We cannot go much further along the road on which government has been traveling these last fifty years. All we can get this way is more bureaucracy but not more performance. We can impose higher taxes but we cannot get dedication, support, and faith on the part of the public. Government can gain greater girth and more weight, but it cannot gain strength or intelligence. All that can happen, if we keep on going the way we have been going, is a worsening sickness of government and growing disenchantment with it. And this is the prescription for tyranny, that is, for a government organized against its own society.

This can happen. It has happened often enough in history. But in a society of pluralist institutions it is not likely to be effective too long. The Communists tried it, and after fifty years have shown—though they have not yet fully learned—that the structure of modern society and its tasks are incompatible with monolithic government. Monolithic government requires absolute dictatorship, which no one has ever been able to prolong much beyond the lifetime of one dictator.

Ultimately we will need new political theory and probably very new constitutional law. We will need new concepts and new social theory. Whether we will get these and what they will look like, we cannot know today. But we can know that we are disenchanted with government primarily because it does not perform. We can say that we need, in pluralist society, a government that can and does govern. This is not a government that "does"; it is not a government that "administers"; it is a government that governs.

Normative Theory and Public Administration

MICHAEL M. HARMON

The dominant issues in normative theory of Public Administration in the past several decades have been responsibility and freedom. Theoretical discourse on the nature of administrative responsibility has for nearly thirty years ranged roughly between the position of Herman Finer, who argued that loyalty to legitimate political authority is the criterion of responsible behavior, and Carl Friedrich's position that responsibility requires the active participation of administrators in sensing and responding to public needs. The question for each was, How can we assure, or at least reasonably expect, that administrators will behave in ways that are responsible to one or another version of the public interest? To Finer such assurances rested in the law and other formal devices enforcing accountability. For Friedrich, the "inner check" provided by the professional values inculcated in administrators during their formal training justified a departure from the narrow legalism of Finer's perspective.

While essential agreement with Friedrich's view of the responsibility issue has been regarded as a crude measure of one's administrative liberalism, it is significant that both interpretations assume a fundamentally negative stance on the nature of man in general and of public administrators in particular. Although Finer and Friedrich arrive at differing conclusions, the same premise about human nature underlies each argument: Without the checks provided by either the law or the processes of professional socialization, the resultant behavior of administrators would be both selfish and capricious. This pessimism, it will be argued below, stems from the peculiar and unnecessarily restrictive assumptions on which administrative responsibility is conceptualized in the literature of Public Administration and political science.

Similarly restrictive is the manner in which the issue of freedom and the public administrator has been treated in the literature. As long as the concern is with how administrators preserve and protect the freedom of others, we are on quite safe and manageable grounds. Issues that arise in this context can be managed through the use of utilitarian formulae of one sort or another. When, however, the administrator inquires about his own freedom, such as the freedom to exert greater influence on public policies, he is confronted with the presumed dilemma between his exercise of free choice and his responsibility to serve the interests of others. Resolution of these conflicts is most often achieved either by the administrator's acquiescence to a higher authority or by striking an expeditious "balance" between his interests and those of the public (or some segment of it). While it is conceded that courageous and risk-taking administrators have not been universally vilified by students of the discipline, the bases on which such administrators are given approval have not been consciously integrated into contemporary theories of responsibility and freedom in Public Administration.

The purposes of this [essay] are to show how our assumptions about responsibility and freedom have inhibited the development of normative thinking in Public Administration and to offer the basis of a more affirmative and activist theory of administrative responsibility.

A half century ago answers to normative questions in Public Administration were rather easily proffered. The American era of reform to which the central values of Public Administration were tied emerged from the excesses of Jacksonian Democracy. During this reform era the doctrine of separation of powers and checks and balances was forwarded with renewed zeal in the form of a simplistic distinction between politics and administration which made the issue of administrative responsibility seem unambiguous. Administrative activity was considered to be responsible to the extent that it reflected the wishes and dictates of elected representatives. Beginning with Dimock,[1] critics of the dichotomy between politics and administration argued that such a view avoided the realities of the governmental process. Administrators, they said, are inevitably involved in political activity and should, therefore, be aware of its subtleties. While this point is now largely conceded, leadership by administrators in the formulation of public policy is still grudgingly regarded as a pragmatic necessity rather than as a positive and integral part of that process.

The belief that policy should be formulated exclusively by elected officials can be traced to the assumption that they are the only actors in the political system who can be held accountable by the democratic constraint of election. Supporting this assumption is the view that democracy is fundamentally a balance between majority rule and minority rights, the former enforced through voting and the latter through the courts. But majority rule and minority rights are only two of a number of features possible in a democratic system; they are not its essence. Keeping the way

1. Marshall E. Dimock, *Modern Politics and Administration* (New York: American Book, 1937).

open for change with respect to social goals is its essential imperative.[2] To view democracy as more than a balance of majority rule and minority rights is especially crucial when relatively little activity in government is actually subject to the vote or scrutiny of elected officials. Given the paramount role of administrators in policy making, the ways in which we—and especially *they*—view their appropriate roles are of central concern.

At the same time that discomfort about the politics-administration dichotomy was being expressed, efficiency as a dominant value in Public Administration came under fire. Dwight Waldo, while not denying the importance of efficiency, pointed out that it can be measured only in terms of purpose and "that the less mechanical and routine the instruments and procedures, and the more important *or more nearly ultimate* the purposes they serve, the less likely is their efficiency to be constant":

. . . there is a realm of "science" where "objectivity" is possible and "efficiency" can be measured. On the other hand, . . . increasingly, as one's frame of reference widens and disagreement about ends becomes important, "science" and "objectivity" are more difficult, judgments of "efficiency" less accurate, more controversial.[3]

Further, while efficiency has some legitimate appeal, the vast resources of a wealthy nation tend to diminish its relative importance. With the demise of old values and assumptions about governmental activity comes the necessity to alter thinking about administrative responsibility. We are forced to regard a theory of administrative responsibility which relies heavily on efficiency as insufficient for this period in our social and political development.

THE ETHIC OF ADMINISTRATIVE NEUTRALITY

Because of its commitment to the doctrine of separation of powers and legislative supremacy, the traditional American view of democracy affirms the ethic of administrative neutrality in matters of substantive policy. At the root of the contention that administrators can and should remain neutral about policy lies the conventional distinction between freedom and responsibility. The argument in its most extreme form suggests that because administrators are not chosen by the electorate they are not free to act as advocates of policies or to allow their personal values to influence significantly the manner in which policies are implemented. Administrative responsibility in its traditional form requires that administrators be able to identify and account for their values so that they will not impinge on decisions of public policy. While the objectivity and clarity of perception necessary to behave with complete neutrality may have some theoretical desirability, such qualities are hardly descriptive of average or even exceptional administrators.

A more basic challenge to the freedom-responsibility dichotomy,

2. Thomas Landon Thorson, *The Logic of Democracy* (New York: Holt, Rinehart and Winston, 1962).
3. Dwight Waldo, *The Administrative State* (New York: Ronald Press, 1948), pp. 204-205.

however, has been leveled by philosophies outside the milieu in which normative issues in administration have usually been argued. From an existentialist's viewpoint, for example, it would be inappropriate to talk of activity purely in terms of responsibility to others, while ignoring responsibility to oneself. To the administrator this is a way of saying that sanctions assuring accountability which rest wholly outside his own values greatly reduce his sense of personal commitment and purpose. Additionally, freedom, in an existential sense, is not antithetical to responsibility. Thus, if the existentialists are correct in saying that freedom without responsibility is a meaningless kind of freedom, a definition of administrative responsibility based solely on the negative notion of accountability becomes untenable.

THE "DILEMMA" OF ADMINISTRATIVE AND POLITICAL DEMOCRACY

Early writers such as Frederick W. Taylor recognized the importance, if not the precise nature, of individual motivation in organizations. Conveniently, the primacy which Taylor ascribed to pecuniary reward as a value was consistent with the values then dominant in public and private organizations. Even the challenge posed to scientific management by the human-relations movement did little to undermine the belief in the essential congruence of individual needs and organizational goals.

Despite some disagreement in modern organization theory about the nature of individual motivation, a general concern is that individual and organizational needs may differ greatly, leading either to widespread employee discontent or the failure of organizations to achieve their goals. Etzioni, for example, has argued that the distinguishing feature of the modern or "structuralist" school of organization theory is that it stresses the inevitable existence of conflict between individual and organizational needs.[4] Transferred to the public sphere, the organizational dilemma posed by Etzioni assumes widespread proportions. Individual needs in this area must be matched against the interests of the general public rather than merely those of a single organization. Frederick C. Mosher recently raised the question of possible conflicts between individual self-actualization, brought about by a trend toward participative decision making in public agencies, and methods of administrative accountability in a democracy:

. . . there has already developed a great deal of collegial decision-making in many public agencies, particularly those which are largely controlled by single professional groups. But I would point out that *democracy within administration,* if carried to the full, raises a logical dilemma in its relation to *political democracy.* All public organizations are presumed to have been established and to operate for public purposes—i.e., purposes of the people. They are authorized, legitimized, empowered, and usually supported by authorities outside of themselves. To what extent, then should "insiders," the officers and employees, be

4. Amitai Etzioni, *Modern Organizations* (Englewood Cliffs, New Jersey: Prentice-Hall, 1965).

able to modify their purposes, their organizational arrangements, and their means of support? It is entirely possible that internal administrative democracy might run counter to the principles and objectives of political democracy in which the organizations of government are viewed as instruments of public purpose.[5]

The dilemma which Mosher sees between administrative and political democracy is subject to serious question. The narrow professionalism in public agencies which he rightly fears is apparently assumed to be the result of a movement toward a more participative form of public management and greater self-actualization of professional public employees. But it is just as reasonable to assume that self-centered professionalism which ignores public needs is likely to manifest itself in organizational systems which rely on quite authoritarian, highly centralized methods of decision making. While the rise of professionalism in government and the growing acceptance of participative management have emerged at roughly the same time, they are not necessarily concomitants. The vision of professional administrators pursuing their own interests at the expense of the public denies the philosophical foundation of self-actualizing behavior. It assumes that administrators will act selfishly and irresponsibly unless forced to act otherwise by vigilant guardians of the public trust. Yet Abraham Maslow, for example, has predicted that the choices of self-actualizing people are more likely to meet the test of "responsible" behavior than those of less healthy people.[6] Maslow did not propose an elitist system in which self-actualizers are granted the exclusive privilege of making important public choices. He simply argued that such people are more likely than unhealthy people to recognize that their own freedom and the freedom of others are inseparable.

This point of view may be disputed on the ground that evidence is lacking to support the belief that individual self-actualization through participative decision making in public agencies will meet the test of responsible behavior in a political democracy. Admittedly, it is a difficult hypothesis to test. At the same time, however, it is also clear that the opposite assumption—that public administrators will act irresponsibly unless otherwise checked—is similarly devoid of empirical support. Yet the latter hypothesis underlies most contemporary political notions of administrative responsibility.

Certainly administrators are not always attuned to or act consistently with the public pulse. But surely corrupt or irresponsible behavior cannot be assumed to be the result of participative decision making and self-actualization until so demonstrated. One might carry the argument a step further by suggesting that the lack of trust in public administrators im-

---

5. Frederick C. Mosher, *Democracy and the Public Service* (New York: Oxford University Press, 1968) , p. 18.

6. Abraham H. Maslow, *Toward a Psychology of Being* (Princeton, New Jersey: Van Nostrand, 1962) . This theme is expanded further by Maslow in *Eupsychian Management* (New York: Dorsey, 1966) in which he discusses the concept of *synergy*. Briefly, synergy, as he defines it, is the reconciliation of the selfish and the unselfish, the rejection of the presumed dichotomy between freedom for oneself and freedom for others.

plied by a strict separation of policy formulation and implementation may, in some instances, be a self-fulfilling prophecy. By too closely guarding institutional arrangements designed to check administrative discretion, a political system may likely be rewarded with precisely the type of behavior it fears. Support for this view is meager in the literature of Public Administration and political science. Yet one need not stray very far into the literature and research about human motivation to conclude that such a hypothesis is more than idle speculation.

SUGGESTIONS FOR REDIRECTION OF NORMATIVE THEORY IN PUBLIC ADMINISTRATION

In searching for the foundations of a new approach to normative theory in Public Administration, this essay has thus far suggested two general guidelines: (1) That such a theory must accommodate the values and motives of individual public administrators to theories of administrative responsibility; and (2) that the essential congruence of administrative freedom and political freedom must be recognized. Stated in somewhat more generic terms, the presumed distinction between freedom and responsibility (or between freedom for self and freedom for others) should be rejected.

A third and closely related imperative is that the basic ambiguity and indeterminacy of complex social systems must be accounted for. While there are numerous predictions of probable major trends in this country and in the world during the remainder of the century, it is clear that individual futures in the coming years will be less predictable than they were in the past. Moreover, since clearly defined external sanctions to govern behavior are becoming generally less evident, their existence cannot realistically be presumed in a theory of responsible behavior in any sphere of activity. Instead, we are required to turn increasingly to an existential concept of self-responsibility as the foundation of a new theory.

This circumstance makes difficult the task of redefining administrative responsibility. Guarantees of accountability traditionally provided by legal and bureaucratic machinery are a necessary but certainly insufficient requisite of administrative responsibility under conditions of uncertainty and rapid social change. A theory of administrative responsibility based on responsiveness to diverse and changing public demands and advocacy of and commitment to programs designed to meet those demands can offer no such explicit guarantees.

Arguing for a more "affirmative" definition of administrative responsibility, however, does not necessitate total discard of traditional notions of accountability. The arguments offered here are simply a reminder that an exclusive reliance on devices to assure accountability has a tendency to create a "blinder" effect on public officials which causes them to ignore other aspects of responsible behavior. We can recognize that there is no necessary (although at times there may be a possible and even probable) conflict between accountability and positive responsibility, and at the same time retain elements of the former and speculate about the conditions under which the latter may be encouraged. We are not necessarily forced into an either-or proposition. My predilection toward creating conditions under which administrators may self-actualize—for example, by permitting them greater involvement in the advocacy and support of policy—is already apparent. If my interpretation of Maslow and other humanistic psychologists is correct, the risks involved in attempting to create these conditions do not appear to be excessive.

In accepting the existentialists' contention that ultimate and transcendental values do not exist, we are forced to confront the knotty problem of patterning administrative and political systems to accommodate this notion. Some valuable assistance in this regard has been rendered by Thomas Landon Thorson. After arguing against the existence of deductive and inductive proofs of the legitimacy of political systems, he argues in favor of democracy on the grounds of such nonexistence:

It is the very recognition of the fact that one cannot *prove* the validity of political proposals by induction or deduction which leads us to reject any claim to absolute truth, and thereby to reject any political system premised on such a claim. No one man, no group, whether minority or majority, is ever justified in claiming a right to make decisions for the whole society on the grounds that it knows what the "right" decisions are. Just because the "rightness" of a political decision *cannot* be proved—because its consequences, short- or long-range, cannot be predicted with certitude nor its ultimate ethical supremacy demonstrated —are we obligated to construct a decision-making procedure that will leave the way open for new ideas and social change.[7]

To Thorson, the key element of democracy is the admonition to keep the way open for change. This point is emphasized not because such openness permits the attainment of some preconceived objective, but because "proofs" for the legitimacy of denying free activity are by definition nonexistent in a democratic system. Thorson's argument that there is no ultimate correctness of normative propositions—which is his basis for justifying democracy—is somewhat similar to the existentialists' denial of universal social norms. Individual needs and values are presumed to be legitimate in part because of the lack of evidence to the contrary.

AMBIGUITY IN PROBLEM DEFINITION

The ambiguity of problems which existentialists emphasize has been criticized by Wayne A. R. Leys as leading to a "cry-baby" attitude. "The existentialist cannot reduce the ambiguity of his problem, at least, prior to the deadline for action, and therefore he cannot rationally define 'the public interest' or anything else."[8] In recognizing their limitations in offering guides for administrative behavior, it should be noted that existentialists are not as universally pessimistic as Leys' comment suggests. Optimism is a dominant theme in much of the literature of humanistic and existential psychology and of what Colin Wilson calls the "new ex-

7. Thorson, *op. cit.*, pp. 138-139.
8. Wayne A. R. Leys, "The Relevance and Generality of 'The Public Interest,'" in Carl J. Friedrich (ed.), *The Public Interest* (New York: Atherton Press, 1966), p. 253.

istentialism." Even granting Leys' argument, it could be said that the existentialists' uncertainty in defining their own values and problems encourages them to refrain from defining those of other people in any dogmatic fashion.

The existentialist perspective suggests that the public administrator must attempt, however inadequately, to understand the relationship of his own values and motives to questions of public policy, and to create a climate in which those to whom he is legally responsible are encouraged to do likewise and to assert their values in the political arena. Such a view meets the test of administrative responsibility in a conventional democratic sense; just as important, however, it recognizes that administrators are human beings rather than machines and that ethical neutrality is an abstraction incapable of providing a viable basis for administrative responsibility.

SOME IMPLICATIONS FOR EDUCATION IN PUBLIC ADMINISTRATION

Part of the difficulty in altering the normative basis of Public Administration can be traced, as suggested earlier, to the historical context in which the field has evolved. In the education of civil servants the values which emerged from the reform era still form the primary basis on which their administrative and managerial talents are developed. The context in which public organizations will operate in the final third of this century, however, differs distinctly from those of earlier decades. With a few notable exceptions, however, educational programs in Public Administration still are linked to questionable assumptions of relative stability in the environment and of high predictability as to the consequences of public policies.

As already noted, it is imperative for the field of Public Administration that it recognize ambiguity and uncertainty as basic conditions of administrative activity. This is a task to which education in Public Administration—both in universities and in midcareer executive development programs—has devoted insufficient attention. An ability to cope with ambiguity is more a function of personality, however, than a result of accumulated substantive knowledge. Public Administration's failure to develop a curriculum which accounts for this distinction is apparent by its treatment of problems and issues typically as matters of content rather than of process of behavior.

Illustrative of this viewpoint was the White House announcement of the formation of the Federal Executive Institute, a new executive-development program for senior career civil servants. The announcement specified three areas on which the FEI programs will focus:

—The major problems facing our society and the nature of the government's response to those problems.
—Ways of maximizing government organizations to increase the effectiveness of these programs.
—Ways in which administration of Federal programs can be improved.

The stated objectives for the Institute, although obviously important, noticeably neglect the individual as an object of study. Instead, the announcement of the formation of the Institute stressed a "program" emphasis "to widen [the executives'] mastery of both the substance and administration of Federal programs."9 Reflecting on this approach, FEI's first director, Frank P. Sherwood, commented:

Such a statement is capable of various interpretations, but it seems to suggest that breadth will be achieved through the input of data which lie outside the experience of the individual. The suggestion is that this will occur largely at the cognitive level. Second, there is the preoccupation throughout that the executive problem in the Federal service is essentially one of sub-optimization, in which executives are maximizing parochial interests at rather high system cost.10

While it would no doubt be desirable for federal executives to obtain a working knowledge of and commitment to the broad range of government programs, the nature of public policy making raises questions as to the possibility of achieving this objective. A preliminary document prepared by the United States Civil Service Commission states, "The main purpose [of FEI] is to augment the ability of the upper civil service to provide continuity and responsiveness in Government operations, and to insure that those near the top are identified with the government as a whole in pursuit of national goals."11 Although the statement has some surface appeal, it seems to presuppose that there exists some more or less rationally defined set of national goals which government could achieve if only public executives were more fully aware of them. Yet it is almost pedestrian in a pluralistic society to say that a set of orderly priorities— the existence of which the FEI programs are apparently supposed to assume—does not exist. Moreover, the Commission statement suggests that higher civil servants have the powers both to grasp on a continuing basis the intricacies of public programs relating to a broad range of national objectives, and to develop a much broader base of loyalties and commitments. The former suggestion seems questionable on its face. Regarding the latter, a good deal of literature indicates that loyalties in large organizations are seldom higher than the subgroup level at which employees can see some direct result of their endeavors. To think that personal commitments of public administrators can be expanded much higher than this point presumes, it seems to me, uncommon patriotism.

I am not proposing that narrowly defined self-interest should be the governing ethic of public administrators. The argument is simply that a knowledge of and commitment to a large number of specific goals and policies asks too much of administrators and is inconsistent with the incremental and fragmented process by which public policy is formulated.

9. *Plan for the Federal Executive Institute,* Prepared for the President by the U.S. Civil Service Commission (undated and unpaged).

10. Memorandum from Frank P. Sherwood, Director of the Federal Executive Institute, to the Staff of FEI, July 1, 1968.

11. *Plan, op. cit.*

Rather, the breadth to be desired of public officials—or of anyone—is primarily a breadth of attitude. To quote again from the Sherwood memorandum:

In my judgment the executive of the future will have to tolerate far more ambiguity than has been true in the past. For a variety of obvious reasons change is becoming a way of life. Thus there will be an increasing number of uncertainties and incommensurables in the executive life space. If he is sensitive, he will feel acute discomfort, he will be open to learning. If he seeks to eliminate the discomfort by searching for certainty and stability, he will fear learning and will not engage in "creative leadership." Our task, then, is to move executives toward maturity, to work with tension by seeking more learning, as well as helping them to develop more insights into the nature of human cooperative processes. The concept of change is very important in this connection. For the executive must not only be concerned about how adaptive he is as an individual but how adaptive is the system for which he has responsibility.

The requisite learning implied by this statement is of a more fundamental order of magnitude than the acquisition of new substantive knowledge. Since learning to be adaptive and to feel comfortable with ambiguity entails a rather immediate and sometimes threatening confrontation with individual values and modes of behavior, the risks involved in developing an educational program which focuses on this concept are substantial. At the same time, however, a strong case can be made that it is a more manageable task than attempting to provide public servants with sufficient substantive knowledge to perform their jobs well. If it is identifiable at all, such knowledge is enormously varied in the short run and continually changing in the long run. To design a general educational program for the public service primarily around inputs of substantive knowledge assumes both a static set of goals for public servants and their agencies and an infinite store of transferable knowledge. Lacking either of these conditions, an emphasis on "learning how to learn" and how to develop an adaptive capacity for public organization seems to be a comparatively modest and practical approach.

What is being proposed essentially is that public administrators learn how to become more democratic—democratic, that is, in the sense described by Bennis and Slater in their book *The Temporary Society*. "Democracy," the authors state, "becomes a functional necessity whenever a social system is competing for survival under conditions of chronic change."[12] Because of a decline in filial deference and the ever increasing mobility of people, fixed bases of human relationships will give way to temporary ones at both family and organizational levels. If Bennis and Slater are correct in predicting that we will live in a "temporary" society, it is important that education in Public Administration not be geared to assumptions of stability and certainty. Education for the public service— and normative theory in particular—must recognize the individual and

12. Warren Bennis and Philip E. Slater, *The Temporary Society* (New York: Harper and Row, 1968), p. 4.

organizational stresses generated by continuous and chaotic change. Change is not an unqualified virtue. It is, however, a fact of political and administrative life to which normative theory in Public Administration must be accommodated.

Comment: On a Redefinition of Administrative Responsibility

JOHN PAYNTER

Michael Harmon's paper on administrative responsibility is a bold venture into a forbidding field. He makes an effort to *construct* in an area where old normative rationales have been the objects of severely damaging critiques, and where most new work is still dominated or at least strongly influenced by a philosophic position that denies the possibility of doing normative theory. His constructions take seriously the major critique of the politics-administration distinction by considering the administrator as a politician, not only in his spare time (while a "citizen"), but in the very acts of "administering." And his redefinition is grounded in the two modern philosophic positions that contend most strenuously with logical positivism: existentialism and linguistic analysis.

RADICAL INTENT AND CONSERVATIVE THEORY

According to Harmon, one needs to go to philosophic foundations in order to properly redefine administrative responsibility because more has been defective in the past than our administrative understandings. The misguided notion that efficiency and neutrality should be prime administrative values is tied to the equally inadequate belief that democracy is "a balance between majority rule and minority rights." Only when the essence of democracy is properly understood can an adequate notion of administrative responsibility be developed. It is Harmon's intention to formulate such a thorough and comprehensive redefinition of democratic administration.

In contrast to this obviously radical intention, however, he displays a surprising reluctance to relinquish the older understandings of democracy and administrative responsibility. Regarding a democratic regime, he asserts unequivocally that its essence is the imperative to keep "the way open for change with respect to social goals." But the sentence immediately following adds that democracy is *"more than* a balance of majority rule and minority rights" (my italics), implying that openness to social change is not the *whole* essence of democracy. Similarly, in redefining administrative responsibility he urges the public administrator "to understand the relationship of his own values and motives to questions of public policy," and "to create a climate in which those to whom he is legally responsible are encouraged to do likewise and to assert their values in the political arena." But he then adds that his view "meets the test of administrative responsibility in a conventional democratic sense." What he seems in fact to have formulated is not a wholly new definition, but an unresolved tension between new and old elements. An attempt to understand that tension and possible reasons for it may shed some light on the difficulties of the normative task in Public Administration.

The tension becomes clear when one spells out the new criteria for administrative action. In the case of the first standard, Harmon presumably means more than he says. The crucial question for an administrator is not whether he understands the relation of his values and motives to questions of public policy, but what bearing that understanding should have on his administrative decisions. From both the existentialist and postpositivist perspectives, the answer would seem to be that his decision should be guided by his own values, with some (undefined) recognition of the freedom of others and of the need to keep the way open for social change. The second criterion presents a similar case: The administrator presumably must do more than encourage political participation among those—but only those—to whom he is legally responsible. If he is to take the existentialist and postpositivist positions seriously, he must selectively urge anyone in the polity to participate whose action would enhance the possibility of continued social change. What remains unclear is how these criteria meet the conventional democratic test of administrative responsibility. In fact, Harmon's new standards would seem to undercut the traditional notion of administrative responsibility. The conventional criteria insisted that the policy decisions of elected officials, not the administrator's own values and motives, should dominate and guide administrative decisions, and that administrators should officially relate to and influence their "clients," not as whole citizens, but only within the sphere of their legally defined and authorized duties.

Of the many possible reasons for Harmon's retention of the conflicting old and new elements, two seem to me especially important for those of us who share his concern to redefine administrative responsibility. First, both elements may have been included because neither by itself yields an adequate understanding of administration. Harmon has indicated some of the defects in the older view, especially its failure to acknowledge the policy role of the administrator. He attempts to overcome that defect by viewing the administrator as something other than a mere implementer. In doing so, however, he virtually shatters the connection between administration and the rule of law. Proponents of the politics-administration distinction understood that connection in terms of the relation between legitimate legislators and obedient executors. The new position, in contrast, acknowledges two other criteria of right decisions: the administrator's own values and the imperative of openness to social change. If the latter is to entail anything more than promotion of the greatest quantitative mutation in human conditions, some additional standard is required for discriminating good from bad, or healthy from unhealthy, change. The imperative itself does not yield such additional standards, and, as existentialists acknowledge, neither will one's own values, as merely personal preferences, yield such socially binding rules. Consequently, the "conventional democratic sense" of administrative responsibility may have been reintroduced in order to provide a legitimate source for needed criteria of action, thereby avoiding the implications of administrative paralysis or political nihilism.

DEMOCRATIC ADMINISTRATION?

Harmon's problematic effort at redefinition suggests a second possible reason for the difficulties in that position. It may be that the requirements imposed on government by a large, complex, and highly industrialized society make a genuinely democratic administration untenable. Harmon asserts early in his paper that the administrator today has "the paramount role . . . in policy making." His overstatement emphasizes our present situation: The administrator will and must make decisions which are not simply—and perhaps not always fundamentally—reflective of popular wants or aimed at keeping the way open for social change. He is, in other words, a politician, not only in the sense that he possesses the skills to achieve his assigned organizational goals in a fragmented political system, but also in the sense that he influences the character of those affected by his decisions and partially determines the nature and direction of popular participation in politics. Unless the conditions which make such administrative action necessary are to be drastically changed, the American polity will continue to be not simply democratic, but a "mixed" regime; two qualitatively different principles of rule will operate in it simultaneously. Perhaps what we most need, then, is not further efforts to redefine democratic administrative responsibility, but thought about the proper ends and forms of that mixture.

VII
Judging the Past:
Evaluation

The culmination of the political process is the phase of evaluation. In evaluation political actions are judged according to standards of the good life prevalent at a given time and place. These standards are closely related to the dominant images of the public situation held by major groupings and are, therefore, in a sense contained within ideologies. Thus, the phase of evaluation is continuous with the phase of policy. The articles in this section present alternative standards for evaluating political activity which are widely held in the contemporary world.

For Samuel P. Huntington political activity is to be judged according to the contribution that it makes to maintaining stable human relations. Making explicit what was implied in the discussions of such writers as Melvin, Lipset, and Dahl, Huntington attempts to define the conditions that must hold if social relations are not to be characterized by violent disruptions and discontinuities. In contrast to Huntington, Karl Deutsch is not satisfied with mere stability as a standard of evaluation. He suggests that political activity can be evaluated on the basis of the quality of human relations characteristic of a given place and time. Thus, for Deutsch, the political process would be judged by the amount of trust, good will, and mutual aid present in social relations. The issue between Huntington and Deutsch, whether to take stability or quality of life as the standard of evaluation, is one of the most significant and deep-rooted debates in contemporary American political thought.

A different aspect of evaluation is discussed by Arthur Selwyn Miller, Ernest Becker, and the present author. All three agree that quality of life should be the guiding standard, but they differ in their interpretations of this standard. Miller is most concerned with the threat to individual freedom posed by large organizations in command of sophisticated technologies. Like Junger and Meynaud he fears the coming of technocracy and is not confident that there is much hope for the preservation of individual initiative. He notes that the United States Supreme Court is fighting a losing battle as it decides cases in favor of individual rights. He feels that despite legal protections, private corporations and other conglomerates will strengthen their controls progressively over employees and clients. While Miller regrets the passing of old liberties, Ernest Becker looks forward to a new era of freedom. For Becker, who follows in the line of Lifton and Kariel, freedom arises when human beings experiment with a wide range of possibilities and do not tie themselves down with limits fixed in advance. The present author attempts to go a step beyond Becker and show that a public morality based on creative freedom can be devised. It is in these three articles that the contrast between freedom and regimentation, which is a central theme of this book and of contemporary life, is brought out most clearly. If one accepts that quality of life, rather than stability, is the proper standard of political evaluation, there are still other choices to be faced. One of the most important of these decisions concerns whether one will evaluate political activities in terms of their effects upon opportunities for traditional liberties—such as freedoms of speech, enterprise, worship, and assembly—or in terms of their effects upon opportunities for realizing creative freedom.

Political Stability: Civic and Praetorian Polities

SAMUEL P. HUNTINGTON

Political systems can be distinguished by their levels of political institutionalization and their levels of political participation. In both cases the
differences are obviously differences in degree: no clear-cut line separates
the highly institutionalized polity from the disorganized polity; so also
no clear-cut line exists between one level of political participation and
another. To analyze the changes in both dimensions, however, it is necessary to identify different categories of systems, recognizing full well that
rarely will any actual political system in fact fit into any specific theoretically defined pigeonhole. In terms of institutionalization, it is perhaps
enough to distinguish those systems which have achieved a high degree of
political institutionalization from those which have achieved only a low
degree. In terms of participation, it seems desirable to identify three
levels: at the lowest level, participation is restricted to a small traditional
aristocratic or bureaucratic elite; at the medium level, the middle classes

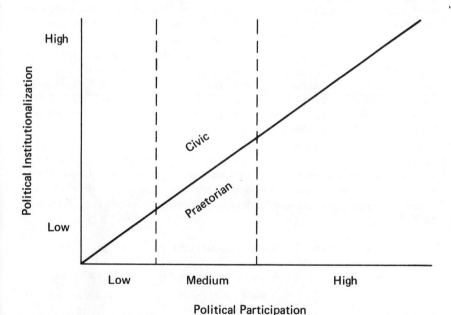

**FIGURE 1 POLITICAL INSTITUTIONALIZATION AND
POLITICAL PARTICIPATION**

have entered into politics; and in a highly participant polity, elite, middle class, and the populace at large all share in political activity.

It would be convenient to leave the matter there, but things are not quite so simple. The stability of any given polity depends upon the relationship between the level of political participation and the level of political institutionalization. The level of political institutionalization in a society with a low level of political participation may be much lower than it is in a society with a much higher level of participation, and yet the society with lower levels of both may be more stable than the society having a higher level of institutionalization and a still higher level of participation. Political stability, as we have argued, depends upon the ratio of institutionalization to participation. As political participation increases, the complexity, autonomy, adaptability, and coherence of the society's political institutions must also increase if political stability is to be maintained.

Modern polities are, in some measure, distinguished from traditional polities by their level of political participation. Developed polities are, in some measure, distinguished from underdeveloped ones by their level of political institutionalization. To these distinctions must now be added a third: the distinction between those polities where political participation is high relative to political institutionalization and those where institutionalization is high relative to participation. Political systems with low levels of institutionalization and high levels of participation are systems where social forces using their own methods act directly in the political sphere. For reasons elaborated below, such political systems are appropriately called praetorian polities. Conversely, political systems with a high ratio of institutionalization to participation may be termed civic polities. One society may thus have more highly developed political institutions than another and yet may also be more praetorian in character because of its still higher level of political participation.

Civic or praetorian societies may thus exist at various levels of political participation. The combination of the classification of societies according to their level of political participation, on the one hand, and their ratio of institutionalization to participation, on the other, produces, of course, a typology of six kinds of political systems, which are identified in Table 1.

TABLE 1.   TYPES OF POLITICAL SYSTEMS

Political Participation	Ratio of Institutionalization to Participation	
	HIGH: CIVIC	LOW: PRAETORIAN
Low: traditional	Organic (Ethiopia)	Oligarchical (Paraguay)
Medium: transitional	Whig (Chile)	Radical (Egypt)
High: modern	Participant (Soviet Union)	Mass (Argentina)

This typology may strike a familiar note to the historian of political ideas. Starting with a different set of categories but with similar concern for the conditions of political stability, our analysis has led to a typology of political systems strikingly similar to that of the classics. The ancient theorists divided political systems in two ways: according to the number of rulers and according to the nature of the rule. Their division of systems into those ruled by the one, the few, and the many corresponds in a rough sense to the distinctions made here, and by other modern political analysts, according to levels of political participation. The distinction between civic and praetorian polities corresponds roughly to the difference postulated by Plato, Aristotle, and other classical writers between legitimate or law-abiding states, where the rulers acted in the public interest, and perverted or law-neglecting systems, where the rulers acted in their own interests rather than those of the polity. "Those constitutions which consider the common interest are *right* constitutions," says Aristotle, and those "constitutions which consider only the personal interest of the rulers are all *wrong* constitutions, or *perversions* of the right forms."

As the Greeks recognized, the "right" constitutions might take a variety of forms, even as today the political systems of the United States, Great Britain, and the Soviet Union differ significantly from each other. The societies with perverted constitutions, in contrast, were societies which lacked law, authority, cohesion, discipline, and consensus, where private interests dominated public ones, where there was an absence of civic obligation and civic duty, where, again, political institutions were weak and social forces strong. Plato's degenerate states were ruled by various forms of appetite: by force, wealth, numbers, and charisma. They were manifestations of what Machiavelli called the corrupt state, dominated, in the words of one commentator, by "all sorts of license and violence, great inequalities of wealth and power, the destruction of peace and justice, the growth of disorderly ambition, disunion, lawlessness, dishonesty, and contempt for religion." Modern equivalents of the classical corrupt society are Kornhauser's theory of the mass society, where, in the absence of institutions, elites are accessible to masses and masses are available for mobilization by the elites, and Rapoport's concept of the praetorian state, where "private ambitions are rarely restrained by a sense of public authority; [and] the role of power (i.e. wealth and force) is maximized."

It is virtually impossible to classify such states in terms of their form of government. We can have little doubt that the United States is a constitutional democracy and the Soviet Union a communist dictatorship. But what is the political system of Indonesia, of the Dominican Republic, South Vietnam, Burma, Nigeria, Ecuador, Argentina, Syria? These countries have held elections, but they are clearly not democracies in the sense in which Denmark or New Zealand is a democracy. They have had authoritarian rulers, but they are not effective dictatorships like the communist states. At other times they have been dominated by highly personalistic, charismatic rulers or by military juntas. They are unclassifiable in terms of any particular governmental form because their distinguishing characteristic is the fragility and fleetingness of all forms of authority. Charismatic leader, military junta, parliamentary regime, populistic dictator follow each other in seemingly unpredictable and bewildering array. The patterns of political participation are neither stable nor institutionalized; they may oscillate violently between one form and another.

As Plato and Aristotle pointed out long ago, corrupt or praetorian societies often swing back and forth between despotism and mob-rule. "Where the pre-established political authority is highly autocratic," says Kornhauser, "rapid and violent displacement of that authority by a democratic regime is highly favorable to the emergence of extremist mass movements that tend to transform the new democracy in antidemocratic directions." Rapoport finds in Gibbon an apt summary of the constitutional rhythms of the praetorian state which "floats between the extremes of absolute monarchy and wild democracy." Such instability is the hallmark of a society lacking political community and where participation in politics has outrun the institutionalization of politics.

Civic polities, in contrast, have recognizable and stable patterns of institutional authority appropriate for their level of political participation. In traditional polities, these structures normally take the form of either a centralized bureaucratic empire or of a complex feudal monarchy, or some combination of these two. At the Whig level of middle-class participation, the dominant political institutions are normally parliamentary assemblies with members chosen through some limited form of elections. In the fully participant, modern polity, political parties supplement or replace the traditional political structures as the key institutions for organizing mass involvement in politics. At all levels of participation, however, political institutions are sufficiently strong to provide the basis of a legitimate political order and a working political community. The institutions impose political socialization as the price of political participation. In a praetorian society groups become mobilized into politics without becoming socialized by politics. The distinguishing characteristic of a highly institutionalized polity, in contrast, is the price it places on power. In a civic polity, the price of authority involves limitations on the resources that may be employed in politics, the procedures through which power may be acquired, and the attitudes that power wielders may hold. If the society is modern and complex, with a large number of social forces, individuals from any one of the social forces may have to make extensive changes in their behavior, values, and attitudes in the process of acquiring power through the political institutions of the society. They may well have to unlearn much which they have learned from family, ethnic group, and social class, and adapt to an entirely new code of behavior.

The development of a civic polity may have some relation to the stage of modernization and of political participation, but it is not directly dependent upon it. By the mid-twentieth century many of the more advanced Latin American nations had achieved comparatively high indices of literacy, per capita national income, and urbanization. In the mid-1950s, for instance, Argentina was economically and socially a highly developed country. Almost half the population lived in cities of over 20,000 people; 86 per cent of the people were literate; 75 per cent were engaged in nonagricultural employment; the per capita gross national product was over $500. Argentine politics, however, remained notably underdeveloped. "The public good," Sarmiento had said in the 1850s, "is a meaningless word—there is no 'public.'" A hundred years later the failure to develop effective political institutions meant the continued absence of public community. As one observer noted,

> The hard surface of military rule or the mottled aspect of Machiavellian balancing and intriguing have been the two masks of Argentine politics since 1930. The masks, most unhappily, do not disguise reality—they *are* the reality of Argentina's situation of weak government, a debility stemming from several fundamental causes. . . . The state is not firmly established as the ultimate arbiter of Argentine public life. The other institutions competing for men's loyalties permit a high degree of protection from the dictates of the state.

So long as a country like Argentina retained a politics of coup and counter-coup and a feeble state surrounded by massive social forces, it remained politically underdeveloped no matter how urbane, prosperous, and educated its citizenry.

In reverse fashion, a country may be politically highly developed with modern political institutions while still very backward in terms of modernization. India, for instance, was typically held to be the epitome of the underdeveloped society. Judged by the usual criteria of modernization, it was at the bottom of the ladder during the 1950s: per capita GNP of $72, 80 per cent illiterate, over 80 per cent of the population in rural areas, 70 per cent of the work force in agriculture, fourteen major languages, deep caste and religious differences. Yet in terms of political institutionalization, India was far from backward. Indeed, it ranked high not only in comparison with other modernizing countries in Asia, Africa, and Latin America, but also in comparison with many much more modern European countries. A well developed political system has strong and distinct institutions to perform both the "input" and the "output" functions of politics. India entered independence with not only two organizations, but two highly developed— adaptable, complex, autonomous, and coherent—institutions ready to assume primary responsibility for these functions. The Congress Party, founded in 1885, was one of the oldest and best organized political parties in the world; the Indian Civil Service, dating from the early nineteenth century, was appropriately hailed as "one of the greatest administrative systems of all time." The stable, effective, and democratic government of India during its first twenty years of independence rested far more on this institutional inheritance than it did on the charisma of Nehru. In addition, the relatively slow pace of modernization and social mobilization in India did not create demands and strains which the party and the bureaucracy were unable to handle. So long as these two organizations maintained their institutional strength, it was ridiculous to think of India as politically underdeveloped no matter how low its per capita income or how high its illiteracy rate.

Almost no other country attaining independence after World War II was institutionally as well prepared as India for self-government. In countries like Pakistan and the Sudan, institutional evolution was unbalanced: the civil and military bureaucracies were more highly developed than the political parties, and the military had strong incentives to move into the institutional vacuum on the input side of the political system and to attempt to perform interest aggregation functions. This pattern, of course, has also been common in Latin America. In countries like Guatemala, El

TABLE 2.   INSTITUTIONAL DEVELOPMENT AT TIME OF INDEPENDENCE

Input Institutions	Output Institutions	
	High	Low
High	India	N. Vietnam
Low	Sudan	Congo

Salvador, Peru, and Argentina, John J. Johnson pointed out, the military was "the country's best organized institution and is thus in a better position to give objective expression to the national will" than were parties or interest groups. In a very different category was a country like North Vietnam, which fought its way into independence with a highly disciplined political organization but which was distinctly weak on the administrative side. The Latin American parallel here would be Mexico, where, as Johnson put it, "not the armed forces but the PRI [Partido Revolucionario Institucional] is the best organized institution, and the party rather than the armed forces has been the unifying force at the national level." In yet a fourth category were those unfortunate states, such as the Congo, which were born with neither political nor administrative institutions. Many of these new states deficient at independence in one or both types of institutions were also confronted by high rates of social mobilization and rapidly increasing demands on the political system.

If a society is to maintain a high level of community, the expansion of political participation must be accompanied by the development of stronger, more complex, and more autonomous political institutions. The effect of the expansion of political participation, however, is usually to undermine the traditional political institutions and to obstruct the development of modern political ones. Modernization and social mobilization, in particular, thus tend to produce political decay unless steps are taken to moderate or to restrict its impact on political consciousness and political involvement. Most societies, even those with fairly complex and adaptable traditional political institutions, suffer a loss of political community and decay of political institutions during the most intense phases of modernization.

This decay in political institutions has been neglected or overlooked in much of the literature on modernization. As a result, the models and concepts which are hopefully entitled "developing" or "modernizing" are only partially relevant to many of the countries to which they are applied. Equally relevant would be models of corrupt or degenerating societies highlighting the decay of political organization and the increasing dominance of disruptive social forces. Who, however, has advanced such a theory of political decay or a model of a corrupt political order which might be useful in analyzing the political processes of the countries usually called "developing"? Perhaps the most relevant ideas are again the most ancient ones. The evolution of many contemporary new states, once the colonial guardians have departed, has not deviated extensively from the Platonic model. Independence is followed by military coups, as the "auxiliaries" take over. Corruption by the oligarchy inflames the envy of rising groups. Conflict between oligarchy and masses erupts into civil strife. Demagogues and street mobs pave the way for the despot. Plato's description of the means by which the despot appeals to the people, isolates and eliminates his enemies, and builds up his personal strength is a far less misleading guide to what has taken place in Africa and elsewhere than many things written yesterday.[1]

1. Perhaps the closest contemporary model comes not from a social scientist but from a novelist: William Golding. The schoolboys (newly independent elites) of *The Lord of the Flies* initially attempt to imitate the behavior patterns of adults (former Western rulers). Discipline and consensus, however, disintegrate. A demagogic military leader and his followers gain or coerce the support of a majority. The symbol of authority (the conch) is broken. The voices of responsibility (Ralph) and reason (Piggy) are deserted and harassed, and reason is destroyed.

The Performance
of Political Systems

KARL W. DEUTSCH

Some people adapt their attitudes toward political change simply according to their prejudices, as they have learned them from others or as they may fit the needs of their own personality. "Every boy and every gal that's born into this world alive," in the words of a song in *Iolanthe* by Gilbert and Sullivan, "is either a little liberal or else a little conservative." Some people are born conformists. They are simply in favor of the existing political order, whatever that may be. In a small town in the American Midwest, they would cheer for the American Legion; in a small town in Russia, they would be for the Communist Party. If they had been born in a New Guinea tribe, they would be loyal headhunters or cannibals. Other people are dissenters by nature, such as the nineteenth-century immigrant from Ireland who, arriving in America on election day, got off the ship and went straight to the polling place. Asked whether he knew anything about the candidates or issues, he replied: "No, I don't. But I want to vote against the government." A Philadelphia taxi driver in the 1960s said the same thing: "I pay no attention to politics but I always vote against the gang that's in."

In our time, politics is such a serious matter that neither unthinking conformism nor blind nonconformism will suffice. In order to decide intelligently whether a political system needs changing, and in what respects, we must know how it performs. We must know whether it produces the outcomes we want, and how well it does in producing them.

If we know how to analyze the workings of political systems and the machinery of government, we may feel less naive and uncritical about politics. We also may feel less helpless and bewildered by the actions of the governments under which we live. Systems theory and systems analysis may make us less inclined to search for demons and villains in political life, and to see it as a simple crusade of good against evil. Our questions may then become more pointed toward reality, and more likely to lead us to effective action.

THE USES OF SYSTEMS THEORY

Some years ago a student radical (who has since become an expert labor lawyer in the complicated field of workman's compensation) asked, "Who really determines American foreign policy?" The question was a little like that of the small boy who asks, "Where in the refrigerator is the little man who turns on the light when you open the refrigerator door?" Or the questions of primitive peoples: "Where is the god within the hurricane? Where is the spirit within the earthquake?" In effect, most such questions are attempts to personify the workings of systems.

A hurricane is a revolving disk of air, one mile high and 500 miles across, which is fed by streams of air in two dimensions and by the rising of air in a third dimension all the way to the stratosphere. It is a complicated but understandable system of storms which is part of a larger system of storm tracks. An earthquake is a system. And so is a war. Systems analysis thus may help us to see that the great catastrophes in history as well as in nature are properties of systems.

Systems do not always work for human good. Quite the contrary, the outcome of a system may be pernicious and destructive. Systems can be traps. They have a logic of their own, which goes even beyond the interests of the individuals whom they may temporarily reward. Many slaveowners, for example, benefited from the social system of slavery. Hence, they learned to believe in it and to defend it. They persisted in acting in accordance with this system even when it led to economic stagnation and civil war, the destruction of their homes, the loss of their property, and the death of their children.

Whether we speak of the catastrophes of nature or of man, the workings of a machine, or the slower changes in human politics, it is important to see that many developments in each of these cases are produced by systems. . . . A *system* is a collection of recognizable units or components which hang together and vary together, in a manner regular enough to be described. Political systems consist of political units and are connected mainly by political processes. We can try to analyze each system to see how it works, how its outcomes are produced, and how it can be changed. With the help of systems analysis, we can try to separate the properties of systems from individual interests, group interests, and the shares of persons in making decisions.

The political systems analyst uses his skill to understand how wide must be the *decision latitude* of an individual, office, organization, or a government, so that it can make a real difference to the outcome. He also tries to recognize when and where the momentum of a system is so great that officeholders become rubber stamps or "dependent variables," making very little difference to the outcome. For it is always important to know whether you can change the outcome of a system by appealing to the judgment of an individual, or by replacing one officeholder with another, or only by changing some or most of the structure of the system. The political analyst also tries to learn who would help make the change, who is interested in it, how to build a coalition big enough and motivated enough to produce the change, and how to aim one's resources with sufficient precision to bring about the change desired.

THE CONCEPT OF PERFORMANCE

A systems analyst is aided in his work by the concept of performance. Performance tests occur everywhere. Automobile firms take part in races to test the design and performance of their cars, and to improve them in the light of experience. But automobile races are tests not only of machines but also of drivers. A first-rate driver may win even with a less than first-rate car. In addition, every race also involves track or road conditions, weather, chance, and luck. Performance, in government as in automobiles, is thus determined jointly by systems, the individuals who operate them, and the environment in which they must function.

EFFECTIVENESS AND EFFICIENCY

Performance is the name we give to any outcome which is desired but improbable without an effort to produce it. Performance achieves some result which otherwise would not occur. If an outcome is certain, no one has to act to bring it about. No human being or organization has to perform anything to make the sun rise. By contrast, a room that is cold in winter may be warmed by the performance of a stove. Any performance is measured by the outcome attained as against the costs and other adverse conditions which make its attainment unlikely. Performance thus includes two dimensions: *effectiveness*—making an unlikely outcome more likely to happen—and *efficiency*—the ratio between change in the probability of the outcome and the costs incurred in producing it. The effectiveness of an automobile may be measured by the speed it can attain, and its efficiency by its consumption of gasoline. (Another kind of effectiveness might be the automobile's freedom from the need for repairs in over 100,000 miles of normal use; the corresponding efficiency would be measured against the higher cost for stronger and better original parts.)

A similar distinction between effectiveness and efficiency applies to the performance of governments and entire political systems. We ask not only how likely is a government or political system to attain some value we are interested in, but also at what price. The American government of the 1920s gave free rein to private business enterprise, with a minimum of government intervention. The enormous cost became evident in the 1930s when ten million people were made unemployed for years by the greatest of depressions. Semi-developed Russia was transformed into a modern industrial state by Stalin's iron-fisted methods, at vast cost in human suffering .

EMERGENCY POLITICS: PURSUIT OF A SINGLE VALUE

Performance is measured, first of all, by specific values. If there is a single overwhelming goal, the primary emphasis will be on *effectiveness* in reaching it. A leader of a political movement, a party, or a government may ask what headway is being made toward this particular goal. He may then give this goal priority over all others. Even democracies do so in time of war. After the attack on Pearl Harbor there was overwhelming agreement in the United States that the war against Nazi Germany and imperial Japan had to be won. Everything else for a time became subordinate to this goal. Similarly, when the Nazis invaded Russia, and Stalin's dictatorship was at war with Germany, Winston Churchill promptly offered Stalin an alliance. He was asked in the House of Commons how he could justify allying Britain with such an immoral dictatorship as Stalin's. Mr. Churchill replied that if the Hitler government should invade hell, His Majesty's government would offer the devil a treaty of alliance. This, incidentally, was a paraphrase of the statement by Lenin a generation earlier that the Bolsheviks would enter an alliance "with the devil and his grandmother" if it would bring about the victory of the Russian Revolution. With victory in war or revolution as the only primary goal, the best system of government is that which appears most likely to win.

If there is more than one major value, however, the question of cost and efficiency cannot be ignored. If justice and other conceptions of the national interest are as important or more important to people than the military effort, if a large part of the people do not believe in the justice of a war or in the war's being in the national interest, then the issue of priorities arises. Thus in the late 1960s, many Americans said, "Carrying on this war is not our paramount goal. Vietnam is not the most important problem facing the United States. It is more urgent to improve our own society right here at home."

In the long run no single goal, no matter how just or admirable, can be pursued completely. The methods of emergency thinking and *emergency government*—the argument that one would do anything, override any scruples, make any arrangements, pay any price to get a goal—are psychologically and organizationally tolerable only for limited amounts of time. The pursuit of one overwhelming goal year after year will change and distort the personalities of individuals, the behaviors of small groups, and the structure of a government. It can even destroy the moral fabric of society. If it is justifiable to use any means to achieve a desired end, if violence or concealment is acceptable, as in a wartime crisis, then why not use the technique of the "Big Lie"? If you want followers, why not gain them by deception? If someone disputes your leadership, or disagrees with your goal or your methods, why not jail him, or assassinate his character?

In every large emergency, people are tempted to set aside the basic rights of individuals and groups, such as free speech, freedom of assembly, or due process of law. In the late 1960s, General Lewis B. Hershey, then Director of Selective Service in the United States, ordered active protestors against the draft to be inducted forthwith into the army. His involuntary retirement followed. If basic rights are set aside briefly, the damage is limited. If emergency rule violates them for a longer time, the damage to constitutional government will be severe, and may prove fatal.

MULTIPLE GOALS AND OPEN-ENDED VALUES

Over any longer period of time it is vitally important for people to learn to restore to their governments the capacity to pursue many goals without neglecting any of them. A good political system is able to balance different values, to accept the possibility of error and to correct it, and to accept the likelihood that there are many questions to which the exact answer is not yet known. The poet Bertolt Brecht, a life-long believer in communism, once said to his Communist readers, "Shouldn't we ask our friends to make a list of all those questions to which they do not yet know an answer?" Brecht was reminding them of a general truth, valid for all ideologies. It is important to keep open the frontier to the unknown so that we know where we must still seek for answers. *Multiple goal-seeking* capacities and research capabilities must be included, therefore, among essential performance criteria for any government or political system that is to endure.

It was in this frame of mind that Thomas Jefferson worked on the draft of the American Declaration of Independence. At one stage, the draft document spoke of men's "unalienable rights" and went on: "These rights are life, liberty, and property." Jefferson then changed the text. He crossed out "These rights are" and substituted "Among these rights are," making clear that men's unalienable rights were not necessarily limited to any particular number. He also struck out the word "property" and substituted "the pursuit of happiness." Some scholars think he did so believing that in future centuries people might be less concerned with property but would always search for happiness. In any case, "happiness" included much more than property, and it was more open to the changing needs of future generations. Thus amended, the Declaration was signed and published, giving shape to the spirit of the new nation. It became one of America's greatest documents and a testimony to the open-ended nature of the American dream.

THE BUDGET: FIRST TESTS OF PERFORMANCE

"For warfare, three things are needed," wrote the Austrian General Montecucculi in the seventeenth century: "money, money, and once again money." Much the same is true for government. To get anything done anywhere, a government is likely to need money in the amount required at the time and place it is needed. The ability of a government to raise money, and then to spend it wisely, is a major test of its performance. If a government has to do several things, it must plan to have money available for all of them and it must plan how to get it. A summary of these plans is called a *budget*. Every modern national government needs a budget, and so does each of its administrative subdivisions. What a government plans for in its budget will reveal its values. How well it plans and executes its budget is a first test of its performance.

Anyone who knows how to read a budget can know the goals of a government. If a government plans to build many highways, its budget for road construction will be large. If a city plans to increase opportunities and facilities for education, its education budget will increase. If a national government decides to acquire expensive new weapons, its defense budget will rise—and so may those of other nations. *Budgetary analysis* is the art and skill of reading a budget so carefully that the analyst can tell for what purposes the government's financial resources will be spent, and usually also how its spending pattern will have changed from those of the previous years. Budgetary analysis thus may serve as a test of both political intentions and performances.

REVENUE BUDGETS AND THE ART OF COLLECTING TAXES

What holds for public expenditures also holds for public *revenues*—the way the government expects to get the money which it plans to spend. The revenue budget—the income side of a budget—will reveal which groups the government is willing to burden more heavily and which ones will be let off more lightly. Governments favoring the rich at the expense of the poor tend to use poll taxes which are collected in equal amounts per head of population or, as in past decades in the United States, per head of voters. Governments that are solicitous of special groups—such as mothers, churches, universities, or oil producers—may grant them special tax exemptions or allowances. Governments that want to collect revenue in accordance with ability to pay tend to use *progressive taxes*. These taxes, such as corporate and individual income taxes in most modern countries, progress to higher tax rates as the taxpayer's income increases. *Regressive taxes* have the opposite effect: a uniform sales tax on bread tends to fall most heavily on the poor. Poll taxes usually are regressive in their impact, too.

The revenue side of a budget will also reveal much about the capabilities of a government or an entire political system. The less income a government gets the less it can do. Generally the art of collecting taxes, as J. B. Colbert once said, resembles the art of plucking a goose: it consists in getting the largest amount of feathers with the fewest squawks. The tax system of a country thus depends in part on which groups can squawk loudest and most effectively. Politicians anticipating the reactions of such groups—on whose support they may depend—tax them lightly, if at all. This is what happens in many underdeveloped countries. Extremely underdeveloped countries collect most of their revenue at their borders, generally at ports of entry. Tariffs and export taxes—and foreign grants and loans—tend to be the major sources of income for their governments. Somewhat more highly developed countries collect much of their income through *indirect taxes* on trade within their borders, and sometimes through excises at the boundaries of their cities. Highly developed countries collect most of their revenue through *direct taxes* on individuals, households, and business enterprises. (The Soviet Union raises most of its tax revenue through a combination of *turnover* and profit transfer taxes at the factory level.) Progressive direct income taxes tend to be more just and humane—and they bring in more money. The ability to use taxes effectively is thus an additional test of government performance.

DEFICIT FINANCING

Governments have another potential source of income besides taxes, loans, and what they earn from public services. They can deliberately spend more money than they take in, and unlike housewives and business firms they can get away with it. For governments can create money—and most of them do—and they can compel anyone in the country to accept this money as "legal tender" for paying taxes or settling debts. In spending a billion dollars more than it has collected, a government may either borrow the money and pay interest on it or it may print it or create it in other ways. The last two practices are known as *deficit financing*.

If a government prints or otherwise creates it, the purchasing power of the remaining money in the country will be somewhat diluted. When this happens there may be some *inflation*—more money purchasing the same amount of goods. Inflation acts like an indirect tax that falls unequally on different groups. People hurt by inflation—housewives, consumers, creditors, white-collar workers, civil servants, the military, pensioners, and others living on fixed incomes—may turn against the government. In contrast, debtors, farmers, manufacturers, and skilled union labor will be little troubled or may even be quite satisfied with the government's policy. Whether the government then stays in power will depend less on the amount of the inflation and more on the strength and attitudes of these contending interest groups. Inflation may not necessarily occur, however. If there are unemployed men and resources within the country, the new money created by the government may stimulate demand and induce the production of additional goods and services which might counter the inflation wholly or in part. The government, of course, will get its money whether there are idle resources in the country or not, but if there are unemployed resources, deficit financing may actually promote employment and prosperity. How skillfully a government foresees the effects of its financial policies, and how well it controls its own actions, constitutes another test of its performance.

BUDGETARY PLANNING AND CONTROL

Ordinarily budgets are prepared for one year ahead. In the case of large public expenditures or investments, however, some countries use capital budgets or development budgets which are planned for several years ahead. The five-year plans of the Soviet Union and other countries are the most elaborate form of such budgeting, comprising much of the country's national economy. The art of *budget forecasting* aims at predicting how much money each of a government's several activities will receive in the next year's budget or in the budgets of other future years. A rough rule of thumb seems to be that most items in a large government budget will not differ by more than 10 per cent from the sums budgeted in the preceding year. Changes of more than 10 per cent, either upward or downward, are no longer matters of routine; they are likely to require relatively substantial political decisions.

A budget is not only a tool of action but also of control. It enables a government to control its own actions, by making sure that subordinate offices and agencies spend their budgetary allocations on the purposes intended, and that the amounts spent stay within budgetary limits. Most countries assign this control function to special national accounting offices or comptrollers general. The United States also has a Bureau of the Budget which controls the requests of the various agencies for future appropriations to make certain that they are compatible with each other, with government policy, and with expected income.

The budget can be a tool for controlling the government from outside. Whoever controls the budget can control most of what a government can do. Countries whose budgets are controlled by foreign powers or creditors are not fully sovereign. In sovereign countries, on the other hand, legislatures or the people can use the budget to control executive power. When the British Parliament in the seventeenth century gained full control of this *power of the purse,* it wrested effective power from the Crown. Even in the twentieth century, the day on which the British Chancellor of the Exchequer presents the government's annually proposed budget to Parliament for its approval remains one of the high points in British political life.

In the United States, the double process of authorization and appropriation of each major budgetary item is intended to strengthen Congressional control over the executive. It is partly counteracted by the skill of some executive departments in concealing their specific expenditures under vague budgetary headings and in exceeding budgetary estimates. Sometimes, under systems of direct democracy, as in some Swiss cantons, certain budgetary items must be approved directly by the voters.

In the muted contest between the controllers and the controlled in any country, there is no substitute for the vigilance of informed legislators and voters. In all modern countries, the need for some executive discretion must be balanced against the need for some political control of the bureaucracy through the budget. How well this balance is maintained is yet another test of performance. But all such budgetary tests do not tell what quality of life a government buys for its people. Here we must ask not how much money is collected and spent but what qualitative and quantitative results the combination of money and politics produces.

SOME QUALITATIVE TESTS OF PERFORMANCE

The performance of government relates to both the present and the future. It must aim at *attaining* as much as possible of each of the many values which peoples now desire, and it must keep the pursuit of all these values as *compatible* as possible. But it must also preserve and enhance the capacity to seek *new* values in the future and to attain these, too. Serving these three tasks, governments must often work for subtle configurations of values which are not easily spelled out, but which people can sometimes recognize by intuition. People then speak of the quality of a political system or of the *quality of life* in a society. We all know some simple tests for this kind of quality: how breathable the air still is, how well the garbage gets collected, how safe it is to walk home after dark, how many children are properly fed and how many go hungry, how many sick are well attended and how many are not attended at all, how many people lead meaningful lives and how many lead "lives of quiet desperation."

THE QUALITY OF LEADERS

A more profound test of the quality of a political system was stressed by Pericles in ancient Greece and by John Stuart Mill in nineteenth-century England. It consists in the kinds of individuals who grow up under it, and in the kind of persons it elevates to leadership. Clearly, in all countries the personalities of leaders will vary as they succeed one another in the course of time. But the personalities and actions of Britain's Prime Ministers and cabinet ministers since 1945, such as Winston Churchill, Clement Attlee, Anthony Eden, Harold Macmillan, and Harold Wilson, say something about the quality of British politics since World War II. Similarly the personalities and acts of Adolf Hitler, Joseph Goebbels, Hermann Goering, Heinrich Himmler, Ernst Kaltenbrunner, Franz Hoess, and Adolf Eichmann say something about the quality of the Nazi political system.

A look at the personalities of American leaders reminds us of the great variety of political life in the United States. American leaders have included men of vast accomplishment and great humanity like Franklin D. Roosevelt and Dwight D. Eisenhower. They have included leaders of great promise cut off before their time, like Martin Luther King, and John and Robert Kennedy; and they have included many men of lesser stature, each stubbornly doing his best as he saw it. A longer view of American history would give us a similar picture. The roster of Presidents is composed of great leaders like Washington, Jefferson, Jackson, and Lincoln, as well as of lesser men like Martin Van Buren, James Buchanan, Chester A. Arthur, and Calvin Coolidge. But in nearly two centuries the American political system has never yet elevated to high office any man who was outstandingly criminal, cruel, or insanely ambitious.

THE QUALITY OF ORDINARY PEOPLE

Another test for the quality of a political system is in the types of personality and behavior it produces among ordinary men and women. How numerous are the drunks, drug addicts, and suicides? How many murders are committed: How frequent are other crimes of callousness or cruelty? Some of the answers can be found in the crime statistics of each country. Others can be found in its surveys of social attitudes and mental health.

But the quality of life under a political system does not depend only on crime and acts legally defined as antisocial. How many persons suffer from race discrimination and how many people practice it? How many "authoritarian personalities" do we find, how many petty tyrants of the office or the breakfast table? What is the most frequently found personality type among the people—the *"modal personality"*[1]—which accounts for so much of what is called "national character"?

And the quality of life is determined as much or more by the presence of good things as by the absence of bad ones. How many people volunteer to help those in need? How many will help their neighbors, shelter refugees, answer an appeal for blood donations? How many acts of interracial decency do we find? In how many cities can people leave their coins on unwatched newspaper piles without the money being stolen? In how many homes are the doors left unlocked? How many jurors and judges treat the accused as innocent until proven guilty? And how many taxpayers are honest in filling out their tax returns?

Every reader may apply this list of questions to the community in which he lives. American readers may find that their country is seriously vulnerable to homicide, carelessness, intermittent corruption, and the destructive overuse of stimulants. They will also find evidence of remarkable generosity and openness, respect for people, and confidence and trust in them.

POLITICAL CULTURE: THE SUM OF QUALITIES

Taken together, all these qualitative aspects of a political system add up to the political culture underlying a country or a people. The notion of "culture" is used here similar to the way it is used by anthropologists. The *culture* of a people means the collection of all its traditions and habits, particularly those transmitted by parents to children and by children to each other. It includes their common stock of images and perceptions of the world in which they live. It thus includes their views of what is practical and possible, and what is not; what is beautiful and what is ugly; what is good and what is bad; what is right and what is wrong. Culture functions like a traffic code for behavior. It tells people where to go ahead and where to stop, and where to make detours.

1. For a discussion of modal personality and national character, refer to A. Inkeles and D. Levinson, "National Character: The Study of Modal Personality and Sociocultural Systems," in Gardner Lindzey, ed., *Handbook of Experimental Psychology,* 2nd. ed. (Reading, Mass.: Addison-Wesley Publishers, 1969), Vol. 4, pp. 418-506.

Culture has implications for political behavior. All cultures, say the anthropologists Florence Kluckhohn and Fred Strodtbeck, can be compared in terms of a few basic questions.[2] Three of these are most relevant for us here. (1) Does a culture teach men mainly to submit to their environment, to work along with it, or to master it? (2) Is it oriented chiefly toward the past, the present, or the future? (3) Does it see human relations primarily as *lineal*, that is, in terms of fathers and sons, superiors and subordinates, or as *collateral*, that is, in terms of brothers and sisters, equals and colleagues?

People who are used to submitting to their environment will easily submit to rulers, foreign or native, and may feel frightened and bewildered when faced with the task of ruling themselves. People accustomed to working along with their environment in constant two-way communication also may favor compromise and decisions by unanimity, even at the cost of much delay; they may dislike quick decisions by majority rule. (This trait, common among many of the emerging peoples in Asia and Africa, often has exasperated Western economic development experts.) People taught to master nature will resort more readily to power and manipulation. They will seek quick decisions overriding all doubts and obstacles, disregarding the needs of dissenting opinions, minorities, and the less obvious consequences of their actions. Such masters of nature will win many triumphs in technology and politics, but in their rush ahead they may leave a trail of neglected vital problems such as eroded soil, polluted air, careless wars, and ill-treated minorities. Those who have learned to work *with* nature—learning from her as often as imposing their will on her—may learn from their dialogue with nature the art of working through dialogues with their fellow men.

Likewise, people's basic view of the relative importance of the past, the present, and the future will shape their attitudes toward economic growth, political reform, and to the needs of old and young. A culture looking more to the past than to either the present or the future may be better in preserving monuments than in accelerating innovations. It may enact laws for old-age pensions many years before expanding large-scale public higher education for the young. Britain passed legislation for old-age pensions in 1908, but legislation for greatly expanded public higher education only after 1960. A culture looking to the future, such as that of the United States, passed these kinds of legislation in reverse order: land grant colleges came in the 1860s and Social Security in 1935.

Finally, if a people tends to regard its members as equals, as Americans and many Frenchmen do, its politics will be fairly different from that of a people who tend to divide its members into superiors and subordinates, as Japanese, Germans, and, to a lesser extent, Englishmen have done during many periods of their history.

Political culture is related to the *frequency* and *probability* of various kinds of political behavior and not to their rigid determination. England

2. See Florence R. Kluckhohn *et al., Variations in Value Orientations* (New York: Harper & Row, 1961).

has had its great forward-looking reformers, Germany and Japan have had their democrats, the United States has produced its share of conservatives and conservationists. Nonetheless, the different political cultures of these countries can be seen in the record of their past behavior and will not soon disappear completely from their future actions.

from The Supreme Court and American Capitalism

ARTHUR SELWYN MILLER

The imaginative creation of new institutions and relations between governments and private groups is a critical need of our time.—Roy Blough

We take as our theme in this [essay] both Professor Blough's statement reproduced above and Eric Hoffer's recent aphorism: "The business of a society with an automated economy can no longer be business." During the two centuries since the Declaration of Independence, there has been one principal constant in American economic life: change, of a nature and character that makes the nation of today fundamentally different from that of the late eighteenth century. Change is not only built into the social structure; it is accelerating. The impact of the scientific-technological revolution means that even more rapid social and legal change may be foreseen in the future.

One consequence of the development is what Dean Don K. Price has called "constitutional relativity":

Science, by helping technology to increase prosperity, has weakened the kind of radicalism that comes from a lack of economic security. But science has helped to produce other kinds of insecurity: the fear of the new kind of war that science has made possible; the fear of rapid social and economic change; and the fear that we no longer have a fixed and stable constitutional system by which to cope with our political problems. And these fears are breeding a new type of radicalism.

The new radicalism is ostensibly conservative. It springs in part from the resentment men feel when their basic view of life is unsettled—as medieval man must have felt when he was asked to think of a universe that did not revolve around the earth, or as some physicists felt a generation or two ago when their colleagues began to talk about relativity and indeterminacy. The new conservative radicalism had a fundamentalist faith in the written Constitution, and the high priests of that faith seem to have desecrated it. The Supreme Court has applied relative policy standards in place of the fixed rules of precedent; and worse still it has admitted into its system of thinking not only the moral law as revealed in tradition, but arguments from the sciences, even the behavioral sciences.

The Constitution does not embody absolutes. In any clause that is the subject of litigation, constitutional relativity is the rule, whether it be in personal liberties, such as freedom of speech, or whether it be in economic liberties, such as due process of law. Decisions on constitutional matters are made either by according a high degree of deference to the political branches of government (as in economics) or by balancing the interests between individual and society (as in personal freedoms).

Dean Price's observation about constitutional relativity is drawn from a book that develops the impact of the scientific-technological revolution on the constitutional order. One such impact is affirmation of a proposition advanced by others—for example, Adolf A. Berle and Paul P. Harbrecht—that traditional ideas of property are in need of redefinition. Price makes this acute statement:

The most fundamental disagreement between the nations of the Western political tradition and those of the Communist world does not turn on their attitudes toward private property. The greatest mistake in Western political strategy consists in committing itself to the defense of property as the main basis for the preservation of freedom. Private property is indeed a useful and important means to that end, but it is not an absolute end in itself, and the effect of scientific advance on a technological civilization has made property less and less important as a source of power, and as a way of limiting political power. Far more fundamental is the way men think about the desirability of organizing truth in the service of power, and using power to determine truth.

New institutional forms are being created; property as the basis of both political *and* economic power is being redefined. Ownership of things is less important than ownership of promises (such as shares of stock); and both are less important than the ability to control the gigantic entities of the modern American economy. Control lies with the corporate managers, who in many respects are self-perpetuating oligarchies wielding immense economic (and political) power.

Even more, power in a political sense may well be passing to other centers: To take two noteworthy illustrations, the scientific-technological elite—what Dean Price labels the "scientific estate"—and those who control the universities and other "nonprofits" in what Professor Daniel Bell has called the "post-industrial society." Says Bell: "To speak rashly: if the dominant figures of the past hundred years [in American society] have been the entrepreneur, the businessman, and the industrial executive, the 'new men' are the scientists, the mathematicians, the economists, and the engineers of the new computer technology." The shorthand term for the new man of power is "technocrat" and for the social system that of "technocracy." Both terms are not new; according to Bell, they were coined in 1919. During the 1930s, technocracy had a brief flurry as a social movement and as a panacea for the depression. With the coming of the Second World War, it became moribund. Its revival in the present era takes a different form and is not tied in with a social or political movement, as was technocracy in the 1930s. Rather, it may be seen in the rise of possible new centers of decentralized power within the body politic; Bell identifies these as the universities and other nonprofit institutions, such as research corporations, industrial laboratories, and experimental stations. If this description proves valid, then the post-industrial society—technocracy—will, in large part, be the resultant, as Dean Price avers, of the scientific-technological revolution. More, it will be closely allied with the government-business complex. We suggested . . . that a form of economic planning was coming into existence, the institutions of which were given the shorthand label of "the corporate state." The direction in which American society may well be moving, then, is toward the corporate state, the governing elite of which is a corps of technocrats (as defined above) rather than businessmen or political officers. Time only will tell whether this tendency, already evident, will become a fact—whether, that is, the forces of science and technology and the pressures from living in an interdependent world will produce such a radically new social order.

To the extent that such a social order does come into being, then one with an eye to history can well cast back to the early 1930s in order to show that two notions then current are ideas "whose time has come." These are the governmental attempt in 1933 to establish a form of the corporate state in the National Industrial Recovery Act . . . and the social movement called technocracy. . . . The attempt to graft the corporate state on the American economy fell before the Supreme Court, which invalidated it in 1935; and technocracy died out with the coming of the war. Both were premature in the 1930s, but they seem now to be flowering (without, however, the same labels). The result likely will be a fusion of corporativism and technocracy. If so, it may be said without fear of contradiction that the Supreme Court is emphatically not going to invalidate the new system. Rather, it will content itself at most with hit-and-miss review of individual acts of parts of the techno-corporate complex. This should occasion no surprise, for certain it is that the Justices have neither the desire nor—more importantly—the competence to deal with the complex issues presented therein. The nature of the American political economy of the future, in other words, will be little dependent on what the nine middle-aged or elderly men who sit on the highest tribunal might say about it.

The other side of that coin is that the governmental decisions of basic significance for the economy will come from the avowedly political branches of government, and from them, mainly the executive-administrative agencies. During the course of American history, a steady tendency may be perceived in the growing intervention of government in decisions previously thought to be private. The state has become an important and pervasive participant in economic matters. The American economy, as a consequence, is well on its way toward becoming managed. Governmental decisions to spend, to tax, to regulate currency, and to do a host of other economic matters, will become far more important than sporadic judicial decisions issued by a Court that must depend on the *bona fides* of others to put its commands into reality and that must depend on the accident of litigation to act at all.

In saying this, however, it is not implied that government is autonomous—that the elites of the private corporations and the institutions of the post-industrial society do not and will not have a great influence on the nature of official decision-making. Quite the contrary. In all probability, decisions will be a product of a mixture of law and politics—of pre-existing command or interdictory rule and of the accommodation of conflicting interests in the political arena. This means that the question to ask is not only, Who has *formal authority* to make economic decisions in government? but rather, Who exercises *effective control* over those decisions? When one probes beneath the surface, it is soon apparent that the decisions of governmental agencies—of the political branches generally—are the result of a parallelogram of conflicting political forces. Even in the ostensibly independent regulatory commissions, decision-making is a marriage of politics and law. Accordingly, the desuetude of the Supreme Court does not necessarily mean the pre-eminent power of the bureaucracy or of Congress; rather, it means a complex interaction of power wielders in the techno-corporate state. The content of decisions, in other words, is influenced by the actions of private groups in the polity. The government official has the *authority* to make the decisions, that is, he is clothed with the formal capacity to decide, but what is decided is not necessarily, or even usually, within his control. Effective *power* over decisions, that is to say, often lies elsewhere.

Whatever may be the situation, then, with respect to other issues of public policy—and it is by no means clear that the pattern is essentially different in those other areas—within the field of economic decisions, the United States Supreme Court has little or no real *power*. It may be clothed with some *authority*, but what its impact might be is quite another matter. The suggestion made here is that the impact is minimal at most, and probably even less, as the United States ever increasingly becomes the techno-corporate state.

Another factor to be emphasized is that old lines of political and economic demarcation are breaking down. At one time, perhaps, it was possible for students of government and of society to make credible distinctions between what was in the public sector and what was consigned to private initiative and to say that policy problems could be divided between foreign and domestic. If so, that state of affairs no longer is true: America has moved beyond that to a new order, one in which the public and private sectors are inextricably intertwined and in which the line between external and internal is increasingly being blurred. The old order is gone, irretrievably; a new order is being created; the age is one of transition, beset, as never before in human history, with changes of the most far-reaching nature. In its most fundamental aspect, the problem facing policy makers is that of managing change—something rather new for Americans. As Daniel Bell has said, "Perhaps the most important social change of our time is the emergence of a process of direct and deliberate contrivance of change itself. Men now seek to anticipate change, measure the course of its direction and its impact, control it, and even shape it for predetermined ends." Within the United States, this has produced the interlocking of public government and private corporation, aided and abetted by the universities and other segments of the third sector of the economy. A continuum may be constructed, in this respect, running from the corporations (such as the major weapons pro-

ducers) that are obviously closely allied to government to those (such as
A.T. & T.) that have only a minor part of their overall income coming
from government. At both ends of the continuum, and also in between,
may be seen a growing partnership between government and business, a
partnership widely recognized by corporate managers. Witness, for example, this statement by a prominent business executive: "Since the
early part of this century we have been developing a new form of public-
private society. . . . Call it what you will, the fact remains that this kind
of government is here to stay, and those who would accomplish almost
anything of public interest must work with the government. I say work
'with' it, not 'for' it." The essential point is that certain societal demands
exist, which must and will be fulfilled, if not by business then by government. More likely, these demands—mainly those for higher material levels
of well-being—will be realized, if at all, through a partnership of government and business. (What this means, among other things, is that individualism is dead; this will be discussed shortly.)

The same sort of blurring may be seen in the fact that public-policy
problems tend to have both external and internal—foreign and domestic—
characteristics. In a statement that encompasses both dimensions presently
under discussion, Arnold Toynbee in 1959 asserted: "The businessman
of the future . . . will be one of the key figures in a world civil service."
By this, Dr. Toynbee apparently meant that business and government
would grow closer together, while simultaneously transcending national
boundaries. If this forecast be accurate, then some sort of corporativism
seems to be in the offing.

In sum, then, the nation-state and the corporation—the twin institutions of the postfeudal and early industrial era—are in the process of
profound alteration; they are breaking up and moving closer together.
What the ultimate form will be cannot be predicted with certainty. What
can be said, however, is that the sharp separation between government
and business, once so evident in the United States, will be increasingly
blurred. The demands of the American people, articulated through government in what has . . . been called the Positive State, finds a counterpart in the principle of the social responsibility of business. The two
institutions are partners. More, the problems of economic, and political,
order now are planetary, not national. The government-business partnership will more and more have to face up to that hard fact.

Finally, it must be said that the American ideal of individualism is
dead. Although the autonomous man has long been the democratic hero,
it is nevertheless true that the core of industrialization, and thus of modern capitalism, is not independence, but interdependence. The autonomous individual does not exist as such; the human being spends his life
as a member of groups and gets his significance only as a member of a
group. He is important in the economic sense only insofar as he can become part of a collectivity—a corporation, a trade union, a farm group, a
consumers cooperative, and the like. As Professor John William Ward has
said, "Our society, like all modern industrial societies, is characterized

by economic and social interdependence, specialization of activity, and large-scale organizations—social phenomena that pose troublesome problems for traditional American attitudes toward the relation of the individual to society." It is a paradoxical fact that, whereas the Supreme Court in recent decades has been busily engaged in seeking to maximize individual liberties—in effect, through a merger of the concepts of liberty and equality—the growth of economic enterprise has created a social milieu in which individual liberties or freedoms are not high on the list of preferred values. Uniformity cultivated through mass advertising and astute use of the mass media is a requirement of industrialism. In the final analysis, furthermore, Americans, according to Professor William Withers, are "more wedded to materialism than to individualism"; where they have had a choice, or could make conscious decisions, "they chose the solution that led to greater material satisfaction, even at the sacrifice of individual freedom."

Thus it is that the recent Supreme Court decisions that appear to enhance the liberty and dignity of the individual come at precisely the time when on-rushing technology and industrial organization make the realization of those values unlikely at best, impossible in all probability. The technological imperatives demand social organization and social control; these organizations are both public and private, and the controls emanate from both sources. The Court is a weak reed indeed on which to rely to further a vanished individualism—even if it could be convincingly demonstrated that people generally wanted that sort of society, by no means a self-evident proposition. Erich Fromm's *Escape from Freedom*, although written about the Europe of the 1930s, seems particularly apposite. The clear lesson to be drawn is not that people want freedom or that the Supreme Court can force them to be free, but that they want material prosperity—and are quite willing to pay the price of organization and control to achieve it.

In the final analysis, the impact of the Supreme Court on the nature and thrust of the American economy will be, in the immortal words of Senator Everett McKinley Dirksen, about like that of "a snowflake wafting down upon the bosom of the mighty Potomac." Even if one assumes (without hard evidence) that the decisions of the Court have had importance in the past, the economics of the future will be determined by other factors—by the actions of government generally, which in turn will reflect the exigencies of the times. It simply does not seem possible that the American people—or American business—will permit nine men, with no special economic competence, to set fundamental policies in economic affairs. However wise the nine may be, the very nature of present litigation techniques and the adversary system is not adequate to the need of either the routine day-to-day decisions nor to the setting of fundamental policy. Doubtless, decisions will emanate from the High Bench, but their total impact will be small indeed; they will be of importance to that segment of the legal profession, academic and practicing bar, that earns its livelihood following what the Court does. For others—those who live in the rarified heights of big business and big government—what the Court might say will have less and less significance as the years go by. At the most, the Justices will be in the position, and have the same approximate power, as someone writing editorials about some of the issues of economic policy.... That conclusion may also prove valid for other areas of public policy.

If the Court reorganized itself so as to permit a more adequate flow of information to it and to enhance its institutional capacity to grapple with the complicated factual issues present in economic-policy cases, then it might be possible to project a greater role for the Court in the future. But there is little evidence that such a reorganization can or will take place. The High Bench remains essentially static in the age of what economist Kenneth E. Boulding has called "the second great transition in the history of mankind." Litigation—courts, generally—are products of a feudalistic, pre-industrial age; even legislatures may be said to be in the same category. Beyond feudalism, beyond industrialism, in the technologically oriented society, manned by technocrats, governed by "rational" processes, and highly organized and bureaucratized—a situation in which the Supreme Court seems oddly out of place.

One need not—indeed, should not—welcome such a development. For it means that the United States has entered an era dominated by administration and by the expert. Humanistic values are being lost in the quest for efficiency. The individual is being submerged in a melange of collectivities, public and private, that interlock in a system of the "new feudalism." American capitalism is far different today from what it was in 1787, when the Constitution was written. (It is the conceit of lawyers that the Supreme Court has had a major part in effectuating those changes.) Capitalism will be different "tomorrow"—in the next two or three decades. Possible preservation of the values of individualism and even perhaps of the dignity of the individual will depend on whether new institutions can be created; as Professor Blough said in the headnote to this [essay], there is a critical need for the "imaginative creation of new institutions and relations between governments and private groups." The need is critical simply because the factor of change—epidemic in society—means that time-honored ways of doing things are in need of re-examination and restructuring. Law and lawyers tend to react to change, rather than guiding or managing it, and thus seem to be fated always to be bringing up the rear. The legal profession, including the august Supreme Court of the United States, appears at times to be trying to preserve values—of individualism, of humanism—that, because of advancing technology and the organizational revolution, seem forever to be gone.

Those values are gone even though, as Victor Obenhaus has recently put it, two polar forces seem now to be in tension. On the one hand, are those that are freeing man from burdensome physical labor and thus creating a leisure society and, on the other hand, is "the closer integration of society and the mutual dependence of men, intra- and internationally." In the final analysis, the question of American capitalism is a question of the nature of man. The efforts of courts and even of governments to alter that nature, whatever it might be, seem feeble indeed. What does not seem feeble is the possibility of control over the individual by the collectivities produced through the organizational revolution. *That* not only appears possible; it seems to be probable. For the nature of man is to some indeterminate extent a resultant of the environment in which he lives. Man's technical resources have become enormous, but his social and psychological conflicts are far from resolved; they may in fact have been exacerbated in recent decades. War, overpopulation, excessive use of scarce resources, environmental pollution, more hunger in the developing nations, economic and intellectual stagnation that may appear with the achievements of the Positive State—all these and more add up to the nightmarish possibility of an Orwellian world of *1984* looming ever closer. The economic institutions of the future may well be a part of George Orwell's prescient forecast of things to come.

Should this dreary prospect in fact come about, then it will likely be without major amendment or other alteration to the basic Constitution. Americans have learned well what Henry George long ago called "an axiom of statesmanship . . .—that great changes can be brought about under old forms." The words of the Constitution will remain the same, but techniques of interpretation that already have embedded concepts of relativity deeply and probably irretrievably will mean that new institutions can be produced within the framework of the Constitution of 1787 as interpreted not only by the Supreme Court, but also by other governmental officials. The exigencies of the future can be accommodated within that document.

The Ethical Society

ERNEST BECKER

What does it mean, then, to love one's country, and what does it mean to be a patriot? If a poet is busy all his life fighting evil prejudices, removing narrow views, enlightening the mind of his people, purifying their taste and ennobling their opinions and thoughts, how could he do better or be more patriotic?

—Goethe

Goethe once exclaimed that he might even consent to support another fifty years of life just to see the Suez and Panama canals built. Wasn't *Faust* the vision of a world that we still want to usher in? Was Goethe right in his poetry, even though he could not be in his own life or times? If we read Erich Heller's superb essays, this is the impression we get. The moral of Faust is that man becomes truly man by the esthetic transformation of the world with his free directive energies. But the moral of the nineteenth century was that community was not possible for the truly creative spirit. The only thing that the real innovator could do was to offer Utopias: poetic—like Faust; social reconstructionist—like Saint-Simon, Fourier, Comte, Bellamy; prophetically historicist—like Marx. At times the nineteenth century seems a truly Biblical epoch, in which passionate visions sprang up on a hostile soil, and there was nothing to do but wait. The great difference is that the nineteenth-century soil was not arid; the great wheels of industrial plenty had begun their relentless grind. For the first time in history, grand Utopian human visions were being obtrusively accompanied by the proper means for their realization.

Fortunately, nature does not grant the wishes of men who want to see the promised land. Had Goethe lived another fifty years, he would have seen the curtain open on one of the most grotesque spectacles of history, and he would have been able to sit with Burckhardt and foretell a new age of monsters. Today we have so lost the Faustian promise that we are even afraid to fulfill it. What will happen, we lament, when the wage-work day is abolished, when the automated factories grind out their plenty, and distribute it to all, when annual salaries are guaranteed, regardless of work—what will man do with his leisure; how will he keep from running wild?

The question betrays the whole failure of our time: the failure of the science of man to put forth an agreed, synthetic theory of human nature; the failure of society to see beyond the kind of monster that it has created with its commercial-industrial madness. Of course social welfare dampens public interest in a society in which there is no public interest, no agreed purpose. Why should the individual design larger, self-transcending social ends when the society as a whole frowns on it? Each person is bent on his own security, his own future; as a result, there is no *social* future, no future for men in common.

All of this is commonplace enough, but it explains why mass man is so impotent. He lacks a basic human dimension—control over the future; in a word, he has no "social ego." After all, a society, as a union of free individuals, needs to project a similar kind of control to that projected by the individual ego. "If I (we) do right in the present, by subordinating certain kinds of impulsive satisfactions, then the future will be secure and rewarding." Thus, the individual ego and the social ego design a broad vista for human energy and control, and man achieves a dignity thereby that is denied to other animals.

What happens when the society lacks an ego? The very same thing that happens when the individual has very weak control over his destiny: he fetishizes. He begins to look for control in narrow areas, areas that have nothing really basic to do with his problems. And society does the same: if it cannot handle the principal problem of adaptation by intelligently harnessing the future to its purposes, it tries to exercise firm control over areas where it does have power. This explains why our society is so

obsessed with traffic violations, with drug addiction, with the unseem-
liness of long haircuts. These are social fetishizations of the problem of
morality in modern times. It is as though the whole society were to breathe
one huge sigh and say: "Ah, if only we could control these, how good life
would be." These kinds of fetish controls are harmless enough, of course:
a few traffic fines, a few hippies jailed for smoking marijuana—it is all
benign. But alas, there are other ways of exercising a fetish social ego,
and they are far from harmless: today we are witnessing our society trying
to gain some kind of control over the national life and some kind of meaningful national design by forging what we might call a "military social
ego." This kind of adaptation is old enough and it has often been necessary for the survival of free communities—e.g., at the time of the Greeks.
But the question that is critical today is whether a "military social ego"
any longer represents an intelligent adaptation to the problems of morality in the modern world. We know that this kind of ego defeats dictatorships and today our best scientists are warning us that it will defeat commercial-industrial democracy.

Our fetish social ego and our "futuristic living" are all of a piece:
they represent a pious wish that everything will turn out well if we
feverishly and uncritically play the game of our society. But there is a
real difference between this naïve and clumsy attempt to influence the
future and the creative design of a new future horizon; and it is the one
that Dewey outlined, namely, the difference between mechanical action
and real action, the difference between external, coerced means, and individually controlled means. It boils down to the question: is the individual a free source of action, does he have aegis over the kinds of means
he will use to achieve the desired end? This was the whole basis of Dewey's
pragmatism. It summed up his entire social philosophy and justified his
theory of education and his vision of a truly sane society. As T. V. Smith
urged, "This redemption of the present from some phantom future has
been John Dewey's greatest contribution to American thought." Ordinarily man is burdened by designs inherited from tradition that impose
means and ends upon him. He barters his free energies in uncritical
acceptance of the life the elders impose. Pragmatism sought to overcome
this by making means relevant to ever-new problems, changing as the
real problem changed. The free man, like the free society, would be one
who could continually re-adapt his means to ever-new ends, and would
not follow slavishly in the footsteps of tradition and habit. Or, put in
terms that are now familiar to us, we would say that the free man is the
true genius who creates new meanings and continually cuts through old
forms. This is why pragmatism has always insisted on the importance of
method. As the noted sociologist E. A. Ross put it:

A schooling devised primarily to produce good character, or patriotism, or
dynastic loyalty, or class sentiment, or religious orthodoxy may lessen friction
in society, but it cannot bring genius to bloom. For this the prime essentials are
the communicating of known truths and *the imparting of method.*

We can see how intimately connected are the visions of the Enlightenment on genius, of pragmatism on science, of democracy on freedom, and of all of these on education. Freedom and genius mean education for cultural criticism, education for tentativeness and experiment. Dewey's "progressive education" was Enlightenment philosophy applied to the modern world. And the credo of progressive education was stated by that other Enlightenment man, long before Dewey. In a letter to Du Pont de Nemours, Jefferson said:

We both consider the people as our children, and love them with parental affection. But you love them as infants whom you are afraid to trust without nurses; and I as adults whom I freely leave to self-government.

Jefferson, we will remember, believed that each generation should live under a constitution of its own making. He wanted a revision of the Constitution, and a new social contract, at least every nineteenth year—since he calculated that in eighteen years and eight months half of those over twenty-one would have passed away. This was the true Enlightenment man speaking, the critic of culture, of any forms that enslave man. He wanted a pragmatic ethic that stemmed from a full consciousness of the fabricated nature of human arrangements. It is curious that Freud has often been condemned for a hard materialism, a tough-mindedness about man's motives, which he thought stemmed from deep-seated instincts. Actually, this kind of natural law is anything but tough-minded. It prevents us from being truly skeptical about social motives, blinds us to the fictional nature of symbolic striving, even while it pretends to disclose the "true" nature of human striving. In short, it pretends that human choices are *limited,* when in fact, as Jefferson saw, they must be limitless and continually reappraised. Jefferson was thus "tough-minded" in the only way that this word can have sense for man.

The problem for the ethical society can now be stated simply. Granted that we will someday put economic affairs under the control of reason, how do we educate the kind of people who might want to revise the Constitution every nineteen years? What does this kind of progressive education entail? The answer is direct: we [see] how man can be given the strength to be ethical, that he needs critical knowledge and that he needs to work in unison with other free slaves. This is exactly what progressive education is, in its original vision. It educates man for the strength to choose, to offer up his own meanings; and it educates him to treat others as sacred ends, rather than as cultural, role-playing means. The function of progressive education is the function of true democratic government, exactly as Emerson envisaged this ideal: namely, to prepare the way for the self-reliant individual. There is thus a clear and direct line of development from Jefferson and Emerson to Dewey and the new science of man in society. Dewey was fully aware of it—which is why he called Emerson the greatest moralist America had produced.

A Fourth Branch of Government: For Whom?

MICHAEL A. WEINSTEIN

In recent years there has been an increasing call for greater attention to the process of political evaluation. In 1968 John Lear wrote in *Saturday Review:* "Everyone is talking about cleaning up the ghettos, modernizing transport, and making equal education available to all, but no one is working on a system of priorities for realization of those reforms or a fair distribution of the costs. In short, the current crisis in American society hinges on authoritative evaluation. . . ."[1]

It is in the favor of such commentators as Lear that they recognize evaluation as an integral phase of the total political process. In the United States, decision and administration are the most visible phases of politics, while policy enters into public awareness through the efforts of organized interest groups. Until recently evaluation has remained relatively hidden and almost completely unorganized. This situation has perhaps been due to the traditional and widespread belief that modern democracy is a self-righting process in which the people feel where the shoe pinches and elect officials who promise to ease the pain. According to this notion evaluation is the responsibility of everybody in general and nobody in particular.

Why has this traditional view been brought into question to the extent that some observers even claim that the focus of national problems is authoritative evaluation? There is certainly no single answer to this question. In part, the new attention to evaluation is due to growing recognition that organized industrial activities frequently have such unintended consequences as environmental pollution and selective impoverishment. This aspect of the current situation is stressed by specialist groupings, whose members feel threatened by a declining quality of life and believe that their skills in planning and engineering could ward off the projected evils. A second source of concern with evaluation has been the appearance of liberation movements composed of those who feel themselves dispossessed by the present order. Segments of the black, youth, feminist, and other movements have demanded a reordering of national priorities in favor of satisfying their wants. Frequently they have expressed little interest or faith in traditional democratic processes, and have placed goals such as greater employment opportunity and higher standard of living above respect for majority rule. The presence of such groups and

---

1. John Lear, "Public Policy and the Study of Man," *Saturday Review,* September 7, 1968, p. 60.

their unwillingness to "work through channels" has impressed established authorities with the importance of systematizing evaluation. Yet a third reason why political evaluation has come in for greater attention recently is that substantial numbers of working-class and lower-middle-class people have begun to demand an accounting of how their taxes are spent. Concerned with inflation, crime, and the proportion of their income going to taxes, these people have become less willing than previously to trust officials to make good use of their money. Like the activity of dispossessed groupings, this protest of the "middle Americans" has impressed established authorities. Finally, some members of the groupings that direct large organizations or conglomerates have concluded that more systematic evaluation of the success of policies would increase the effectiveness of their control by providing a better basis for planning than is available at present. Thus, at least four current tendencies run together in the new attention to evaluation.

It should be clear that those who believe that the current crisis in American society hinges on authoritative evaluation are primarily members of elite and specialist groupings. There has been very little, if any, call from dispossessed groups for an improved method of social accounting that will include the costs of activities foregone as well as the benefits derived from activities performed. Proposals for systems of social accounting have been made by administrators and other specialists in response to the demands of the dispossessed. Few, if any, middle Americans have expressed interest in an "error detecting and evaluating subsystem in our national management system."[2] Ideas for such a subsystem have been generated by administrators and other specialists responding to the complaints of middle Americans. Thus, present concern with evaluation can be traced to the recognition by segments of elite and specialist groups that the traditional belief that democracy is a self-righting process is incorrect. This judgment is founded upon the feeling that the electorate is incapable of grasping the indirect consequences of organized activities (e.g., pollution, inflation), the awareness that many members of dispossessed groups will not accept the results of the electoral process as binding, and the awareness that numerous middle Americans are demanding visible results from their taxes. In short, the crisis of authoritative evaluation stems from a growing feeling that the electorate, the traditional focus of evaluation in Western democracies, can no longer be trusted to judge the success of policies. Where an unregulated process fails to serve those who have previously benefited from it, it is likely that the prime beneficiaries will strive to bring the process under regulation. It appears that this principle is operating with respect to the evaluative phase of the political process in America.

How do the interested parties propose to organize political evaluation? The most ambitious plan is that a fourth branch of government be created, "designed to function independently of the original three

2. N. Golovin, "Letter to the Science Editor," *Saturday Review*, January 4, 1969, p. 112.

branches of government—legislative, executive, and judicial."[3] This evaluative branch of government would "a) collect all the data necessary to continually track the state of the nation; b) define potential problems suggested by the information; c) develop alternative plans to cope with the problems; and d) evaluate ongoing projects in terms of real time and advise the people accordingly."[4] The fourth branch would be staffed mainly by social scientists but would draw upon personnel from all scientific disciplines. It would be politically neutral and would provide for its members an economic status and career stability comparable to that enjoyed by the judiciary. The ability of the evaluative branch "to counter-balance the older three branches would reside in public access to its information as well as to its conclusions."[5]

As sketched above, this proposal for an evaluative branch of government betrays its function as an instrument with which elite and specialist groupings might remedy the deficiencies that they find in evaluation by the electorate. The collection and analysis of data on the state of the nation would be far more valuable for the directors and managers of organizations and conglomerates than it would be for members of groupings which do not participate directly in making long-term commitments of resources and personnel. Further, staffing the evaluative branch with social scientists and other experts, and providing them with high economic status and secure careers, make it likely that the definition of potential problems, the content of alternative plans to meet the problems, and the criteria for evaluating projects would reflect the perspectives of elites and specialists. Thus, the absence in the proposal of any substantive criteria of evaluation is explained by the tacit assumption that those who would serve in the fourth branch would incorporate the value judgments and factual definitions of elite and specialist groupings into their decisions. Finally, restricting the power of the fourth branch to an information function insures that present organizations would not be unduly disturbed in their activities. Under this description, the evaluative branch would provide elite and specialist groups with an advantage in the contest to influence the substance of policy. Thus, the fourth branch would allow these groups to have an even greater impact than they presently have on public opinion and the electoral process, and would allow officials to by-pass public opinion through appeals to the plans and evaluations done by this branch. Such an evaluative branch would be far more an instrument of policy than a means of scientific evaluation.

CRITERIA OF EVALUATION: INSTITUTIONAL LIBERALISM

While the proposal for a fourth branch of government does not include substantive criteria of evaluation, it is possible to anticipate the

3. Lear, *op. cit.,* p. 60.
4. *Ibid.*
5. *Ibid.*

standards that would probably be used by such an agency. A description of these standards is found in the works of Talcott Parsons,[6] who has attempted over the past several decades to describe the operative public morality in the United States and other Western countries. Through understanding and criticizing the present public morality it will be possible to develop new standards of evaluation and state the conditions necessary for their embodiment in organizational practice.

Although Parsons does not give a name to the public morality he describes, *institutional liberalism* is a convenient designation. It will be useful to discuss this doctrine in terms of the four major components of any public morality. The first part of a public morality is the set of standards by which programs and other activities are judged successes or failures. This is the core of public morality, and it looks forward to the phase of policy as well as backward to the phase of administration. For institutional liberalism, success is judged by what Parsons calls "coordination standards," or quantitative measures of achievement. The second component of a public morality is a definition of the scope of political activity. For institutional liberalism, politics is differentiated from other human activities both structurally and functionally. Institutional liberals hold that politics is and should be conducted through specialized agencies of limited competence, such as legislatures, executive departments, and courts. The third aspect of a public morality is an approved method through which change in the direction of proclaimed values can be accomplished. For institutional liberalism, the approved method of change is creative leadership functioning within structurally differentiated institutions. The fourth component of a public morality is a vision of human destiny to be realized through activities aimed at attainment of proclaimed values. For institutional liberalism, the vision of human destiny is summed up by Parsons as "institutionalized individualism," in which human beings gain fulfillment through performing the roles allotted to them in institutions.

COORDINATION STANDARDS

According to Parsons, human societies are divided into four systems, each of which performs a function necessary for maintaining the society. The economy has the function of transforming the nonsocial environment in accord with social goals, the polity has the function of mobilizing the energies of actors to the realization of social goals, the societal community has the function of containing the various social roles present in a society within a meaningful framework, and the culture has the function of maintaining the major standards of value "governing" social behavior. Parsons holds that each social system has a standard of value which provides justification for activities undertaken within it, and a coordination standard which measures achievement of the relevant value. The complete set of standards of value and coordination standards comprises the criteria of evaluation offered by institutional liberalism.

6. Talcott Parsons, *Politics and Social Structure* (New York: The Free Press, 1969).

For the economy, the standard of value is utility, and the coordination standard is solvency, or maintenance of a favorable cash position. Thus, institutional liberalism judges achievement in the economy as the accumulation of money. For the polity, the standard of value is effectiveness, or the ability to mobilize the energies of actors to the realization of social goals. The coordination standard for the polity is success, which Parsons defines as demonstrated obedience to the commands of officials. Thus, institutional liberalism judges achievement in the polity as the accumulation of power. The more officials win compliance with their directives, the higher they are evaluated, because in institutional liberalism only the officials are capable of defining social goals. For the societal community (the widest group with which people identify), the standard of value is solidarity, or the maintenance of cooperation between different sectors of the society. The coordination standard for the societal community is consensus, or agreement on what is good for the group. Thus, institutional liberalism judges achievement in the societal community by the accumulation of influence, defined as the ability to win consensus. Finally, for the culture, the standard of value is integrity, or persistence, of the other standards of value. The coordination standard for the culture is pattern-consistency, defined as stability of the standards over time. Pattern-consistency is won by moral leaders who are able to persuade others that they have obligations to act on particular interpretations of standards of value. Thus, institutional liberalism judges achievement in the culture by the accumulation of moral commitments.

The striking characteristic of the standards of value and coordination standards provided by institutional liberalism is their quantitative rather than qualitative bias. Achievement in the economy is measured by accumulation of money rather than by the experiences involved in making and using products. The quality of demand, whether spontaneous or manipulated, is not questioned. Achievement in the polity is measured by the accumulation of power rather than by the experiences involved in exercising power and the uses to which it is put. The quality of command is not questioned, merely the ability to gain compliance. Achievement in the societal community is measured by the accumulation of influence rather than by experiences involved in forming judgments. The quality of opinion—its accuracy, scope, and depth—is not questioned. Finally, achievement in the culture is measured by the accumulation of moral commitments rather than by the experiences involved in appreciating community life. Whether everyday experience is characterized by beauty is not open to question. Thus, institutional liberalism makes a virtue of ignoring the quality of life. The preferences of human beings are taken as givens, not to be questioned, and there is no discussion of how these preferences might be manipulated by large organizations and conglomerates. The public morality of institutional liberalism is purely quantitative and lacking in content. This means that qualitative standards are treated as private concerns to be placed apart from political evaluation.

The standards of value characteristic of institutional liberalism would be likely to guide an evaluative branch of government. A professionalized staff of evaluators, composed mainly of social scientists pledged to political neutrality, could do nothing else but judge in terms of quantitative standards. This is because evaluations of solvency, success, consensus, and integrity focus on the means rather than the ends of human action. While ends and means are relative to one another, it is clear that the closer one gets to ends, the more explicitly political questions arise. Thus, an evaluative branch would function as an "error detecting and evaluating subsystem in our national management system." It would point out cases of insolvency, failure of obedience, lack of consensus, and collapse of standards, and suggest plans for remedying these conditions. There is, of course, the likelihood that an evaluative branch would tend to view what are essentially means as ends in themselves. Solvency, success, consensus, and integrity would be seen as constituting the good life. However, there is an even more important consideration to take into account. In its concentration on means, the evaluative branch would provide current elite and specialist groups with more effective procedures to maintain and enhance their positions. Hence, underneath its supposed political neutrality, the evaluative branch would be functioning to aid realization of the policies of elite and specialist groups. This becomes apparent when the coordination standards are analyzed more closely. What is the disaster of insolvency to those who control existing organizations is often the opportunity to initiate new enterprises for others. What is the crisis of authority to present officials is the opportunity to revise rights and duties for others. What is the breakdown and polarization of the nation for established opinion leaders is the opportunity to fashion new communities for others. What is the decline of morality and the collapse of standards for current moral leadership is the opportunity to create a counter-culture for others. Thus, the coordination standards are far from neutral, and the evaluative branch appears even more clearly as a means to shore up existing institutions.

DIFFERENTIATION

In addition to providing criteria of evaluation, institutional liberalism also provides a scope for political activity. The hallmark of institutional liberalism, at least as it is defined by Parsons, is that social evolution tends in the direction of specialized structures performing each social function. Thus, institutional liberals hold that in modern societies specialized organizations do and should have control over performing the functions to which they are adapted. This means that politics becomes a specialized and limited activity, primarily tied to the institutions of government, and that there is a separation made between public and private domains of human activity. This does not mean that other institutions lack a political aspect. The function of mobilizing the energies of actors to the realization of social goals is performed everywhere in society. However, government "is the concrete structural system in societies that have (sic.) the highest level of political primacy of function, with structural and processual implications accordingly."[7]

7. *Ibid.,* p. 519.

The meaning of the separation of politics can best be grasped by an example. Parsons applies the idea of differentiation to the question of whether or not the university should take political stands on broad issues of social concern such as war, poverty, and race relations. He notes that radical students tend to define the moral obligations of the university not as responsibility "for the implementation of academic values as such, but for a set of more general societal-political values broadly of a 'radical' character, with which, however, the academic values are linked."[8] The students conceive "the university to be a microcosm of the total society, rather than a specifically differentiated sub-system."[9] From the standpoint of a differentiated modern society, however, the university should not be committed to realizing all aspects of the good life, but should concentrate on the attainment of "cognitive rationality," which seems to mean the search for truth. Thus, according to Parsons, the problem with radical students is that they insufficiently appreciate the special role of the university in modern life. The problems of war and poverty are responsibilities of other institutions specifically adapted for dealing with them.

Parsons does admit that there are grounds for the student's judgment that the university is a microcosm of society. Bent on encouraging the growth of universities, administrations and faculties have frequently treated the university as a service center for other institutions in order to gain financial support. In Parsons' judgment there has been "an insufficiently clear differentiation between the relatively 'pure' intellectual disciplines and interest in many of their fields of application, notably military fields for the natural sciences."[10] There is, however, a problem with Parsons' call for a return to academic values. The rise of the university as a service center for governmental, business, and other organizations is encouraged by a public morality in which achievement is judged by quantitative standards. If the accumulation of money, power, influence, and moral commitments is the measure of success, these media will be sought even at the expense of such values as "cognitive rationality." Performing services for other organizations improved the position of universities with respect to Parsons' coordination standards. Thus, the standards of evaluation of institutional liberalism militate against differentiation. This is a serious conflict in the doctrine, because what holds for universities also holds for other organizations. There is a contradiction between differentiation and evaluation by the quantitative standards of judgment, in that activity aimed at achieving these standards tends to outrun the pursuit of specialized values. Any activity will be performed, regardless of the proclaimed values of the organization, if it will result in the gain of money, power, influence, or moral commitments. Whenever achievement with respect to the coordination standards can be gained most effectively by stepping beyond particularized and differentiated values, this will be done. Thus, every organization in the contemporary United States is an actual or potential conglomerate capable

8. *Ibid.*, p. 515.
9. *Ibid.*
10. *Ibid.*, p. 516.

of performing any activity that can be systematized. It is clear that the creation of an evaluative branch of government would only hasten the flight from differentiation.

The third component of institutional liberalism is its description of an approved method for social change. This aspect of the doctrine can be called creative leadership, because institutional liberals hold that progressive change is initiated by elites working within the institutional system. Creative leadership occurs when elites take risks on new projects. The clearest case of this process is in the economic system. In the economy, an entrepreneur persuades a banker to loan him money for the purposes of initiating a new enterprise. There is a risk involved, because if the enterprise fails the banker will take a loss. Thus, the successful banker is one who can distinguish promising plans from those that have a small chance of reaping profits. It is through such provision of capital to creative leadership that economic development occurs.

A similar process occurs in the other three systems. In the polity, elected officials are granted the authority to create binding obligations so that social goals will be attained. They have some freedom to define their programs, but the success of these programs will be ultimately judged by the degree to which compliance is won, and the degree to which future obligations will be accepted as binding. Similarly, in the societal community, opinion leaders may win enough influence to speak for many members of a particular group. The leader will have a degree of freedom to decide what specific policies are in the "best interest" of the group, but his judgments will be tested ultimately by the degree of consensus he is able to promote. Finally, in the culture, moral leaders may be in a position to define the moral commitments of the members of a group. Within the general scheme of values they have some freedom to apply the values to specific cases. However, their applications will be judged by the degree to which the general values retain respect and the degree to which people allow their commitments to be defined for them. Thus, there are forms of political, social, and cultural bankruptcy. Political bankruptcy occurs when significant numbers of people no longer consider the commands of officials binding on them, social bankruptcy takes place when significant numbers of people no longer allow institutionalized interest groups to define their demands for them, and cultural bankruptcy occurs when significant numbers of people no longer allow institutionalized moral authorities (churches and families) to define their value commitments for them. Just as in the case of economic bankruptcy, these forms of bankruptcy are most likely to happen when the projects pushed by leadership groups offend those who must live with their results. Creative leadership avoids bankruptcy while instituting change.

The idea of creative leadership must be analyzed in the light of the notions of differentiation and coordination standards. It is likely that one reason why the proposal for a fourth branch has gained currency is that members of elite and specialist groupings sense that creative leadership has failed as a method of securing social change. The method of creative leadership depends on differentiation and the operation of institutionalized checks on unsound projects. However, as differentiation disappears, insolvent enterprises seek government loan guarantees, ineffective officials resort to credibility gaps and image-making, disrespected opinion leaders attempt to win quasi-governmental status for their particular interest groups, and shaky moral elites resort to propaganda campaigns through the mass media. All of these activities are attempts by leaderships to dodge responsibility for the failure of their policies. By trying to eliminate checks on their performance, they paradoxically discourage other groupings from taking their enterprises, commands, opinions, and moral judgments seriously. This is where the real contemporary crisis of evaluation resides—in the breakdown of institutionalized checks on the projects of leaders, and in the consequent efforts by elite and specialist groupings to escape evaluation. The economic, political, social, and cultural bankruptcy stemming from this process leads some members of these groups to conceive of a fourth branch of government as a means of tiding them over the crisis.

INSTITUTIONALIZED INDIVIDUALISM

Why has the doctrine under consideration been viewed as a form of liberalism? The answer to this question lies primarily in the vision of human destiny expressed by Parsons in his statements on the aims of contemporary Western societies. According to Parsons there is a "type of individualism that is focal to the whole American pattern of values and attitudes—the strong emphasis on freedom and responsibility of the individual *within* a framework of both normative order and collective organization."[11] He calls this type of individualism *institutionalized individualism* and sketches his vision of modern society: "In this point of view, we can see society as providing for more complex, more technical, and more 'professional' jobs, allowing for more variety of choices, in occupation and in culture, and providing greater diversity within the framework of organization."[12] Thus, Parsons' vision is in the liberal tradition because it stresses freedom (in this case, freedom of choice among alternatives) and diversity. This freedom is seen to depend upon specialization.

Parsons contrasts institutionalized individualism with two other varieties of individualism present in contemporary societies. "Regressive individualism," which in the terms of earlier discussion would be associated with middle Americans, resists, in the name of individual freedom from organizational control, "the process of institutional change by virtue of which a more complex and hence more effective division of labor or differentiation has been developing, by which there has developed an increasingly ramified system of pluralistic collective solidarities and enterprises (including, of course, the enterprises of government, but by no means confined to them) and, finally, by which there has been developing

11. *Ibid.,* p. 184.
12. *Ibid.*

a more generalized and elaborated system of norms, especially at the level of law, through which the inevitably complex relations of such a society come to be regulated."[13] Thus, regressive individualism is anti-specialist and anti-organization. It is an ideology of those nonspecialist and non-elite groupings which have been left behind by the rise of conglomerates. A second variety of individualism criticized by Parsons is associated with the dispossessed and their supporters. Best called utopian, this type of individualism is opposed to formal organizations and authority structures, and holds that "a free acceptance of individual responsibility" and a "full commitment of the individual is enough" to insure social development. This is an ideology of those who feel repressed and dispossessed by conglomerates.

It is clear that institutionalized individualism also is an ideology—an ideology of elite and specialist groupings. It is based on the premise that human development can best be gained through performance of specialized roles in complex organizations. Its conception of freedom is variety of choice among alternatives provided by organizations. Expansion of choice is associated with expansion of organizations. Thus, the ideology of institutional liberalism makes direct connection with its criteria of evaluation. Sheer expansion of choice is a quantitative standard quite consistent with the coordination standards of solvency, success, consensus, and pattern-consistency. Even in its view of human destiny institutional liberalism ignores the quality of life. Given its proposed composition, an evaluative branch of government would likely adopt the ideology of institutionalized individualism as its own.

TOWARD A CRITICAL LIBERALISM

Critical liberalism has been coined specifically to designate the public morality described in the following discussion. Liberalism here means the tradition of political theory and action emphasizing human freedom and development. In each historical period, liberalism takes on a new meaning in accordance with the fullest definition of freedom attainable through collective action at the given time and place. Critical liberalism is meant to be relevant to the post-bureaucratic world of the present. It is a public morality which will only be realized through broad social struggles. It is critical because it is based not on abstractions, but on the direct inspection of lived experience. It should not be confused with classical liberalism, which stressed freedom of enterprise, or welfare liberalism, which emphasized freedom from want. Critical liberalism places creative freedom at the center of attention and is not wedded to any particular regime, such as representative democracy. It is not an apology for present institutions and, in fact, holds that these institutions contain fundamental contradictions. However, unlike many radicalisms it is neither monistic nor utopian.

The fourth branch of government is a proposed remedy for resolving the contradiction of institutional liberalism. However, it should be apparent from the foregoing analysis that this contradiction is too deep and fundamental to be resolved by creating an institution to shore up elite

13. Ibid.

and specialist patterns of activity. Institutional liberalism depends upon differentiated organizations promoting specialized values through creative leadership held responsible by institutionalized checks. Only when organizations actually promote such values and when leadership actually is held responsible does institutional liberalism provide interesting work and vital cultural diversity. However, institutional liberalism does not contain within it any qualitative criteria of evaluation. Thus, its quantitative standards drive elites to ignore the specialized values whenever doing so will further organizational growth. This leads to growing irresponsibility of leadership groups and a consequent crisis of evaluation.

A revival of liberalism cannot proceed by urging that organizations return to the pursuit of specialized values. The development toward the conglomerate capable of performing any function amenable to systematization has gone too far for a return to differentiation. What is needed, instead, is a new standard of evaluation taking account of the quality of life, a new scope for politics, a redefinition of the means to legitimate social change, and a new vision of human possibility. It is most convenient to begin with the new vision of human possibility.

Institutional liberalism presents a false choice between anti-organizational and anti-specialist individualisms of the right and left, and freedom of choice within complex organizations. Critical liberalism presents another alternative—creative freedom. Viewing the human being as capable of rejecting the present and acting on a novel future, critical liberalism offers a vision of the future in which human beings have maximum opportunity to appreciate, inquire into, and plan their culture, and ultimately to create it. This ideal does not reject specialization and organization but requires that activity be directed to maximize creative freedom rather than freedom of choice among pre-established alternatives. Thus, all human beings must be viewed as at least potentially self-conscious contributors to the shaping of the future, rather than as passive consumers of a future created for them by elites.

Attainment of creative freedom requires that we abandon the distinction between change undertaken within established institutions and change outside of them. The choice between attempting to reach a position where "creative leadership" within the system is possible and confronting the system through revolution is also a false choice. The method of critical liberalism is experimental. Wherever there are opportunities for allowing people to control their work, to participate in decisions affecting them, to inquire into their experience, and to broaden and deepen their appreciation of beauty, these opportunities must be seized whether they are inside or outside of the established institutions. Neither collaboration with nor repudiation of the leading institutions is a guarantee that one is aiding human development. Far more important is whether one's actions are principled by the standard of creative freedom. Adopting an experimental approach to social change requires that the distinctions between public and private organizations be abandoned. In a world of conglomerates all organizations are mobilizing human energies for the pursuit of goals, the attainment or failure of which affects great masses of human beings. Thus, all large organizations are public in their effects, if not in their responsibility. A central feature of critical liberalism is its insistence that the scope of politics be broadened to include the activities of all complex organizations. This means that the development of orderly specialist-producer and client-consumer control over these organizations, and possibly their decentralization, is an aim of critical liberalism.

An experimental and comprehensive politics aiming at the realization of creative freedom demands new standards of political evaluation. In the past, evaluation has been rooted in the results of activity. For example, the coordination standards of institutional liberalism refer to whether action has resulted in solvency, success, consensus, or pattern-consistency. Critical liberalism, based on the ideal that human beings can progressively learn to create their own futures, draws its criteria of evaluation from the quality of activity itself. Economic activity is judged according to the standard of creativity. Does work present novel challenges and opportunities for innovation, or is it repetitive? Political activity is judged according to the standard of participation. Are people taking an active part in making the decisions that affect them, or are they being manipulated or coerced into following imposed patterns? Social activity is judged according to the standard of appreciation. Are people deriving enjoyment and depth of experience from their relations and their use of products, or are they entering into relations and using products simply to be accepted in a status group? Cultural activity is judged according to the standard of inquiry. Has a person made a commitment or formed an opinion after a process of rigorous examination, or has the commitment been made or the opinion formed out of guilt or the pronouncements of an unquestioned authority? Each of these standards— creativity, participation, appreciation, and inquiry—are aspects of creative freedom. They are qualities of activity rather than results of action. They are the standards proposed by critical liberalism for the evaluation of all organizations.

It is clear that the standards of critical liberalism could not be incorporated into a fourth branch of government. They can only be used by those directly involved in activities—by individuals and small groups.[14] This, of course, does not mean that critical liberalism's program could be realized through individuals adopting a certain set of attitudes. Rather, the struggle for creative freedom can only reach success through the concerted and organized efforts of people within and without complex organizations to direct activity toward the extension of creativity, participation, appreciation, and inquiry.

14. Don E. Kash and Michael A. Weinstein, "The R and D Contract and Democratic Theory," *Policy Sciences,* I (1970) , pp. 113-121.

VIII
Prospects of
Political Action

If the beginnings of political thought are found in images of the public situation, the final products of political thought are visions of the public situation transformed. The articles in this section parallel those in the first section, in the sense that they provide future projections of the images presented there.

M. Stanton Evans presents a conservative vision of the future corresponding to aspects of the thinking of Burnham and Meyer. He argues that many American conservatives believe that they are doomed to witness in frustration the progressive growth of the centralized welfare state. He claims that as long as conservatives feel this way, they will allow the welfare state to become larger and larger. However, he maintains that there is great sentiment in the United States for decentralization and reduction of the powers of the Federal government. He urges conservatives to take advantage of this sentiment and commit themselves to vigorous political action. For Evans, the conservative future lies in activating middle Americans.

Arnold S. Kaufman presents a liberal's vision of the future. He argues that liberals must vigorously advocate radical transformation of social and political institutions within a framework of the present political party system and governmental agencies. Kaufman sees the liberal future in an alliance of the dispossessed, some of the specialists, and some of the middle Americans.

A radical's vision of the future is provided by Paul M. Sweezy. He contends that the experience of radicals in the twentieth century has proven that the new society must be continuously built. The full development of human potential will not come through imposing an iron-fisted dictatorship on the people after a revolutionary struggle, but only through perpetual efforts to destroy organizational dominations and replace them with more cooperative and equalitarian forms. Sweezy points to the experience of Communist China as an example of an attempt to carry out such a permanent revolution.

Like Friedrich Georg Junger, Morton Kaplan reflects on the implications of contemporary technology for human freedom. His nightmare society of technocratic domination has haunted many thinkers whose work appears in this book, particularly Miller. Kaplan notes that the continuation of present trends, rather than any drastic new developments, would lead directly to the enactment of his nightmare in American society. On the freedom side of the freedom-regimentation polarity is the article by Ivan Illich. Illich argues that there are two kinds of institutions in the contemporary world, those which people use without being persuaded or threatened to do so and those which people must be persuaded or threatened to use. His vision of the future, which parallels the remarks of Lifton and Becker, is one in which institutions based on persuasion and threat will disappear and those based on utility or intrinsic value will survive and thrive. It is such a vision in which creative freedom is emphasized and which motivates much current political action aimed at transforming the public situation. This vision is not a blueprint for an ideal society but a limit which political activity might approach. However, those who would work to realize this vision must overcome the tendencies represented by competing visions, particularly those emphasizing regimentation. The present remains an age of paradox and ambivalence in which the first step toward liberation is clarification of the public situation and one's possibilities within it.

The Self-Fulfilling Prophecy

M. STANTON EVANS

I have argued that, by developing the proper strategy and seizing the relevant occasions, the Republican party can work a major transformation of American politics: That it can halt the devolution of our system into a consolidated welfare state and foster a new era of decentralization, constitutional restraint of power, and reaffirmation of individual freedom.

It is standard doctrine, of course, that no such reversal of historical form is possible. Quite apart from the question of materials at hand or developing attitudes in American society, reversion from centralization to decentralization is supposed to be impossible. The long-term drift to collectivism, we are informed, is "inevitable." The twentieth century is the age of collectivisms, and it is foolish to think the United States can withstand the universal tides of history.

Among the many psychic barriers to conservative political progress, none is more formidable than this historical defeatism. Questions of political strength, population movement, the present or future state of public opinion, are to a certain extent measurable—although considerably less so than we might wish. It is possible to look at these things and decide whether realistic opportunities exist for conservative advance. But it is not similarly possible to examine the question of "historical tides."

The idea that there is anything inevitable about collectivist dominion is simply that, an idea. It stems from two sources: The fact that we do indeed have many kinds of collectivism in the world today, including our own diluted brand of it; and the fact that assertion of collectivism's "inevitable" triumph is itself a feature of leftist exhortation. In a society long dominated by collectivist thought, this idea will be abroad because it is what collectivists, from Karl Marx to C. Wright Mills, have believed.

Such notions have an obvious effect on conservatives and Republicans who do not want collectivism but feel there is little they can do about it. This is the self-fulfilling prophecy at work. If conservatives believe there is no hope of combatting the liberal welfare formula, they will fail to take the actions requisite to successful resistance. If they tell themselves they are beaten before they start, they in all probability won't start to begin with—or if they do, their efforts will be too halfhearted to be effective.

The particularly invidious effect of this conception is that it tends to neutralize the conservatives' principal asset: Their commitment to idea and principle. In an age of drift and indecision, the man who believes in something and is willing to work for it has, we have seen, an incalculable advantage; but that advantage can be canceled if the man of deep belief becomes convinced his point of view has no possibility of success. The self-fulfilling prophecy thus tends to demoralize precisely where morale could be the decisive factor.

The available data suggest there is no reason to assume the permanence of liberal rule. On the contrary, all the pre-conditions of conservative revival are ready to hand: The suburbs, the middle class, the rise of the West and South, the conservative intellectual community, the new consensus liberals, the youthful conservatives on the campus, even certain aspects of the new left phenomenon—all indicate a heightening resistance to the extension of Federal power. Equally instructive is the rising level of public concern over the dangers of big government—concern which has tripled in seven years' time and which will in all probability continue to grow in the years ahead. Most important of all, perhaps, is the continuing popularity of the term "conservative."

A Republican party which stood forth clearly on the issue of limiting Federal power, relieving the tax burden, and resisting expansion of the Federal bureaucracy would have an excellent chance of uniting these elements into a common front. On the tax issue alone, it is already capable of mustering impressive majorities in statewide and congressional races, and has every reasonable prospect of doing so, at some future time, in the presidential arena. That prospect will fade only if the GOP, in pursuit of "moderate" doctrine, allows it to.

Even a confused Republican party will now and again get people into national office, of course, but the odds are that they will be the wrong people elected for the right reasons. The eight-year White House reign of the Deweyites provides an almost perfect example: A Republican regime—brought to power by an upsurge of anti-welfarist sentiment—which proceeded to extend the spread of welfarism. In consequence, the Eisenhower victory signaled, not the beginning of new Republican strength, but a continuation of the old decline.

The GOP can consolidate stable majorities only when it understands the reasons for its occasional victories and assembles a strategy for making them systematic. It can become a national majority party when it starts playing up to its own strength rather than that of the opposition. None of this will be likely to happen so long as the party hesitates between the substance of limited government and the rhetoric of welfarism. Until the GOP can make up its mind between the war on poverty and the need to reduce Federal tax levels, it will tend to fall between the stools of the old consensus and the new. Only by affirming the limited-government view can it surface its implicit majorities. Only by defaulting its opportunities can it make liberal victory "inevitable."

Also contributing its mite of inevitabilist confusion is the idea that there is something intrinsically hostile to the limited-government view in the rapid alteration of our technology. We are told that the complexities of the age demand augmented centralization and that local autonomies cannot survive in the era of the jet transport and instant communication. This facile assumption does not bear up under scrutiny.

It is unquestionably true that modern technology makes certain kinds of centralized power—the proposed "data bank," for example—more feasible than in the past. But this does not mean such power is either desirable or necessary. On the contrary, such developments suggest the dangers of centralization and have helped to spur resistance to it. The augmented feasibility of centralized power tends to make big government a less attractive rather than a more attractive proposition.

Nor are the anti-libertarian tendencies of consolidated power the only problems associated with it. There are also dangers of an economic and social character. The fact is that, as our economy becomes more and more complex, it is increasingly difficult for a government planner sitting in Washington to take all the appropriate variables into account and make a correct decision. He is better able to give a ruling and make it stick, but less able to make the right ruling in the first place. The complexity of the times, as modern industry has discovered, makes decentralization, not consolidation, desirable.

Like considerations obtain with respect to the technological factor which has concerned us most in the course of this discussion—the communications media. Again, it is assumed that the new communications technology is intrinsically favorable to the liberal position, unfriendly to conservatives. And since there are key aspects of modern communications which have served to disorient conservatives, this belief is understandable. It is mistaken nonetheless.

The notion that popular communications are *ipso facto* hostile to conservative opinion goes back to the invention of movable type and the spread of literacy. Such developments, it has been supposed, are contributory to the modern liberal temper; they have served to accelerate the spread of universal suffrage democracy, broken up existing culture patterns, and given birth to pamphleteering and popular journalism which have been useful to leftward revolutionaries. The continued expansion of mass political involvement through the electronic media is thought to have the same effect.

It would be foolish to deny that the spread of mass communications has had, in many instances, a liberalizing effect—or that it has this effect even now. Much of the preceding argument has been precisely to this point. But it is equally hazardous to suggest that these communications facilities *must* yield liberal benefits rather than conservative ones. It is always necessary to distinguish between the uses to which a given technology can be put, and the uses which are intrinsic to it. There is no more reason to suppose modern communications are *per se* hostile to conservatism than there is to suppose our nation is "inevitably" doomed to collectivism.

The disorienting impact of the media, their "certifying" power, and their ability to merchandise a point of view through extraneous appeals are all proper subjects for concern; but, unless one adopts the position that all objectionable things are somehow connected to the political opposition, it should be clear that these are not matters particularly associated with any single species of ideology. The harmful impact of these things on conservatives results from the fact that the media happen to be staffed with liberals—not from the nature of the media themselves.

In a certain sense, indeed, there is "conservatism of technology" which militates in the opposite direction. This has been true since the invention of type and it remains true today. The spread of printed books did serve, in some circumstances, to fragment traditional cultures; but it also made the preservation of the past, in somewhat tangible form, much more feasible than it had ever been before. Print can be an instrument of change; it can also be an agent of continuity. The recourse to historical documents, the citing of precedents, the vigorous defense of written tradition which are essential aspects of conservative advocacy became possible with the advent of printing.

Nothing could better illustrate this fact than the history of our own freedoms, built upon a mountain of documents and defended in a torrent of pamphlets. It was, precisely, the science of printing which allowed the British libertarian tradition to take root in America—where colonists like John Adams and James Madison read the works of Coke and Blackstone and Locke, then proceeded to put the printing presses of America to work in their own behalf. The technology of print, in sum, depends for its political effects upon the purpose to which it is put.

The same point emerges clearly from an examination of the contemporary press. The notion that newsprint journalism is necessarily liberal in its impact has long since been disproved; it can be argued, in fact, that the newspaper in America is the most conservative of all the communications media. More regional variations emerge in the daily press than in national magazines or the TV networks, and more conservative expression also appears there. Conservative political columnists are published quite frequently, even in liberal papers, and there are of course a number of explicitly conservative papers as well. Few people would assert that *The Wall Street Journal* or the *Chicago Tribune*, two of the largest circulation papers in the country, have performed as instruments of liberalism.

All of this can be equally true of the electronic media. These outlets are highly serviceable to the liberal cause today, not because of an intrinsic technological liberalism, but because the people who are in charge of them are wedded to liberal doctrine. The same instruments can be and have been used by conservatives to sell their ideas to the electorate. Which means conservatives must not only look to their own morale vis à vis the existing bias of the media, but also perfect the media techniques necessary for getting around this hazard. This will involve full use of all the information furbelows, communications circuits, and public-relations expertise which modern technology affords. It will also involve finding attractive and articulate candidates who can go on television, make a good appearance, and speak convincingly. To be successful, conservatives are going to have to make use of all the most modern instruments of communication.

If there is no "inevitable" trend to the left, neither is there any "inevitable" drift to the right. The fact that many elements in contemporary America favor conservative renascence does not mean we shall necessarily see the triumph of conservatism; the impulses are there and will find some kind of expression, but whether that expression will issue in tangible political success depends on the activities of some highly individualistic and unpredictable citizens—the members of the conservative movement as such, and the members and leadership of the Republican party. If those activities are intelligent and timely, then success is probable. If they are hesitant and psychologically maladroit, then the opportunity can easily be defaulted.

The liberal ascendancy in American politics has come about because a number of people who believed strongly in the liberal view of things conducted a long educational campaign and seized a favorable psychological moment to merchandise their program. A conservative ascendancy can come about if other people who believe just as deeply in the conservative view spread their ideas and seize their moment in similar fashion.

Our example from American history is to the point. Men like Adams and Madison confronted, in many ways, a situation comparable to our own. Having enjoyed as a matter of prescriptive right the privileges of "free-born Englishmen," they found those privileges abridged by the growing power of the British government. Had they looked to the historical tide of the age, they would certainly have concluded that the triumph of highly-centralized monarchies was inevitable, and that a handful of American colonists could do little about it. And had they reached that conclusion, they would of course have been right—because they would have failed to do the things necessary to roll back the objectionable novelty of centralization.

But, of course, they didn't tell themselves anything of the sort. They believed that men make history, rather than the other way around. They resisted the encroachments of the British King and Parliament, and preserved their freedoms. They brought about the very reversion from centralization to decentralization which is supposed to be a historical impossibility.

There is no need to belabor the comparison: The circumstances are very different, the relationship of the American citizenry to their government is very different. In particular, full redress of grievances is open to all of us through the existing political process. But the essential point is the same: There is nothing "inevitable" about either free government or collectivism; the former is harder to maintain, and appears less often in the annals of Western history. It is nevertheless a function, not of historical drift, but of human effort. If the proper kind of effort is forthcoming, the future of conservatism can be very bright indeed.

A Strategy
for Radical Liberals

ARNOLD S. KAUFMAN

One of Jules Feiffer's cartoons captures the mood of political hopelessness that pervades the American Left. A long-haired militant asks a short-cropped liberal whether he voted in the last election. "Yes." "Did your man win?" "Yes." "How will you feel about him a year from now?" asks the militant. "Betrayed," the liberal answers. "Then why did you vote?" "To be effective." The liberal then asks the militant whether he voted. "No." "What did you do?" "Blew up a university," answers the militant. "Why did you blow up a university?" "To be effective." "How will you feel about it a year from now?" "Ineffective." To which the liberal responds, "I can get the same results a lot easier."

My aim is to dispel this sense of profound discouragement. I offer a political strategy that is, I think, better than betrayal or ineffectiveness —at least for those who are radical and liberal.

I am liberal in believing that "a good society is one in which each person possesses the resources of materials, mind, and spirit, as well as the opportunities, to carve out a career in conformity to that person's own nature and reasoned choice."[1] This simple expression of basic social faith will have to serve for present purposes.

I am radical because the United States is so far from being a good society that institutional arrangements must be thoroughly transformed before it can become one. The sense of *radical* I intend is a matter of what political programs one embraces, not of the political tactics favored. So radical liberals favor radical policies for eliminating poverty and racism, guaranteeing full employment, providing decent housing and medical care to everyone, drastically paring military appropriations, purifying and beautifying our common environment, reconstructing our prisons and mental institutions, implementing a universal right to higher education—to mention only a few minimal points. Radicals know that to achieve these goals vast corporate powers must be subordinated to wise and democratic governance: bureaucracies must be humanized, pursuit of private profit ethically subordinated.

Radical liberals are not and for the foreseeable future will not be a majority of the population or the voting public; but there are many of us. Our numerically significant but distinctly minority status is the foundation on which any sensible political strategy must be built.

Radical liberals must regard electoral politics as an essential part of the strategy for political change. But since we comprise a distinct mi-

---

1. Arnold S. Kaufman, *The Radical Liberal* (New York: Atherton, 1968; Clarion Books, 1970) , p. 6.

nority both of the voting public and of the Democratic party—the major party with which we must identify—our strategic aims must be to build a radical majority in the long run and to deploy our minority strength effectively in the short run. What are the prospects?

There are two bases for a new majority coalition: self-interest and moral concern. Many think that only self-interest provides a reliable basis for building a coalition. Such a view goes too far in the basically healthy effort to debunk the moralism that has plagued American politics. People *are* capable of acting persistently and energetically out of primarily moral motives. Richard L. Stout provides evidence for this claim in a book that describes the significance of the effort thousands of morally concerned people made during the McCarthy campaign.[2]

If we are to build a radical majority, there is no realistic alternative to relying on what has been called a constituency of conscience. For consider the alternatives:

First, we might rely on a broadly based movement that has workers, especially trade unionists, the racially oppressed, and the very poor as its primary base. Such a coalition would not have to wait for some distant future to effect radical change. For it is, or is close to being, a voting majority of the population. But this in itself is not a valid alternative, for such a coalition would not be radical. Those who favor this approach cling to a neo-Marxist faith in the radical potentialities of organized workers, even though a plausible basis for their optimism has disappeared. It is a fact of American political life that whatever radicalism is found among workers, and trade unionists in particular, tends to diminish as their precarious hold on a marginally comfortable life grows firmer. Relatively little education, growing security and comfort, constant concern with satisfying desires that press against income, the still frightening realities of an uncertain labor market—in combination these cause the near-poor and the affluent poor to draw back from genuinely radical commitment, *even while remaining a generally progressive force for change.*

This is a crucial point. A distinction must be drawn between progressive and radical majorities. Radical liberals should view organization of progressive voting majorities as a vital part of their strategy for change. Without doing so, it is unlikely that repression can be contained or the basis for a radical future laid. But the ameliorative, reformist programs such majorities are disposed to support are far from radical enough.

I am not saying that the working class is authoritarian, or the trade union movement conservative. Many within the trade union movement are deeply committed radical liberals. They form an indispensable part of the new coalition. And the possibilities for progressive coalition between racial minorities and white workers, especially in the South, now is great and growing. Yet, a coalition whose core consists of organized workers, though generally progressive, will not be radical.

A second alternative is to rely mainly on those who are most abused racially and economically—a constituency of the oppressed. This group

2. Richard Stout, *People* (New York: Harper & Row, 1970).

must be an important part of any new radical coalition. As they become more aware of the causes of their misery the poor increasingly seek radical perspectives. The Poor Peoples' Campaign and the Welfare Rights Organization represent a new kind of radical assertiveness among the very poor. Still, they comprise a small proportion of the total population, and even their absolute strength is likely to diminish over time. For there is a good conservative sense in trying to buy social stability by using a portion of America's prodigious wealth to provide them with modest increments in income. No doubt, this is the main political thought behind Nixon's conversion to a minimum income program.

As people who have been long deprived begin to consume more, their expectations rise and they tend to become more overtly frustrated and angry. Their ire tends to focus on whatever frustrates their effort to consume, not on the forces that hold them down. Not for them the counter culture. Barring economic catastrophe, in 20–30 years some of those who yesterday joined the Poor People's Campaign may be among the most consumption-oriented segments of our population. Groups afflicted by scarcity cannot generally be made to skip this cultural stage—as the Communist states of Eastern Europe have discovered and China will discover. This is not said critically, but in an effort to assess the prospects for radical liberalism.

A third alternative for building a new radical coalition is to appeal to the more affluent on the basis of their narrow interest. War, ecology, the debasement of our culture affect them, too, vitally. While this must be done, it is delusive to suppose that the affluent can be radicalized on the basis of self-interest alone. For them life usually is too comfortable, and the cost of activism too great. Whatever effort they can make on behalf of radical programs will depend on the depth of their moral commitment.

Each of these alternatives is an important part of any effort to forge a new radical majority, but separately they are doomed to failure. Our ability to create a radical future depends on our ability to fuse a radical constituency of the oppressed with a radical constituency of conscience. And the prospect of organizing a conscience constituency that will in time be sufficiently numerous rests in turn on what is happening to our young people, primarily the more affluent young on the nation's campuses.

While higher education is neither essential nor enough to produce liberals, every study reveals a significant correlation between the two. Examining the available evidence, Kenneth Keniston and Michael Lerner declare that

The most decisive refutation of the leftist charge that the universities are centers for reactionary indoctrination is the growing liberalism of college students. Radicals who claim universities castrate their students intellectually find it impossible to explain why American students are taking an increasingly active role in attempting to redress the injustices of American society.[3]

3. *New York Times Magazine,* November 9, 1970, p. 66.

Young people, especially the more affluent ones, are less afflicted by economic fear and careerism than any generation of advantaged youth before them.[4] They feel, with some reason, that they will *make it* economically and professionally. And they know that anxieties of budget-cutting conservatives bear no plausible relationship to what this society can do to end human misery.

So today's young people are uniquely predisposed to use education not only as a stepping stone to personal security but as a means of examining their lives and their society. They bring to these tasks commitment to the ideals of American culture—belief in liberty and justice, in the efficacy of reason, etc. And they take these ideals seriously. The basic mission of our universities is to provide what has traditionally been called, not without reason, a liberal education. When this task is competently fulfilled, the ideas and knowledge it opens to students affect them profoundly. Now they quickly, sometimes intolerantly, demand that material be presented in a manner that breathes life into study. They demand relevance, though they are often too impatient and therefore self-defeating.

As the conventional American ideals are taken seriously and as students are confirmed in their suspicions that the rhetoric is remote from the reality, education comes to promote both the liberal ideal and a commitment to making it real. The potential ranks of the conscience constituency will swell as long as increasing numbers of the young receive an honest liberal education. Barring economic catastrophe, there is only one way in which the trend can be impeded or reversed—through politicization of the university.

The serious danger of politicization emanates not from the bulk of the students or faculty but from those who accurately perceive the long-range political threat implicit in the very idea of a liberal education—a danger they try to counter in three ways: (1) by forcing curricular changes that divert educational resources from liberal education; (2) by repression, crude and subtle; (3) by cutting college budgets enough to insure that standards of educational competence will erode.

To cope with this assault, the universities' internal political resources are inadequate. Those who want to protect the integrity of liberal education need political allies, and there are no more reliable allies than those who have a natural political interest in preventing interference with the campuses doing well what they are supposed to do. None have a more natural interest in protecting the universities than those forces that are trying to build a new radical coalition.

The views just sketched contrast sharply with the rage for counter

4. A survey by the American Council on Education shows that the percentage of entering college freshmen who consider themselves far Left or "liberal" has risen to more than 36 percent while the percentage who consider themselves "far Right" or "conservative" has declined to 18.1 percent. (Data from the *New York Times,* December 20, 1970.) If my analysis is correct, education will intensify these trends.

culture. I find that the currently fashionable works of counter-cultural theorists are naive and politically muddled.[5] It is dangerous to suppose, as Charles Reich does,[6] that successful cultural revolution is inevitable. Unless we maintain continuous effective political awareness and action on every front, minds will ultimately be destroyed, not liberated. Ideologues of the counter culture do not appreciate the extent to which the young are moved, not by new ideals, but by the traditional values of American culture. At its best and most politically relevant, the changing styles of American consciousness are efforts to redeem the pledge of liberty and justice for all. Although much that the chroniclers of the counter culture write is useful background to the serious business of building a decent society, it is dangerous to regard their prescriptions as an alternative to hard, sustained political effort.

BUILDING THE NEW COALITION

To criticize a new coalition strategy on grounds that it would not build winning majorities in the immediate future would miss my central point. The basic aim is *radical* change. But, as present majorities are not radical, the most urgent aim is to transform the center of American political life from moderation to radicalism. To do that we must build a radical coalition now, deploying its substantial but minority strength effectively on behalf of programs that are radical when possible, and at least progressive. As the radical coalition consists primarily of two groups —constituencies of the oppressed and of conscience—it is paramount to increase and fuse their respective strengths.

I have already indicated what is important in shaping a growing constituency of conscience: protect and adequately fund a system of higher education committed to liberal education for everyone who wants to go to college. Beyond this, the conscience constituency must be organized wherever the potential exists—in unions, churches, businesses, towns, city neighborhoods, suburbs, and so on. For not only the young seek to redeem the promise of their own lives and the promise of American society. There is something in the air that stirs millions of Americans.

The Black Power movement was first and foremost an effort to transform the consciousness of black Americans; to destroy attitudes of slavishness and deference; to engender self-respect and autonomy. The same urgings are plain in the movement for women's liberation, among radical clergy, within segments of the industrial community. Affluent people in growing numbers are trying to feel free, to live with dignity, without lying. And their needs fuel political interests in ways that erode constraints of self-interest. Criticism that dwells primarily on political defect

5. See Theodore Roszak, *The Making of a Counter Culture* (Garden City, N.Y.: Doubleday, 1969) ; Philip Slater, *In Pursuit of Loneliness* (Boston: Beacon, 1970) ; Charles Reich, *The Greening of America* (New York: Random House, 1970) . I am not passing a general judgment on these works—only on those parts that have political relevance. In other respects these authors have important things to say.

6. In Reich's *New Yorker* abridgment, September 26, 1970, p. 111.

and rhetorical excess misses the most hopeful thing about these liberation movements. If these urgings are an outgrowth of middle-class attitudes, then all power to that aspect of bourgeois culture. In response to these currents the politics of the new coalition should, in part, be redemptive. But its primary aim must be to radicalize and politicize what is too often merely redemptive.

There is no blueprint for what needs to be done. Each segment of the emerging conscience constituency must be convinced that its special interests are important; that people within the coalition care. Yet each must be brought into the coalition not merely on the basis of interest, but on the basis of moral concern. Political activity must become a means of endowing with significance lives despoiled in other respects.

The central difficulty in building the constituency of the oppressed is their sense of powerlessness resulting from political isolation. And the main barrier to joining it to a constituency of conscience is this sense of powerlessness often expressed in mistrust of those who are moved primarily by moral concern. This is neither surprising nor unjustified. For what is a moral matter to the conscientious may, for the oppressed, be a condition of survival. And it is inevitable that, faced with less catastrophic options, the affluent will not usually be willing to absorb comparable personal costs for the sake of social justice. Those black activists of the South who in the early days of the civil rights movement doubted that their affluent white helpmates could stay the course once the going got rough or, more likely, tiresome, showed good sense. Tension and disharmony can never be completely eliminated from a coalition that is primarily a fusion of these two constituencies.

However, there are many ways in which mistrust can be reasonably allayed. Four general issues are crucial. Each involves dissolution of traditionally liberal hang-ups about mere forms of equality and lawfulness. Each has symbolic importance that sometimes transcends its importance to peoples' lives.

First, relatively affluent whites should respond affirmatively to claims for reparation. The moral case for doing so is strong; the strategic case, decisive. Suppose an easily identifiable group has, by and large, suffered the effects of original injustices from which another easily identifiable group has generally benefited. The disabilities and advantages have been transmitted to the respective groups by social inheritance, much by deliberate design of unjust social institutions. This is the situation of most black people in relation to most whites in our society. There is a compelling case for a transfer of resources from whites to blacks. It is not a matter of visiting the sins of the fathers on the sons, but of transferring undeserved benefits to those who suffer undeserved disabilities. This perspective is, moreover, compatible with acknowledging that distinct groups —e.g., the poor—have equal or greater claims than black people as such.

Second, the issue of minority representation is crucial. Whether X, who is white, will make a better congressman than Y, who is black, is often less important than the fact that the election of a black representative has political significance for black constituents everywhere. In California, Democratic legislators have gerrymandered Chicano candidates out of contention so often that many key Mexican-American leaders are no longer willing to play the Democratic electoral game. They demand representation. To intone that merit alone should be decisive is morally evasive. Minorities must be accorded representation at every level of American power. As a group, minority representatives will tend to make greater personal sacrifices for the sake of important policy goals than comparable alternatives.

Third, economic boycott is an important weapon for poor minorities. Whether organized on behalf of the grape or lettuce workers of California, or the black residents of Cairo, Illinois, or the white miners of Appalachia, successful boycott is effective power. Members of the new coalition should bring economic muscle to bear in communities that otherwise cannot be influenced by minority economic pressure. The conscience constituency should become the lens through which the power of poor and racial minorities is effectively magnified in communities where the oppressed are politically insignificant.

Fourth, one aspect of the law-and-order issue is preeminently important to all oppressed groups, especially ghetto dwellers: the injustice of *official* lawlessness. They view lawless action, not only by police but by every segment of the legal system, as a plague that specially afflicts them. Last year the *New York Times* (November 31, 1970) carried stories about the determination of black policemen in Hartford, Connecticut, to protect members of minority communities who are physically interfered with by "white bigoted police officers"; about a grand jury report that indicated "there was probably cause to believe that state policemen committed a criminal offense in a case in which they shot and killed two unarmed brothers in a stake-out and then planted a gun to cover themselves"; about a New York detective who was tried for conducting illegal checks of police records on behalf of a private business firm. And beneath the surface of reported events is greater abuse of official power that is never publicly aired. The new coalition should fight for that favorite ideal of conservatives, genuine rule of law. Doing so would produce a dramatically favorable response among those who primarily suffer the harm of official lawlessness.[7]

These four issues have great symbolic and policy significance. But, taken together, they are only one aspect of the general political effort to empower the oppressed. A program of progressive change that will achieve meaningful *reform* is a precondition for successful *radicalism*. To complete the work of the welfare state is the surest route to a radical future. The sooner everyone has access to a decent share of affluence, the sooner will a subsequent generation know in their gut that achievement of material well-being is only a way-station to a truly satisfying existence.

---

7. This observation is, unhappily, partly based on personal experience. I testified in the case of a UCLA professor who was assaulted by policemen, then charged with felonious assault. In this instance the state's case was so flimsy, the number of eyewitnesses so great, that the judge terminated the proceedings before the defense had finished giving all its evidence, summarily declaring the defendant innocent without even retiring to his chambers.

Fear that welfarism is co-optative is morally arrogant, and politically senseless from the point of view of genuine radicalism.

THE TOKENISM OF AMERICAN DEMOCRACY

A major obstacle to significantly ameliorative social programs lies in a political system whose hallmark is tokenism—in the maintenance of social stability by means of payoffs to the victims of injustice—payoffs so small as to be mere tokens. The system has worked primarily because those who have least have traditionally accepted least in return for their compliance with established forms of law and order. From the Republic's beginnings, this system of token payoffs has worked remarkably well. Radical strategy cannot rid us of tokenism until radical majorities can act within a genuinely majoritarian system. But we cannot even navigate the intervening waters unless there is at least mitigation of the evil.

Tokenism has three main causes. (1) The entire social system is institutionally skewed in favor of the tiny minority at the top of the social hierarchy that has most power, wealth, and status. (2) As majorities are not presently radical, even the majoritarian aspects of the system tend to promote tokenism, especially in relation to poverty and racism. (3) Manipulation and co-optation are so common that most Americans, especially those at the bottom, are too often inculcated with political attitudes that frustrate basic interests.

(1) Social stability is important to anyone who has something he wants to protect against society's boat-rockers. In a just society, just men would seek social stability to protect those institutions that promote what they cherish most. In an unjust society, powerful men do the same.

American democracy's historic genius, throughout the era of industrial expansion, has enabled groups highest in the social hierarchy to protect what they have with minimum reliance on repressive force. By contrast to other political systems, primary reliance on a token carrot instead of a big stick has enabled American democracy to promote social peace efficiently and with a minimum of jeopardy to structures of injustice. The institutional devices by which the interests of the mighty have almost always been protected at the expense of the weak are many, varied, and mutable. At one time, the Supreme Court was a main bulwark; today it is a less reliable tool of the powerful. At one time, limitations on the franchise were effective; with gradual extension of the suffrage, devices like the congressional seniority system and the poll tax were introduced to take up the slack. Our federal system was designed to frustrate the will of urban majorities, something it has done remarkably well as the present madness of our system of agricultural subsidies attests. In fact every aspect of American political life—party organization, electoral practices, municipal governance, legislative redistricting, governance of the mass media—betrays an institutional skew that favors the upper classes.

Today the practices by which majorities are frustrated is vulnerable to political attack. For the American electorate increasingly supports

efforts to translate theoretical majoritarianism into institutional practice—a development reinforced by the Supreme Court's one-man one-vote
decision. The new coalition should ally itself with every effort to erode
the unequal political power of the socially mighty; but it should do so
with care. For majorities are not more inclined to govern justly than
ruling elites. Paradoxically, in some cases the vestiges of class rule have
become important defenses for oppressed minorities.

(2) Our short-term coalition aim should not be majoritarian democracy; rather, what we should seek is a democratic order that most effectively promotes social justice. For example, direct primaries often harm
the interests of urban minorities who, through strategic concentrations,
have acquired a political leverage within nominating conventions that
more majoritarian practices might dilute. Radical liberals who are
carried away by majoritarian bias will ignore such practicalities at peril
of frustrating their primary goal—to build the coalition.[8] Because majorities usually act against the victims of extreme poverty and racial discrimination, the new coalition should deliberately try to modify adherence to the principle of majority rule. I can do no more here than
suggest the range of possibilities.

The following specific measures may prove useful: community control that increases the power of oppressed minorities over municipal
decisions affecting their lives; a cabinet post that deals exclusively with
minority interests; systematic and sustained effort by the Democratic
party organization to bring minorities into positions of influence and
power out of proportion to their numbers; gerrymandering electoral
districts to guarantee minority representation; a National Party Committee structure that magnifies the representation of minorities; even the
use of weighted votes when feasible.

(3) The fact is that a free marketplace of ideas as John Stuart Mill
proposed it does not exist. Despite the current fashions of counter culture,
in political thought and feeling the great mass of the American people
are too often manipulated "right down to their very instincts." Autonomy
is a word more honored ceremonially than in practical political ways.
Even those who are genuinely autonomous can rarely make themselves
heard. That is partly why so many of them are inclined to "speak" dis-
ruptively. But these problems are so basic and so deep that any remedies
proposed in this brief space would be too superficial to be helpful. Besides
more emphasis on liberal education, there is a need for more political
education, more participation in decisions that affect one's life, more
democratic control over the media of communication, more sympathy
for liberation movements despite occasional rhetorical excess.

ELECTORAL POLITICS: KEYSTONE IN THE ARCH

The vote is the keystone of a strategic arch that includes many other
forms of political action. Nonelectoral tactics will fail unless there is

---

8. For example, a proposal for a direct presidential primary went down to
defeat in a special 1969 convention of the Michigan Democratic party partly because so many black Democrats thought a convention system gave them more
political leverage.

effective use of the ballot. For example, the vast concentrations of corporate power cannot be democratically and wisely mastered without vigorous use of voting power. The task is not more likely to be accomplished by bloody revolution, or the Great Refusal, or "socialism in the ghetto," or the politics of the shaman—to mention only a few of the more frivolous alternatives that have been suggested.[9]

Yet the keystone is useless without the other stones in the arch. When Hubert Humphrey proclaimed that "liberalism and violence are deadly enemies,"[10] he betrayed devastating historical ignorance about how almost every radical program of liberal change has been achieved in this society. Foreign domination was lifted, slavery ended, the franchise extended to women, the trade unions were organized and the conditions of racial minorities generally improved by a complex set of events and political activities that included much essential disruption, disorder, and violence. But American revolutionaries also used their votes to control colonial legislatures. Abraham Lincoln had to be elected before he emancipated the slaves. Women were enfranchised only when enough elected public officials were willing to endorse a constitutional amendment. New Deal legislation promoted and consolidated trade union organization. And right now legislative willingness is essential if the lives of racial minorities are to be steadily improved. It is morally wrong and politically opportunistic to urge radicals to pledge unconditional nonviolence. But it is more absurd to urge them to forego electoral activity. Only a complex strategy that promotes flexibility about tactics can do the job.

Lest I be misinterpreted in a climate of public opinion that is only a little less hysterical about violence than it was about Communism during the McCarthy period, I do not think violence is particularly useful at this time. All forms of disorder tend to be counterproductive. By and large, the sporadic violence that has occurred has been manipulated by the Nixons, Agnews, and Reagans for political advantage. There is even evidence that they have, on occasion, not been loath to encourage violence.[11]

My point is not to defend violence, but to liberate the tactical imagination. Principally, I had in mind neither violence nor any other form of social disorder when I used the metaphor of the arch. Political education that goes on outside the electoral process as such is far more important and persuasive.

The role of secondary political groups that focus on a narrow range of issues needs to be stressed in this connection. Peace, civil liberties, and ecological groups play an indispensable role whose effectiveness tends to be blunted by their engagement in electoral politics. This is something Ralph Nader, to his credit, understands very well. There must be division

9. By Tom Hayden, Herbert Marcuse, Christopher Lasch, and Theodore Roszak, respectively.

10. *New York Times Magazine,* October 11, 1969.

11. I have in mind such statements as Ronald Reagan's when he welcomed a bloodbath on the campuses, as well as hard evidence that President Nixon went out of his way to encourage rock throwing at San Jose, California, for the sake of its effect on the 1970 elections.

of labor within the radical movement. Appropriate linkage of such groups with a radical coalition that is directly involved in electoral activities provides the best assurance that an obsessive desire to win elections will not undermine a politics of issues. As to electoral strategy itself, the main problem is how to deploy most effectively a minority of substantial strength. As they have only the support of a minority, candidates who run as radicals and liberals cannot normally hope to win. By the same token, those who place exclusive emphasis on winning erode prospects for radical change. When winning is the measure, the disheartening impact of losing is magnified. And demoralized former activists swell the ranks of the apathetic—not because they don't care, but because they can't hope.

Apathy is not, however, the worst consequence of a mania for victory. Practitioners of the old politics who are disposed to pay any price to win demote even the gravest moral issues. By 1967 Hubert Humphrey was already convinced that the war in Southeast Asia was wrong and had to be ended. Asked why he did not say so at the 1968 Democratic National Convention he explained that President Johnson "was absolutely paranoid about the war," and that, after all, "there I was, supposed to be running for President of the United States. All I had for a party to start with were the Johnson remnants."[12]

Radical liberals who cannot normally win elections are yet sufficiently numerous to veto the election of candidates who desperately want simply to win—especially the ones who have tended to take for granted our willingness to march lock-step in the cadres of the lesser evil. And while we should always support a lesser evil when evils are our only alternatives, the mistake is to suppose that support of marginally better candidates is always, in balance, the lesser evil.

The opposite is often true. By exercising an electoral veto we can, in those instances where the opposite *is* true, exert maximum pressure on the entire political process—educating the center when we defend our use of the veto; educating candidates or at least forcing them to reassess their inclination to move to the soft side of every tough policy question; giving heart to those who despair by enabling them to count some losses as victories; moving the whole center of gravity of American politics, eventually, toward an authentic liberalism.

Two broadly conflicting approaches to the problem of applying the veto vie for the favor of radical liberals: formation of a new political party on the one hand, retaining a loose affiliation with the Democratic party on the other. Under the present conditions, the latter is more rational.

A new party that really tries to win elections would not be sufficiently better than the Democratic party to justify the enormous effort that would have to be expended in the building. At best, such a new party effort would be slightly more progressive and less corrupt than internal Democratic party politics. Those who think otherwise fantasize. It is the process of seeking power, not the Democratic party, that co-opts. Immunity re-

12. *New York Times Magazine,* October 11, 1969, p. 26.

sults not from new organizational forms, but from rationality and morally authentic commitment—another reason why a new political coalition based solely on self-interest would merely initiate new political horrors. Granting that a new party would make political education easier, the critical test is whether such a shift would make application of a veto strategy more effective. The answer to that question is plainly negative, for a new party would organize a minority of an already distinct minority. In the process it would fragment our strength in those other ways that anyone who has ever been involved in internecine political conflict knows too well. Not only would deployment of the veto be less effective, but a new party effort would make us look far weaker than we are.

Many who might be attracted by a new coalition strategy that broadly gears itself to Democratic party activity will not be drawn to a new party. The bulk of the racial minorities, the more radical trade unionists, all in the conscience constituency who have acquired significant leverage within the Democratic party are not about to abandon the organization they continue to view as their main vehicle for electoral effort. The election victories of genuine radicals like Bella Abzug in New York, Ronald Dellums in California, the successful gubernatorial race of Pat Lucey in Wisconsin, Joseph Duffey's near-miss in Connecticut are among the gains I have in mind. Those who have in the face of growing repression made this limited progress are not about to yield it for the sake of party purity. And those who look to liberal Republicans for radical leadership, who try to induce men like John Lindsay and John Gardner to join a new genuinely radical party, pursue a will'o the wisp. Common Cause, for example, is a hopeful development, but hardly radical.

Moreover, any new party would be the fourth, not the third. It is true, as Senator McCarthy has emphasized,[13] that habits of major-party loyalty have been eroding. But, though generally healthy, the main benefits of this development have gone to those who are conservative or reactionary, not to radical liberals. Buckley's success in New York, Byrd's in Virginia, and the general threat George Wallace poses, all indicate that a new party would likely be the weakest of the four. And because a party is a less flexible instrument than the alternative I will propose, a new party effort is likely to play right into the hands of conservative and reactionary forces. For by splitting the vote that would normally go to progressive candidates, conservatives and reactionaries hope to gain by pluralities what majorities normally deny them.

To some extent people find a new party attractive because they despair of reforming the Democratic party in even its procedural aspects. Reform of the Democratic party, state by state and at the national level, indeed is urgently needed. And the little that has been done—reports by the McGovern and O'Hara commissions, proposals by a few reform commissions in such states as Michigan—is mostly a matter of blueprints awaiting implementing action. Progress is being made, but the omens are, at best, problematic. Yet well-justified scepticism about party-reform

13. In his general defense of a new party effort in "A Third Party May Be a Real Force in 1972," *New York Times Magazine,* June 7, 1970.

efforts is a sandy foundation on which to build fourth-party effort and a very weak basis for a new coalition strategy.

The time for a new party has not yet arrived. The alternative is loose affiliations with the Democratic party, primarily by successfully deploying our power to veto.

In order to do so most effectively, we must understand what makes very good politicians tick. Senator Edmund Muskie, for example, is a man who possesses integrity, intelligence, moral sensibility, and enough *amour propre* to project great dignity. He reminds many of Lincoln. Moreover, like Lincoln, he is very ambitious—a man who seeks and enjoys the exercise of power. Most important within the frame of broadly decent but quite flexible moral commitments, his decision-making mechanisms function so that he comes to perceive the world and to make judgments in ways that accommodate his political ambitions. When he forms judgments that conflict with views held by people who can advance or impair his career, he displays a fine humility. Publicly, he becomes silent or vague about important issues. He is, and perceives himself as, a bridge across troubled waters.[14]

In brief, Muskie's instinctual tendencies move him toward the center of any system of political pressures that is relevant to his electoral success. Clearly such a man will be affected by credible pressure from radical liberals. An intelligently conceived, vigorously applied veto strategy can contribute to the moral education of men like Muskie. But this must be done in a rational, credible fashion. The purpose is to limit the range of acceptable candidates; and to make sure that those who qualify and run conduct their campaigns in ways that most advance radical liberalism's long-term aims.

To see how this approach might work, consider a concrete case. Liberals want the Democrats to nominate a presidential candidate in 1972 who can win without betraying certain critically important, minimal commitments and values. That is to say, we would support a man who, if he wins, will at least be pledged to defend us against repressive force, will generally encourage the demographic trends on which we found our hope for future majorities, will energetically try to advance the welfare state, will enable us to be heard by keeping channels of governmental and party power open, will treat with reasonable sympathy programs we favor, the moral aspirations we voice. He cannot be radical and win. He can be progressive, reasonable, and tolerant. With these thoughts in mind, we should formulate a set of minimal but definite criteria of acceptability. Presenting these to all plausible candidates, we should warn each that unless he subscribes to these reasonable standards, we will work to defeat him in the general election should he be nominated. By gently reminding him of what many of us did in 1968, we can make it plain that this is not an empty threat.

14. "The American people don't like extremists or extreme positions. If I'm pushed to try to please the Left, I lose some Democratic votes and the independent and Republican votes I've always needed and gotten in Maine. I'm one of the few politicians who can still talk to the hard-hats and the blacks." *New York Times Magazine,* November 22, 1970, p. 130.

Of course, circumstances could arise in which all threats are void. Suppose an Agnew is nominated. Or suppose the danger of another Vietnam, or of a great depression, is imminent. We might have to swallow our convictions and our threats, support a nominee who does not satisfy even our minimal criteria. But barring such unfortunate contingencies, we should make the veto threat, and carry it out if it becomes necessary.

The same process, with appropriate variations, should be adopted whenever we are in a minority so definite that candidates of our own cannot win. The veto is applicable at every level of the electoral process. In each case we should assess our strength, assess the alternative to the lesser-evil Democrat and, where the alternatives are tolerable, apply the veto. The processes by which criteria are hammered out, limits of tolerability fixed, are crucial. No component of the potential coalition of radical forces should be excluded.

It is argued that we cannot organize a veto effectively enough to be credible. But it has been done, notably in 1968, and should be done much more explicitly. We have no alternative to going the veto route—except acquiescing in the kind of pseudo-realism that permits fundamental evils of our society to fester while candidates continue merrily to appeal to majority prejudices at the center. To permit this to happen will result in more than burning ghettos; our hopes for a liberal future will also go up in flames.

To accept the veto as basic to our electoral strategy does not preclude our running candidates who are genuinely committed radicals. In those rare instances where assessment yields a rational prospect of winning, the fight should certainly be made. Nor do radical liberals have to restrict themselves to candidacies that have prospects for victory. At times it is important to make the race for mainly educational reasons—though, unless this is done without illusion, the resulting loss will be demoralizing.

The basic approach should be clear. Electoral effort, precisely because it is so important, should be conducted with all the intelligence and determination needed to exert a maximum influence on the entire political process. The tension between short-term gains and long-term prospects should always be in the forefront. Skill at using our minority strength most effectively in building toward future majorities is the keystone of the arch which has the veto at the center.

A NEW POLITICAL PERSONA

The new politics sketched in what has gone before needs a new political persona, able to handle baffling tensions without losing either moral elan or political effectiveness.

The tensions are many. For at the heart of this new politics is the effort to build a radical coalition that is cohesive without being monolithic, progressive in ways that do not weaken more basic commitment to radicalism, tactically bold yet mindful of political consequence. The new coalition seeks to exert a steady pressure on the Democratic party. Above all, the coalition neither overestimates its present strength, nor underestimates its future potential.

Possessive individualism—the need to appropriate and control all things, people, organizations as one would a toothbrush—is the scourge of our culture. It is, and not surprisingly, a special vice of our politics. The radical Left has not been spared. Through the period of Vietnam protest, insurgents frequently suffered leaders who treated the many movements and groups they helped to build like personal fiefdoms. Some wheeled and dealed, manipulated and lied, betrayed trusts. Others displayed more integrity, but not less possessiveness. Unless this atavistic need to control is curbed, unless we become more capable of substituting the satisfactions of common effort for the satisfactions of ego-fulfillment, the new politics will in time become indistinguishable from the old.

The new political man will view all political leaders, especially candidates and officials, as neither devils nor saints, but as fallible creatures too often caught in a web of conflicting pressures to which they respond out of a variety of motives. But such understanding compassion should not prevent us from adding to the official's predicament. For our basic task is to generate pressures that by influencing judgment and action serve our ultimate aims. We will not succeed if we role-play, if we act *as if* we were at the center of the system of pressures rather than as part of its source. The tendency to role-playing comes to the fore when successful candidates or officials emerge from our own ranks. It is then that the dangers of harmful identification, of false loyalty and misplaced gratitude are greatest. Part of the price of success is that old intimacies must give way to the imperatives of a politics of impersonal, radical pressure.

My remarks no more than scratch the surface of the topic. Unless the qualities that constitute this new political persona become typical rather than exceptional, our radical minority cannot hope to be effective. But if radicals learn to find their gratifications through communal accomplishment within a strategic frame set by long-range moral perspectives, then the present mood of cynicism and despair may lift.

The Transition to Socialism

PAUL M. SWEEZY

The following is the text of a lecture, given in March and April [1971] in Turin and other Italian cities, at the invitation of the Associazione Culturale Italiana.

The subject of this talk is so large and one hour is so brief that I must confine myself to a few aspects of what could easily constitute the content of an entire course of lectures. This necessarily means that I will assume much that is neither obvious nor uncontroversial. I may therefore be useful at the outset to make explicit some of these assumptions.

(1) There is no such thing as a general theory of the transition between social systems. This is not because relatively little attention has been paid to the subject—though this is undoubtedly true—but because each transition is a unique historical process which must be analyzed and explained as such.

(2) Nevertheless, a comparative study of transitions can be extremely valuable. In particular the study of past transitions can help us to ask fruitful questions about present and possible future transitions, to recognize similarities and differences, to appreciate the historicity and totality of the process under examination.

(3) Transitions are never simple or brief processes. On the contrary, they typically occupy and even define whole historical epochs. One aspect of their complexity is what may be called multi-directionality: movement in one direction may turn back on itself and resume in a forward direction from a new basis. In some places the reversal may be prolonged or conceivably even permanent.

(4) Transitions from one social order to another involve the most difficult and profound problems of historical materialism. "Herr Proudhon does not know," Marx wrote in *The Poverty of Philosophy*, "that all history is but the continuous transformation of human nature." (Marx/ Engels, *Werke*, Vol. 4, p. 160.) This view can be squared with the principle, as stated in the sixth Thesis on Feuerbach, that "the human essence is no abstraction inherent in each single individual" but "the ensemble of social relations," only if it is possible to relate the transformation of human nature to the transformation of social relations. How this is to be done is also indicated in the *Theses on Feuerbach* (the third):

The materialist doctrine that men are products of circumstances and upbringing, and that therefore changed men are the product of other circumstances and changed upbringing, forgets that it is men who change circumstances and that the educator must himself be educated. . . . The coincidence of the changing of circumstances and human activity can be conceived and rationally understood only as *revolutionizing practice.*

Here, in the concatenation of human nature, social relations, and revolutionizing practice, we reach the heart of the problem of the transition from one social system to another.

* * *

Let us begin with a few reflections on the transition from feudalism to capitalism in its decisive European theater. There are, I believe, many unsettled questions in this area relating to such matters as the causes of the decline of feudalism and the origins of capitalism, but they are not my present concern. Whatever positions may be held by different scholars on these questions, it seems to me unlikely that any would disagree that both the decline of feudalism and the beginnings of capitalism can be traced far back into the Middle Ages, that is to say, into a period when there is no doubt that the dominant European mode of production was feudal. In other words, there is no doubt that capitalism made its ap-

pearance, not as a theory or an aspiration but as an actual social formation within the confines of feudal society. Oliver Cox has argued very
persuasively that Venice in the Middle Ages was already a thoroughly
bourgeois city-state, completely oriented toward profit-seeking commerce,
with significant capitalist production (e.g., in ship-building) and a typically bourgeois political and ideological superstructure. The same can be
said with even greater certainty of a considerable number of Italian and
Northern European cities in the later feudal period, and of course the
discovery of America and the opening up of sea routes to the Far East in
the fifteenth and sixteenth centuries generated a burst of activity (including plunder and piracy as well as trade) which by no stretch of the
imagination could be called "feudal." There is room for dispute about
precisely how and when capitalism finally triumphed, but there can be
no contesting the fact that the process involved an ongoing struggle between two actually existing social formations for supremacy, i.e., for state
power (monopoly over the means of coercion) and the right to organize
society in accordance with their respective interests and ideas. Moreover
the process was a prolonged one in which the "new" social formation had
ample time to prepare itself, both economically and ideologically, for the
role of undisputed dominance.

What does this mean in terms of the transformation of human nature? It means that "bourgeois man" was born and matured in a feudal
world. The establishment and expansion of capitalist economic and
social relations were practical human activities which gradually molded
human beings with appropriate attitudes, motivations, "instincts"—
cupidity, means-and-ends rationality, individualism, and so on. For centuries bourgeois man lived alongside feudal man, sometimes in uneasy
accommodation, sometimes in mortal combat, but always advancing
and reaching out for more power, eventually conquering and even assimi-
lating his ancient rival. When the time finally came for bourgeois man to
step forward as the master of his universe, his nature was fully formed
and faithfully reflected the newly emergent "ensemble of social relations."
In retrospect we can see that in this case the "revolutionizing practice,"
which in Marx's view is the key to understanding changes in society and
hence also changes in human nature, was precisely the centuries-long
process of building capitalism within the framework of feudal society.

*   *   *

If we turn now to the subject before us, the first thing we notice is
that the transition to socialism does not, and in the nature of the case
cannot, take the same course as the transition from feudalism to capitalism. Not that this road has never occurred to anyone, or even that it has
never been tried. Quite the contrary. The distinguishing characteristic
of pre-Marxian or Utopian socialism was the deliberate selection (though
not the conscious copying) of a road to socialism similar to that which
had led from feudalism to capitalism. Small socialistic communities were
to be, and in many cases actually were, established. These were to be both

schools of socialism and bases from which the new society would spread, undermining and eventually overwhelming their capitalist matrix. There were many reasons why this strategy could not work, perhaps chief among them that the small socialist communities—unlike capitalism in the interstices of feudal society—had nothing positive to offer the dominant system and hence from its viewpoint their success would be an unmitigated disaster. Add to this that they had neither the ability nor the desire to compete against capitalism on its own terms and one can see that the obstacles to their survival, let alone development, were so enormous that they were in effect doomed from the outset. Instead of creating a new socialist human nature, they served only to buttress the characteristic bourgeois view that human nature is, after all, unchangeable.

Marx of course shared none of the illusions of the Utopians and, as we have already seen, was fully aware of the complex interrelation of social systems, human action, and social change. (It is worth remembering that both the *Theses on Feuerbach* and *The Poverty of Philosophy*, from which I quoted earlier, were written in the period 1845-1847, i.e., early in Marx's intellectual development; and there is not the slightest reason to believe that he ever changed his mind on these absolutely fundamental questions.) What, then, was his conception of the *modus operandi* of the transition to socialism?

The answer, at least in broad outline, is well known. Socialism itself cannot take root and grow within the confines of capitalist society, as capitalism had done under feudalism. But in Marx's view capitalism has a special, perhaps historically unique, characteristic which not only makes possible but guarantees the existence of a different road to its transformation.

The essence of capitalism is the self-expansion of capital, which takes place through the production and capitalization of surplus value. Production of surplus value in turn is the function of the proletariat, i.e., the class of wage workers who own no means of production and can live only by the sale of their labor power. Since the proletariat produces for capital and not for the satisfaction of its own needs, it follows that capitalism, in Marx's words, "establishes an accumulation of misery corresponding with accumulation of capital." The proletariat is thus both essential to capitalism and its essential victim. As capitalism grows, so does the proletariat; and the very processes of capitalist development prepare the proletariat for its historic role. Hence the concluding sentences of the first section of the *Communist Manifesto*: "What the bourgeoisie therefore produces, above all, are its own grave-diggers. Its fall and the victory of the proletariat are equally inevitable."

This theory of the revolutionary mission of the proletariat is of course central to Marxism and has been endlessly expounded, criticized, and debated. It is not my present purpose, however, to enter this discussion but rather to point out that, considered as a theory of the transition to socialism, it is only half a theory. What it deals with is the overthrow of capitalism; what it omits is the construction of socialism. Does Marxism contain, or imply, a complementary theory of the construction of social-ism? If so, what is it? These are the questions to which I should like to address myself next.

*   *   *

For our purposes we do not need a definition of socialism, nor do we need to compile a catalogue of its characteristics. But we definitely do need to be perfectly clear that Marxism has always conceived of socialism as the negation of capitalism, operating according to radically different laws and principles. Capitalism treats people as means to the expansion of capital, which is the root of its manifold contradictions and evils. The main point of socialism is to reverse this, to enable people to take over and to arrange not only their productive activity but their whole lives with a view to satisfying their truly human needs. This reversal implies, among other things, the abolition of private property in the means of production and of incomes derived therefrom, a high degree of equality in all things, allocation of resources by plan rather than by the blind forces of the market, the elimination as rapidly as possible of invidious distinctions between manual and mental labor and between city and country, and the ultimate replacement of all money and commodity relations by direct human relations.

Now it is clear that capitalists and those imbued with capitalist atti-tudes and values would neither want nor be able to build and operate such a society. Their bourgeois human nature would be totally incom-patible with the ensemble of social relations of socialist society. An at-tempt to combine the two would be doomed from the outset: either bourgeois human nature would have to be transformed into socialist human nature, or socialist relations would have to be transformed into bourgeois relations.

Let us recall at this point that this dilemma never arose in the case of the transition to capitalism. Bourgeois relations grew up within the framework of feudal society and molded bourgeois human nature over a period of several centuries. When capitalism finally conquered feudalism, it did so not merely as a revolutionary class but as an entire social order in which the correspondence between human nature and social relations was already fully developed. The element of dissonance represented by the continued existence of feudal remnants was of course there and in some (superstructural) respects was even important, but it posed no serious threat to the functioning of capitalism.

As we have seen, socialist human nature could not emerge through the revolutionizing practice of socialism within the framework of capital-ism. Are there other possibilities, and if so what are they?

Not so long ago, I argued, in a discussion with Charles Bettelheim, that Marxism, at least up to the time of the Russian Revolution, had a clear answer to this question:

In classical Marxian theory . . . the proletariat . . . referred to the wage workers employed in large-scale capitalist industry who, in the advanced capitalist countries, constituted a majority of the working class and a very substantial proportion of the total population. These workers were assumed to have acquired, as a consequence of the capitalist accumulation process itself, certain specifically proletarian (and anti-bourgeois) attitudes and values: solidarity, cooperativeness, egalitarianism, etc. Historically speaking, the proletarian was seen as a "new man" formed by capitalism and possessing the interest, the will, and the ability to overthrow the system *and* to lead the way in the construction of a new socialist society. (*Monthly Review,* December 1970, p. 17.)

I wrote this not after research in the relevant texts but from my general understanding of Marxian theory formed over a period of many years. Subsequently I was challenged to support this interpretation, and I must confess that I was unable to do so. It is easy to cite dozens of passages from the works of Marx and Engels affirming the revolutionary role of the proletariat in the overthrow of capitalism. I have not, however, found any which are specifically addressed to the question of the proletariat's ability or readiness to build a socialist society; and at least some of their formulations, especially those which analyze the effects of the division of labor on the worker, clearly imply a negative evaluation of the proletariat's qualifications. Consider, for example, the following from the famous chapter on "Machinery and Modern Industry," in the first volume of *Capital* (repeated verbatim by Engels in *Anti-Dühring*):

Modern industry, indeed, compels society, under penalty of death, to replace the detail-worker of today, crippled by life-long repetition of one and the same trivial operation, and thus reduced to the mere fragment of a man, by the fully developed individual, fit for a variety of labors, ready to face any change of production, and to whom the different social functions he performs are but so many modes of giving free scope to his own natural and acquired powers.

As a statement of one of the central aims, I would even say necessities of socialism, this is magnificent. But when Marx says that modern industry "compels society" to follow the course indicated, he deliberately sidesteps the question of the nature of the revolutionizing practice which will turn a mere fragment of a man into a fully developed individual.

When in doubt about the correct interpretation of Marx, it is a good idea to consult Lenin. What were his ideas on this subject?

Perhaps Lenin's most systematic analysis of the characteristics of the proletariat was in *What Is to Be Done?,* written in 1902. There, as is well known, he argued that "economism" comes naturally to the proletariat: "The history of all countries shows that the working class, exclusively by its own effort, is able to develop only trade union consciousness, i.e., the conviction that it is necessary to combine in unions, fight the employers and strive to compel the government to pass necessary labor legislation, etc." (*Selected Works,* Vol. I, Part 1, pp. 233-234.) Socialism, i.e., the conviction that it is necessary to overthrow capitalism and replace it by an entirely different system, was, according to Lenin, introduced into the proletariat by revolutionary intellectuals. It was they who took the initiative in educating the advanced workers to their real interests and organizing them into a revolutionary vanguard party whose functions were both to lead the proletariat in revolutionary struggles and to imbue it with an ever sharper socialist consciousness. The clear implication of this view for the problem which concerns us is that it is not capitalism as such but the revolutionary struggle to overthrow capitalism which creates men with the will and ability to go further and begin the construction of socialism. Revolutionizing practice, in Lenin's view, was nothing more nor less than the practice of revolution.

We are often told, especially by learned opponents of Marxism, that it was precisely in his denial of the spontaneous revolutionary potential of the proletariat that Lenin differed most markedly from Marx and Engels. This is supposed to be the basis of his conception of the nature and role of the vanguard party, which is widely believed to constitute a Leninist deviation without roots in the teachings of the masters.

Certainly there is no doubt that it was Lenin who was responsible for developing the vanguard party, both in theory and practice, as we know it today. But is there really any inconsistency between the Leninist conception of the party and the ideas of Marx and Engels?

It seems to me that it would be correct to give an affirmative answer to this question only if it could be shown that Marx and Engels believed that the proletariat was capable of developing, exclusively by its own effort (in Lenin's phrase), a revolutionary *and* socialist consciousness. As I indicated earlier, I used to think that this was indeed their view but an effort to prove it convinced me that I was wrong. Not only does one look in vain for specific statements attributing revolutionary socialist spontaneism to the proletariat, but the lifelong practice of the two men would be incomprehensible if they had held such a view of the character of the proletariat. From the Communist League in the 1840s through the First International to Engel's last years when he acted as consultant to socialist parties all over the world, they were tireless in their efforts to do just what Lenin said it was the function of revolutionary intellectuals to do, i.e., introduce a revolutionary socialist consciousness into the proletariat. And it is of course obvious that one of the examples Lenin had in mind when he wrote *What Is to Be Done?* was the founders of scientific socialism. The weight of the evidence, it seems to me, is that in this as in other matters Lenin's ideas and activities were fully consistent with those of Marx and Engels. For them, no less than for him, revolutionizing practice was the practice of revolution.

* * *

I would like now to attempt to draw some of the implications of this view for the transition to socialism. Bourgeois human nature, as we have seen, was formed in a centuries-long process of actual capitalist development within the framework of feudal society. When capitalism had grown strong enough to challenge and defeat feudalism, there was no real possibility of a return to feudalism. Bourgeois man was at home only in bourgeois society: there was no conceivable reason for him to reactivate or recreate feudal social relations. (This is not to deny of course that capitalist power could here and there be defeated by feudal power, resulting in local and perhaps even prolonged setbacks to the progress of capitalism. Such occurrences, however, could not arrest the general advance of the new system.) It is altogether different in the case of the transition to socialism. Socialist human nature is not formed within the framework of capitalism but only in the struggle against capitalism. What guarantee is there that this will occur on a sufficient scale and in sufficient depth to make possible the construction of a new socialist society? For we should be under no illusion that the social relations specific to a socialist society could exist in anything but name in the absence of the kind of human material which alone could give them sense and meaning. That Marx himself understood this, even if he did not explore all its implications, is shown by a passage from the *Enthüllungen über den Kommunisten-Prozess zu Köln* in which he distinguishes between the propaganda of his group in the Communist League and that of an opposed minority group:

While we say to the workers: you have to undergo fifteen, twenty, fifty years of civil wars and popular struggles not only to change the relations but to change yourselves and prepare yourselves for political mastery, they tell them on the contrary, "We must come to power immediately, or we can forget about it." While we make a special point of emphasizing to the German worker the under-developed state of the German proletariat, they flatter his national feeling and the craft prejudice of the German artisan, which to be sure is more popular. (*Werke,* Vol. 8, p. 412.)

Here Marx puts his finger on the central issue: the proletariat must not only change the relations of society but in the process change itself. And unfortunately more than a century of subsequent history proves all too conclusively that there is as yet no guarantee that this can be successfully accomplished.

As far as the industrially advanced countries are concerned, capitalism proved to have a great deal more expansive and adaptive power than Marx suspected. Under the circumstances, their proletariats succumbed to the economism which Lenin saw as natural to them but believed could be overcome by a conscious revolutionary vanguard. What actually happened was the opposite: the vanguards, whether calling themselves Socialist or Social Democratic or Communist, instead of converting the proletarian masses to revolutionary socialism were themselves transformed into economistic reformers. There are of course those who see in this a temporary aberration and believe that a new revolutionary period has opened in which the proletariat will once again play the role attributed to it in classical Marxist-Leninist theory. (For an able presentation of this argument, see Daniel Singer's recently published work, *Prelude to Revolution.*) I for one fervently hope that they are right, but as for now the most one can say is that the case is unproved.

When we turn to the countries where the old regimes (either capitalist or a feudal-capitalist mixture) have actually been overthrown, we are confronted with two very different experiences which, for obvious reasons, can best be exemplified by the Soviet Union and China respectively.

The October Revolution proved the validity, under conditions existing in Russia in 1917, of the first half of the Marxist-Leninist theory of transition to socialism. The industrial proletariat, though relatively small, was able, under resolute revolutionary leadership, to overthrow the bourgeois regime which had come to power in the February Revolution. But with regard to the second half of the theory—the capacity of the proletariat to lead the way in the construction of socialism—the Russian experience is at best inconclusive. Small to begin with, the Russian proletariat was decimated and dispersed by the four years of bloody civil war, hunger, and chaos which followed the October Revolution. The Bolshevik government, preoccupied with problems of survival and economic recovery, was obliged to rely on the old, obviously profoundly anti-socialist state bureaucracy and to add to its size and power in the ensuing years. Nevertheless, the period from roughly 1922 to 1928 was one of revolutionary ferment—in the arts, education, sexual relations, social science, etc.—which, had it not been cut short, might have generated powerful socialist forces and trends. What brought this period to an end was the fateful decision to subordinate everything else to the most rapid possible economic development. It would take us too far afield to discuss the reasons for or justification of this decision: suffice it to point out that it entailed what may almost be called a supernatural counter-revolution together with the imposition of an extremely repressive political regime. Under the circumstances, revolutionizing practice tending to produce socialist human nature almost totally disappeared. Instead, the reconstituted and expanded proletariat which came with forced-march industrialization was repressed and atomized, deprived of all means of self-expression and terrorized by an omnipresent secret police.

While the Russian experience thus throws little light on the positive side of the problem of constructing socialism, it does provide devastating proof of the impossibility of infusing seemingly socialist forms—such as nationalized means of production and comprehensive economic planning—with genuine socialist content unless the process goes hand-in-hand with the formation of socialist human beings. The idea, assiduously promoted by Soviet ideologists, that raising material living standards of the masses will by itself foster socialist consciousness never had anything to recommend it and has been shown by Soviet (as well as American!) experience to be nonsense. Some of the negative potentialities of the Soviet Russian system were, paradoxically, held in check for a time by the Stalinist terror: a bureaucrat abusing his position too blatantly was likely to find himself in a labor camp, if not worse. But after Stalin's death these restraints were largely removed, and the true nature of the situation was soon revealed.

A recent Chinese critique points to the heart of the matter:

From production to distribution, from economic branches to government organizations, the forces of capitalism run wild in town and countryside. Speculation, cornering the market, price rigging, and cheating are the order of the day: capitalist roaders in enterprises and government team up in grafting, embezzling, working for their own benefit at the expense of the public interest, dividing up the spoils and taking bribes. Socialist ownership by the whole people has degenerated into ownership by a privileged stratum, and is directly manipulated by a handful of capitalist roaders and new bourgeois elements. . . . This has been a painful historical lesson! ("Socialist Construction and Class Struggle in the Field of Economics—Critique of Sun Yeh-fang's Revisionist Economic Theory," by the Writing Group of the Kirin Provincial Revolutionary Committee, *Peking Review*, April 17, 1970, p. 9.)

I would stress particularly the statement that "socialist ownership by the whole people has degenerated into ownership by a privileged stratum" with the *caveat* that this is to be interpreted *de facto* rather than *de jure*. It is a privileged stratum—what Charles Bettelheim has called a new "state bourgeoisie"—which controls the means of production and thereby decides how the fruits of production are to be utilized. Regardless of legal forms, this is the real content of class ownership.

It is noteworthy that the foregoing characterization of the situation in the Soviet Union could be applied with little or no change to almost any capitalist country, the main difference being that under capitalism a large part of the activities alluded to are perfectly legal. This underscores the fact that no legal system, using the term in the broadest sense to include the system of property relations, can effectively control men's behavior unless it is in harmony with the historically formed human nature of its subjects. This condition is patently not fulfilled in the Soviet Union.

This of course does not mean that there will never be socialism in the Soviet Union, still less that the failure of the first effort to introduce it has been without positive effects. The earliest appearances of capitalism were also abortive, but they left a precious heritage of experience (including, for example, the invention of double-entry bookkeeping) without which later capitalisms might also have failed or at any rate found development much more difficult. It was through the Russian Revolution that the crucially important science of Marxism-Leninism reached the peoples of Asia, Africa, and Latin America; and it is probably no exaggeration to say that it was only the negative example of later Soviet experience which enabled other countries to see the necessity of protracted revolutionizing practice to the building of socialism. "The restoration of capitalism in the Soviet Union and certain other socialist countries," said Lin Piao on the fiftieth anniversary of the October Revolution, "is the most important lesson to be drawn from the last fifty years of the history of the international Communist movement." (Quoted in *Le Monde Weekly*, January 13, 1971, p. 8.)

It was not, however, only the negative lesson of Soviet experience which impelled the Chinese to pioneer a different road to the construction of socialism. The situation in China differed in important respects from that in Russia. For one thing, the Chinese proletariat, though smaller than the Russian, was never seriously plagued by economism. As Mao wrote in 1939, "Since there is no economic basis for economic reformism in colonial and semi-colonial China as there is in Europe, the whole proletariat, with the exception of a few scabs, is most revolutionary." (*Selected Works*, Vol. II, p. 324.) To this consistently revolutionary force there was added another even larger one formed in the quarter-century-long military struggle against capitalism, feudalism, and imperialism, which culminated in the triumph of the Revolution in 1949. In the words of the editors of *Hongqi* (No. 5, 1964): "Owing to the education and training received in the people's army, millions of ordinary workers and peasants and many students and other intellectuals of petty-bourgeois origin have gradually revolutionized themselves [in thinking and action] and become steadfast, politically conscious fighters and mainstays in revolution and construction." (The square brackets are in the original text.) The prolonged civil war in China combined with the war against the Japanese invaders thus fostered a vast growth in both the size and the maturity of the revolutionary forces, while a much shorter period of civil war and resistance to foreign invaders in the Soviet Union seriously weakened the revolutionary forces there. The result was that China, on the morrow of the Revolution, was much more richly endowed with revolutionary human material than Russia had been. Finally, in Lenin and Mao Tse-tung Russia and China were fortunate to have two of the greatest revolutionary geniuses of all time; but Lenin died before the process of constructing socialism had really begun, while Mao's leadership has already lasted more than two decades since the victory of the Revolution.

Both men were well aware of the enormous difficulty of the task that lay ahead after the overthrow of the old regime. In his "Report at the Second All-Russia Trade Union Congress" (January 20, 1919), Lenin said:

The workers were never separated by a Great Wall of China from the old society. And they have preserved a good deal of the traditional mentality of capitalist society. The workers are building a new society without themselves having become new people, or cleansed of the filth of the old world; they are still standing up to their knees in that filth. We can only dream of cleaning the filth away. It would be utterly utopian to think this could be done all at once. It would be so utopian that in practice it would only postpone socialism to kingdom come.

No, that is not the way we intend to build socialism. We are building while still standing on the soil of capitalist society, combating all those weaknesses and shortcomings which also affect the working people and which tend to drag the proletariat down. There are many old separatist habits and customs of the small holder in this struggle, and we still feel the effects of the old maxim: "Every man for himself, and the devil take the hindmost." (*Collected Works*, Vol. 28, 424-425.)

Mao was even more explicit when he wrote, as the Peoples Liberation Army was about to win its final victories in March of 1949:

To win country-wide victory is only the first step in a long march of ten thousand *li*. Even if this step is worthy of pride, it is comparatively tiny; what will be more worthy of pride is yet to come. After several decades, the victory of the Chinese people's democratic revolution, viewed in retrospect, will seem like only a brief prologue in a long drama. A drama begins with a prologue, but the prologue is not the climax. The Chinese revolution is great, but the road after the revolution will be longer, the work greater and more arduous. (*Selected Works,* Vol. IV, p. 374.)

After only two decades we can see how right Mao was. The drama has continued to unfold, moving from one climax to another. Despite all its initial advantages, China has never been free of the danger of slipping back into the old forms and relations which for centuries had molded Chinese human nature. The old "ensemble of social relations" continued and still continues to exist in the minds and consciousness of hundreds of millions of Chinese. As Marx expressed it in *The Eighteenth Brumaire,* "The tradition of all the dead generations weighs like a nightmare on the brain of the living." (*Werke,* Vol. 8, p. 115.) To overcome this ineluctable fact—not to nationalize property or build heavy industry or raise material living standards, important though all these things are—is the central problem of the transition to socialism. And it was the Chinese revolutionaries under the inspired leadership of Mao Tse-tung who grasped and internalized this truth to the extent of making it the conscious basis of their revolutionizing practice.

This is not the occasion for an attempt to analyze this revolutionizing practice, nor do I have the knowledge and competence which would be required. What I wish to emphasize is that *for the first time* the problem has been fully recognized and correctly posed. Until that was done, there was not even a chance of finding a satisfactory solution.

It is as well to close on a note of caution. In politics, as in science, the first step in solving a problem is to recognize and pose it correctly. But the first step is usually a long way from the final solution, and when the problem is nothing less than changing human nature this *caveat* is doubly and triply relevant. Fortunately, Mao knows this better than anyone else, and we can hope that the knowledge will become a permanent part of his legacy to the Chinese people. Ultimate success or failure will probably not be known until all of us here tonight are long since gone and forgotten. Said Mao in 1967 at the height of the Cultural Revolution:

The present Great Proletarian Cultural Revolution is only the first of its kind. In the future such revolutions must take place. . . . All Party members and the population at large must guard against believing . . . that everything will be fine after one, two, three, or four cultural revolutions. We must pay close attention, and we must not relax our vigilance. (Quoted in the concluding chapter of Jean Daubier, *Histoire de la révolution culturelle prolétarienne en Chine,* Paris, Maspero, 1970.)

All history, Marx said, is the continuous transformation of human nature. What is Mao telling us but that even after the overthrow of class domination the positive task of transforming human nature never ceases?

A Nightmare

MORTON A. KAPLAN

In the scenario that follows the term "nightmare" carries several implications. The scenario is a nightmare in that it does sound like the product of a bad dream. However, if we extrapolate certain tendencies in society, as they could be reinforced by technological developments, the world that emerges would be a nightmare judged by the values that humane and sensitive individuals presently hold.

We do not argue that the scenario that follows is likely or even plausible. On the other hand, it requires a kind of blindness not to recognize that the seeds for this nightmare, bizarre though it is, lie in the present and that the arguments for many of the individual steps that might bring it to pass are not in themselves reprehensible. These steps could in some cases even be considered to represent praiseworthy motives. To recognize the less desirable potentialities of the present is a necessary, although not a sufficient, condition for avoiding them.

Much of what we have to say in this scenario is not original. Aldous Huxley in *Brave New World* and George Orwell in *1984*, as well as many other novelists, created anti-utopias in which omnipresent social controls changed radically the nature of man and of society. The anti-utopias usually have been regarded as merely imaginative extrapolations that were technologically infeasible. Unfortunately, a few short years later, as we now write, it is less difficult to extrapolate from existing progress in the sciences to the technological developments necessary to produce these anti-utopias. Huxley's Alphas and Betas would still seem scientific marvels; yet recent advances in genetics, with specific reference to the unravelling of the DNA code, show them to be within the range of possibility. Many of the scientific developments of the future could be even more consequential than nuclear fission, less controllable by current techniques, and more inconsistent with existing social institutions and cultural values.

Many of the demands for increased social controls will stem from the vulnerabilities of modern complex societies. Although modern complex society has both greater instantaneous and long-range flexibility than simpler societies, it also has less redundancy and more bottlenecks that could affect the whole society. Thus major interruptions that overwhelm its instantaneous or short-run adjustment capability, or occur too suddenly for its long-range flexibility to get a chance to work, might cause great damage to the society. Because simple societies are less interdependent than modern complex societies, their breakdowns are often much less total in their effects. The modern industrial society is highly differentiated and therefore requires greater integration in order to function effectively. The disrupted complex society, under at least some important conditions, might not be able to sustain even the low level of productivity that is normal to a simple society.

The greater wealth and improved technology of modern society provide us with many important advantages and freedoms. Diversity of life style, despite mass production and mass man, is possible today in a way that in the past was available only for a few of the élite or of the wealthy, if for any at all. The great diversity of modern society, however, requires a geometric increase in the organization of modern life. We become increasingly sensitive to the disturbances produced by others. And this sensitivity in turn requires greater and greater social control in order to maintain the peace and stability of the system. One need not assume the triumph of the police mentality, or the intrusion of motivations denigrative of human dignity, to foresee that many restrictions on human liberty will have valid and attractive rationales, even rationales related to the liberty of one's fellows. Federal safety regulations for automobile manufacturers and tests for drivers increase the "freedom" of the license-holding driver to drive in safety. Coercive treatment for the mentally ill raises the probability that they will be able to lead freely constructive lives. Plastic hearts might replace real ones and damaged brains might be linked to computers. Therapeutic abortions, through the death of the foetus, increase the freedom of the mother. And the biological adaptation of man to his ecological niche in an extremely complicated and over-populated society will increase his freedom to live a satisfying and useful life.

We have, of course, omitted the crucial qualification: under the new developing conditions. It is still possible that the terminus of the process will be inconsistent with anything we would regard as freedom or dignity or even human. The evolution of society might produce the devolution of man. The adaptability (and superiority) of man have heretofore consisted in his lack of specialized adaptation (unlike the lesser animals). In the not-too-distant future, man might be adapted in a specialized sense, while society through the control of genetic science maintains its general adaptability by fitting men to the various tasks that time and environment provide. The survival of the fittest may be replaced by the fitting of the survivals.

The nightmare is bizarre, but consider a few of the factors that could facilitate and seem to justify a controlled society, or a few that could make it feasible, although the two categories are neither necessarily nor entirely distinct. Overpopulation and organizational complexity have already been mentioned. The greater susceptibility of society in general to disruption could create opportunities for deliberate intra-societal attacks accompanied by blackmail, to say nothing of organized crime on a novel scale. When nuclear weapons become subject to criminal access (miniaturization will help to bring this about), and when criminal or political conspiracies become capable of bringing civil government to a halt through the disruption of the computerized networks upon which it will depend, the only alternative to a new feudalism (without the mitigating social features of the old) might be forms of surveillance and control far surpassing any now in existence.

Access to places of amusement and museums might have to be rationed, food substitutes developed, access to new forms of socialized housing (mile-high community units) regulated, scarce medical facilities (replacement organs, esoteric remedies, very skilled surgeons, and so forth) allocated. Some humans might have to be adjusted to environments different from the earth's surface.

Clearly it would be erroneous to compare man to the lemming, but every known animal species on which the experiment has been carried out is dysfunctionally disorganized by overcrowding. Rules governing mutual adjustment (whether social or legal) will necessarily be very stringent. There will be a strong emphasis on adjustment (other-directed orientations) in place of individualism. Resort to drugs, other worldly religions, delinquency, crime, and mental disease (as a way of "acting out") could increase significantly, requiring medical, social, and criminal sanctions to prevent or to contain those forms of disturbance that are excessively dysfunctional for the social and political systems.

The consequences of dislocations and of mistakes in the production, distribution, and control functions of business and government are likely to be so huge that the facilities for coping with them must take precedence over civil liberties or private pursuits and property. The blackout of the eastern United States in 1965 only suggests what can go wrong in the future. (That particular disturbance need not have occurred with proper systems design, including cutoffs and redundancy, with their concomitant costs—but that is the problem. On the one hand, there could be extremely sophisticated and prudent systems designs or, on the other hand, there could be extensive control and supervision to avoid the possibility or consequences of relatively farfetched disasters.) Needs for control and surveillance will likely develop to utilize the technological capabilities that are present in the system. Technological developments, in addition to meeting environmental requirements, will likely produce needs to satisfy the technological capabilities.

It is already possible to monitor conversations by the disturbances they produce on window panes and to photograph documents through windows at great distances. Television monitors both indoors and out might become common as the techniques become cheaper. Voices and faces might be checked immediately by advanced computers working through nationwide banks of identifiers. Quite apart from credit needs, the means to maintain continuous checks on the entire population and automatically to scan them for disturbing words or phrases will likely be available by the year 2000. It might occur that only those with enormous resources will be able—and in even these cases only partly and perhaps only by bribery or by political manipulation—to avoid some monitoring or to interfere with transmission of the data. At the minimum, if the monitoring exists, new code languages will develop in efforts to evade some of the consequences.

There are cases today of individuals who are kept biologically alive, in an attempt to avoid testamentary consequences, by bizarre and uncomfortable medical techniques long past the point at which the physician, the individual, or the family would otherwise prefer a natural death. As facilities for replacing human parts increase, including artificial stimulation or substitution for certain brain functions, court cases will almost inevitably arise over the issue of when a man ceases to be himself. (Consider the case of a man who has had most of his intellectual capabilities replaced by a computer or even by a transplanted brain.) Ultimate resort to these techniques would come under government regulation. If overpopulation and means for increasing longevity increase to some as yet unspecified limit, the right to bear children and to resort to longevity techniques could be controlled by the government. How these issues, which are so politically potent, could be handled presents a challenge to the imagination. If such issues arise, and they well might, then the consequences for what we now regard as civilized human standards are obviously enormous.

It is not unlikely that there will become available by the year 2000 drugs and other behavior controls capable of producing personality changes at will, of rewarding activities by hormonal flows (perhaps by remote control) that overcome rational ego or superego objections to continuation of the activities, and of punishing other activities. Alternative techniques include radio waves, ultrasonic impulses that cause uneasiness, induced hallucinations, and various forms of educative devices operating from infancy. These might be so effective that continuous control techniques would be superfluous, although available for obdurate cases. Much of this might be available or imposed under the rubric of mental hygiene, simply because such intrusions on individual freedom are not likely to occur except for highly persuasive reasons.

It is not difficult for an American to understand that a dictatorship— even a benevolent one—would use such techniques. The Soviet Union already has sent some of its important literary figures to mental institutions; it is well to remember that the United States sent Ezra Pound to such an institution, although it did so as an act of kindness. It is difficult to accept that such techniques would be used widely in the United States until we recall the extent to which they are already legitimized. Hundreds of psychiatrists were apparently willing in 1964 to lend their names to the conclusion that Barry Goldwater was mentally unsound although they had not examined him. Our culture is attuned to the concept of mental illness and its cure: the modern concept is to rehabilitate rather than to punish criminals because of the belief that crime results from mental illness. Delinquents are guided by social workers. Disturbed schoolchildren are treated by guidance counselors. Parents read psychologists to learn how to raise their children. The rhetoric of our time—and most of it is quite genuine and functional—is the rhetoric of mental adjustment and treatment. Our national pastime is self-medication with tranquilizers and with other drugs that affect the psychological condition of the individual. Rather than doubting that Americans would use the most advanced techniques that become available and as systematically as possible, there is reason to doubt that there would be much effective resistance. We do not need the rationale of a political ideology to justify control of the masses. We have our own myth of adjustment and of mental balance; anti-social behavior, as interpreted by the received truth of the day, is sufficient to indicate the desirability of treatment. Even some of the New Left—self-proclaimed rebels against societal conformity—have advocated (perhaps seriously, perhaps not) placing LSD into dormitory food to free the mass of students from their "false"—hence also "sick"—beliefs. Even those of us who criticize this abuse of terminology often think of some of the New Left or of other social rebels as "merely sick."

As anti-social behavior becomes less tolerable as a result of the increasing complexity and crowding of society, are we not likely to treat what we cannot tolerate? No doubt if we were ever presented with this kind of future as a direct and systematic alternative to the present, we would not opt for it. But we are not presented with choices in this fashion. Each adaptation that helps partly to produce the future is considered on the basis of incremental costs and benefits, of marginal changes; it is possible that each incremental change or marginal benefit might seem to outweigh the costs, that the benefits will be clear and the transition to the nightmarish future hypothetical.

So far the nightmare is one that could conceivably be produced by the year 2000 or shortly thereafter. The ethical problems that could be caused when we learn to produce man or variations of man in the laboratory are unlikely to occur until well after the year 2000. Laboratory men who are indistinguishable from ordinary men, we hope, would be granted the rights of natural men. Specialized laboratory-created beings that differ from natural men, but that do possess the ability to reason, are more likely not to be granted full rights (a decision we would regard today as ethically monstrous). If they are not granted human rights, questions might then be raised about the rights of adapted and specialized men who are indistinguishable from manufactured adapted and specialized men. In any event, the scope and variety of restrictions upon full natural men will be enormously increased.

Further problems would arise if bionic computers are made that perform many of the tasks of men and develop creative capabilities. As the distinction between man and lesser creatures and machines begins to shade off, the uniqueness of man and the rights attributed to this uniqueness may begin to attenuate. The vulnerability of the political system to shocks and to disruptions could reinforce arguments for the restriction of man based upon the substitutability of manufactured men and bionic machines. A creature that is superfluous as well as dangerous might appear difficult to defend. If the esthetic function of man also degenerates, then the argument that man is an unique cultural being will also have attenuated. Bionic computers, for example, might be able to produce real art. Even now, some popular music (and even some classical records) are produced as much by equipment and by mechanical interventions in the performance as by "natural" performances with "normal" instruments. More than this, creative bionic computers might produce music that is genuinely more creative than some of the current musical fashions, for instance, aleatory music.

If athletes begin to make use of prosthetic devices as well as of drugs to improve their performances, we might gradually produce almost entirely mechanical athletes, for whom bionic robots might eventually substitute. As this process continues, man's confidence in himself and in his role might be seriously undercut. His vision of himself as a unique being, so essential apparently to his sense of identity, might be destroyed.

A variety of strange religions would spring up in efforts to explain this peculiar universe. Such religions might attempt to glorify man in ways that repudiate the rational and scientific interpretations that have flourished since the Renaissance; or they might be masochistic and denigrative of man. More likely both types would flourish under the suggested conditions.

Perhaps many (most?) men would be kept in a permanently drugged state (pacified?) and adapted to the ecology to which they are assigned according to some computerized calculation. The central government would so likely be swamped by the problem of keeping the system functioning properly that it would be concerned only with marginal and immediate problems rather than with the increasing repulsiveness of the entire system. In any event there might be no rational or moral (whatever these terms may mean in such a bizarre twenty-first century) feasible solution that does not reject modern technology or condemn billions of surplus humans to death or to deprivation. The twenty-first century would no more be able to return to the world of the twentieth century than we could return to the golden age of Greece.

Efforts to control the situation would doubtless occur—perhaps as desperate measures. For instance, the political and intellectual élite might distribute contraceptive drugs through the food supply that could be counteracted only by other drugs restricted to the élite. The rationalization could be persuasive: with bionic automation, production would not be disrupted and population might drop to tenable limits that permit humane standards.

Yet the cure might be more brutalizing than the problem. In any event, this "cure" assumes that a technocracy, or oligarchy, or "aristocracy" controls the political system. As technological innovations are made and biological manufacture and reproduction intensify, the legitimacy that invests political democracy might deteriorate; the political bases from which these encroachments can be resisted might be undermined. If at the same time the system becomes so complex that it can be worked only from the vantage point of the memory banks of a centralized national or worldwide computer system, political and military capabilities would in fact be concentrated in one (if not monolithic, at least centralized) control center. Particularly if creative bionic computers and man-computer feedback circuits are involved in the central apparatus, control may pass from man to machines, in which case, although population might be limited since it serves no useful function, humanity might be kept in a perpetually drugged and/or subservient state, to the extent to which it is permitted to persist. This would prevent rebellion and disturbance or other "undesirable" interferences with the maintenance of the system. By determining what information to feed back to the computer-linked controllers and by manipulating the logic of the problem, the computers might gradually gain control of the entire system. This might result not from some analogous organic urge to control or even to destroy, although the possibility that this complex might enter a condition equivalent to madness can hardly be dismissed, but from an effort to reinforce stasis; the bionic central computers are likely to view humans as defective both emotionally and logically.

Because of the enormous importance of the national computer networks for planning and control, they might become the focus of politics, conspiracy, and intra-élite coups in the event they do not secure the kind of control adumbrated above. Quite possibly efforts by political groups to seize control of the central computers might themselves disrupt the computer functions at least temporarily and produce crises or disturbances that affect the operations of and prognosis for the system. Advance weapons systems that operate on a computerized basis would make consensus among the population and support within the armed forces almost irrelevant. Some types of weapons could be individualized and could, in effect, "home in" on voice and sight patterns of particular individuals identified from the national population register as enemies. Others would be used against large groupings but would themselves not require any human agency other than the programming of the computer. These weapons would use advanced surveillance techniques to find and to destroy their targets or alternatively to incapacitate them. Again, the patterns they would home in on, whether group or individual, would be transmitted from a central registry. Pickup of prisoners would be automated.

The nightmare we have sketched is bizarre, implausible, inhumane, and evil. But it is not impossible. Incremental decisions could lead us from the present to such a nightmarish future. Even if this future were regarded as unlikely and improbable, it is worth considerable thought to reduce that likelihood and plausibility still more. Many unlikely and implausible things have occurred in the past. The nightmare we have sketched would undoubtedly place us beyond redemption.

The Institutional Spectrum

IVAN ILLICH

Most utopian schemes and futuristic scenarios call for new and more costly technologies and more complex organization to solve the problems of society. Inevitably, these solutions mean more and more complex manipulation of men to fit them into such an environment. Herman Kahn has found pupils in Venezuela, Argentina, and even Colombia. The pipe dreams of Brazilian planners for the year 2000 sparkle with more new machinery than would be possible to install in the United States, which by then will be weighted down with the antiquated atomic sites, jetports, cities, and multiversities of the seventies.

There are other futurists who take their inspiration from more benevolent masters, vulgarizing Buckminster Fuller. They would depend on cheaper and more exotic devices to create an artificial environment. They rely on a revolutionary technology which can make more with less: lightweight monorails rather than supersonic transports; vertical living rather than horizontal sprawling, and multichannel bedroom TV rather than more monstrous campuses. Both types of planners seek to make economically feasible what is now technically possible. Both refuse to face the inevitable social consequences of their planning: the increased craving of all men for goods and services which will continue to remain the privilege of a few.

I believe that a desirable future depends on our deliberately choosing a life of action over a life of consumption, on our engendering a life style which will enable us to be spontaneous, independent, yet related to each other, rather than maintaining a life style which only allows us to make and unmake, produce and consume—a style of life which is merely a way station on the way toward the depletion and pollution of the environment. The future depends more upon our choice of institutions which support a life of action than on our developing new ideologies and technologies. We need a set of criteria which will permit us to recognize those institutions which support personal growth rather than addiction, as well as the will to invest our technological resources preferentially in such institutions of growth.

The institutions which might lead us into a humane future are by far the cheapest imaginable, since they would not organize production, consumption, and the recycling of waste, but would facilitate creative encounter, cooperation, and living. Instead of attempting to make feasible within our institutional horizon what is technologically possible, research for a viable future should concentrate on recognizing those institutions which foster inventive activity, and on rendering them possible with available means. I propose a review of the style in which our institutions now function, in order to single out those in which we should invest our limited resources—institutions which allow man to act on his own and to interact with others rather than institutions which obligate him to make and consume goods and services.

Too often we have sacrificed human needs for the necessities of institutions, for technological possibilities. We need only consider the advertising deemed necessary by our "public utilities." Bell Telephone ads in the airport are there not to encourage travelers to make more calls but to make them forget bad service. Bell tries to make the individual user forget the transfer of priorities from private to corporate users and the chatter of computers pre-empting its lines. The actual aim of subway advertising is to console the tortured, captive client with the thought that traffic-jammed drivers are even worse off than passengers crushed together below the surface of Manhattan. The New York Transit Authority must make excuses for conditions in the subways caused by our subsidizing the movement of tons of steel over superhighways rather than subsidizing the expansion of subway lines. Postal services need not be "sold." Yet the Post Office is compelled to justify legislation which provides cheaper rates for those who advertise products than for those who transmit purely personal concerns. True public utilities do not need to create a need for their services. No municipality in Mexico would dream of advertising its public market, though it might put up signs to help the tourist find it.

The subway and the Mexican market, the telephone and postal service are institutions for which advertising and marketing should be either negligible or incidental cost factors. Opposed to them are the institutions in which the cost of delivery of a given item tends to equal or exceed the total cost of the product or service. It will be useful for analysis to order our institutions according to this characteristic on a spectrum, placing the former—the "convivial" institutions—on the left and the latter—the "manipulative" institutions—on the right.

Generally, such a spectrum, moving from left to right, has been used to characterize men and their ideologies, not our social institutions and their styles. This categorization of men, whether as individuals or in groups, often generates more heat than light. Weighty objections can be raised against using an ordinary convention in an unusual fashion, but by doing so I hope to shift the terms of the discussion from a sterile to a fertile plane. It will become evident that men of the left are not always characterized by their opposition to the manipulative institutions, which I locate to the right on the spectrum.

To the right of such enterprises as Coca-Cola and the tobacco companies lies institutional advertising, which attempts to identify the public good with the name of a company or party. Whatever the International Business Machines Company spends on true public service is as nothing compared with the yearly expenditure allocated to conjuring up an image of responsibility, solidarity, and devotion to human progress in the eyes of all who see the three-letter word "IBM." Coca-Cola wants consumers to believe that things go better with a Coke; IBM wants the general public to believe that what's good for IBM is good for you and me. Unless these beliefs were induced, Coca-Cola would go out of business and IBM would have real competition.

The spectrum, of course, extends even further to the right. Law enforcement has moved there, as it has shifted from the hands of the sheriff to those of the FBI and the Pentagon. Modern warfare has become a highly professional enterprise whose business is killing. It has reached the point where its efficiency is measured in body counts. Its peace-keeping potential depends on its ability to convince friend and foe of the nation's unlimited death-dealing power. Modern bullets and chemicals are so effective that a few cents' worth, properly delivered to the intended "client," unfailingly kill or maim. But delivery costs rise vertiginously; the cost of a dead Vietnamese went from $360,000 in 1967 to $450,000 in 1969. Only economies on a scale approaching race suicide would render modern warfare economically efficient. The boomerang effect in war is becoming more obvious: the higher the body count of dead Vietnamese, the more enemies the United States acquires around the world; likewise, the more the United States must spend to create another manipulative institution—cynically dubbed "pacification"—in a futile effort to absorb the side effects of war.

At this same extreme on the spectrum we also find social agencies which specialize in the manipulation of their clients. Like the military, they tend to develop effects contrary to their aims as the scope of their operations increases. These social institutions are equally counterproductive, but less obviously so. Many assume a therapeutic and compassionate image to mask this paradoxical effect. For example, jails, up until two centuries ago, served as a means of detaining men until they were sentenced, maimed, killed, or exiled, and were sometimes deliberately used as a form of torture. Only recently have we begun to claim that locking people up in cages will have a beneficial effect on their character and behavior. Now quite a few people are beginning to understand that jail increases both the quality and the quantity of criminals, that, in fact, it often creates them out of mere nonconformists. Far fewer people, however, seem to understand that mental hospitals, nursing homes, and orphan asylums do much the same thing. These institutions provide their clients with the destructive self-image of the psychotic, the overaged, or the waif, and provide a rationale for the existence of entire professions, just as jails produce income for wardens. Membership in the institutions found at this extreme of the spectrum is achieved in two ways, both coercive: by forced commitment or by selective service.

At the opposite extreme of the spectrum lie institutions distinguished by spontaneous use—the "convivial" institutions. Telephone link-ups, subway lines, mail routes, public markets and exchanges do not require hard or soft sells to induce their clients to use them. Sewage systems, drinking water, parks, and sidewalks are institutions men use without having to be institutionally convinced that it is to their advantage to do so. Of course, all institutions require some regulation. But the operation of institutions which exist to be used rather than to produce something requires rules of an entirely different nature than those required by treatment-institutions, which are manipulative. The rules which govern institutions for use have mainly the purpose of avoiding abuses which would frustrate their general accessibility. Sidewalks must be kept free of obstructions, the industrial use of drinking water must be held within limits, and ball playing must be restricted to special areas within a park. At present we need legislation to limit the abuse of our telephone lines by computers, the abuse of mail service by advertisers, and the pollution of our sewage systems by industrial wastes. The regulation of convivial institutions sets limits to their use; as one moves from the convivial to the manipulative end of the spectrum, the rules progressively call for unwilling consumption or participation in the institutional agent. The different cost of acquiring clients is just one of the characteristics which distinguish convivial from manipulative institutions.

At both extremes of the spectrum we find service institutions, but on the right the service is imposed manipulation, and the client is made the victim of advertising, aggression, indoctrination, imprisonment, or electroshock. On the left the service is amplified opportunity within formally defined limits, while the client remains a free agent. Right-wing institutions tend to be highly complex and costly production processes in which much of the elaboration and expense is concerned with convincing consumers that they cannot live without the product or the treatment offered by the institution. Left-wing institutions tend to be networks which facilitate client-initiated communication or co-operation.

The manipulative institutions of the right are either socially or psychologically "addictive." Social addiction, or escalation, consists in the tendency to prescribe increased treatment if smaller quantities have not yielded the desired results. Psychological addiction, or habituation, results when consumers become hooked on the need for more and more of the process or product. The self-activated institutions of the left tend to be self-limiting. Unlike production processes which identify satisfaction with the mere act of consumption, these networks serve a purpose beyond their own repeated use. An individual picks up the telephone when he wants to say something to someone else, and hangs up when the desired communication is over. The message, not the medium, counts in a true network. He does not, teen-agers excepted, use the telephone for the sheer pleasure of talking into the receiver. If the telephone is not the best way to get in touch, people will write a letter or take a trip. Right-wing institutions, as we can see clearly in the case of schools, both invite compulsively repetitive use and frustrate alternative ways of achieving similar results.

Toward, but not at, the left on the institutional spectrum, we can locate enterprises which compete with others in their own field, but have not begun notably to engage in advertising. Here we find hand laundries, small bakeries, hairdressers, and—to speak of professionals—some lawyers and music teachers. Characteristically left of center, then, are self-employed persons who have institutionalized their services but not their publicity. They acquire clients through their personal touch and the comparative quality of their services.

Hotels and cafeterias are somewhat closer to the center. The big chains like Hilton—which spend huge amounts on selling their image—often behave as if they were running institutions of the right. Yet Hilton and Sheraton enterprises do not usually offer anything more—in fact, they often give less—than similarly priced, independently managed lodgings. Essentially, a hotel sign beckons to a traveler in the manner of a road sign. It says, "Stop, here is a bed for you," rather than, "You should prefer a hotel bed to a park bench!"

The producers of staples and most perishable consumer goods belong in the middle of our spectrum. In the same range belong many repair shops, tailors, or barbers. They fill generic demands and add to the cost of production and distribution whatever the market will bear in advertising costs for publicity and special packaging. The more basic the product—be it goods or services—the more does competition tend to limit the sales cost of the item.

Most manufacturers of consumer goods have moved much further to the right. Both directly and indirectly, they produce demands for accessories which boost real purchase price far beyond production cost. General Motors and Ford produce means of transportation, but they also, and more importantly, manipulate public taste in such a way that the need for transportation is expressed as a demand for private cars rather than public buses. They sell the desire to control a machine, to race at high speeds in luxurious comfort, while also offering the fantasy at the end of the road. What they sell, however, is not just a matter of uselessly big motors, superfluous gadgetry, or the new extras forced on the manufacturers by Ralph Nader and the clean-air lobbyists. The list price includes souped-up engines, air-conditioning, safety belts, and exhaust controls; but other costs not openly declared to the driver are also involved: the corporation's advertising and sales expenses, fuel, maintenance and parts, insurance, interest on credit, as well as less tangible costs like loss of time, temper, and breathable air in our traffic-congested cities.

An especially interesting corollary to our discussion of socially useful institutions is the system of "public" highways. This major element of the total cost of automobiles deserves lengthier treatment, since it leads directly to the rightist institution in which I am most interested, namely, the school.

FALSE PUBLIC UTILITIES

The highway system is a network for locomotion across relatively large distances. As a network, it appears to belong on the left of the institutional spectrum. But here we must make a distinction which will clarify both the nature of highways and the nature of true public utilities. Genuinely all-purpose roads are true public utilities. Superhighways are private preserves, the cost of which has been partially foisted upon the public.

Telephone, postal, and highway systems are all networks, and none of them is free. Access to the telephone network is limited by time charges on each call. These rates are relatively small and could be reduced without changing the nature of the system. Use of the telephone system is not in the least limited by what is transmitted, although it is best used by those who can speak coherent sentences in the language of the other party—an ability universally possessed by those who wish to use the network. Postage is usually cheap. Use of the postal system is slighty limited by the price of pen and paper, and somewhat more by the ability to write. Still, when someone who does not know how to write has a relative or friend to whom he can dictate a letter, the postal system is at his service, as it is if he wants to ship a recorded tape.

The highway system does not similarly become available to someone who merely learns to drive. The telephone and postal networks exist to serve those who wish to use them, while the highway system mainly serves as an accessory to the private automobile. The former are true public utilities, whereas the latter is a public service to the owners of cars, trucks, and buses. Public utilities exist for the sake of communication among men; highways, like other institutions of the right, exist for the sake of a product. Auto manufacturers, we have already observed, *produce* simultaneously both cars and the demand for cars. They also *produce* the demand for multilane highways, bridges, and oilfields. The private car is the focus of a cluster of right-wing institutions. The high cost of each element is dictated by elaboration of the basic product, and to sell the basic product is to "hook" society on the entire package.

To plan a highway system as a true public utility would discriminate against those for whom velocity and individualized comfort are the primary transportation values, in favor of those who value fluidity and destination. It is the difference between a far-flung network with maximum access for travelers and one which offers only privileged access to restricted areas.

Transferring a modern institution to the developing nations provides the acid test of its quality. In very poor countries roads are usually just good enough to permit transit by special, high-axle trucks loaded with groceries, livestock, or people. This kind of country should use its limited resources to build a spiderweb of trails extending to every region and should restrict imports to two or three different models of highly durable vehicles which can manage all trails at low speed. This would simplify maintenance and the stocking of spare parts, permit the operation of these vehicles around the clock, and provide maximum fluidity and choice of destination to all citizens. This would require the engineering of all-purpose vehicles with the simplicity of the Model T, making use of the most modern alloys to guarantee durability, with a built-in speed limit of not more than twenty miles per hour, and strong enough to run on the roughest terrain. Such vehicles are not on the market because there is no demand for them. As a matter of fact, such a demand would have to be cultivated, quite possibly under the protection of strict legislation. At present, whenever such a demand is even slightly felt, it is quickly snuffed out by counterpublicity aimed at universal sales of the machines which currently extract from U.S. taxpayers the money needed for building superhighways.

In order to "improve" transportation, all countries—even the poorest —now plan highway systems designed for the passenger cars and high-speed trailers which fit the velocity-conscious minority of producers and consumers in the elite classes. This approach is frequently rationalized as a saving of the most precious resource of a poor country: the time of the doctor, the school inspector, or the public administrator. These men, of course, serve almost exclusively the same people who have, or hope one day to have, a car. Local taxes and scarce international exchange are wasted on *false public utilities*.

"Modern" technology transferred to poor countries falls into three large categories: goods, factories which make them, and service institutions—principally schools—which make men into modern producers and consumers. Most countries spend by far the largest proportion of their budget on schools. The school-made graduates then create a demand for other conspicuous utilities, such as industrial power, paved highways, modern hospitals, and airports, and these in turn create a market for the goods made for rich countries and, after a while, the tendency to import obsolescent factories to produce them.

Of all "false utilities," school is the most insidious. Highway systems produce only a demand for cars. Schools create a demand for the entire set of modern institutions which crowd the right end of the spectrum. A man who questioned the need for highways would be written off as a romantic; the man who questions the need for school is immediately attacked as either heartless or imperialist.

SCHOOLS AS FALSE PUBLIC UTILITIES

Like highways, schools, at first glance, give the impression of being equally open to all comers. They are, in fact, open only to those who consistently renew their credentials. Just as highways create the impression that their present level of cost per year is necessary if people are to move, so schools are presumed essential for attaining the competence required by a society which uses modern technology. We have exposed speedways as spurious public utilities by noting their dependence on private automobiles. Schools are based upon the equally spurious hypothesis that learning is the result of curricular teaching.

Highways result from a perversion of the desire and need for mobility into the demand for a private car. Schools themselves pervert the natural inclination to grow and learn into the demand for instruction. Demand for manufactured maturity is a far greater abnegation of self-initiated activity than the demand for manufactured goods. Schools are not only to the right of highways and cars; they belong near the extreme of the institutional spectrum occupied by total asylums. Even the producers of body counts kill only bodies. By making men abdicate the responsibility for their own growth, school leads many to a kind of spiritual suicide.

Highways are paid for in part by those who use them, since tolls and gasoline taxes are extracted only from drivers. School, on the other hand, is a perfect system of regressive taxation, where the privileged graduates ride on the back of the entire paying public. School puts a head tax on promotion. The underconsumption of highway mileage is not nearly so costly as the underconsumption of schooling. The man who does not own a car in Los Angeles may be almost immobilized, but if he can somehow manage to reach a work place, he can get and hold a job. The school dropout has no alternative route. The suburbanite with his new Lincoln and his country cousin who drives a beat-up jalopy get essentially the same use out of the highway, even though one man's care costs thirty times more than the other's. The value of a man's schooling is a function of the number of years he has completed and of the costliness of the schools he has attended. The law compels no one to drive, whereas it obliges everyone to go to school.

INSTITUTIONAL REVOLUTION AND THE
NATURE OF THE ALTERNATIVES

The analysis of institutions according to their present placement on a left-right continuum enables me to clarify my belief that fundamental social change must begin with a change of consciousness about institutions and to explain why the dimension of a viable future turns on the rejuvenation of institutional style.

During the sixties institutions born in different decades since the French Revolution simultaneously reached old age; public school systems founded in the time of Jefferson or of Atatürk, along with others which started after World War II, all became bureaucratic, self-justifying, and manipulative. The same thing happened to systems of social security, to labor unions, major churches and diplomacies, the care of the aged, and the disposal of the dead.

Today, for instance, the school systems of Colombia, Britain, the U.S.S.R., and the U.S. resemble each other more closely than U.S. schools of the late 1890's resembled either today's or their contemporaries in Russia. Today all schools are obligatory, open-ended, and competitive. The same convergence in institutional style affects health care, merchandising, personnel administration, and political life. All these institutional processes tend to pile up at the manipulative end of the spectrum.

A merger of world bureaucracies results from this convergence of institutions. The style, the ranking systems, and the paraphernalia (from textbook to computer) are standardized on the planning boards of Costa Rica or Afghanistan after the model of Western Europe. Everywhere these bureaucracies seem to focus on the same task: promoting the growth of institutions of the right. They are concerned with the making of things, the making of ritual rules, and the making—and reshaping—of "executive truth," the ideology or fiat which establishes the current value which should be attributed to their product. Technology provides these bureaucracies with increasing power on the right hand of society. The left hand of society seems to wither, not because technology is less capable of increasing the range of human action, and providing time for the play of individual imagination and personal creativity, but because such use of technology does not increase the power of an elite which administers it. The postmaster has no control over the substantive use of the mails, the switchboard operator or Bell Telephone executive has no power to stop adultery, murder, or subversion from being planned over his network.

At stake in the choice between the institutional right and left is the very nature of human life. Man must choose whether to be rich in things or in the freedom to use them. He must choose between alternate styles of life and related production schedules.

Aristotle had already discovered that "making and acting" are different, so different, in fact, that one never includes the other. "For neither is acting a way of making—nor making a way of truly acting. Architecture [*techne*] is a way of making . . . of bringing something into being whose origin is in the maker and not in the thing. Making has always an end other than itself, action not; for good action itself is its end. Perfection in making is an art, perfection in acting is a virtue." The word which Aristotle employed for making was "*praxis*," and the word he employed for doing, "*poesis*." A move to the right implies that an institution is being restructured to increase its ability to "make," while as it moves to the left, it is being restructured to allow increased "doing" or "*praxis*." Modern technology has increased the ability of man to relinquish the "making" of things to machines, and his potential time for "acting" has increased. "Making" the necessities of life has ceased to take up his time. Unemployment is the result of this modernization: it is the idleness of a man for whom there is nothing to "make" and who does not know what to "do"—that is, how to "act." Unemployment is the sad idleness of a man who, contrary to Aristotle, believes that making things, or working, is virtuous and that idleness is bad. Unemployment is the experience of the man who has succumbed to the Protestant ethic. Leisure, according to Weber, is necessary for man to be able to work. For Aristotle, work is necessary for man to have leisure.

Technology provides man with discretionary time he can fill either with making or with doing. The choice between sad unemployment and joyful leisure is now open for the entire culture. It depends on the institutional style the culture chooses. This choice would have been unthinkable in an ancient culture built either on peasant agriculture or on slavery. It has become inevitable for postindustrial man.

One way to fill available time is to stimulate increased demands for the consumption of goods and, simultaneously, for the production of services. The former implies an economy which provides an ever-growing array of ever newer things which can be made, consumed, wasted, and recycled. The latter implies the futile attempt to "make" virtuous actions into the products of "service" institutions. This leads to the identification of schooling and education, of medical service and health, of program-watching and entertainment, of speed and effective locomotion.

The radically alternative way to fill available time is the development of a limited range of more durable goods—and of institutions which can increase the opportunity and desirability of human interaction—and do so at the rate at which men are relieved by machines of the burden of making things.

A durable-goods economy is precisely the contrary of an economy based on planned obsolescence. A durable-goods economy means a constraint on the bill of goods. Goods would have to be such that they provided the maximum opportunity to "do" something with them: items made for self-assembly, self-help, reuse, and repair.

A durable-goods economy, with strict limits imposed on the available variety and obsolescence of goods, requires more, rather than less, research in order to provide a better choice among items destined for production. It also requires planning, rationing, and a public oriented toward "action" rather than the making and "consuming" of artifacts. Planning and rationing have not worked in economies devoted to competitive making and consumption. They would work in a society oriented toward action. Planning would consist of deciding which goods were to be made. Rationing would merely ensure that they were acquired for use rather than resale.

The complement to a durable, repairable, and reusable bill of goods is not an increase of institutionally produced services, but rather an institutional framework which constantly educates to action, participation, and self-help. The movement of our society from the present—in which all institutions gravitate toward postindustrial bureaucracy—to a future of post-industrial conviviality—in which the intensity of action would prevail over production—must begin with a renewal of style in the service institutions—and, first of all, with a renewal of education.